LEBANON

ALSO BY ANISSA HELOU

Saudi Feast

Feast

Sweet Middle East

Levant

Savory Baking from the Mediterranean

Modern Mezze

The Fifth Quarter

Mediterranean Street Food

Street Café Morocco

Lebanese Cuisine

LEBANON

COOKING THE FOODS OF MY HOMELAND

ANISSA HELOU

ecco

An Imprint of HarperCollinsPublishers

DÉDICACE

To my beautiful late mother, Laurice Helou, and the rest of my family, whose support from when I was born has been unfailing!
&
For my friend Ilaria Borletti, whose support when I switched to writing about food has also been unfailing!

CONTENTS

TRANSLITERATION viii
INTRODUCTION xi

PANTRY 1
FLATBREADS AND SAVORY PASTRIES 25
SOUPS 55
DIPS AND SPREADS 67
SALADS 79
ON THE GRILL 105
COOKED IN EXTRA VIRGIN OLIVE OIL 117
YOGURT DISHES 133
KIBBÉ 153
STUFFED VEGETABLES 185
FISH 211
POULTRY 231
OFFAL 245
GRAINS AND LEGUMES 257
STEWS AND BRAISES 277
SWEETS 293

ACKNOWLEDGMENTS 341
INDEX 345

TRANSLITERATION

The modern Lebanese transliteration of the Arab words is to replace the letters that are difficult for Westerners to pronounce with numbers:

7 is for ح, for a very deep h that is practically impossible for non-Arabic speakers to achieve.
2 is for ق, a q that only the Druze pronounce, while the rest of us silence it.
3 is for ع, another impossible letter for Westerners to pronounce; it comes from deep in the throat and has no equivalent in the Western alphabet.

I was going to use this transliteration, but then I decided not to because it is little known in the West. Instead, I tried to stay as close to the classical transliteration (i.e., ü for oo and é for a hard e, i for ee, and so on) as possible, and used the apostrophe symbol for both the letters ع and ق, as well as for making a distinction between letters that needed to be pronounced separately.

INTRODUCTION

I lived in Beirut for the first twenty-one years of my life, in what would now be considered a foodie family. My strict and rather ascetic father was nevertheless a gourmet, and my beautiful mother was an amazing cook. She essentially made everything at home and, of course, she cooked for us every day. Because she came from a Christian Maronite family (her mother from Rechmaya, a beautiful hilltop village in the Aley district, and her father from Bhamdoun, a summer resort in the same district), her dishes were from this mountainous region. I never questioned whether they were anything but national dishes, mainly because our country is so small (about half the size of New Jersey). Until, that is, I started researching this book. When I wrote my first book on Lebanese cuisine more than thirty years ago, it was soon after the end of the civil war, when I had not been to the home country for more than ten years. That first book was all about my mother's recipes, whereas this one, for which I traveled the country, is all about our regional culinary diversity.

As I crisscrossed Lebanon with my friend Dalia Khamissy, who took the location photographs, I realized that the size of the country had no bearing on the breadth of our cuisine. In fact, it is remarkable that such a tiny nation should have so many distinct regional specialties, not to mention different names for the same dish depending on where you are. There is a very good reason for this, which is that it wasn't a country, at least not as we know it, until fairly recently.

The history of Lebanon is both complex and fascinating. It is mentioned in the Bible as the land of milk and honey, and its Arabic name, Lubnan, from the Phoenician root *lbn*, means "white," an allusion to the snow-covered peaks of its two mountain ranges, the Lebanon and anti-Lebanon.

Its recorded history starts with the coastal Phoenician city-states of Tyre and Sidon in the south, Beirut (or Beritos as it was known then) and Byblos in the center (the latter is claimed to be one of the world's oldest inhabited cities), and Tripoli in the north. The Greeks came with Alexander the Great, then the Romans, followed by the Byzantines, under whom the region became a major center for Christianity. The Muslims took over in the seventh century, soon after the birth of Islam, and after belonging to different Muslim Caliphates, the country reverted to Christian control under the Crusaders, who settled the County of Tripoli, from where they ruled over most of the country for nearly a century. Following their defeat, the Ayyubids took over, then the Mamluks, who were replaced by the Ottomans in the mid-fifteenth century.

Our modern history begins with the Emirate of Mount Lebanon, established as an autonomous region under the Ottomans in the late sixteenth century, a mountainous territory that had long been a place of refuge for persecuted communities, from the Druze (a secretive religion where the tenets are only known to the religious leaders), to the Christian Maronites, to the Alawis, an offshoot of Shiite Muslims.

The first meaningful ruler of the Emirate was Fakhreddine Ma'an or Fakhreddine II, who introduced the production of silk to the region and was often referred to as the Merchant Emir. Together with Druze feudal lords, he employed Maronites for farming as well as administrative work, and he was instrumental in displacing Shiites farther south, replacing them with Christians whom he had encouraged to move from the far north of Mount Lebanon.

The Shihabs brought power to Sunni Muslims until, that is, Emir Fakhreddine Shihab II converted to Christianity in the early nineteenth century, drawing closer to the Maronite church, already an impressive economic, social, and cultural institution. Shihab II proceeded to dispossess the Druze feudal lords, distributing most of their properties to Christian relatives. Following his death in 1850, the Druze rebelled and asked for their lands back. This eventually led to the conflicts of 1860, when the Druze killed around ten thousand Christians. Until then, the story was about displacement, with Shiites, Druze, and Christians vying for control of various parts of the Emirate, having lived more or less in harmony beforehand—the Sunnis were mostly in the coastal areas, both in the center and up north. After the massacres of 1860, the Ottomans sent a governor to restore peace, following which the balance of power shifted in favor of the Christian Maronites.

The end of the First World War marked the fall of the Ottoman Empire, at which point the French took a mandate over the country and drew up its constitution in 1920, allocating different political powers to different confessions. However, it wasn't until 1943 that the country became fully independent. Regardless, the confessional system was here to stay, another reason why our small country has so much diversity, both culinary and otherwise.

Not too long after independence, we had our first civil war, in 1958, which was quickly brought to an end with the help of the Americans. After that, the country enjoyed a dolce vita period where Beirut was called the Paris of the Middle East and the country as a whole the Switzerland of the region—a myth that was destroyed with the outbreak of the civil war in 1975, which lasted, with a few lulls in the fighting, until 1990.

Rebuilding and prosperity were brought to a halt when the Israelis attacked in 2006, trying to bring an end to Hezbollah, followed by the 2019 revolution, then the port of Beirut explosion and the subsequent economic collapse. This said, the country continues to function somehow and to be attractive to the Lebanese diaspora, which is as large, more or less, as those living in the country.

As I delved deeper into the history of my country, it made sense to me why such a young and tiny nation should have such a rich and varied culinary tradition. Apart from its complex history with successive invaders and refugees leaving their mark, the country was stitched together by a foreign power, together with their Christian allies, who never took into account the different confessions and factions, some of whom had been and, more importantly, had wanted to remain under those ruling them, with many Muslims, both in the north and the south, preferring to remain as part of Greater Syria within the Ottoman Empire.

In the south, I discovered dishes that were closer to those of Palestine than to those of Mount Lebanon, where my mother comes from, as well as a whole range of kibbés that neither Beirutis nor those in the north knew much about; not to mention mishtah, a spiced flatbread that is typical of that region. In Beirut, I uncovered many interesting Sunni and Greek Orthodox variations on familiar dishes together with specific dishes that were completely new to me. And in the north, I was told by the mother of one of our greatest artists, Akram Zaatari, about her Sufi family, who lived and practiced their faith in the family

Playing backgammon in the Mar Elias neighborhood, Beirut

takiya (Sufi lodge) in Tripoli, that is, until the government took it over. Farther up north, in Beino, a beautiful, unspoiled village near the Syrian border, I had meat cooked with fruit, which was a revelation. I had been convinced that no one in Lebanon cooked meat with fruit like they do in Syria, but I guess the proximity of the village to the northern part of Syria explains it.

Farther east in Baalbek, I spent a morning in a bakery watching a group of hulking hairy men make hundreds of dainty sfiha baalbakiyeh, mesmerized by how delicately they handled the soft dough and how in perfect sync they were, each concentrating on one task, whether it was dividing the dough, flattening it, adding the meat filling, or shaping the hand pies.

As for the Bekaa, our most fertile region in the southeast, it is there that I learned about a superb range of dishes using bulgur wheat as a base, most of which were again new to me.

As I researched and wrote the book, I came to look at the food of my own country afresh, realizing that it is far more fascinating to view a cuisine through a regional rather than a national lens, given that our national borders had been so recently drawn, and not by us but rather by the colonizing powers who had taken over from the Ottomans. The recipes I have included reflect this. Of course, I could have included many more, but I didn't want to be repetitive, notwithstanding the lack of space and time. As a result, I chose dishes that are most representative of their community or region, together with universal classics that you find throughout the country. I hope you will enjoy them as much as we do and that you will be inspired to share them with both family and friends.

Anissa Helou
London
July 2024

INTRODUCTION XIII

لبنة ماعز

PANTRY

Müneh is the Arabic word for the foodstuffs that we keep in our pantry, that are meant to last us through the year, until the next season of plenty when we can replenish preserves such as awarma (lamb confit, page 15), pickles, and essential ingredients such as bulgur wheat, extra virgin olive oil, tahini, and nuts, to name a few. I have also included in this chapter a section on the fresh ingredients that we use the most, such as herbs, cheese, labneh, lemons, and so on, together with the seasonal delights that make us happy while their season lasts.

In the old days, most people made their own müneh at home and stored it in earthenware jars and canvas bags kept in cold rooms or cellars. Now things have changed. Instead of making their own, most source it from trusted suppliers and keep it in glass jars or bottles that they store in the pantry or refrigerator depending on how cool it needs to be. That said, many rural folk still make their own, but instead of preparing them at home, they go to communal kitchens to prepare the industrial quantities they need for their family. They do this toward the end of summer or early fall—both ideal times for preparing müneh—because the produce is plentiful then and cheaper to buy.

I visited one of those communal kitchens, Matbakh Ors el-Shams (meaning the kitchen of the sun), up in Mükhtara in the Shouf Mountains, the seat of the Druze leader Walid Jumblatt. It is in the heart of Druze country, where both men and women still dress in traditional black with the men donning a white cap, while the women cover their head with a very large, light white shawl. The kitchen is run by the very lovely and welcoming Liliane Ghannam. It was first set up as an NGO, but when the grants dried up after a couple of years, Liliane and her partner decided to lease the kitchen and equipment on a daily basis to those locals who still prepare their müneh, charging nominal fees because they wanted to continue to help the community rather than prioritizing making a profit.

On the day I visited, the kitchen was buzzing. One lady had brought bucketloads of pomegranate seeds (she had seeded the fruit at home) to juice in their industrial juicer before taking the juice back home to boil it down into pomegranate molasses. Another lady had trimmed an enormous quantity of tiny eggplants, which she boiled in the huge pots they had in the kitchen, before salting and pressing them using a remarkable large contraption made of a metal cylinder with holes in it and a flat metal disk that she slowly lowered onto the eggplants to press them and extract the excess liquid, which you could see seeping out of the holes. Not doing this would mean the eggplants, which she was using to make makdüss (page 14), would rot. She then took the eggplants back home to fill with a mixture of chopped garlic, walnuts, and red pepper before stacking in jars and covering with extra virgin olive oil. At the entrance was a wonderful Druze lady in traditional black and white making stacks of saj bread for locals who had commissioned them. As for Liliane, she was on the balcony, overseeing the winching up of crates of tomatoes that another lady had brought to make her year's supply of tomato paste.

While Dalia was photographing the action, I started talking to the ladies. I was fascinated by their patience and endurance given that they could have easily bought their müneh from trusted sources, but they all told me the same thing. Apart from it being more economical, they loved the community spirit of the kitchen and the satisfaction they derived from making their own, the way their mothers and grandmothers had done. They actually reminded me of my grandmother in Rechmaya, not too far from Mükhtara. She also made her own müneh, with the help of my mother and aunt. I was also reminded of how in Sicily, where I spend much of my time now, many

LEBANON

families buy large quantities of tomatoes in the summer to make their own passata and pelati (puréed and peeled tomatoes). Many families have their own olive groves, and when the harvest season comes, they pick the olives themselves or have workers do it before carrying them to the frantoio (olive press) to press into the precious extra virgin olive oil that, like us, they use for everything.

In Ehden, another village way up north, I walked past a charming small group chatting on a veranda, and on a whim, I decided to barge in on them to ask if they had any plans to make their own müneh—it was early fall, which is when people prepare it. I was also curious about what they would be cooking that day, and if kibbé (Ehden is famous for its kibbé) was on the menu. The house belonged to three siblings, two ladies and a gentleman. One of the sisters was disabled, but the other two were very active, and they had already prepared much of their müneh, which they kept in glass jars and bottles placed in crates wedged between the beds they slept on.

They had only one large room, where all three slept, the covered veranda, where I found them with their neighbor, which acted as their living room (in the warm months, that is; in the winter they go down to their home in Zgharta), and one small kitchen. All around the veranda were strings of green beans that they had hung to dry. It was quite a wonderful impromptu visit, and we promised to go back to spend a day making kibbé with them. Sadly, we never managed to, but I will go back to give them a copy of the book!

CONCENTRATED

Verjuice ('Asir Hosrum)

The juice of unripe, sour grapes, which we call *hosrum* in Arabic, and which we sometimes use instead of lemon juice in salad dressings and cooked dishes. The fresh juice is boiled

The siblings' müneh stored in between their beds, Ehden

with a little salt until it is slightly reduced and has turned pink. It is then bottled to use throughout the year. The tartness of our verjuice is very different from that of lemon juice, or sumac for that matter, and my mother often used it instead of lemon juice in her tabbüleh.

Grape Molasses (Dibss 'Enab)

Made from cooked grape juice, it can be a lovely golden color, or a dark brown depending on how it is processed. We use it as a natural sweetener, and we also eat it with bread, although without the tahini that we add to carob molasses.

Carob Molasses (Dibss Kharrüb)

The carob is a typical Mediterranean tree, and it has been growing in Lebanon for centuries. The pods are picked when mature, that is, dark and practically dry, seeded, then coarsely ground before being boiled with water, strained, and pressed to extract as much liquid as possible. Then it is boiled again until it turns into a thick dark syrup. Carob molasses is usually mixed with tahini and served as a sweet breakfast or as dessert after meals, scooped with pita bread. You can also chew on the mature pods the way we did as children to have as a natural sweet snack. I still do this in Sicily sometimes, whenever I come across a carob tree with ripe pods hanging from it—there are plenty there as well.

Tomato Paste (Rebb el-Banadüra)

Tomato paste is basically very reduced crushed tomatoes. I still remember when my grandmother and mother made ours in a huge pot, which they put over a portable gas fire in the middle of the kitchen. They first quartered the tomatoes, passed them through a food mill, then poured the juice/purée into the pot. They added a fair amount of salt and let the juice bubble over medium heat for what seemed like hours, stirring regularly, until it

was reduced to a thick, dark red paste. I loved dipping my finger into the pot at the very end to taste the salty, freshly made tomato paste. I could only do this when my mother's back was turned or if she had stepped out of the kitchen; otherwise, I would have been told off—she was very strict and did not allow us to eat or taste anything outside mealtime. I am sure this is why I am obsessed with tasting whatever is cooking, in my kitchen and others.

Pomegranate Molasses (Rebb el-Rümman)

I call it syrup, others call it molasses. Either way, it is made with the juice of slightly sour pomegranates known as *abu leffan* in Arabic. The seeds are pressed and the juice is strained, then boiled down until reduced to a thick, dark brown sweet/sour syrup, which adds an intriguing flavor to various cooked

dishes as well as salads. The syrup is used a lot more in the north than in the rest of the country, perhaps because of its proximity to Syria, where it is much more common.

DISTILLED

Orange Blossom Water (Ma' el-Zahr)

A fragrant water distilled from the macerated blossoms of the Seville orange (*bou-sfayr*). The water has a slightly bitter taste and is used sparingly, mostly in puddings but sometimes also in fruit juices. It is also used to make what we call "white coffee" (*ahweh baydah*), which is not actually coffee but rather a tisane made with orange blossom water and hot water. I love to have it after meals instead of real coffee. You simply add a teaspoon of ma' el-zahr (meaning "water of flowers") to a small cup (the same that we use for Turkish coffee) full of boiling water. Apparently, it also has a tonic effect and is given in tiny quantities to people who have fainted. I have not yet tried it as a tonic, and I wonder if this grandmother's tale is actually correct! The blossoms are cooked into sugar syrup to have a beautiful confection that is a cross between candied blossoms and blossom jam, which is used to garnish creamy or cream-filled sweets.

Rose Water (Ma' el-Ward)

Ma' el-ward, meaning "the water of roses," is another fragrant water but one distilled from the petals of the Damascus rose, or *ward jüri* as it is known in Arabic. It is used to flavor sweets as well as ice cream. The petals are also made into an exquisite jam.

DRIED

Burghul/Bulgur Wheat

Until not so long ago, bulgur wheat was our main staple, and it wasn't until rice became cheap that people started using it instead in dishes such as müjaddarah (pages 259 to 260) or stuffed vegetables (pages 187 to 208). Now, both are staples, although bulgur wheat is still the favored grain of rural folk. It comes in two grades, fine (*na'em*), to be used in tabbüleh and kibbé, and coarse (*kheshin*), for cooked dishes. There is also a very coarse grade that goes by different names depending on where you are, such as fa'sh (meaning broken or split open) or kasr el-ameh (meaning breaking the wheat). This grade is used primarily to cook in a tomato sauce. It is also called *zmatiyeh* or *zullayt* or *rüss*. Anyhow, there is also a very fine grade called *sraysirah*, which is like flour and is basically the very fine residue left after the fine and coarse grades are milled and sifted.

PANTRY

Bulgur wheat is made by parboiling, drying, and milling whole wheat. It comes in two colors, dark brown, known as *asmar* and *baladi*, meaning brown or local because it is locally produced, and golden, known as *abyad* (meaning white), which is imported.

My grandmother's family is from Rechmaya, and before my mother married, she used to spend her summers there. She still remembered how they prepared bulgur wheat once the wheat was harvested—by the time we grew older and started going there during the summer, they no longer made their own. As a result, I missed out on seeing the process. In those days, my grandmother would order sacks of wheat to be delivered to the family home. They would empty them one by one onto white sheets to pick it clean of any impurities—she and the other women in the family spent hours doing this painstaking work. Once the wheat was clean, they parboiled it, drained it, then took it up to the flat roof to spread on white sheets again, but this time to dry it in the sun. They left it there for several days, regularly turning it over until it was completely dry.

The wheat was put back in the same sacks for the men to carry it to special stone mills, where they ground it into bulgur wheat. The finished product was brought back home and sifted to produce the different grades before being stored in canvas bags and labeled according to the grade. It lasted them the year, until the next harvest. In poorer or more remote homes, they ground their own on a millstone to only produce the coarse grade and the very fine one.

Frikeh

Frikeh is produced by harvesting the wheat when it's still green. It is then burned in the field before threshing and drying it in the sun. Then it is left either whole or it is coarsely cracked. Because of the burning, frikeh has a distinctive smoky flavor. It is cooked the same way as bulgur wheat or rice. The best, in my opinion, is green with slightly charred bits and cracked. The greener the color, the better, because it means that it was harvested very early.

Dried Vegetables (Khodrah M'addadeh/Myabasseh)

Most vegetables are dried by home cooks and are not often found commercially except for beautiful strings of dried okra that you could almost wear as a necklace—they also make a rather attractive decoration for your kitchen, until, that is, the weevils get to it. The vegetables are trimmed as if they are to be cooked—in the case of eggplant and zucchini they are also cored—then spread on cotton sheets or strung onto cotton thread and hung

over wooden frames to dry in the sun, except for green vegetables, which are put in the shade to keep their color. Then, when the time comes to use them, they need to be soaked in water first to rehydrate them.

Kishk

Kishk was until not so long ago mostly prepared at home by mountain folks and rural communities in the Bekaa, where most of the wheat is grown. It is now produced commercially. It is used in hearty breakfast soups, often with awarma (lamb confit, page 15) and garlic. The soup is so thick that you can scoop it with pita bread, which is how it was eaten traditionally. Kishk is also used to make a topping for mana'ish (page 34) or in soups and salads (pages 58, 63, 88, 170, 274). It is one of our most classic preserves, and when made commercially, it looks almost like regular flour with a pale ivory color, whereas when made at home, it is speckled with brown flecks. Fall is when it is made. The weather is cooler than in the summer but not yet cold, so perfect for a slow fermentation.

It is not difficult to make kishk. The classic ratio is one measure coarse bulgur wheat to eight salted yogurt. First, place the bulgur wheat in a large bowl and cover it with two parts yogurt. Let soak for 24 hours. During that time, salt the rest of the yogurt and pour into a colander lined with a double or triple layer of cheesecloth. You can then tie up the ends and hang it somewhere over a sink or washbasin to drain off the excess liquid or you can leave it as is—the liquid will drain off but more slowly. The next day, unmold the yogurt that is now labneh into a bowl and divide into three equal parts. Mix one part with the bulgur wheat/yogurt mixture and let sit, covered with a kitchen cloth, in a cool place. The next day, mix in the second part, and the following day, the third. Once you have added all the labneh, let the mixture ferment for a week, stirring every now and then, until it has become quite sour. When ready, lay clean kitchen towels over straw mats, then start pinching off small lumps of the bulgur wheat/yogurt mixture to spread on the cloth. Put out to dry in the sun— this will take a couple of days. When the lumps are dry enough, rub between the palms of your hands to break them into a coarse powder. Sift the coarsely ground kishk to make a fine powder. You can keep it in the freezer or in airtight jars in a cool, dark place. Do not discard the bigger pieces left in the sifter. Instead, mix with awarma and a little labneh to make a filling for savory pastries.

Mastic (Miskeh)

Mastic is often described as gum arabic, which is not quite right, given that the latter is glue, whereas mastic is a dried resin used mostly in baking. The resin seeps through the bark of the *Pistacia lentiscus* tree, an evergreen

PANTRY 7

native to the Mediterranean that is now mostly found on the island of Chios, in Greece. In the summer, mastic producers there go out very early in the morning to their mastic tree groves to make incisions in the tree bark so the resin can seep out, a process called *kentima*. It takes a few days for the resin to dry and to drop either on the ground or onto rocks placed around the trees. The transparent resin is then collected and rinsed in barrels. After that, it is spread out and left to dry before being sorted by hand to make two kinds: clear, tiny crystals that are called *dahtilidopetres* (flintstones) or larger, spotted soft ones known as *kantiles* (blisters). The latter is a lesser grade, normally used for chewing—the resin is a natural chewing gum that makes the most horrible cracking noises when people chew it—while the finer grade is used in cooking and baking. Small amounts go a long way, imparting an intriguing exotic flavor to some breads, sweets, and ice creams, even some savory dishes. It is no longer so easy to find the flintstones. For some reason, most mastic available commercially now is the blisters, which is fine, as the taste is the same. It is just a little softer and less pure than the transparent one.

Lebanese Couscous (Moghrabiyeh)

A large-grain couscous that must have been brought over from the Maghreb, as its name indicates. The grains are the size of small

beads, about ¼ inch (5 mm) in diameter, and you can buy them fresh or dried. Either way, moghrabiyeh is cooked more or less like pasta first, then finished in the sauce.

Sahlab/Salep

A fine powder ground from a variety of dried wild orchid tubers that is used to thicken milk, for either a hot drink or ice cream. Pure salep is light gray in color with tiny flecks. If it is very white, it probably has been mixed with cornstarch. Turkish salep is the purest as far as I know and the one I use. In winter I boil it with milk to make sahlab, a thick drink that is served in soup bowls or cups with ka'k (sesame galette) (page 51). In some places, you may get croissants; in fact, a similar drink was common in France in the seventeenth century. In summer, I use it to thicken milk for ice cream (page 337) to give it a surprising stretchy, chewy texture that extends the pleasure of eating it. You can substitute with cornstarch, although the texture will not be quite the same.

Semolina (Smid)

Normal semolina (*smid*) is used for spongy cakes and creamy fillings, whereas fine semolina (*firkha*) is used instead of flour to make cookies with a lighter, crumblier texture.

Sesame Seeds (Simsüm)

The seeds of *Sesamum indicum* or *S. orientale*, a plant that grows in hot countries. Apparently, the best come from Sudan. We use the seeds liberally, both raw and toasted, in breads, biscuits, ka'k, za'tar, and falafels. They are also prepared with caramel to make a chewy sticky sweet called *simsmiyeh*, or a brittle of the same name.

Soapwort (Shirsh el-Halaweh)

The basis for an intriguing sweet dip known as *natef* (page 302), which is served solely with karabij. The dip is also an essential ingredient in halva, and, like meringue, it is

used to top some pies. The secret to a proper natef lies in the saponin found inside the root of *Saponaria officinalis* or that of *Gypsophila struthium*. The root is rinsed clean before being boiled for a long time, until the liquid is reduced by three-quarters. The resulting murky liquid is cooled, then whisked, and as it is whisked a miraculous transformation takes place where the brown water starts turning into a stiff white foam—this is a result of the saponin, which is basically soap. Sugar syrup is then whisked into the white foam to make natef. I only found out more about it after the publication of *Lebanese Cuisine*, when Helen Saberi, Esteban Pombo-Villar, the late Alan Davidson, and I embarked on a serious but also fun investigation to establish whether *shirsh el-halaweh* was soapwort or bois de panama (a South American bark that can be used as a substitute)—I had seen the latter mentioned in some recipes. We published our findings in a series of articles in *PPC (Petits Propos Culinaires)*, which were then reprinted in *The Wilder Shores of Gastronomy: Twenty Years of the Best Food Writing*, published in 2002. In fact, both soapwort and the bark of bois de panama have saponin, and, as a result, you can use either to produce the same white foam as tested by Charles Perry, who wrote about his experiment in the *Los Angeles Times* a year or two after our investigation. The white foam is also used in the spring to clean the carpets before they are rolled and put away for the summer months.

Sumac (Summa')

Sumac is a coarse powder ground from the dried berries of *Rhus coriaria* (tanner's or elm-leafed sumach, not to be confused with other poisonous plants of the same family). The purplish brown berries are harvested on the stalk at the end of summer and spread to dry in the sun. Once dry, the berries are rubbed off the stalks, ground, and sifted into the coarsely ground, lemony seasoning that ranges in color from deep maroon to brighter red. It is used to season salads, stuffings, fried eggs, and grilled fish or meat. Its pleasing tart flavor is a change from that of lemon juice or verjuice, and because it is completely dry, it doesn't add any moisture to the dishes it's used in.

Dried Figs (Teen M'yabass)

Fig trees grow practically everywhere in Lebanon, and in the old days, figs were peddled in wicker baskets from house to house by hawkers shouting *yalla ala teen men el-jabal* (meaning "come and get figs from the mountain"). More often than not, the vendors were the ones who had picked them early in the morning. Given how plentiful they are, a good part of the crop is dried so as not to waste it. The figs are squashed flat to slightly open them and spread on straw mats laid on flat roofs or in the fields for the fruit to dry in the sun. Once completely dry, they are stacked in tin boxes and stored away. Some will first dip them in boiling water flavored with anise seeds to ward off insects before drying them again and storing them. They can then be chopped up and made into a thick jam that you eat with bread or simply off the spoon "to sweeten the mouth" (*tat'halli el-temm*), as we put it.

ZA'TAR

Za'tar means "thyme" in Arabic, and it describes both the fresh herb and the wonderful, lightly salted mix made with ground dried thyme, sumac, and toasted sesame seeds that has now gone global, with chefs and home cooks sprinkling it on practically everything. We, on the other hand, mostly use it mixed with olive oil, as a topping for mana'ish (page 34). In many traditional households, like my mother's and grandmother's, there will always be a small bowl of za'tar mixed with olive oil on the kitchen counter ready to dip bread into or to mix with labneh (page 22). The mix is very simple to make, though make sure you have the right dried za'tar (called *zübe'* in Arabic or *Origanum syriacum* in Latin). You can buy it fresh in season to dry it yourself, or you can buy big dried bunches and pick both leaves and buds off the stalk—the more buds there are on the branches, the better the za'tar—before grinding them. You can also buy it already ground, but only from a reliable mat'haneh (meaning press) or mahmassa (meaning roastery), as some unscrupulous ones will also grind the stalks to bump up the weight, and as a result their profit. That said, the picking of the dried leaves and buds off the stalks is a bit of a chore. Here are the proportions for the za'tar mix:

1½ cups (75 g) pure dried za'tar

½ cup (30 g) ground sumac

1 cup (100 g) toasted sesame seeds

1 tablespoon fine sea salt

Mix all the ingredients in a large bowl, then transfer to a large frying pan and place over medium heat. Toast, stirring, for a few minutes, until the aroma rises. Heating the za'tar makes it last longer. We also have another type of za'tar, *Thymbra spicata*, which is for eating fresh or pickling. Unlike the furry leaves of zübe', this za'tar has long, slender leaves and is somewhat less sharp.

Floral Tisane (Z'hürat)

A wonderful mixture of mostly dried flowers that mountain folk collect in the fields and dry for home use or to sell. You can buy them ready-mixed in a beautiful medley or separately so as to mix your own. Each has beneficial properties, especially for minor ailments. Among the mix you will find chamomile (or *babünge* in Arabic), corn silk (*shoshat al-dara*), a type of hibiscus (*khatmiyah*), a herb similar to wild thyme (*qos'ayn*), and roses (*ward*), to name a few. To make the tisane, use 1 teaspoon of z'hürat for a medium teapot. Add boiling water and let infuse for about 10 minutes before serving. We also make tisanes with individual herbs, such as fresh mint (*na'na'*), hyssop (*al-zoffa*), and sage (*maramiyeh*), or with seeds such as anise (*yansün*). The individual herbs or seeds are boiled in water for a couple of minutes, then left to infuse for five minutes or so before straining and serving.

Nuts

The nuts we use the most in our cooking are pine (*snübar*), pistachios (*fcstü' halabi*), almonds (*loz*), and walnuts (*joz*). Our pine nuts, from *Pinus pinea*, are long and rather fat, and in the shops they are graded and priced according to their size. I consider them the best, but perhaps I am prejudiced. The rounder, shorter, and less tasty ones come from North America (*P. edulis*, *P. monophylla*, and *P. cembroides*), or from Korea or China (*P. koraiensis*). The latter are the least expensive and the most commonly used these days, but I don't like them, mainly because they are not as attractive or as good. Pakistani and Afghan pine nuts are longer and thinner than Mediterranean ones, but the taste is not as intense. Also, oddly enough, they don't toast so well.

Pine nuts are precious to those growing or harvesting them, and they consider them as their white gold, but unfortunately our pine forests have been ravaged by two pests. The pine shoot beetle, which dries out the tree, and is currently affecting roughly just one in one thousand trees thanks to a system of locally produced traps. The western conifer is a seed bug that feeds on young pine cones, blighting their seeds. These pests have reduced our pine nut production by nearly 90 percent, hence the price increase. As a result, many no longer use them, using instead either Chinese pine nuts or slivered almonds. Fortunately, there is still enough of a production for me to be able to source what I need, albeit at a higher cost, but I personally don't mind—I don't believe there is a good substitute, and I advise you to use Mediterranean pine nuts over any other.

The nuts are inside hard shells that are nestled individually inside the scales of the pine cone. When the cones are dry enough, the scales open and the kernels fall or are shaken out. The hard shells are then cracked open with the help of a machine to reveal pine nuts wrapped in a brown skin that is then rubbed off, also by machine. The whole process is done automatically, from shaking the kernels out to cracking the shells open, to rubbing the thin skins off, but when I was a child, I would venture out, together with my sisters, to the woods behind our summer house (my parents rented a house in the mountains to get away from the city's heat) to pick pine cones, which we shook to get the pine kernels. We gathered these in a bag and took them to an opening where there were flat stones, on which we could crack the shells open using a smaller flat stone. The hard shells were beautiful, dark brown with lighter brown stripes, and we had to adjust the strength of our hit so as to break the shell without crushing the nut, a feat we didn't always achieve. Regardless, crushed or not, the freshly cracked pine nuts were delicious and one of my favorite summer treats.

OILS AND FATS

Clarified Butter/Ghee (Samneh)

You can buy samneh or you can make your own, which is very simple. It is a good idea to make a large batch at a time, as ghee lasts much longer than butter. First, heat unsalted butter in a saucepan until the milky solids separate from the clear fat, which we describe in Arabic as the eye's tear (*dam'at el-'eyn*). If there are any milky solids floating to the surface, carefully skim them before slowly pouring out the clear fat, leaving the milky solids that have settled on the bottom in the pan—I don't throw away the milky solids but use them when I cook rice. Keep the ghee in a sealed container in the refrigerator. It doesn't really have an expiry date and until not so long ago, most home cooks used it instead of butter.

Tahini (T'hineh)

An absolutely essential ingredient that was once not so easily available in the West but is now part of the global ingredients repertoire. I was fortunate enough one day, before the Syrian uprising, to see tahini being made at a halva maker in the old souks of Aleppo. They first toasted the seeds, then put them to soak in large stone vats to loosen the hull, which they then removed (I think) before pressing the seeds to get that wonderful creamy "fat," which is the main ingredient in tarator (page 77) and an essential one in hommus (page 68), among other dips. Tahini is also used in cooked dishes, such as kibbeh arnabiyeh (page 165), where it is seasoned with the juice of different citrus. What is not so obvious, though, is which tahini to use. I prefer the smooth, light-colored one and always go for an imported Arab label rather than a Western one. This said, I have found very good tahini made in the US, both artisanal and mass produced. Simply check the color, which is easy enough if it is packed in glass jars, otherwise you will have to wait until you open the container. Most of the imported tahini is packed in plastic containers. The color should be light cream and the texture needs to be very smooth. Tahini separates when left for a long time, and all you need to do is to stir the oil that floats to the surface back into the creamy part before using. It seizes up as you first add liquid to make whatever sauce or dip you are preparing, but do not worry, it loosens up again as you add more liquid.

Extra Virgin Olive Oil (Zeyt Zeytün)

Olive oil was the main oil used throughout the country until not so long ago, for frying, cooking, and seasoning, of course. Most families buy their yearly supply directly from trusted producers, either relatives, or

PRESERVED

Pickling Solution (Khall al-Kabiss)

You can use this pickling solution with any vegetable you would like to pickle. I don't usually add anything, but you can add a few garlic cloves and one or more chilies to give your pickles a spicy, garlicky taste. If you are pickling turnips, you need to add a few slices of raw beet to give the turnips a deep purplish color. The ratio is 1 part vinegar to 2 parts water and 7 percent salt. You can add a little sugar if you want, or you can leave it out. Be sure to use a very good vinegar. My mother would use apple vinegar, but I go for either champagne vinegar, which is quite mild, or a good wine vinegar.

friends, or friends of friends. At home, my mother used to ask her uncle in Rechmaya (her maternal family village), who had olive groves, to send her about 75 quarts (75 liters) as soon as he pressed the new harvest. In those days, most people picked olives by hand and carefully selected them to produce three different grades. The first and best is khadir (meaning "green"), and it is extracted from totally unblemished early-harvest green olives. The second best, bab awal (meaning "first door"), is pressed from slightly blemished olives, while the third, bab thani (meaning "second door"), is the oil extracted from the rest of the crop. The olives that had already fallen on the ground are pressed to produce oil for soap.

EGGPLANTS IN EXTRA VIRGIN OLIVE OIL

MAKDÜSS

Here the eggplants are preserved in extra virgin olive oil rather than pickled, but first they need to be blanched, salted, then pressed to get rid of any excess liquid. Then they are filled with a mixture of minced garlic, crushed mild fresh chilies or red bell peppers, and coarsely ground walnuts. Makdüss is often made with tiny white eggplants, but you can use small Japanese eggplants or tiny round black eggplants like those that the lady at Matbakh Ors el-Shams (page 2) was preparing. The smaller, the better, but my mother also used regular-size Japanese eggplants. Anyhow, makdüss is not usually served as part of a selection of pickles but separately, to eat with or without bread. My friend Feryal (page 342) adds them as a garnish to her fattüsh (page 87).

MAKES 1 QUART (1 LITER)

1 pound 14 ounces (750 g) very small round or Japanese eggplants, stalk and husk peeled off without cutting into the eggplant

1 tablespoon coarse sea salt, plus extra for rubbing the eggplants

Extra virgin olive oil

FOR THE FILLING

2 heads garlic, peeled, minced to a fine paste

⅔ cup (100 g) coarsely chopped walnuts

¼ teaspoon cayenne pepper or 1 fresh red mild chili, topped, seeded, very finely chopped

1 teaspoon fine sea salt

1. Fill a pot with water and place over medium-high heat. Bring to a boil, then add the eggplants together with the salt. Cook for 5 minutes. Drain and let cool, then slit each eggplant down the middle, cutting halfway into the flesh—make sure you do not cut through to the other side—to create a large enough pocket to eventually take in the filling. Rub a little coarse salt inside each and place in a flattish colander. Put a large plate over the eggplants and either put a heavy weight on it or, with your hands, press on the eggplants to extract as much excess liquid as you can. Wipe dry inside and out and spread on a kitchen towel. Let dry.

2. To make the filling: Put the minced garlic cloves in a medium bowl. Add the chopped walnuts and cayenne or chili together with the fine salt and mix well.

3. Take one eggplant and pry the flesh open. Press a teaspoon of the filling into the eggplant. Smooth the filling with your finger or spoon to level with the eggplant skin. Place on a plate and finish filling the rest of the eggplants the same way.

4. Pack the eggplants in layers inside a 1-quart (1 liter) jar, filled-side up or against the sides—fit them quite snugly but without crushing them. Cover with olive oil. Close the jar and store in a cool, dark place. They will be ready after a month or so.

AWARMA

Long ago, when I lived in Lebanon, we would often go to Rechmaya, my maternal grandmother's village, which was very exciting because it was when my grandmother, together with her sister, Tante Marie, who lived there all year round, would be preparing awarma, a kind of lamb confit. My mother's sister, Tante Jeannot, who never married and lived with my grandmother, also helped, as did my mother of course.

Tante Marie's house had a lush garden at the back that overlooked the spectacular valley below. It was there that she kept the lamb she had bought earlier in the season to make awarma. She tied it to a tree and, together with the other women of the family, they took turns in fattening it as soon as it was brought back, treating it like a precious child and hand feeding it on mulberry and vine leaves. However, the lamb's pampered existence came to a brutal end the moment it grew plump enough to be killed.

The slaughter may have been bad news for the poor lamb, but for the family, it was an occasion for feasting. After it had been butchered by one of the uncles—most of my grandmother's family lived in the village all year round—the women would set about preparing the meat. The bones were used in h'risseh (page 240) or to enrich stocks and sauces. The liver, still warm out of the animal, was reserved for our breakfast, cut up into small pieces and served on a plate, together with a little mound of diced fat from the tail—I always sat next to my grandmother while she made me the liver bites (page 247).

With breakfast over, the backbreaking work began. My grandmother, mother, and aunts used razor-sharp knives to trim and dice both meat and tail fat into very small pieces, keeping them separate. They then melted the fat before cooking the meat in it to create the year's stock of awarma. The proportions for making awarma change from family to family, but here is how it was done in our family. I doubt you will be able to find tail fat in the West. This said, the fat from around the kidneys is a good enough substitute. As for which cut of meat to use, either shoulder or neck is good, and your awarma will definitely be superior if you cut everything by hand.

MAKES 3 500-GRAM JARS

2 pounds 4 ounces (1 kg) tail fat, hand-chopped into small pieces

2 pounds 4 ounces (1 kg) lamb, from the neck or the shoulder, trimmed of most fat and skin, hand diced into ¼-inch (½ cm) pieces

2 tablespoons sea salt

1. Put the tail fat in a large pot and place over medium heat. Let the fat melt, stirring occasionally, and bring to a boil. Let bubble until completely melted and golden—there will be tiny crisp pieces of fat left but you do not have to worry about them.

2. In the meantime, put the meat in a bowl. Add the salt and mix well. Then, add to the boiling fat and let bubble gently for 20 to 30 minutes, until the meat is completely cooked. Turn off the heat and let cool for 15 minutes before transferring to sterilized glass jars. Eventually the fat will solidify and lighten in color. Use for the recipes on pages 35, 63, and 83.

Zeytun (Olives)

The olive tree is as much the symbol of Lebanon as the cedar of Lebanon. There isn't a single traditional home that will not have a yearly supply of their own cured olives or those bought from small artisanal producers who cure olives for sale that are as good as the home-cured ones. My mother, like her mother and other traditional women, always would finish her meal with an olive or two wrapped in pita, a kind of palate cleanser. I have learned to cure my own in Sicily, and every year, when I cure the freshly harvested olives I buy from an old couple at my local farmers market, I feel as if I am back in my mother's and grandmother's kitchens.

Our most famous olive groves are in Hasbaya, Deir Meymas, and Marja'yün in the south, the Shüf region, southeast of Beirut, and the Koura region in the north.

We have three different ways of preparing green olives for curing. One where we crush the olives with a clean stone or pestle, to burst the flesh open but without breaking the stone. Another where we make a slit lengthwise into the olives with a sharp knife. And the third where we keep them intact, in which case they take longer to be ready. Whichever way we prepare them, the curing method remains the same, but both taste and texture will differ slightly.

Regardless of how you choose to prepare them, you first need to soak the olives for three days, changing the water twice a day to get rid of some of the bitterness. Once this is done, drain the olives, then cut a few lemons into thin slices. Wash a few fresh chilies (the chili and lemon to taste), and if you have access to citrus leaves, wash a few, also to add to the olives. Then take as many sterilized glass jars as you need for the quantity of olives you are curing and spread a thick layer of olives over the bottom, arrange a few lemon slices on top and a couple of citrus leaves if you are using them, and continue making layers, interspersing each two or three with one or two chilies until you have filled the jar. Cover the olives with brine, which is salted water (5 tablespoons coarse sea salt per 1 quart/1 liter water). In the old days, they checked the salt content by putting a raw egg in its shell in the water; if it floated, the solution was salty enough for the olives—a method called in Arabic *fowshet el-baydah*, or "floating of the egg." The uncut olives take the longest to ripen, about six months; the slit ones will be ready after one to two months and the crushed ones after three weeks.

As for black olives, which are basically ripe green olives, they are preserved in olive oil.

You need to first wash them in several changes of water until very clean. Then put them in a large crock and sprinkle liberally with sea salt. Mix well twice a day for about four days, so all of the olives have absorbed the salt, then cover with extra virgin olive oil. You can add a little wine vinegar, or not, according to taste, and continue mixing well for another couple of days. Pack in sterilized glass jars and, depending on how ripe they were to start with, eat immediately or after one or two weeks. Both black and green olives will last the year if kept in a cool, dark place.

SPICES

The Arabic word for spices is *b'harat*, which simply means "spices," and, to my knowledge, it is only in Tunisia that the word describes a specific mixture. Everywhere else, b'harat is followed by the name of the dish that the mixture is for, such as b'harat shawarma (page 112) or b'harat moghrabiyeh (page 233). If I have a recipe for a mix, I make my own, otherwise I buy premixed, from either one of my two favorite spice shops, known as mat'haneh (mill) or mahmassa (roastery) because the spices are ground and roasted there. In Beirut, I go to Mat'hanet Khoury, which my friend Jacquot (see Acknowledgments) introduced me to. I absolutely love their ready meghli mixture (page 330). All you have to do is soak it for two hours in the required amount of water before boiling. This considerably shortens the time for stirring. *Meghli* means "boiled" because you need to boil it for a long time for it to thicken to a custard-like consistency, and all the while you need to keep stirring so as not to have any lumps! And when I am in the south, I go to Moussa Ibrahim in Dibbine, whom I got to know through another friend, Zelfa Hourani, who has a beautiful Ottoman house in Marja'yün, a lovely southern village very near the border. Obviously, they are not the only places. There are also pretty good prepacked spice mixtures that you will find in any well-stocked Middle Eastern grocery store.

We also have what I like to call the trinity of spices, used in almost all of our dishes, and that is cinnamon (*erfeh*), allspice (known in Arabic as *b'har helü*), and black pepper. White pepper is occasionally used instead of black, and sometimes a seven-spice mixture (page 19) is added.

The other spices that are also frequently used are anise, both seeds and ground (*yansün* in Arabic), mahlep (*mahlab*), and chili (*harr*).

Allspice (B'har Helü)

We describe allspice as a sweet pepper (*b'har* means pepper and *helü* sweet) because of its subtle flavor that hints of cloves, cinnamon, and nutmeg. Its aroma is pretty central to almost all of our savory dishes.

Cinnamon (Erfeh)

Cinnamon belongs to the Lauraceae family, and there are two types. One is thin sheets from the inner bark of *Cinnamomum zeylanicum* that are dried, then rolled into thin quills. In the West, you buy them all cut to the same short length, whereas in Lebanon you can buy them as long as 12 inches (30 cm), and it is left to you to break off the length you need for your recipe. Cassia is the other type, and it is the thick, dark bark of *Cinnamomum cassia*. It is the one that we use most commonly because it tastes stronger. Cinnamon sticks are an essential seasoning in most soups, stocks, and stews. A medium stick is about 2 inches (5 cm) long. We also use ground cinnamon, and it is a good idea to keep a stock of ground cinnamon as well.

Mahlep (Mahlab)

The grains of mahlab are found inside the kernel of prunus mahaleb, a species of cherry. They are small, pear-shaped, with a light brown husk and a pale soft core. You can buy them whole or ground to use mainly in baking. Mahlab has a rather intriguing, slightly bitter flavor. As a result, it is used sparingly.

PANTRY

KAMMÜNEH

An essential spice mixture from the south that is mainly used in kibbé, both meat and vegetarian. There are many versions, varying from village to village and from family to family. This one comes from my friend Feryal (page 342), who makes her own to sell in her lovely eponymous shop in Beirut. It is different from others that I have tasted in that it is very heavy on cumin, which is not surprising given its name—*kammün* means cumin in Arabic.

MAKES ABOUT 1½ CUPS (140 G)

Just over ½ cup (70 g) cumin seeds

Just under 2 tablespoons (10 g) black peppercorns

½ teaspoon (3 g) ground allspice

Just over ½ cup (12 g) dried rosebuds, shell and core discarded

2 tablespoons (3 g) dried chilies, seeded

2 tablespoons (12 g) dried mint

¾ cup (25 g) dried marjoram

1½ teaspoons (3 g) dried basil

Put the cumin seeds, peppercorns, allspice, rosebuds, and chilies in a spice grinder and process to a fine powder. Transfer to a small mixing bowl. Add the dried mint, marjoram, and basil and mix well. Store in an airtight glass jar in a cool, dark place.

Feryal Osseyran in front of her mise en place for tomato kibbé, which is seasoned with her kammüneh

SEVEN-SPICE MIXTURE
SABE' B'HARAT

The quintessential Lebanese spice mixture that is made of seven different spices—*sabe'* meaning seven. It varies slightly from region to region and from family to family. Here is the one I make.

MAKES JUST OVER ½ CUP

2 tablespoons finely ground black pepper

2 tablespoons ground allspice

2 tablespoons ground cinnamon

2 teaspoons ground coriander

2 teaspoons ground cloves

2 teaspoons ground ginger

2 teaspoons freshly grated nutmeg

Put all the spices in a small mixing bowl and mix well. Store in an airtight glass jar in a cool, dark place.

Spice display at a müneh shop, Saida

FRESH ESSENTIALS

Lemons (Hamüd)

If anyone asked me which single flavor to associate with Lebanese cooking, I would have to say lemony. I don't think I am ever out of lemons on the kitchen counter when the weather is cool, and in the refrigerator otherwise. We use lemon juice extensively, in lemonade of course, our ultimate summer drink, in dips and salads, in cooked dishes, and also in sugar syrup. And we use lemon wedges or slices as a garnish, so make sure you have lemons on hand whenever you are planning a Lebanese meal.

Buttermilk (Ayran)

Real ayran is a slightly sour, frothy drink that we often have with kebabs (pages 107 and 111) or lahm bil-ajine (page 43). It is the whey that is left over from when yogurt is churned to produce butter. A much faster version, although not as strong in flavor, is made by mixing yogurt with enough water to have a thin creamy drink to which you add salt before whizzing with a handheld blender to make it frothy.

Herbs (A'shab)

There are two herbs that are essential to our cooking, and they are parsley (*Petroselinum crispum*) and mint (*Mentha x piperita*). I usually

Fresh vine leaves

Fresh chickpeas

keep both in my fridge, washed, dried, and layered in between paper towels inside an airtight container. The paper absorbs the excess moisture; as a result, the herbs last longer. We use other fresh herbs, such as cilantro, basil (*Ocimum basilicum*), purslane, and za'tar, but not almost daily like the first two.

Seasonal Treats (Bil-Mawssam)

Our food still follows the seasons, and all of us impatiently wait for seasonal treats to appear in the markets, at greengrocers, or simply on carts in the street. In the fall, we feast on fresh pistachios (*festü' halabi*), jujube (*ennab*), and pomegranates (*rümman*). When spring comes, it is time for unripe greengages (*janarek*), which we eat dipped in salt, and fresh green almonds (*loz akhdar*), which we eat whole also dipped in salt. Later, as the green shell becomes too hard to eat, we crack

LEBANON

them open to get at the fresh nut. Soon after, it is the short season of loquats (*akki dünya*). And when summer comes, we get our fingers red eating mulberries (*tüt*). We also pick fresh vine leaves (*wara' enab*) to roll around various fillings for mehshi (pages 187 to 208), and we press unripe sour grapes (*hosrum*) and boil the juice to have verjuice, which we often use instead of lemon juice. However, the seasonal treat that takes the prize is the desert truffle, which, unlike its Western counterparts, has no particular aroma but a very subtle nutty flavor. The truffle is found in the desert sand after the first rains, and it needs careful washing and brushing to get rid of the last grains of sand before it is peeled and, depending on its size, kept whole or cut into medium chunks. You can prepare it in different ways: boiled and dressed as a salad; marinated and grilled; or stewed with or without meat (page 130). I personally do not see the point of paying the relatively high price it commands (nothing like that of black or white truffle) for something that has more texture than flavor. Still, I recently had it, cooked with black truffle cream and served alongside a braised leg of lamb. I also had it with meat in a stew flavored with cardamom and I enjoyed both more than I thought I would.

Cheese (Jibneh)

Once most of our cheeses were made with ewe's or goat's milk, but these days cow's milk is most commonly used, while those made from the other two are fairly seasonal.

My favorite cheese is what we describe as green (*jibneh khadrah*), meaning "freshly made." Springtime is when goat's and ewe's milk cheeses are at their best because the animals graze over green pastures, mostly in the mountains. And like ricotta, jibneh khadrah needs to be consumed within two or three days.

Arisheh is a type of curd cheese traditionally made from the whey left after extracting butter from yogurt, but these days, it is commonly made by bringing yogurt to a boil then adding lemon juice to curdle the yogurt. It is then strained and the curds are refrigerated, where they will keep for a couple of days unsalted, longer if salted.

Arisheh is the base for shanklish, a fermented cheese from Akkar in the far north and the Bekaa in the east. The process is long but simple enough for you to make—my aunt used to make it for us in Mashta el-Helou in Syria, on the other side of the border from Akkar. Because she made her own butter, she had arisheh, which she first kneaded with salt and cayenne pepper until smooth enough to roll into balls the size of tennis balls. She put the balls of shanklish to dry on cotton sheets laid over straw mats for a few days before storing them inside airtight glass jars to let them ferment for up to a week. By then, they would have developed mold all over. She rinsed them clean, then rolled the balls in plain dried za'tar before packing them in glass jars—traditionally, cheese makers and home cooks used the same earthenware jars from year to year because of the enzymes from previous batches, which facilitated the fermentation. If shanklish is consumed within a week, it is described as akhdar (literally meaning green but describing something fresh). The longer it is kept, the softer and more pungent it becomes, a bit like Roquefort.

We also have what I like to describe as medium fresh cheeses, such as feta, either Bulgarian (*bolghari*) or one made in Tripoli (*jibneh trabülsiyeh*). Both are white, crumbly, and salty. Hallüm is another salty but harder white cheese, with an elastic, chewy texture that makes it perfect for grilling. It is sometimes flavored with nigella seeds (*habbet el-barakeh*, meaning the grain of grace). Hallüm can come in individual square blocks with rounded corners, or it can be shaped in long thick tresses (*jibneh majdüleh*). The latter is looser because the cheese is stretched and as a result kind of shredded. It is a good idea to rinse these cheeses under cold water before eating to get rid of some of the saltiness. If still too salty, simply soak them in a few changes of fresh water. Akkawi is a softer, slightly less salty variation on hallüm, which is also used in sweets such as k'nafeh (page 298). Darfiyeh is a crumbly goat's cheese from the north that is matured in goat skin.

The most popular non-white hard cheese we have is an imported, mature ewe's cheese known as *ash'awan*. It is similar to the Romanian kashkaval, Greek kasseri, and Turkish kaser.

Yogurt (Laban)

Yogurt is very important in our cuisine, both as a refreshing side and as a cooked sauce for meat, eggs, or vegetables. Many home cooks still make their own yogurt. I also do in Sicily because I can get unpasteurized milk from a wonderful lady who keeps a large herd of milking cows and lives in a village not too far from where I am in Trapani. Some of her cows graze in the mountains, while others are in fields by the sea. Their milk differs noticeably. However, unlike my mother's, my yogurt making skill is inconsistent even if I follow her instructions to the letter by first boiling the milk, then letting it cool to a temperature where I can hardly keep my little finger in, counting to ten. I then add 3 tablespoons yogurt that I have kept from the previous batch for each quart (1 liter). I cover the pan and wrap it in a towel like she did and let it sit for at least 4 hours before uncovering the pan, being mindful not to disturb the setting yogurt and to let it cool completely for another couple of hours. Sometimes my yogurt comes out perfectly, while other times it fails to set. I still do not know why. My suspicion is that I should make it regularly from the same batch because not all commercial yogurts have enough necessary enzymes or whatever it is that makes the milk set into yogurt—some may have been too homogenized. If you are using store-bought yogurt, always use plain full-fat, tangy yogurt, and preferably locally made.

Labneh

Many describe labneh (also known as labaneh) as cheese, but it is not. It is simply yogurt that has been strained in a cheesecloth until most of the excess liquid has dripped away. If you let all the excess liquid drain, you get a very dense labneh, which you can then roll into balls to preserve in extra virgin olive oil, whereas if you leave it creamier, you get the labneh that we mix with olive oil to eat as a dip or use as a sandwich spread.

Lebbah/Lebba

Lebbah is the first milk that cows produce after giving birth. It is very thick and slightly curdled, and utterly delicious, eaten with a sprinkling of sugar or a drizzle of honey. We used to spend some of our summer holidays at *amto* (aunt in Arabic) Zahiyeh's in Mashta el-Helou, where my father's family comes from. And, for a long time, she kept two cows in a shed on one side of her courtyard. I loved to go with her when it was time to milk them, and I was absolutely mesmerized by how my aunt squeezed the nipples to make the milk spurt out into the bucket. And my greatest excitement was when they gave birth, and my aunt brought back steaming bowls of lebbah for us to enjoy. An absolute delight that is practically impossible to have nowadays.

Wild Greens (Sli')

Foraging has always been an integral part of our cuisine, long before it became a trend in

the West. I am not sure where the word *sli'* comes from, but it describes a whole range of wild greens, from the common hommaydah (rumex), which is similar to sorrel and which we picked and chewed on when we were kids because we loved its tart flavor, to ba'leh or wild purslane (*Portulaca oleracea*), to wild fennel or shummar (*Foeniculum vulgare*), to the thin leaves of mokho bi ebboh (*Tarxacum*), to rashad, a kind of misticanza that we eat with olives, to hindbeh barriyeh, a wild chicory, and so on. People start foraging at the end of October, beginning of November after the first rains, and stop in early May when it starts to get hot and the wild stuff either dies or becomes overgrown. Wild asparagus (*Asparagus acutifolius*) and akküb (*Gundelia tournefortii*), an edible thistle, also belong to the sli' family. In fact, there are so many different wild edible plants that I wouldn't be able to list them here, not to mention that I don't know them all. What is interesting, though, is that you find the same in other Mediterranean countries, such as Greece, where sli' is called horta, and Sicily, where some greens like qualeddo appear in the farmers market in season.

SPECIAL UTENSILS

Vegetable Corer (Man'ara)

A long, narrow scoop that is used to core eggplants, zucchini, and marrows. It comes in two lengths, one fairly short for coring Japanese eggplants and zucchini and a longer one for the marrows.

Falafel Scoop (Aleb falafel)

You don't need a falafel scoop to shape falafel, but using one will make your job much easier, and faster. It is what commercial falafel makers use, to mesmerizing effect given how fast they work. The traditional scoop is brass. It looks like a short candlestick without a base with a round tray with raised sides at the top.

Inside the tray is a levered flat sheet. The round base column is about ¾ inch (2 cm) in diameter and the tray is about 2¼ inches (5½ cm) wide with the rim about ¼ inch (5 mm) high. The levered sheet is 2 inches (5 cm) wide, and it sits on a column that sinks inside the column when you press the lever down. The falafel maker pulls the tray down before filling the cup with the falafel mix. He then smooths the mix into a round or pointed top before releasing the lever over the hot oil to let the plate pop up and eject the falafel.

Ma'mül Molds (Tabe')

These molds come in three basic shapes: round and flat, round with a pointed top, and oval, also with a pointed top. They are deeply carved inside so when the ma'mül is pressed into the mold, it comes out incised with a geometric pattern. The round and oval ones are for nut-filled pastries (round for walnuts and oval for pistachios, although some sweets makers invert them), while the flat round ones are for those filled with dates. The decoration changes for the flat molds. Those used by the Christian community have a cross pattern, whereas those used by Muslims have simple geometric patterns. The carvings vary slightly depending on where the molds are made, but the size is more or less the same, about 2 inches (5 cm) in diameter, or long at the base. They all have a thick handle and a flat rim above the carved cup so you can tap the mold against your work surface to eject the ma'mül.

FLATBREADS AND SAVORY PASTRIES

FLATBREAD FROM THE SOUTH
MISHTAH

Mishtah is the typical flatbread of the south, rather like Italian focaccia but with none of the crispy bubbles that are so typical of focaccia. The Arabic name means "stretched," and depending on which bakery you buy it from, it can be long and wide or round. The texture of the bread is interesting because it has cracked wheat mixed in with the dough, while the flavor is intense because of the added spices, such as anise seeds, mahlep, and a spice mixture called *ka'k* (pages 50 and 51). You can also buy the mixture from specialty spice stores. In Lebanon they are called *mahmassa* (meaning the place where you roast) or *mat'hana* (meaning mill), both indicative of how the spices are processed, first by roasting then by grinding.

When I wrote my first book on Lebanese cuisine more than thirty years ago, I had never tasted mishtah, nor did I know about it. This is what is so interesting about our tiny country, where regional specialties are kept practically a secret from those who are not from there. It wasn't until I met my friend Nayla Audi, whose father comes from a notable political family in Kfar Rumman, a small town far south, that I finally discovered this fabulous bread. Nayla's family hardly ever serves pita bread with their meals. It is either homemade "handkerchief" bread (page 30) or mishtah from their local bakery. They, and most people in the south, also use the mishtah dough to make mana'ish (page 34).

MAKES 6 BREADS

1 cup (125 g) unbleached all-purpose flour, plus extra for kneading and rolling out

2⅓ cups (250 g) whole wheat flour

2¼ teaspoons instant (fast-acting) yeast

1 teaspoon fine sea salt

3 tablespoons (20 g) sesame seeds

3 tablespoons (20 g) anise seeds

½ teaspoon ground mahlep

1. Put the flours, yeast, salt, sesame seeds, anise seeds, mahlep, ground anise seeds, and ka'k in a large mixing bowl and mix well. Stir in the drained cracked wheat and make a well in the center. Gradually add 1¼ cups (310 ml) warm water, bringing in the flour as you go along. Mix until you have a rough ball of dough.

2. Transfer the dough to a lightly floured work surface and knead for a couple of minutes. Shape into a ball. Cover with a clean kitchen towel (you can also invert the bowl over it) and let rest for 15 minutes—this will help hydrate the dough and reduce the kneading time. Knead for a few more minutes, until the dough is soft and malleable.

3. Brush a large clean bowl with olive oil. Shape the dough into a ball and place in the bowl, turning it to coat all over with the oil. Cover with plastic wrap. Let rise in a warm, draft-free place for 1 hour, or until more or less doubled in size.

4. Transfer the dough to your work surface. Divide into 6 equal pieces. Shape each into a ball. Cover with a very damp, although not dripping wet, kitchen towel and let proof for another 45 minutes.

½ teaspoon ground anise seeds

½ teaspoon ka'k (page 50) (optional)

½ cup (85 g) cracked wheat (jrish) or coarse bulgur wheat, soaked for 30 minutes in cold water, drained

Extra virgin olive oil for the bowl

5. Flatten each ball with your hands or a rolling pin until you have a 6-inch (15 cm) disk. Transfer to a nonstick baking sheet, or one lined with parchment paper or a silicone baking mat. You can also divide the dough into 12 pieces to make smaller mishtahs to serve with drinks, in which case, make them about 4 inches (10 cm) in diameter. With your fingers, make dimples here and there all over the breads. Let rest while you preheat the oven to its highest setting.

6. Bake the mishtah in the preheated oven for 12 to 15 minutes, until lightly golden. Serve warm or let cool on a wire rack and serve at room temperature.

Sahjouneh's mishtah dough

OLIVE OIL CRACKERS
MALLET EL-SMID

A rather unusual, textured cracker from Dar el-Qanün in Ras el-Ayn, a village in the south, where a women's cooperative known as Mawasem al Dayaa (meaning "the seasons of the village") revived the tradition of making these dry breads that once were an essential staple for those going into the fields to till the land. They were also an essential foodstuff for those going on the Hajj pilgrimage. The farmers both snacked on them and offered them to those around them. Because they are dry, they keep very well. The dough is basically a combination of flour and bulgur wheat with the hydration essentially olive oil. Sesame and nigella seeds are added for flavor, and a little salt is added too. They are not so easy to make given the lack of water, and they need longer kneading than regular dough. Regardless, they are definitely worth making given how good and unusual they are.

MAKES 20

4 cups (500 g) unbleached all-purpose flour, plus extra for kneading and rolling out

1 teaspoon kosher or fine sea salt

¼ cup (35 g) sesame seeds

Heaping 1 cup (200 g) coarse bulgur wheat, soaked for 30 minutes in room-temperature water

1¼ cups (310 ml) extra virgin olive oil

Nigella seeds to garnish the crackers

1. Put the flour, salt, and sesame seeds in a large mixing bowl and mix well. Drain the bulgur wheat and add to the flour mixture. Mix well, then make a well in the center. Add the olive oil and ¼ to ½ cup (60 to 125 ml) water and knead for 5 to 10 minutes—the ladies of Dar el-Qanün knead the dough for about 20 minutes; they say it takes that long for the gluten to develop. Let sit for 30 minutes.

2. Divide the dough into 18 to 20 equal pieces, place them straight onto one or more nonstick baking sheets, or one or more lined with parchment paper or silicone baking mats, and with your fingers flatten each into a 5-inch (12½ cm) disk. Prick each with a fork here and there, then sprinkle with nigella seeds, and let rest while the oven is preheating.

3. Preheat the oven to 450ºF (220ºC).

4. Bake in the preheated oven for 12 to 15 minutes, until golden brown around the edges and completely dry—these are crackers after all. Remove from the oven and transfer to a wire rack to let them cool. These will keep for at least two weeks stored in airtight containers.

HANDKERCHIEF BREAD

MAR'Ü'

Also known as *khobz saj* (meaning saj bread), mar'ü' is a paper-thin bread that is a specialty of the mountains. It used to be prepared solely by women, but now you see more and more men preparing it, mostly in commercial bakeries. Once the dough is kneaded and rested, it is divided, then each piece is rolled into a ball before being flattened into a medium disk. From this point onward, the baker starts flipping the dough from one hand to the other, and with each pass, it expands until it becomes impossibly thin with a diameter as large as the baker's arm. A mesmerizing transformation that requires real skill. Personally, I have not mastered it, and I suspect that most of you will not either. Still, there is no need to lose heart because there is always the rolling pin. You will not be able to roll the dough out as thin as when it's flipped from one hand to the other, but you will still be able to produce a beautifully thin bread that you can bake in a large nonstick frying pan if you don't have a saj. The saj looks like a large inverted wok, and traditionally it was fired by wood, but more often than not these days, it is gas.

MAKES 10 SMALL SAJ BREADS

2 cups (250 g) unbleached all-purpose flour, plus extra for kneading and rolling out

1 teaspoon fine sea salt

1. Mix the flour and salt in a large mixing bowl and make a well in the center. Gradually add ⅔ cup (180 ml) water, bringing in the flour as you go along. Mix until you have a rough ball of dough.

2. Remove the dough onto a lightly floured work surface and knead for a couple of minutes. Shape into a ball. Cover with a clean kitchen towel or invert the bowl over it and let rest for 15 minutes—this will help hydrate the dough and reduce the kneading time. Knead for a few more minutes, until the dough is smooth and elastic.

3. Divide the dough into 10 pieces, each weighing just over 1¼ ounces (40 g). Shape into small balls, rolling the dough in between the palms of your hands and then cupping your hand around it to roll against your work surface, which should not be floured—keep the side with the seam against the work surface to seal it. Sprinkle a tray or part of your work surface with flour and place the balls of dough on it. Cover with a very damp, although not dripping wet, kitchen towel and let rest for 30 minutes.

4. Roll out each ball of dough, dusting with flour every now and then, until you have a 7- to 8-inch (17½ to 20 cm) disk. Place the disks of dough in between floured baker's couches—if you don't have any, use floured kitchen towels.

5. Place a large nonstick frying pan over medium heat, and when the pan is very hot, cook the disks of dough, one after the other, for a minute or so on each side. They should be lightly golden with small burned spots where they have bubbled up. Stack in between clean kitchen towels. You can serve these immediately, or use them to make wraps. You can also freeze them. If so, all you have to do when you want to serve them is put them in a hot oven, preheated to 450ºF (220ºC) for 2 to 3 minutes, to defrost and soften them.

Wonderful Druze sheikha making handkerchief bread at Matbakh Ors el-Shams, Mükhtara

PITA

KHOBZ

Hardly anyone in Lebanon makes pita at home. Almost everyone buys it from commercial bakeries, where the pita divides into two extremely thin layers. The homemade one, on the other hand, splits into thicker layers. As a result, everyone prefers commercial pita. This said, it is totally rewarding to make your own, even if you do not have the fully automated system commercial bakeries have where the dough is kneaded and divided and shaped by machines before the loaves are carried on a conveyor belt that allows them to rest before they make their way to the oven. Once baked, it is out onto another conveyor belt, where the bread cools slightly before arriving to the sales window or packing room. It is fascinating to watch the process. At home, the fascinating part is watching your disks of dough puff up in the oven, giving you a real sense of achievement. Good pita is available throughout the country, both from bakeries and at grocery stores. It is the main staple and a pretty universal one without any particular religious or regional association.

MAKES 10 MEDIUM LOAVES

4 cups (500 g) unbleached all-purpose flour, plus extra for kneading and rolling out

1 packet (7 g) instant (fast-acting) yeast

2 teaspoons fine sea salt

¼ cup (60 ml) extra virgin olive oil

1. Mix the flour, yeast, and salt in a large mixing bowl and make a well in the center. Add the olive oil to the well and, with your fingertips, rub the oil into the flour until well incorporated. Gradually add 1⅓ cups (330 ml) warm water, bringing in the flour as you go along. Knead until you have a rough, rather sticky ball of dough.

2. Remove the dough onto a lightly floured work surface. Sprinkle with flour and knead for a couple of minutes, sprinkling with more flour if the dough is too sticky. Shape into a ball. Cover with a clean kitchen towel or invert the bowl over it and let rest for 15 minutes—this will help hydrate the dough and reduce the kneading time. Knead for a few more minutes, until the dough is smooth, elastic, and rather soft. Shape into a ball and place in a clean lightly floured bowl. Lightly dust the top with flour and cover with plastic wrap. Let rise in a warm, draft-free place for 1 hour, or until more or less doubled in size.

3. Remove the dough onto your work surface and divide into 10 equal pieces. Roll each piece into a ball. Cover with a very wet, although not dripping, kitchen towel and let rest for 45 minutes.

4. Preheat the oven to its highest setting.

5. Roll out each ball of dough to a circle 6 to 7 inches (15 to 17½ cm) in diameter, dusting your work surface and dough with flour if the dough

sticks. Try to form as perfect a circle as you can—a good way to achieve this is to give the circle of dough a quarter turn between each rolling out. Cover the disks of dough with a floured baker's couche or a dry kitchen towel. Let rest for 15 to 20 minutes.

6. Bake the pitas in the preheated oven for 6 to 8 minutes, until well puffed and very lightly golden. The baking time will vary depending on your oven. It is a good idea to start checking on the breads after 5 minutes. Bake in separate batches if your oven is not large enough. These are best served immediately or still warm. Otherwise, let them cool on a wire rack and store or freeze in plastic bags. Simply defrost them while still in the bag, then reheat in a warm oven, preheated to 375ºF (180ºC).

TABÜNEH

Tabüneh is a typical although rather rare bread from the mountains to the north and east of Batroun, a now fashionable northern seaside town. Tabüneh starts out in a very similar way as the thin Sardinian cracker pane carasau, which begins as a giant pita before being split open and baked again to turn it into paper-thin crackers. Tabüneh is basically a super-thin large pita made with a slightly different dough, which results in a drier bread that is meant to last longer. It is then rehydrated by sprinkling it with water and letting it sit wrapped in a kitchen towel until it softens. I have seen it baked in a very primitive wood-fired oven in a tiny village where the baker had built his oven in the same shed he kept his milking cow. His bread was amazing, with a slightly different taste from pita, even if it was not flavored with anything. And while I was researching this book, I found a dedicated tabüneh baker in Abrine who used a mixture of whole wheat and all-purpose flour and possibly also a little bran, which accounted for the difference in texture and appearance from the tabüneh I knew. One baker flattened the disks of dough in a machine, then passed them one by one to a second baker manning the gas-fired oven, who picked up a disk using a long, thin rolling pin and laid it on the floor of the oven. It puffed in seconds, at which point he took it out and laid it on a stack he had already baked. It deflated as quickly as it puffed up, releasing a huge plume of steam. An absolutely fascinating spectacle. The owner then gave us a taste, and I brought back a bundle to my beautiful mother, who was very happy to taste a bread she didn't know. There is no need here for a recipe for tabüneh, as it really needs professional knowledge and very high heat to reproduce, but I thought I would describe it for you.

The owner of the bakery in Aabrine showing us his tabüneh

FLATBREADS AND SAVORY PASTRIES

MANA'ISH

Mana'ish are the quintessential Lebanese breakfast, flatbreads that can be topped with a variety of toppings ranging from za'tar (page 10) and extra virgin olive oil, to kishk (page 7), mixed with tomatoes, onions, walnuts, and extra virgin olive oil, to awarma (page 15), or simply grated white cheese. Sometimes the cheese and za'tar toppings are used together for a richer man'üsheh (singular of mana'ish). You can make these using either the dough for pita (page 32), like they do almost everywhere, or that for mishtah (page 26), like they do in the south. Most people still make their own topping/s at home to send or take to the local baker, who will make the mana'ish using their own dough. Mana'ish can be found all over the country. The kishk topping is more of a mountain or Bekaa specialty, and in a tiny bakery in the south, I saw Sahjüneh, a wonderful woman baker, use a tomato and onion salad as a topping, which made for a very refreshing man'üsheh. A kind of Lebanese take on Italian pizza! Here, I give a selection of toppings that you can use with either pita or mishtah dough (pages 32 and 26). Once you have made the dough, rolled it out, and let it rest, all you need to do is divide your selected topping/s equally among the disks of dough and bake in a preheated oven on maximum heat for 6 to 12 minutes. Check on the mana'ish after 6 minutes and either remove from the oven if ready or bake for a few more minutes, until the edges are puffed and browned and the topping/s are cooked.

MAKES 6

FOR THE DOUGH

Pita dough (page 32)

or

Mishtah dough (page 26)

Preheat the oven to its highest setting for the pita or mishtah. Make the dough according to the instructions on page 26 or page 32 and make the toppings while it rests.

THE TOPPINGS

FOR THE TOMATO TOPPING

4 medium firm ripe tomatoes (about 500 g), diced into medium-small cubes

1 medium onion (about 150 g), peeled, finely chopped

3 tablespoons (45 ml) extra virgin olive oil

1 teaspoon ground allspice

Sea salt

Coarsely ground black pepper

Put the tomatoes, onion, oil, and allspice in a large mixing bowl. Add salt and pepper to taste and mix well. Use a perforated spoon to pick up and divide the toppings evenly among the disks of pita or mishtah dough and spread all over. Let rest for 10 to 15 minutes, then bake in the preheated oven for 6 to 12 minutes. By the time they are ready, the tomatoes should have softened but not become completely mushy. Serve hot or warm.

FOR THE ZA'TAR TOPPING

1 cup (75 g) za'tar mixture (page 10)

1 small onion (about 100 g), peeled, finely chopped

1 cup (250 ml) extra virgin olive oil

Kosher or fine sea salt

Mix the za'tar, chopped onion, and olive oil in a small bowl. Divide the za'tar mixture equally among the disks of pita or mishtah dough and spread all over, making sure you oil the edges. Bake in the preheated oven for 6 to 12 minutes. The oil in the za'tar should be bubbling by the time they are ready. Serve hot or warm.

FOR THE CHEESE TOPPING

1 pound (500 g) firm akkawi cheese or fior di latte (cow's milk mozzarella), coarsely grated

Divide the cheese equally among the disks of pita or mishtah dough, spreading evenly all over. Bake in the preheated oven for 6 to 12 minutes, until the edges have bubbled up and the mana'ish are golden all over. The cheese should be melted and brown in places.

FOR THE KISHK TOPPING

½ cup (50 g) kishk (page 7)

1 medium onion (about 150 g), peeled, finely chopped

1 medium tomato (about 125 g), diced into small cubes

⅓ cup (50 g) coarsely chopped walnuts

2 tablespoons (13 g) toasted sesame seeds

1½ tablespoons tomato paste

½ cup (125 ml) extra virgin olive oil

½ cup (125 ml) plain full-fat runny yogurt

½ teaspoon cayenne pepper

Sea salt

Put all the ingredients in a medium mixing bowl and mix well. Taste for salt before adding any because kishk is already quite salty, and adjust to your liking. Spread the kishk mixture evenly over the disks of pita or mishtah dough. Bake in the preheated oven for 6 to 12 minutes, until golden around the edges and the mixture is bubbling slightly.

FOR THE AWARMA TOPPING

1½ cups (about 200 g) awarma (page 15), fat softened

6 small organic eggs, whisked

Put the awarma and eggs in a large mixing bowl and mix well, then divide the topping equally among the disks of pita or mishtah dough. Spread evenly all over. Bake in the preheated oven for 6 to 12 minutes, until the eggs are set and the dough is crisp and golden brown around the edges. Take out of the oven and serve immediately.

FLATBREADS AND SAVORY PASTRIES

DOUGH FOR FATAYER AND SAMBÜSAK
AJINET AL-FATAYER WAL-SAMBÜSAK

These two savory pastries, one fried (sambüsak) and the other baked (fatayer), are made with the same dough; and from the name, I am guessing that sambüsak are the Lebanese variation on the Indian samosa. Both are filled and fried, although the shape differs and the fillings too. The most common filling for sambüsak is ground meat and pine nuts, but they can also be made with vegetarian fillings. There are, of course, regional variations both in the fillings and the dough, with some making the latter with milk instead of water. As for the triangles, they can be made large, although this is usually done in bakeries where they are sold as a snack or light meal. Commercial bakers only make them small when home cooks bring their own filling and ask the baker to use his dough to make the fatayer. At home, they are usually made small, but you can also make them large to save time, in which case divide the dough in four and follow the instructions for making the small triangles, using a quarter of the filling for each.

MAKES ABOUT 28 PIECES

1 cup plus 3 tablespoons (150 g) unbleached all-purpose flour, plus extra for kneading and rolling out

¼ teaspoon fine sea salt

2 tablespoons (30 ml) vegetable oil, plus extra for frying the sambüsa

Mix the flour and salt in a medium mixing bowl and make a well in the center. Add the vegetable oil to the well and, with your fingertips, work it into the flour until completely absorbed. Gradually add ⅓ cup (80 ml) water, bringing in the flour until you have a rough dough. Remove the dough onto a lightly floured surface and knead for a few minutes. Invert the bowl over it or cover with a clean kitchen towel and let rest for about 15 minutes—this will hydrate the dough and reduce kneading time. Uncover the dough and knead for a few more minutes, until smooth and malleable. Shape into a ball and cover with a damp cloth. Let rest for 10 to 15 minutes.

TO MAKE SAMBÜSAK

1. Divide the dough in two and roll each half into a ball. Slightly flatten the first ball and lightly dip each side in a little flour. Roll out into a large disk, about ¹⁄₁₀ inch (2 mm) thick, regularly turning the dough over. Take a 3-inch (7 cm) round pastry cutter and cut as many circles as you can, starting from the edge and working your way round the outside first, then the inside. This size will make medium crescents. You can also make smaller ones using a 2-inch (5 cm) round pastry cutter, but that can be quite fiddly. Pick up any excess dough. Knead together and let rest before rolling out.

2. Turn the dough circles over. Take one and lay it on the fingers of one hand. Put a teaspoon of the stuffing of your choice (pages 39 to 42) in the middle and fold the dough over the filling into a half-moon, aligning the edges. With your free thumb and index finger, pinch the edges together into a thin flat rim. Slide the filled pastry onto the tips of your fingers so the flat edge is free. Pinch one end to flatten the edge further and fold it toward you in a small diagonal pleat. Continue pinching and pleating the rim until you have a fluted edge (or until the edge resembles a twisted cord). This is done as much to decorate the sambūsak as to seal it so it does not open during frying. Continue making these, putting the finished ones onto a lightly floured surface, until you finish the first lot of circles.

3. Fill a medium frying pan with enough vegetable oil to deep-fry the sambūsak. Place the pan over medium-high heat, and when the oil is very hot—test by dipping a piece of bread in it, if the oil immediately bubbles around it, it is ready—slide the crescents in and fry on both sides until golden all over, about 5 minutes in total. Remove with a slotted spoon onto a wire rack placed over a baking sheet to let any excess oil drain off. Take the oil off the heat while you roll out the second half of the dough. Knead the cut-outs together. Let rest, then make more crescents and fry them. Roll out the leftover dough and finish making the crescents. You should end up with about 28 pieces. Serve immediately or warm.

TO MAKE FATAYER

1. Preheat the oven to 450°F (220°C).

2. Prepare and cut the pastry as per the instructions for sambūsak above. Put a teaspoon of the stuffing (or less depending on the size of the disks of dough) of your choice (pages 39 to 42) in the middle of each circle. Then lift two sides, each one-third of the circle, and with your thumb and index fingers, pinch together, halfway down, making a thin raised seam. Lift the remaining open side and, aligning it to have the middle against the raised seam, pinch the loose edges together to have a triangle with the closed edges forming a thin raised inverted "y" in the middle. Make sure you pinch the dough tightly together so it does not open during baking. Gently transfer the filled triangles onto a nonstick baking sheet, or one lined with parchment paper or a silicone mat. Continue filling and shaping the triangles until you have finished both the dough and filling. You should end up with about 28 pieces.

3. Bake in the preheated oven for about 10 minutes, until golden. Transfer to a wire rack and let cool to serve warm or at room temperature. Both crescents and triangles will freeze well either before or after cooking. If frozen raw, defrost them slightly before frying or baking. And if frozen already baked or fried, just pop them into an oven preheated to 375°F (180°C) for about 10 minutes, until warm in the case of the triangles and hot in the case of the crescents.

CURD CHEESE SAMBŪSAK
SAMBŪSAK BIL-ARISHEH

The filling for this sambūsak is traditionally made with a kind of local curd cheese called arisheh, which you cannot really buy in the West but can be made by curdling yogurt and straining it (page 21). You can also use commercial curd cheese as an acceptable substitute or a mild sheep's and goat's milk feta kept in brine, which you need to rinse, pat dry, and crumble before using.

MAKES ABOUT 28

Dough for Fatayer and Sambūsak (page 36)

FOR THE FILLING

2 tablespoons (30 g) unsalted butter

1 free-range organic egg, beaten

7 ounces (200 g) arisheh (page 21)

A few sprigs flat-leaf parsley (about 30 g on the stalk), most of the stalks discarded, very finely chopped

Handful mint leaves, very finely chopped

2 scallions, trimmed, very thinly sliced

¼ teaspoon ground cinnamon

½ teaspoon ground allspice

½ teaspoon finely ground black pepper

Sea salt

1. Prepare the dough following the instructions on page 36.

2. To prepare the filling: Melt the butter in a small frying pan over medium heat. Add the egg and scramble it, leaving it somewhat soft. Transfer to a medium mixing bowl. Add the arisheh, parsley, mint, and scallions. Season with the cinnamon, allspice, and pepper. Taste before adding any salt, as the cheese may be salty enough. Adjust to your taste and mix well. Shape, fill, and fry the sambūsak following the instructions on page 37. Serve immediately after frying or warm.

MEAT SAMBÜSAK

SAMBÜSAK BIL-LAHMEH

You can vary the taste here by replacing the lemon juice with vinegar, verjuice (the juice of unripe grapes, page 3), or pomegranate molasses.

MAKES ABOUT 28

Dough for Fatayer and Sambüsak (page 36)

FOR THE FILLING

3 tablespoons (45 g) unsalted butter or ghee

3 tablespoons (25 g) Mediterranean pine nuts

4½ ounces (125 g) lean ground lamb

¼ teaspoon ground cinnamon

½ teaspoon ground allspice

⅛ teaspoon finely ground black pepper

1 tablespoon lemon juice (or one of those mentioned above)

Sea salt

Vegetable oil for frying

1. Prepare the dough following the instructions on page 36.

2. To prepare the filling: Put the butter in a medium frying pan and place over medium heat. Once the butter has melted, add the pine nuts and toast, stirring constantly, until golden brown—be very careful at the end, as they will quickly turn from golden brown to burned, and you really don't want this to happen given how expensive Mediterranean pine nuts are these days. Remove with a slotted spoon onto a double layer of paper towel to drain any excess fat. Then transfer onto clean paper towels.

3. Cook the meat in the same butter until it loses all traces of pink. Keep stirring and mashing the meat with a wooden spoon so you don't have any lumps. Season with the cinnamon, allspice, and pepper. Add the lemon juice (or vinegar, verjuice, or pomegranate molasses). Then add the toasted pine nuts and salt to taste. Cook, stirring, for another minute or so. Taste and adjust the seasoning if needed. Let cool.

4. Shape, fill, and fry the sambüsak following the instructions on page 37. Serve immediately after frying or warm.

SWISS CHARD FATAYER
FATAYER BIL-SIL'

These fatayer can be made with different greens, ranging from spinach, which is the most common, to purslane, or to any of the wild greens, which we call sli' (page 22). My favorite are those filled with Swiss chard. You can also use sorrel for a particularly sour taste, or chicory for a slightly bitter one, or fresh za'tar (page 10) for a more pungent one. The instructions below do not change whichever green you choose, except perhaps as far as squeezing them, as some will have more excess liquid than others. You will also need to adjust the seasonings to fit the green of your choice.

MAKES ABOUT 28 SMALL FATAYER OR 4 LARGE ONES

Dough for Fatayer and Sambüsak (page 36)

FOR THE FILLING

7 ounces (200 g) Swiss chard, thinly shredded into strips about ¼ inch (5 mm) wide

Sea salt

1 small onion (about 100 g), peeled, very finely chopped

¼ teaspoon finely ground black pepper

1 tablespoon sumac

1 tablespoon Mediterranean pine nuts

Juice of ½ lemon, or to taste

1 tablespoon extra virgin olive oil

1. Prepare the dough following the instructions on page 36. Let rest while you prepare the filling.

2. Put the chopped Swiss chard in a large mixing bowl. Sprinkle a little salt all over, and with your fingertips, rub the salt in until the Swiss chard is wilted. Put the chopped onion in a separate bowl that will eventually be large enough to take the greens. Add a little salt and the pepper and again rub the seasonings in with your fingers to soften the onion.

3. Squeeze the chard dry and pull apart the chopped leaves, making sure you don't have any clumps. Add the onion, sumac, and pine nuts. Then add the lemon juice and olive oil and mix well. Taste and adjust the seasoning if needed. The taste should be quite strong to offset the plain dough. Cover with a clean kitchen towel. Set aside.

4. Preheat the oven to 450°F (220°C).

5. Fill, shape, and bake the fatayer following the instructions on page 37. Serve hot or warm.

STRAINED YOGURT FATAYER
FATAYER BIL-LABNEH

These are probably my favorite fatayer. I love how with the first bite, the crust breaks to release the hot tangy juice of the melting labneh. A perfect contrast and a moment that is filled with nostalgia, as I remember my mother and grandmother making these for us when I lived in Beirut. Labneh—or *labaneh*, as Palestinians call it—has gone global now. It is also universal throughout our country, changing only with which milk is used to first make the yogurt, which is then strained for labneh. In the north, it will be more often than not goat's milk, whereas it is often sheep's milk in the mountains. It is not common to find it made with goat's milk in stores, and it is almost impossible to buy a commercial one made with sheep's milk. Fortunately, we have the choice in the West—simply buy your favorite yogurt and strain it through a cheesecloth to have either goat's milk or sheep's milk labneh.

MAKES ABOUT 28

Dough for Fatayer and Sambüsak (page 36)

FOR THE FILLING

1 small onion (about 100 g), peeled, very finely chopped

¼ teaspoon ground cinnamon

¼ teaspoon ground allspice

⅛ teaspoon finely ground black pepper

Sea salt

1 small firm ripe tomato (about 100 g), diced into very small cubes

5 ounces (150 g) very thick labneh (page 22)

1 teaspoon unsalted butter, softened

1. Prepare the dough following the instructions on page 36. Let rest while you prepare the filling.

2. Put the chopped onion in a medium mixing bowl. Add the cinnamon, allspice, pepper, and salt to taste and rub the seasonings into the onion with your fingers to soften it.

3. Add the diced tomato, labneh, and softened butter and mix well. Taste and adjust the seasoning if needed. Cover with a clean kitchen towel and set aside.

4. Preheat the oven to 450°F (220°C).

5. Shape, fill, and bake the fatayer following the instructions on page 37. Serve hot or warm.

MEAT "PIZZA"

LAHM BIL-AJINE

You can vary the above topping by drizzling a little yogurt or tahini sauce (page 77) over the meat mixture and baking as above. Or you can add a little pomegranate molasses to the meat mixture for an intriguing sweet and savory flavor.

MAKES 4 MEDIUM "PIZZAS"

Pita dough (page 32)

FOR THE TOPPING

1 medium onion (about 150 g), peeled, grated over the fine side of the grater

1 medium tomato (about 125 g), grated over the coarse side of the grater

5 ounces (150 g) lean ground lamb

1 teaspoon lemon juice, or to taste

¼ teaspoon ground cinnamon

½ teaspoon ground allspice

¼ teaspoon seven-spice mixture (page 19)

⅛ teaspoon finely ground black pepper

½ teaspoon Aleppo pepper

Sea salt

⅓ cup (50 g) Mediterranean pine nuts for garnish

1. Prepare the pita dough following the instructions on page 32.

2. Put the grated onion and tomato in a large mixing bowl. Drain off any excess liquid, then add the meat, lemon juice, cinnamon, allspice, seven-spice mix, black pepper, and Aleppo pepper. Mix well. Add salt to taste and mix again. Taste and adjust the seasoning if needed—if you are reluctant to taste raw meat, make a small patty and sear it in a small pan to make sure it is well seasoned. Place in a colander over a bowl to drain off any excess juice to avoid a soggy dough. Cover with a clean kitchen towel and set aside.

3. Follow the instructions for mana'ish (page 34) to make, divide, and shape the dough. If you are making small lahm bil-ajine, spread ½ teaspoon meat topping flatly and thinly all over; if you are making medium ones, divide the topping evenly among the disks of dough and spread thinly over each. Scatter a few pine nuts over each and bake in the preheated oven for 10 to 12 minutes, or until the dough has bubbled up around the edges and is golden brown. Serve hot or warm.

FLATBREADS AND SAVORY PASTRIES

MEAT-FILLED HAND PIES FROM BAALBEK
SFIHA B'ALBAKIYEH

These hand meat pies are a specialty of Baalbek, a UNESCO World Heritage site and one of the most beautiful archeological sites in Lebanon. It was known as Heliopolis during Hellenistic times, and before that, it was a Phoenician city, with a triad of deities worshiped there. It retained its religious function in Roman times, with thousands of pilgrims flocking to the sanctuary of the Heliopolitan Jupiter, where its colossal structures count among the finest examples of Imperial Roman architecture at its apogee. Apart from its historical attraction, Baalbek is also where you find Eastern culinary delights, such as these irresistible hand pies, shaped square and filled with a highly seasoned ground meat mixture. I saw them being made at a great bakery in the heart of the city, where the men worked in tandem, first dividing the very soft dough into tiny balls, then slapping them into flat disks before piling the meat mixture in the middle. They then lifted the meat-topped disks of dough and flattened the meat with their thumb before quickly lifting the corners to make square hand pies. The size differed according to the clients, who each brought their meat mixture for the bakers to use with their dough. The classic mildly spiced filling is meat, tomatoes, and onion, but there is another one with meat, onions, yogurt, tahini, and pomegranate molasses. Both versions are scrumptious, but remember to put your meat mixture in a sieve before you start using it so it is not too wet.

MAKES 25 TO 30

FOR THE DOUGH

2 cups (250 g) unbleached all-purpose flour, plus extra for kneading and rolling out

¼ packet (just under 2 g) instant (fast-acting) yeast

½ teaspoon fine sea salt

1½ teaspoons baker's or superfine sugar

1 tablespoon vegetable oil

⅔ cup (160 ml) organic whole milk

FOR THE FILLING

Double the amount of topping for Meat "Pizza" (page 43)

1. To make the dough: Mix the flour, yeast, salt, and sugar in a large mixing bowl, then add the vegetable oil and milk and mix until you have a rough dough. Remove your dough onto a lightly floured work surface and knead for a couple of minutes. Roll the dough into a ball and invert the bowl over it. Let rest for 15 minutes—this will help hydrate the dough and reduce kneading time. Uncover the dough, knead for a few more minutes, and then invert the bowl over it again. Let rise for 45 minutes to 1 hour.

2. To make the filling: While the dough is resting, prepare the topping for Meat "Pizza" and place in a sieve over a bowl to get rid of any excess liquid.

3. Preheat the oven to 450ºF (220ºC). Line two baking sheets with parchment paper or silicone mats or use nonstick ones.

4. To make the hand pies: Divide the dough in two and roll each half into a ball. Cover and let rest for 15 minutes. Then roll out one ball into a thin sheet, about 1/10-inch (2½ mm) thick. Use a 3¼-inch (8 cm) pastry cutter to cut out as many circles as you can. You should be able to cut at least 12. Gather the excess dough and knead together into a ball. Let rest, covered, while you make the first batch of pies. Turn the circles of dough over and put 1 tablespoon of meat filling in the middle of each, leaving about ½ inch (1¼ cm) free all around. Then lift two free sides and pinch to have something like two "ears" on either side of the meat. Do the same with the other two free sides to end up with a square cup with "ears" on all four corners. Pinch the "ears" really tight and cup the dough against the meat. Transfer to the baking sheet and shape the remaining pies in the same way. Let rest for about 10 minutes, then bake in the preheated oven for 20 minutes, until the meat filling is cooked through and the pastry is golden brown around the edges.

5. Take out of the oven and serve hot or warm, either as a snack or as part of a mezze spread.

Sfiha in the making at a bakery in Baalbek

ANJAR CHEESE "PIZZA"
SFIHA FROM ANJAR

Even though this is called *sfiha*, the shape is not square like that from Baalbek but round like mana'ish. What's really interesting about this recipe is that, like the name indicates, it comes from Anjar, where there is a large community of Armenians, although I don't think that this recipe is Armenian given its use of shanklish, a kind of blue cheese that is more northern Lebanese/Syrian. Again, the topping was new to me, but the combination of the mild akkawi and pungent shanklish, sweetened by the onion with the added dried thyme, makes for a wonderful variation on the regular cheese mana'ish (page 34).

MAKES 10 MEDIUM SFIHAS

Pita dough (page 32)

FOR THE TOPPING

2 large onions (about 400 g), peeled, very finely chopped

1 teaspoon fine sea salt

7 ounces (200 g) akkawi cheese, coarsely grated, soaked in a couple of changes of cold water to make it less salty

1 ball of shanklish (about 125 g), crumbled

1½ tablespoons crushed dried thyme or oregano

⅓ cup (80 ml) extra virgin olive oil, plus extra for the baking sheet and to brush the edges of the sfiha

1. Prepare the pita dough following the instructions on page 32. Let rise while you prepare the topping.

2. Put the chopped onions in a large mixing bowl. Add the salt and rub it into the onions with your hands to soften them.

3. Add the cheeses, thyme, and olive oil and mix well. To make one large sfiha, using your oiled hands, flatten the dough to cover an oiled nonstick baking sheet measuring 18 x 12 inches (45 x 30 cm), making dips here and there as you would with focaccia. Then spread the topping all over and let rest while you preheat the oven to 500°F (250°C).

4. Bake in the preheated oven for 20 minutes, or until the cheese is melted and the edges of the sfiha are crisp and golden brown. Take out of the oven and let rest for 5 minutes or so. Serve hot.

SWEET SAJ BREAD

TALAMI

These are small, rather thick sweet breads from the west Bekaa, where the dough is hydrated with butter and milk rather than oil and water. They are flavored with mahlep (page 17) and anise seeds and can be baked on the saj or in the oven. You can emulate the saj in your kitchen by using a large well-seasoned cast-iron or nonstick flat pan and turning over the bread to bake on both sides, whereas you won't need to do this if you bake it in the oven. These are great for breakfast, or served as a snack with labneh, za'tar (page 10), and extra virgin olive oil, or at teatime with butter and honey or jam.

MAKES 6 BREADS

4 cups (500 g) unbleached all-purpose flour, plus extra for kneading and rolling out

1 teaspoon instant (fast-acting) yeast

1 cup (200 g) baker's or superfine sugar

¼ teaspoon mahlep (page 17)

¼ teaspoon anise seeds

½ teaspoon fine sea salt

4 tablespoons (60 g) unsalted butter, softened

1 cup (250 ml) organic whole milk

Fine semolina to rest the shaped bread on

1. Put the flour, yeast, sugar, mahlep, anise seeds, and salt in a large mixing bowl and mix well. Add the butter and, with the tips of your fingers, rub it into the flour. Add the milk and knead until you have a rough ball of dough. Remove onto a lightly floured work surface and knead for a few minutes. Shape into a ball. Cover with a kitchen towel or invert the bowl over the dough and let rest for 15 minutes—this will allow the dough to hydrate and reduce the kneading time. Knead for a few more minutes, then dust a clean bowl with flour and place the dough in it, dusting it with a little more flour. Cover with plastic wrap and let proof in a warm, draft-free place overnight, or for 10 hours.

2. Remove the dough onto a lightly floured surface and divide into 6 equal pieces. Roll each into a ball and let rest, covered with a clean kitchen towel, for 15 minutes. Sprinkle one or more baking sheets with fine semolina. Then, with your hands, flatten each ball of dough to a ½-inch- (1¼ cm) thick circle, making dimples with your fingers here and there, and place over the semolina so it doesn't stick while resting. Dust with a little semolina and cover with a clean kitchen towel.

3. Here I am assuming that you don't have a saj, which is not a problem, because you can bake the breads in the oven. To do so, preheat the oven to 450°F (220°C), then bake in the preheated oven for about 15 minutes, until golden. Or place a large nonstick frying pan over medium-high heat. When the pan is hot, reduce the heat to medium and place as many disks of dough as will fit comfortably in the pan. Cook for 3 to 4 minutes on each side, until golden brown all over. Serve hot, warm, or at room temperature.

SACRED BREAD
ORBAN

Orban is a typical bread that is taken to church in most Christian communities, and in particular in the Metn region, east of Beirut. The Greek Orthodox make a plain version without the sugar, spices, and fragrant waters, which they use for communion instead of the wafer, while the Greek Catholics prepare it the way described below. I do not give a recipe for the plain version because it is too bland. This version is far more flavorful and as a result more interesting.

MAKES 4

4 cups (500 g) unbleached all-purpose flour, plus extra for kneading and rolling out

1 tablespoon instant (fast-acting) yeast

1 teaspoon fine sea salt

1 cup (200 g) baker's or superfine sugar

½ teaspoon ground nutmeg

½ teaspoon ground mastic (page 7)

1 teaspoon ground mahlep (page 17)

½ cup (125 ml) orange blossom water

½ cup (125 ml) rose water

1. Mix the flour, yeast, sugar, nutmeg, mastic, and mahlep in a large mixing bowl and make a well in the center. Gradually add the orange blossom and rose waters, bringing in the flour and sugar mixture as you go along. Knead until you have a rough dough. Remove onto a lightly floured work surface and knead for a couple of minutes. Roll the dough into a ball and cover with a damp kitchen towel or invert the bowl over it and let rest for 15 minutes—this will help hydrate the dough and reduce the kneading time. Then knead for a few more minutes, until smooth and malleable. Shape into a ball. Lightly dust a clean bowl with flour and place the ball of dough inside the bowl. Cover with plastic wrap and let proof in a warm, draft-free place for 1½ hours, or until doubled in size.

2. Divide the dough into 4 pieces. Roll each into a ball and place on a lightly floured work surface. Cover with a damp, although not dripping wet, kitchen towel and let rest for 1 hour.

3. Preheat the oven to 450ºF (220ºC) about 15 minutes before you are ready to bake the breads.

4. When the time is up, roll out each ball of dough into a circle about ½ inch (1¼ cm) thick. Transfer onto a nonstick baking sheet, or one lined with parchment paper or a silicone baking mat. Stamp deeply with a cross pattern, or a Greek or Bulgarian wooden stamp that has a cross pattern.

5. Bake in the preheated oven for 15 to 17 minutes, until golden but still soft. These breads are taken to church the day after and distributed to the faithful.

OLIVE OIL GALETTES
KA'K BIL-ZEYT

A savory variation on the Easter Rings (page 324) that I assume belongs to the Muslim community rather than the Christian one.

4 cups (500 g) unbleached all-purpose flour, plus extra for kneading and rolling out

1 teaspoon instant (fast-acting) yeast

3 tablespoons (24 g) powdered milk

1 teaspoon mahlep (page 17)

½ teaspoon fine sea salt

1 cup (250 ml) extra virgin olive oil, plus extra for shaping the dough

1. Mix the flour, yeast, powdered milk, mahlep, and salt in a large mixing bowl and make a well in the center. Add the olive oil and, with the tips of your fingers, rub the oil into the flour. Then add ¾ cup plus 1 tablespoon (200 ml) warm water and knead for 3 minutes, until you have a rough ball of dough. Remove onto a lightly floured work surface. Invert the bowl over the dough and let hydrate for about 15 minutes. Knead again for a few minutes and divide into 8 small balls. Let rest for 30 minutes.

2. Preheat the oven to 400ºF (200ºC).

3. Use a rolling pin to flatten each ball into a disk about 8 inches (20 cm) in diameter. Roll each disk into a cylinder and join the ends to shape a ring. Transfer to a nonstick baking sheet, or one lined with parchment paper or a silicone mat. Let rest for 30 minutes, then bake in the preheated oven for 25 minutes, or until golden brown all over. Let cool and serve at room temperature with coffee or tea or simply as a snack.

ABBAS GALETTES
KA'K AL-ABBAS

Named in remembrance of the Prophet's son-in-law Imam Ali's son, Abbas, these dry "cookies" are from the south, specifically from Nabatiyeh, a town southeast of Sidon. Imam Ali was the first leader of Shiism, and the recipe dates back hundreds of years. These galettes were first made to take on trips in trade caravans or for the Hajj pilgrimage, because they lasted for a long time given that they are baked until dry. These days, they are prepared for Eid al-Adha (the Feast of the Sacrifice and the most important in Islam) as well as for Ashura, to distribute to the faithful during the procession. They are also prepared for special occasions. The mixture of the spices in the dough makes them really tasty, and they will keep for at least a month in an airtight container.

MAKES 24 GALETTES

- 2¾ cups (345 g) unbleached all-purpose flour, plus extra for kneading and rolling out
- 2 cups (250 g) fine semolina
- 1 teaspoon instant (fast-acting) yeast

- 1 tablespoon anise seeds
- 1½ teaspoons ka'k spice mixture (½ teaspoon each ground nutmeg, ginger, and cinnamon)

- 1 tablespoon fine breadcrumbs
- ½ cup (100 g) toasted sesame seeds
- 1 cup (250 ml) organic whole milk
- 1½ teaspoons ground turmeric

- 1 cup (200 g) baker's or superfine sugar
- ⅓ cup (80 g) unsalted butter, melted
- ¼ cup (60 ml) extra virgin olive oil, plus extra to brush the galettes when they come out of the oven

1. Mix the flour, semolina, yeast, anise seeds, ka'k spice mixture, breadcrumbs, and sesame seeds in a large mixing bowl and make a well in the center.

2. In another bowl, mix the milk with the turmeric and sugar and stir until the sugar is completely dissolved and the milk is yellow. Add the melted butter and olive oil and mix well. Gradually add the liquid mixture to the flour, bringing it in as you go along, and knead until you have a rough ball of dough. Remove onto a lightly floured work surface and knead for a few minutes. Roll the dough into a ball. Lightly dust a clean bowl with flour and place the ball of dough in it. Cover with plastic wrap and let proof overnight, or for about 8 hours, in a draft-free place.

3. The next day, divide the dough into 24 equal pieces and roll each into a ball. Let rest for about 15 minutes, then roll out to about 4 inches (10 cm) in diameter. If you have the special stamp that makes circular incisions

in the top of the bread, use it to stamp the breads, otherwise stamp two circles, one larger than the other, in the dough without pressing too hard.

4. Preheat the oven to 350°F (180°C).

5. Bake in the preheated oven for 15 to 18 minutes, until dry and lightly browned around the edges. Brush with olive oil as soon as they come out of the oven and let cool on a wire rack. Serve at room temperature or store in an airtight container.

KA'K

Ka'k can be either a dry rusk coated with sesame seeds, a staple of my childhood in Lebanon that we often had for breakfast dipped in hot milk; or it can be a soft, round pita-like loaf coated with sesame seeds that have been slightly sweetened with date or grape syrup. And, of course, there is the ka'k that looks like a handbag and that is sold on the street.

The rusks once came in only one shape, long and narrow with a slight gap in between the thick top and bottom layers, but nowadays they come in all kinds of shapes and forms: tiny or not so tiny balls, long (and not so long) thin sticks (somewhat like grissini), fat sticks, rings, and, of course, the classic shape that I knew and loved as a child.

It would be futile for me to give a recipe for the rusks here, as I doubt they can be reproduced successfully given the long and complex process. In fact, it took the baker who explained it to me three years to perfect his and achieve consistently good results.

First, there is no yeast involved. The leavening agent is produced by soaking split chickpeas in boiling water for about 12 hours, until they start to ferment. Throughout this time, the water is kept at a very high temperature to help the fermentation process. Then the water is strained and the chickpeas are discarded. A batter is then made by mixing the chickpea water with flour and baking soda, which is left to ferment for a while longer before more flour and baking soda are added together with sugar, ghee, mastic (page 7), and mahlep (page 17). The mixture is kneaded into a soft dough and left to rise. It is only then that the baker can start shaping it. The different-shaped ka'k are then allowed to rise before being baked until completely dry. The end result is a light, crunchy rusk with a half biscuit, half dry bread texture and a subtle exotic flavor.

The method of creating a leavening agent by soaking chickpeas in hot water is not reserved only for the making of ka'k in Lebanon. It is used in both Turkey and Greece, but my guess is that you have to be a really dedicated baker to go to all the trouble of keeping the soaking water hot for so long. Even then, you cannot be sure that the fermented solution will actually leaven the bread. However, the recipe that seemed to me easiest to follow is one I found in Diana Farr Louis's *Feasting and Fasting in Crete*. It is not her recipe but one she had found in a booklet published by the department of agriculture in Heraklion in Crete. The leavening is made by soaking chickpea flour in hot water and letting the batter ferment. Then flour, flavorings, and more water are added to make a dough, which is then shaped into bread or rusks. Whichever method you choose, it is highly unlikely you will succeed until you've tried several times. So, I decided to save you the trouble and not give a recipe for any of the rusk versions. However, making the Tripolitan ka'k that is similar to pita is not so difficult, and here is a recipe that the bakers at Furn el-Qal'ah in Tripoli have given me. Their ka'k is among the best I have had, and they are the ones who supply the top sweets makers in that town.

THE CITADEL BAKERY'S SESAME GALETTES

KA'K FURN AL-AL'A

Thanks to my friend Ziad Mikati, I discovered an amazing ka'k bakery in Tripoli. Ziad sent me there with his driver Ibrahim. The bakers there received Dalia and me with open arms, and they let us take as many pictures as we wanted; not only that, but they also gave me their recipe. The taste is slightly sweet and the two layers are very thin, which makes this ka'k a perfect vehicle for k'nafeh (page 298), as well as ma'jü'a (page 295). Obviously, the homemade version is not as perfect as theirs, given that they have been at it for years, not to mention that they churn out hundreds of loaves on a daily basis. Anyhow, these soft disks of ka'k are typical of Tripoli, both to use with sweets and to make cheese sandwiches, which you find sold on the street. So, it is well worth trying to make them. The way they coat the dough with the sesame seeds in the bakery is by spreading the seeds on a jute bag and very quickly flipping the dough over them to coat both sides. You can try to emulate this by using a rough kitchen cloth or simply spreading the seeds over a baking sheet.

MAKES 10 KA'K

4 cups (500 g) unbleached all-purpose flour, plus extra for kneading and rolling out

2½ tablespoons (30 g) baker's or superfine sugar

1 packet (7 g) instant (fast-acting) yeast

½ cup (50 g) sesame seeds, soaked in enough water to cover them overnight, mixed with 2 tablespoons (30 ml) date syrup, drained, spread on a rough kitchen cloth

1. Mix the flour, sugar, and yeast in a large mixing bowl and make a well in the center. Gradually add 1¼ cups (310 ml) warm water, bringing in the flour as you go along. Knead until you have a rough, rather sticky ball of dough.

2. Remove the dough onto a lightly floured work surface. Sprinkle with flour and knead for a couple of minutes, sprinkling with more flour if the dough is too sticky. Shape into a ball. Cover with a clean kitchen towel or invert the bowl over it and let rest for 15 minutes—this will help hydrate the dough and reduce the kneading time. Knead for a few more minutes, until the dough is smooth, elastic, and rather soft. Shape into a ball and place in a clean, lightly floured bowl. Lightly dust the top with flour and cover with plastic wrap. Let rise in a warm, draft-free place for 1 hour, or until more or less doubled in size.

3. Remove the dough onto your work surface and divide into 10 equal pieces. Roll each piece into a ball. Cover with a very wet, although not dripping, kitchen towel and let rest for 45 minutes.

4. Preheat the oven to its highest setting.

5. Roll out each ball of dough into a 5- to 6-inch (12½ to 15 cm) circle, dusting your work surface and dough with flour as you go along. Try to form as perfect a circle as you can—a good way to achieve this is to give the circle of dough a quarter turn between each rolling out. Dip each disk in the sesame seeds on both sides and transfer to a nonstick baking sheet, or one lined with parchment paper or a silicone mat. Let rest for 15 to 20 minutes.

6. Bake in the preheated oven for 6 to 8 minutes, until well puffed and very lightly golden. The baking time will vary depending on your oven. It is a good idea to start checking on the breads after 5 minutes. Bake in separate batches if your oven is not large enough. These are best served immediately or still warm. Otherwise, let them cool on a wire rack and store or freeze in plastic bags. Simply defrost them while still in the bag, then reheat in a warm oven heated to 375°F (180°C).

SOUPS

LEMONY SWISS CHARD SOUP
ADASS BIL-HAMÜD

We do not have many soups in our repertoire, as we normally start our meals with salads, dips, or savory pastries. In fact, soup is often served as a main rather than as part of a mezze. Perhaps this is why I am not very fond of soups, except for this one and a couple of others. And like gazpacho, this soup is served chilled and is a particular summer favorite. You can of course serve it hot or warm, but the refreshing flavors come through best when served slightly chilled. The classic recipe calls for more garlic, but I like to tone it down so as not to become a social leper! I also use less lemon so I can serve it with wine.

SERVES 4 TO 6

1 cup (200 g) large green lentils, soaked in cold water for 30 minutes

14 ounces (400 g) Swiss chard, trimmed, washed, dried, shredded into thin strips about ½-inch (1¼ cm) wide

6 to 8 large cloves garlic, peeled, minced into a fine paste

Juice of 2 lemons, or to taste

⅔ cup (160 ml) extra virgin olive oil

Sea salt

1. Drain the lentils and put them in a large pot. Add 1½ quarts (1½ liters) water and place over medium-high heat. Bring to a boil, then add the shredded chard. Reduce the heat to medium. Cover the pot and let bubble gently for about 15 minutes. Stir to mix the softened chard and lentils and let bubble, covered, for another 10 to 15 minutes, until the lentils are tender.

2. Mix the minced garlic with the lemon juice, then whisk in the olive oil. When the lentils and chard are done, add the garlic/olive oil/lemon juice mixture. Mix well. Add salt to taste and simmer uncovered for 5 more minutes. Taste and adjust the seasoning if needed. Serve hot, warm, at room temperature, or slightly chilled.

MIXED LEGUME AND GRAIN SOUP
MAKHLÜTA

This is a typical mountain soup that can be made with or without meat. It is quite substantial either way. The recipe below is for the vegetarian version, which I prefer. If you want the meat, simply add ½ pound (225 g) lean lamb meat diced into small cubes. There is another version of makhlüta (which means "mixed" in Arabic) from Mükhtara, a town in the Shouf, which is the seat of the leader of the Druze political party Walid Jumblatt Jr. Theirs has no grains and fewer legumes, but what makes it really interesting and different from the other two versions is that the broth is made with kishk. You will find the recipe for that version on page 58.

SERVES 4 TO 6

¼ cup (50 g) dried cannellini beans, soaked in plenty of water overnight with ¼ teaspoon baking soda, then drained and rinsed

½ cup (75 g) dried chickpeas, soaked overnight in plenty of water with ¼ teaspoon baking soda, then drained and rinsed

¾ cup (150 g) dried brown lentils, soaked in water for 1 hour, then drained

2 tablespoons (30 g) coarse bulgur wheat, rinsed under cold water

2 tablespoons (30 g) short-grain white rice, rinsed under cold water

⅔ cup (160 ml) extra virgin olive oil

2 medium onions (about 300 g), peeled, finely chopped

2 teaspoons ground cinnamon (or ground cumin)

2 teaspoons ground allspice

½ teaspoon finely ground black pepper

Sea salt

1. Put the drained and rinsed beans and chickpeas in a large pot. Add the drained lentils to the pot. Add 2½ quarts (2½ liters) water. Cover the pot and place over medium heat. Bring to a boil, then reduce the heat to medium-low and let bubble gently for about 1 hour, until the legumes are tender.

2. Put the olive oil and chopped onions in a large frying pan and place over medium heat. As soon as the oil starts sizzling around the onions, reduce the heat to medium-low and cook, stirring regularly, until soft and golden, 10 to 15 minutes.

3. Drain the bulgur wheat and rice and add to the pot when the time for the legumes is up. Add the fried onions together with their oil. Season with the cinnamon (or cumin if you prefer), allspice, pepper, and salt to taste and simmer for another 15 minutes.

4. If the soup is too thick, add a little boiling water to adjust the consistency to your taste. If it is too liquid, boil for a little longer. Taste and adjust the seasoning if needed. Serve hot or warm.

MIXED LEGUME AND KISHK SOUP FROM MÜKHTARA

MAKHLŪTAT MÜKHTARA

In this variation on the makhlūta (page 57), the soup is more substantial and is served as a main course with pita bread. Mükhtara is in the heart of the beautiful Shouf Mountains, once the preserve of both Druze and Christians. The region was often the scene of violent strife between the two, with massacres enacted on both sides. Despite the region's gruesome history, the Shouf Mountains remain the best preserved and most beautiful part of the country.

SERVES 4 TO 6

- ¾ cup (125 g) dried chickpeas, soaked overnight in plenty of water with ¼ teaspoon baking soda
- ¾ cup (125 g) dried cannellini beans, soaked overnight in plenty of water with ¼ teaspoon baking soda
- ¾ cup (125 g) small dried fava beans, soaked overnight in plenty of water with ¼ teaspoon baking soda
- 4 tablespoons (60 g) unsalted butter
- 3 tablespoons (45 ml) extra virgin olive oil
- 1½ teaspoons ground coriander
- ½ cup (65 g) kishk (page 7)
- Sea salt

1. Drain the chickpeas, cannellini beans, and fava beans and rinse under cold water. Put them in a large pot and cover well with water. Place over medium-high heat. Bring to a boil, then reduce the heat to medium-low, cover the pot, and let bubble gently for about 1 hour. Take off the heat and drain. Set aside.

2. Put the butter and olive oil in a wide, deep sauté pan and place over medium heat. When the butter has melted, add the cooked legumes and stir well. Add the coriander and mix again.

3. Add the kishk. Mix well, then add ½ quart (½ liter) water. Stir until the kishk is completely dissolved in the water and let bubble gently for about 10 minutes, stirring regularly. Taste before adding any salt—kishk is already salted—and mix again. The soup should be rather thick but not as thick as porridge, and the legumes should not be mushy, so be careful as you stir the soup. Taste and adjust the seasoning if needed. Serve hot with good bread.

LENTIL SOUP
SHORBET ADASS

A delectable and simple soup that is a Ramadan fixture for Lebanese Muslims. You can vary the taste by replacing the cinnamon with cumin, both being perfect spices for this soup.

SERVES 4 TO 6

2 cups (400 g) dried brown lentils, soaked in water for 30 minutes

¼ cup (60 ml) extra virgin olive oil, plus more to drizzle over the soup

2 medium onions (about 300 g), peeled, finely chopped

1 teaspoon ground cinnamon (or ground cumin)

Freshly ground black pepper

Sea salt

1. Drain the lentils and put them in a large pot. Add 3 quarts (3 liters) water and place over medium-high heat. Bring to a boil, then reduce the heat to medium. Stir the lentils in case some have stuck to the bottom and let bubble gently for 45 minutes.

2. While the lentils are cooking, put the olive oil and onions in a large frying pan and place over medium heat. As soon as the oil starts sizzling around the onions, reduce the heat to medium-low and cook, stirring regularly, until golden, 10 to 15 minutes.

3. Take the lentils off the heat and let sit for about 15 minutes. Add the onions and their oil to the lentils and process the soup into a purée using a handheld blender or a food processor. Return the puréed lentils and onions to the pot and place over medium heat. Season with the cinnamon (or cumin) and pepper and salt to taste. If the soup is too thick, add a little water to achieve the right consistency—be careful not to make it too runny, as it is meant to be thick. Simmer for 10 more minutes. Taste and adjust the seasoning if needed. Serve hot or warm with a drizzle of olive oil.

YELLOW SPLIT PEA SOUP

SHORBET ADASS ASFAR

This soup is quite different from the previous one because it is made with split yellow lentils with lots of vegetables and a fair amount of chili. I got the recipe from the lovely Nadine Souheil, whom I met through her sister, Zeinab, the chef at Dar Zefta, a charming boutique hotel in the south (see page 342). Both Zeinab and Nadine are wonderful southern cooks, and Nadine very generously invited me over more than once to sample particular dishes from her region. This soup was one of them. It is very simple to prepare, and you can make it as spicy as you like. Nadine made it quite hot, which I liked, but here I tone down the chili, as it is not to everyone's taste.

SERVES 6 TO 8

2½ cups (500 g) yellow split peas

2 large carrots (about 300 g), peeled, cut into chunks

1 medium onion (about 150 g), peeled, quartered

1 large potato (about 250 g), peeled, cut into chunks

2 Romano peppers or one red bell pepper (about 150 g), trimmed, seeded

1 to 2 fresh chilies, trimmed, seeded

2 medium tomatoes (250 g), seeded

1 teaspoon ground cumin

Just over 1 stick (125 g) unsalted butter

Sea salt

1. Put the split peas, carrots, onion, potato, both peppers, and the tomatoes in a large pot. Add 2½ quarts (2½ liters) water and place over medium-high heat. Bring to a boil, then lower the heat to medium-low and let bubble gently for 1¼ to 1½ hours, checking on the water level toward the end, until the vegetables are very tender.

2. Add the cumin and butter and mix until the butter is completely melted and fully incorporated into the lentils. Season with salt to taste and mix again. Take off the heat and process, using a handheld blender or food processor, until you have a completely creamy soup. Serve hot with good bread.

THE SOUP OF THE FEAST
SHORBET EL-EID

The feast here can be either Christian or Muslim. Both communities prepare this soup with slight variations. It is festive because of the chicken (once considered precious meat) and the added kibbé balls, which take a fair amount of time to prepare, but if you make them ahead and keep them in your freezer, then you will be able to put together this soup without having to think much ahead. It is fairly substantial, and again it is served as a main course and not as a starter.

SERVES 6 TO 8

FOR THE STUFFING

14 ounces lean minced lamb

¾ cup (150 g) Egyptian, Calasparra, or bomba rice, soaked in cold water for 30 minutes, drained

⅓ cup (50 g) Mediterranean pine nuts, toasted in a little butter

2 teaspoons ground cinnamon

2 teaspoons ground allspice

Sea salt

FOR THE SOUP

1 free-range organic chicken (about 3½ pounds/1½ kg)

1 cinnamon stick

Kibbé Balls (page 162) but without the stuffing

1. Put the stuffing ingredients in a large mixing bowl and mix well. Add 2 tablespoons (30 ml) water to moisten it so it cooks well inside the chicken.

2. Fill the chicken cavity and neck with the rice and meat stuffing, leaving enough space for the rice to expand during cooking, and sew the openings shut so no stuffing comes out into the broth.

3. Put the stuffed chicken in a large pot and cover with water. Place over medium-high heat and bring to a boil. As the water is about to boil, skim the surface clean so you have a beautiful clear broth in the end. Then reduce the heat to medium-low, add the cinnamon stick, and cover the pot. Let bubble gently for 45 minutes to 1 hour, until both the chicken and stuffing are cooked through.

4. While the chicken is cooking, prepare your kibbé balls, but do not stuff them. If you find shaping them empty too difficult, simply shape them into smaller balls. Drop into the pot with the chicken at the last 10 minutes of cooking.

5. When the soup is ready, carefully remove the kibbé balls onto a plate, then remove the chicken onto a large serving platter and position it in the middle. Pour the broth into a soup tureen. Return the kibbé balls to the broth. Serve very hot—the idea is for diners to first help themselves to the broth together with a kibbé ball, then add a piece of chicken and a little stuffing.

KISHK SOUP
SHORBET KISHK

You can make this thick wintery soup with or without awarma (page 15). It is a typical hot breakfast in rural places, both in the mountains and the Bekaa, where much of the kishk (page 7) is made. I prefer it with awarma, which I make myself when I am in the home country because it is practically impossible to find tail fat in Europe or America. If you don't have awarma, and would like to make it with meat, use 2 tablespoons (30 g) butter to sauté the garlic until golden before adding 2 ounces (60 g) lamb meat diced very small and proceeding with the recipe as below. The soup has a slightly sour taste because of the fermentation process during the making of kishk. It is normally eaten with pita. You tear the bread in pieces and use them by shaping them a little like a cornetto to scoop up the soup. Both kishk and awarma are very much part of the müneh (see page 2). In the not-so-distant past, they were prepared in large quantities at the end of the summer to keep for the cold winter months, with awarma often used instead of fresh meat, particularly when there was no refrigeration.

SERVES 4

2 ounces (60 g) awarma (page 15)

4 large cloves garlic, peeled and quartered

1¼ cups (150 g) kishk (page 7)

1. Put the awarma and garlic in a medium pot and place over medium heat. Cook, stirring occasionally, until the fat starts to bubble and the garlic is lightly golden.

2. Add the kishk and stir to mix with the awarma and garlic, then gradually add 1 quart (1 liter) water, stirring all the time so you don't have any lumps. Depending on the kishk, you may need a little more or a little less water to achieve the right consistency, which should be like that of a thick soup. Bring to a boil, still stirring, then reduce the heat to low and let bubble very gently for a few minutes, stirring regularly. Taste before adding any salt, as both kishk and awarma are already salted. Serve very hot with pita bread. You can also serve the soup with very good, crusty sourdough or baguette even if neither is traditional.

ZINKOL WITH VERJUICE
ZINKOL BIL-HOSRÜM

I had two versions of zinkol when I was traveling through the country. One was a typical vegetarian soup from the west Bekaa and the other was served chilled with the tiny boiled bulgur wheat balls dropped into watered-down minty yogurt, while another is the recipe below. The chopped onion is traditionally fried in ghee, but I prefer to use olive oil, while the broth is flavored with verjuice for an interesting sour flavor. The bulgur wheat balls are flavored with dried mint, which makes for a more intriguing soup than the yogurt-based one. If you want to prepare the chilled yogurt version, simply dilute a little yogurt with water, then add salt and dried mint to taste before adding the blanched bulgur wheat balls. Serve chilled or at room temperature. You can also prepare zinkol with lentils instead of chickpeas and use awarma (page 15) instead of olive oil following the recipe below but omitting the verjuice.

SERVES 4 TO 6

FOR ABOUT 50 SMALL BULGUR WHEAT BALLS

1 cup (200 g) fine bulgur wheat

½ cup (60 g) unbleached all-purpose flour

1 tablespoon crushed dried mint

½ small onion (about 50 g), peeled, finely grated

Sea salt

Freshly ground black pepper

FOR THE SOUP

3 cups (450 g) cooked chickpeas

1 cup (250 ml) verjuice

4 large cloves garlic, peeled

½ cup (125 ml) extra virgin olive oil

2 medium onions (about 300 g), peeled, very finely chopped

4 large cloves garlic, peeled, minced to a fine paste

1. To make the bulgur wheat balls: Mix the bulgur wheat, flour, and dried mint in a large mixing bowl. Season with salt and pepper to taste and mix again. Add the grated onion and ½ cup (125 ml) water and knead together until the mixture is well blended and malleable enough to shape into tiny balls the size of cherries. Finish making the bulgur wheat balls, lining them on a baking sheet. Refrigerate while you prepare the soup.

2. To prepare the soup: Put the cooked chickpeas in a pot and add 1 quart (1 liter) water. Place over medium heat and bring to a boil. Reduce the heat to medium-low and let bubble gently for 10 minutes. Add the verjuice together with the whole garlic cloves and simmer for 10 more minutes.

3. While the soup is bubbling, put the olive oil and chopped onions in a large frying pan and place over medium-high heat. When the oil starts sizzling around the onions, reduce the heat to medium-low and cook, stirring every now and then, until soft and golden, 10 to 15 minutes. Add the minced garlic and cook, stirring, for another couple of minutes. Take the onion mixture off the heat and process into a fine purée with the help of a handheld blender. Add it to the soup.

4. Remove the bulgur wheat balls from the refrigerator and drop into the soup. Cook for another 15 to 20 minutes, stirring occasionally. Serve hot, warm, or at room temperature.

In the souks of Saida

DIPS AND SPREADS

HOMMUS

HOMMUS BI-TAHINI

Hommus is now a global dish with endless and sometimes rather bizarre variations, such as red velvet and pumpkin pie hommus, to name a few. Thankfully, our country has resisted the various Western interpretations. This is not to say that there are no regional variations. In fact, there are a few. In the north, hommus is mostly made with no garlic and the garnish is often walnuts toasted in melted ghee and scattered all over with the ghee replacing the olive oil, which means you have to eat the hommus fairly fast before the fat cools down. In Beirut, on the other hand, the classic garnish is boiled chickpeas, chopped parsley, and olive oil, and lines of paprika made by dipping a fork in the spice then impressing it at regular intervals along the edges. There is also the famous awarma (page 15) garnish, which is often not awarma but rather sautéed diced lamb and toasted pine nuts, except that these days the pine nuts are often replaced with slivered almonds because the Mediterranean kind has become a lot more expensive due to a disease that hit the trees, which has reduced production dramatically. Also, people are poorer because of the economic crisis.

I always make my own hommus, but I no longer bother to cook the chickpeas. Instead, I buy very good precooked ones preserved in salt water in glass jars with no added preservatives. They taste just as good as those freshly cooked, and all I need to do is rinse them to get rid of most of the saltiness. Sometimes, if I feel patient enough, I rub them gently between the palms of my hands to loosen the skins, which I then pick off before processing with the tahini, lemon juice, and garlic.

SERVES 4 TO 6

1 (1½-pound/675 g) jar cooked chickpeas (preferably a Spanish brand), about 3 cups (475 g net volume/weight)

⅔ cup (180 ml) tahini

1 garlic clove, peeled

Juice of 2 lemons, or to taste

Sea salt

Aleppo pepper and extra virgin olive oil for garnish

1. Drain the chickpeas in a colander and rinse under cold water. If you have the time, gently rub them between the palms of your hands to loosen the skin, then pick off and discard as much of the loose skins as you can.

2. Transfer the chickpeas to a food processor. Add the tahini, garlic clove, and lemon juice and process until you have a very smooth purée. Add a couple of ice cubes at the very end and process again until the ice is completely melted and incorporated into the hommus—this will lighten the dip and make it smoother. Transfer to a large mixing bowl. Taste before adding any salt—the chickpeas remain fairly salty even after rinsing. Mix well. If the dip is too thick, add a little water to loosen it—the dip needs to be soft and creamy but not runny. Taste and adjust the seasoning if needed. Scoop the hommus into a shallow round or oval serving bowl and spread across the bowl, raising it over the edges, or make waves as you spread it. Drizzle a little olive oil into the dips and sprinkle the raised edges with Aleppo pepper. Serve with pita, saj, or any other good bread, crackers, or crudités.

EGGPLANT DIP
BABA GHANNÜGE

Another Levantine dip that has gone global is baba ghannüge. It also goes by another name, *mütabbal*, meaning "seasoned." As such, the recipe can be used with other vegetables, in which case the name of the vegetable in Arabic is added to the mütabbal to indicate what the dip is made with. If made with eggplant, it will be mütabbal batinjan, if zucchini, it will be mütabbal küssa, and with beets, it will be mütabbal shmandar. The latter is originally Syrian but has been adopted by us. All follow the same principle of first cooking the vegetable, then puréeing and mixing it with tahini, lemon juice, and minced garlic. Sometimes a little labneh or yogurt is added. My mother liked to add a tiny amount of pomegranate molasses for a hint of sweet and sour. As for the garnish, my favorite is pomegranate seeds, and depending on the type, the seeds can be pearly pink or ruby red. Either will create a gorgeous effect, making the seeds look like precious embroidery against the raw, silky dip; and their tangy, juicy bite with a slight crunch makes for a delightful contrast to the creamy dip.

SERVES 4 TO 6

3 large eggplants (about 2 pounds/900 g)

⅓ cup (80 ml) tahini

Sea salt

Juice of 1½ lemons, or to taste

1 garlic clove, peeled, minced to a fine paste

Aleppo pepper or pomegranate seeds (preferably the sour type)

Extra virgin olive oil for garnish

1. Preheat the oven to 450°F (220°C).

2. Prick the eggplants in several places with the tip of a small knife so as to keep them from bursting during grilling. Place over a gas fire—traditionally they are grilled over a live fire until completely done, but I find the process messy. Instead, I char the skin over the gas fire to get the smoky flavor that is so typical of this dip, and finish cooking the eggplants in the oven. Once the skin is charred, transfer the eggplants to the preheated oven and roast for 30 to 45 minutes, until they are very soft.

3. Remove from the oven and cut in half lengthwise. Scoop out the flesh with a spoon. Put in a colander and let drain any excess liquid for about 15 minutes.

4. Put the grilled eggplant in a wide mixing bowl and mash with a potato masher or a fork. Add the tahini and salt to taste and mix well. Add the lemon juice and minced garlic and, again, mix well. Then taste and adjust the seasoning if needed.

5. Transfer to a round or oval shallow serving bowl and spread across the dish, raising it along the edges, or make waves all over. One garnish option is to sprinkle Aleppo pepper over the raised edges. Another is to scatter pomegranate seeds all over. In both cases, drizzle olive oil in the dips. Serve with pita, saj, or any other good bread, crackers, or crudités.

BEET DIP

MÜTABBAL SHMANDAR

I first learned how to make this dip in Aleppo, where I used to lead culinary tours before the uprising. One of the highlights of my tours was a cooking lesson with Maria Gaspard, a charming chef who taught my groups all kinds of fabulous dishes, including this one, which is also widely made in Lebanon. Not only is it very beautiful with its vibrant purple color, but it is also delectable. Maria boiled the beets, but I like to roast them so they don't get watery and their flavor is more intense.

SERVES 6

1 pound 5 ounces (600 g) beets

⅓ cup (80 ml) tahini, or to taste

1 clove garlic, peeled, minced to a fine paste

Juice of 1½ lemons, or to taste

Sea salt

Extra virgin olive oil to drizzle over the dip

1 tablespoon finely chopped flat-leaf parsley or slivered pistachios for garnish

1. Preheat the oven to 450°F (220°C).

2. Wash the beets and cut off any excess stalks but without cutting into the beets. You do not want them to bleed during baking. Wrap each beet with aluminum foil and place on a baking sheet. Bake in the preheated oven for 1 to 1½ hours depending on their size, until soft but not mushy.

3. Remove from the oven onto a large cutting board and let rest until cool enough to handle. Unwrap each, then peel and cut into chunks. Place in the bowl of a food processor. Add the tahini, garlic, and lemon juice and process until you have a smooth purée.

4. Transfer to a large mixing bowl. Add salt to taste and more lemon juice and/or tahini if you feel the dip needs it. Spread in a shallow round or oval serving bowl, making grooves here and there. Drizzle a little olive oil in the grooves and sprinkle with the chopped parsley or slivered pistachios. Serve with good bread.

ZUCCHINI SPREAD

TRIDET EL-KÜSSA

The Lebanese have a wonderful no-waste philosophy when it comes to food, and one perfect example of this approach is stuffed vegetables. If they are coring zucchini (page 188), they will use the cored inside to prepare various dishes, including the one below, which I had never come across until the day I met Akram Zaatari, one of our greatest artists, who hails from Saida in the south. Akram told me about his mother, Nazek, who was born into a Tripolitan Mawlawi (i.e., Sufi) family who had their own religious seat in the northern city until the government took it over. When Nazek married Akram's father, who is from Saida, she moved south and learned the regional dishes of her husband's family, including this one. The name is intriguing given its connection to tharid, which is said to be the Prophet's favorite dish. In Akram's family, they add the bread to the cooked core and let it soak up the juices, while in other families, like Mazen Sabbagh's, who are Sunnis from Beirut, they use the bread to scoop the cooked zucchini core. Mazen's mother doesn't like the texture of soggy bread, even if it ends up disappearing. Also, she doesn't boil the core. Instead, she cooks it with chopped onion and a little minced garlic in olive oil before adding toasted pine nuts for crunch. Another variation is to toast or fry the pita bread and spread it over the seasoned zucchini core or serve it on the side. Here I give Nazek's version. I have also made bruschetta with this spread, using toasted sourdough, garnishing them with fresh mint leaves fried in olive oil!

SERVES 4 TO 6

Sea salt

Cores from 4 pounds 6 ounces pale green zucchini (about 2 kg)

2 medium day-old pita breads, split open and torn into small pieces

Juice of 1 lemon, or to taste

4 cloves garlic, peeled, minced to a fine paste

½ cup (125 ml) extra virgin olive oil, plus extra to drizzle over the dip

Powdered dried mint for garnish

1. Bring a large pot of water to a boil. Season with salt as you would for pasta. Once the water starts bubbling, drop in the zucchini cores and poach for about 5 minutes. Drain (reserving some of the water in case you need it) and transfer to a large, wide mixing bowl.

2. Add the torn bread pieces, lemon juice, minced garlic, and olive oil and mix well. Taste and adjust the seasoning if necessary. Let sit for about 15 minutes to let the bread soak up the juices, stirring the mixture every now and then. Transfer to a serving dish and spread over the plate. Drizzle with a little olive oil and sprinkle with dried mint to taste—the spread should be somewhat moist though not soupy. Serve warm or at room temperature with more fresh or toasted pita bread.

SUMAC EGGPLANT SPREAD

TRIDET EL-BATENJAN

I was given this recipe at my first lunch at the Charafeddine family's in Meshref, where both Yasmine, our hostess, and Feryal, her daughter's mother-in-law, were cooking. At that lunch, I met Maha Mroue, who hails from the south, and as we started talking about typical dishes from there, she told me about this one, which somewhat resembles Akram Zaatari's tridet el-küssa (page 72) except that it is made with eggplant. Maha makes it with whole grilled eggplant, and that is how I made it the first time, but for some reason I preferred the idea of making it with sliced grilled eggplants for a slight contrast in texture. The recipe is typical of the city of Tyre as well as villages in the south. If you prefer the idea of grilled eggplant, cut the eggplant into medium-thick slices and brush with extra virgin olive oil on both sides. Bake in the oven, preheated to 450ºF (220ºC), until soft and golden all over with slightly crisp edges. Then cut into strips and use as below.

SERVES 4

2 large eggplants (about 500 g)

1½ tablespoons sumac, soaked in 1 cup (250 ml) water

2 cloves garlic, peeled, minced to a fine paste

1½ tablespoons coarsely ground dried mint

Sea salt

1 day-old medium pita, torn into bite-sized pieces

¼ cup (60 ml) extra virgin olive oil

Fresh mint leaves for garnish

1. Preheat the oven to 450ºF (220ºC).

2. Prick the eggplants in several places to stop them from bursting during grilling and place over an open flame—you can grill them all the way over the flame, but I like to char the skin over the fire to get the smoky flavor, then finish them in the oven so as not to have burnt skin flying all over, which is what will happen if cooked completely over gas. Once the skin is charred, transfer the eggplants to a baking sheet and roast in the preheated oven for about 30 minutes, until they have completely shrunk and are very soft. Remove from the oven and let cool briefly. Cut the eggplants in half and scoop the flesh out. Discard the skin and put in a colander to drain off any excess liquid.

3. Strain the sumac liquid into a mixing bowl. Add the minced garlic and dried mint and mix well. Add salt to taste.

4. Spread the pita on a serving platter and drizzle the sumac water all over. Then chop up the grilled eggplant and spread it over the bread. Drizzle the olive oil all over and season with a little salt. Garnish with fresh mint leaves and serve immediately.

FAVA BEAN AND MÜLÜKHIYEH SPREAD

BISSARA

There are two ways of preparing this very interesting recipe, which I got from Batoul Charafeddine, who is from Tyre, a charming coastal town all the way down south. In fact, because there was a lot of exchange between southern Lebanese and Palestinians, this recipe belongs to both. It also belongs to Egyptians, who had a lot of exchange in the past with Tyre as a trading port—the use of mülükhiyeh here points to Egypt, as it is essentially an Egyptian green. Anyhow, you can prepare bissara as described below to have a dip or you can use more liquid to let it set flat in the plate like with müjaddarah m'saffayeh (page 261). I like it both ways, but it is easier to serve as a dip if you have friends over for drinks. It needs a fair amount of lemon juice to lift it, and the spicier it is, the more delicious. I use Aleppo pepper, but you can also use red chili flakes if you want it to have more kick. Bissara is one of those regional dishes that remains a mystery to most who are not from Tyre. I personally didn't even know it existed until Batoul's brother, Mohamed Charafeddine, described it to me one day when I was lunching at their home. I then prepared it for some of my friends in Batroun (who also didn't know it), and it was a complete hit.

SERVES 4 TO 6

1¼ cups (250 g) dried peeled fava beans, soaked overnight in plenty of water with ½ teaspoon baking soda

¼ cup (60 ml) extra virgin olive oil

3 small onions (about 300 g), peeled, very finely chopped

4 large cloves garlic, peeled, minced to a fine paste

½ bunch cilantro (about 100 g on the stalk), washed, dried, most of the stalks discarded, finely chopped

1. Drain and rinse the fava beans under cold water. Put in a medium pot and add 2 cups (500 ml) water. Place over medium heat and bring to a boil. Lower the heat to medium-low, partly cover the pot, and let bubble gently until completely mushy, about 30 minutes—if you want to serve it like müjaddarah m'saffayeh (page 261), increase the water to 2½ cups (625 ml).

2. While the fava beans are cooking, put the olive oil and onions in a large frying pan and place over medium-high heat. As soon as the oil starts sizzling around the onions, reduce the heat to medium-low and cook, stirring regularly, until soft and golden, 10 to 15 minutes. Add the minced garlic and cook, stirring, for a couple of minutes, then add the chopped cilantro. Cook, stirring constantly, until the cilantro has wilted. Set aside.

¼ cup (20 g) powdered dried mülükhiyeh (page 237)

1 tablespoon Aleppo pepper

Juice of 2 lemons, or to taste

Sea salt

Lemon wedges to serve on the side

3. When the fava beans are ready, take them off the heat. Add the onion, garlic, and cilantro mixture and process with a handheld blender until very smooth. Then add the powdered mülükhiyeh and Aleppo pepper and mix well. Add the lemon juice and salt to taste and mix again. Taste and adjust the seasoning if needed. If you have made it to serve like müjaddarah, pour into soup plates and let it set. If you have made it to serve as a dip, transfer to a round or oval serving platter and spread it all over the plate, creating a raised edge, or make grooves here and there. Drizzle with olive oil, and garnish with either sliced fresh chilies or the quartered cherry tomatoes. Serve warm or at room temperature with good bread and lemon wedges for those who would like it tarter.

DIPS AND SPREADS

GARLIC DIP

TÜM

Tüm is an essential accompaniment to grilled chicken, grilled quail, and chicken shawarma. It is also served with our goat or lamb tartare (habrah nayeh, which is like kibbeh nayeh but without the bulgur wheat and spices), and in some restaurants, it is served with large beefsteak tomatoes that are cut across in half and sprinkled with sumac. Before the economic crisis, most restaurants served these at the beginning of a meal with nuts and seeds and the obligatory crudité platter, but these days the initial complimentary offering is kept to a minimum. Anyhow, they are served as an appetite opener before any of the mezze is brought in. I like dipping Persian cucumbers in tüm to have as a snack, but whichever way you have it, you are bound to have a strong garlicky breath for a good twenty-four hours after you eat it. Still, garlic is reputed to be healthy, and as long as you share this dip with those you will be spending time with afterward, there is no need to worry about your garlic breath. Traditionally, this dip is made with only garlic, lemon juice, and oil (vegetable oil in restaurants and extra virgin olive oil at home). Many restaurants use citric acid instead of lemon juice to preserve the dip longer, but I don't. This said, it will keep for a few days in the fridge in an airtight container. If you find the taste too strong, add a little labneh or mashed potatoes.

SERVES 4

20 large cloves garlic, peeled, brown ends sliced off and discarded

½ teaspoon fine sea salt, or to taste

1 cup (250 ml) extra virgin olive or vegetable oil, or a mix of both, plus more if needed

Juice of ½ lemon, or to taste

Labneh to taste to soften the sharpness of the dip, if needed

1. Put the garlic and salt in a food processor and process until as smooth as you can get it, scraping the sides with a spatula every now and then.

2. Slowly drizzle the olive oil through the open part of the lid while still processing as if you are making mayonnaise. The garlic paste will eventually emulsify with the oil to become fluffy without the need to add an egg yolk—some chefs add a little whipped egg white to make the dip whiter and fluffier. Once you have used up all the oil and the dip is completely fluffy, drizzle in the lemon juice, with the blade still turning. Finish with one or two ice cubes with the blade still turning. Taste and adjust the sharpness if needed—if it's too pungent, drizzle in up to an extra ¼ cup (60 ml) oil and whisk in a little labneh.

3. Keep in a glass jar for later or transfer to a bowl to serve with chicken wings (page 108) or kebabs (page 107), or whatever else takes your fancy.

TAHINI DIP
TARATOR

Tarator is a lemony tahini dip that is served with falafel, fried cauliflower, and fried fish. It is also used as a dressing with boiled or roasted vegetables such as Swiss chard stalks or beets. If you are going to use it as a dressing, you may want to thin it down with a little more water or lemon juice depending on your preference until it is the consistency of heavy cream. As a dip, you can vary it by adding very finely chopped herbs, such as parsley (¼ bunch parsley/50 g on the stalk, washed, dried, most of the stalk cut off, very finely chopped), cilantro, or tarragon, or spices such as Aleppo pepper, pepper paste, or any other flavoring that takes your fancy. Add whatever flavoring you choose at the end after you finish mixing the dip.

SERVES 4

⅔ cup (160 ml) tahini

Juice of 1½ lemons, or to taste

1 to 2 cloves garlic, peeled, minced to a fine paste

Sea salt

1. Put the tahini in a small mixing bowl and gradually add the lemon juice, stirring constantly. The tahini will thicken at first before it starts diluting again as you start adding just over ⅓ cup (100 ml) water. Taste the dip to adjust the tartness to your liking. If you think it needs more lemon juice, add the juice of another ½ lemon. Keep stirring until the sauce has the consistency of creamy yogurt.

2. Add the minced garlic and salt to taste and mix well. Taste and adjust the seasoning if needed. Serve with the Swiss chard salad and falafel recipes (pages 97 and 266), or simply as a dip on its own with pita chips or a selection of crudités.

LEMON AND GARLIC DRESSING

This is the classic dressing for most of our salads. In the home country, they go strong on both lemon juice and garlic, but I often omit the garlic and use less lemon juice if I am serving wine. You can freshen the dressing by adding crushed fresh herbs such as fresh mint or basil. The mint lends itself particularly well when paired with grilled vegetables such as eggplant (page 94) or with fresh fava beans (page 92). It is best to crush the herb/s in a mortar with a pestle for maximum flavor, always adding a generous pinch of salt to absorb any juices that are released. And always mix the dressing with the salad at the last minute just before serving so it stays fresh and crisp. If making the salad with cooked vegetables, do the opposite. You can replace the lemon juice with verjuice (page 3) for a slightly different tart flavor or even sumac for a drier mixture.

SERVES 4

1 to 2 garlic cloves, peeled

A few fresh mint, basil, or cilantro leaves, washed, dried, crushed (optional)

Sea salt

Juice of 1 lemon, or to taste

¼ cup (60 ml) extra virgin olive oil

Chop the garlic coarsely (with the herb of your choice, if any) and put it in a mortar. Add a pinch of salt and pound with a pestle until you have a smooth paste. Stir in the lemon juice, then the olive oil. Taste and adjust the seasoning if needed. Add to the salad of your choice and serve immediately.

Fresh garlic display in Hasbaya in the south

POMEGRANATE MOLASSES DRESSING
REBB EL-RÜMMAN BIL-ZEYT WAL-TÜM

A rather unexpected combination that adds another dimension to fried vegetables.

SERVES 4

2 tablespoons (30 ml) pomegranate molasses

1 large clove garlic, peeled, minced to a fine paste

⅓ cup (80 ml) extra virgin olive oil

Sea salt

Put the pomegranate molasses in a small mixing bowl. Add the crushed garlic and olive oil. Add salt to taste and mix well. Use with grilled or baked eggplants (see page 124) or fried cauliflower.

Pomegranate seeds, ready to be juiced at Matbakh Ors el-Shams, Mükhtara

TABBÜLEH

The most important step in this salad, which has now gone global with many reiterations that really have nothing to do with the classic recipe, is how you chop the herbs, which you need to do by using a shaving action rather than a chopping one. You need to slice the herbs into thin, crisp slivers—this is called *chiffonade* in chef's terms. And even if some recipes tell you to use a food processor to save time, don't! You do not want to bruise the herbs. If you do, you will end up with a mushy salad that will oxidize very quickly. Also, how you dice the tomatoes is important—use a very sharp or serrated knife to cut neatly into the skin without pressing on the flesh. This will also make a difference in the result. And one last bit of advice: Be sure to use the minimum amount of fine bulgur wheat. If you prefer more grain in your tabbüleh, simply adjust the amount to your liking, bearing in mind that it is basically an herb and tomato salad and not a grain salad. In fact, the ratio used varies according to region or family, but it will always be the herbs and tomatoes, not the grains, that dominate. Tabbüleh is usually served with lettuce or fresh vine leaves or white cabbage leaves, all of which are used to scoop the salad.

SERVES 4 TO 6

2½ tablespoons (30 g) fine bulgur

3 large firm ripe tomatoes (about 600 g), diced into ¼-inch (5 mm) cubes

1 bunch scallions (about 50 g), trimmed, very thinly sliced

2 bunches flat-leaf parsley (400 g on the stalk), washed, dried, most of the stalks discarded, sliced into thin slivers

⅓ bunch mint (75 g on the stalk), leaves only, washed, dried, sliced into thin slivers

¼ teaspoon ground cinnamon

¼ teaspoon ground allspice

¼ teaspoon seven-spice mixture (page 19)

¼ teaspoon finely ground black pepper

Sea salt

Juice of 1 lemon, or to taste

⅔ cup (160 ml) extra virgin olive oil

4 gem lettuces, washed, dried, quartered (or fresh tender vine leaves, or white cabbage leaves, washed and dried)

1. Rinse the bulgur wheat under cold water. Drain and set aside to fluff up. Stir the bulgur wheat with a fork every now and then to separate the grains.

2. Put the bulgur wheat in a large mixing bowl. Add the diced tomatoes—drain the juices if any—then add the sliced scallions. Add the sliced parsley and mint, the cinnamon, allspice, seven-spice, pepper, salt to taste, the lemon juice, and olive oil and mix well.

3. Taste and adjust the seasoning if needed. Serve immediately with either gem lettuce, fresh vine leaves, or white cabbage leaves.

WINTER TABBÜLEH
TABBÜLEH SHATAWIYEH

This is a very interesting recipe from Soghbine, in the west Bekaa, which doesn't really have much to do with the classic tabbüleh apart from the name and the use of fresh parsley and mint. The bulgur wheat here is coarse and the whole dish is cooked and served either hot or warm with blanched cabbage leaves. It also has awarma (page 15), which is unusual for a salad. I don't expect you to find awarma in the West, in which case simply use lean lamb, diced into tiny cubes, and sauté it in butter (7 ounces/200 g trimmed lamb from the shoulder or leg and 4 tablespoons/60 g unsalted butter).

SERVES 4 TO 6

1 cup (200 g) awarma (page 15)

2 medium onions (about 300 g), peeled, finely chopped

1 cup plus 2 tablespoons (200 g) coarse bulgur wheat

¼ teaspoon ground cinnamon

½ teaspoon ground allspice

½ teaspoon ground caraway

Sea salt

Freshly ground black pepper

2 cups (300 g) cooked chickpeas

1 bunch flat-leaf parsley (about 200 g on the stalk), washed, dried, most of the stalks discarded, finely chopped

½ bunch fresh mint (about 100 g on the stalk), leaves only, washed, dried, finely chopped

1 small spring cabbage to serve on the side, trimmed, quartered, and steamed until the leaves are just soft

1. Put the awarma in a pot and place over medium heat. When the fat has completely melted, add the onions and sauté until soft and golden, 5 to 10 minutes. If using lamb meat (see headnote), sauté the onions in the butter first, then add the meat and brown it.

2. Add the bulgur wheat and mix well with the onions and awarma. Then add 2 cups (500 ml) water and stir until the water starts bubbling. Add the cinnamon, allspice, and caraway together with salt and pepper to taste. Mix well. Cover the pot and lower the heat to medium-low. Simmer for 10 minutes. By then the water should have been completely absorbed. Add the chickpeas and mix well. Take off the heat and add the chopped parsley and mint. Mix well again, then taste and adjust the seasoning if needed. Transfer to a shallow serving bowl and serve hot with the steamed cabbage—you will use the leaves to scoop the tabbüleh.

WHITE TABBÜLEH
TABBÜLEH BAIDAH

I am not sure where this version of tabbüleh comes from. Initially, I thought it was a winter one from days long past. However, tomatoes are definitely summer produce. It may be a regional variation, although I have yet to find a person who can tell me where it comes from. I found the recipe in Ibrahim Mouzannar's *Lebanese Cooking* and liked it. However, I adapted it to make it lighter on the bulgur wheat and oil. And I use the fine-grade bulgur wheat, whereas Mouzannar recommends medium-grade. I also season the salad with Aleppo pepper rather than the paprika he suggests to give it a light kick. In fact, I often make it without bulgur wheat, which makes it more like a regular salad than tabbüleh, and it is just as delicious.

SERVES 4 TO 6

½ cup (100 g) fine bulgur wheat

1 pointed white cabbage (about 500 g), outer damaged leaves discarded, finely shredded

1 bunch scallions (about 100 g), trimmed, thinly sliced

½ bunch fresh mint (about 100 g on the stalk), leaves only, washed, dried, finely chopped

4 firm ripe medium tomatoes (about 500 g), seeded, diced into small cubes

1 tablespoon Aleppo pepper

Juice of 1 lemon, or to taste

Just over ⅓ cup (100 ml) extra virgin olive oil

Sea salt

1. Rinse the bulgur wheat under cold water. Drain and set aside to fluff up. Stir with a fork every now and then to separate the grains.

2. Put the bulgur wheat, shredded cabbage, sliced scallions, chopped mint, and diced tomatoes in a large salad bowl. Sprinkle the Aleppo pepper all over. Add the lemon juice, olive oil, and salt to taste and mix well. Serve immediately.

MIXED HERB AND TOASTED PITA SALAD
FATTÜSH

Fattüsh is one of the most popular and adaptable Lebanese salads. You can make it with whatever salad ingredients you have, as long as you add toasted pita and use sumac in the seasoning to give the salad an intriguing tart flavor. Some cooks add pomegranate molasses, while others add garlic. In some villages, they use stale bread rather than toasted, while in others, they fry the bread. I don't like frying, so sometimes I imitate fried pita by simply brushing the rough side with olive oil before toasting it in the oven. That said, more often than not, I toast the bread plain, then toss it with the sumac and olive oil before adding to the salad to keep it crisp longer. You can find purslane in Middle Eastern grocery stores in spring and summer. If it is not available, use an equivalent amount of parsley. And for those on a gluten-free diet, just omit the bread. Your fattüsh will still be delightful. I often make mine without bread, although technically it is no longer considered fattüsh.

SERVES 4

FOR THE SALAD

4 gem lettuces or 1 large cos lettuce (about 400 g), outer damaged leaves discarded, washed, dried, cut across into ½-inch (1¼ cm) strips

1 bunch scallions (about 100 g), trimmed, thinly sliced

3 Persian cucumbers (about 300 g), cut in half lengthwise, thinly sliced

3 medium firm ripe tomatoes (about 300 g), cut into bite-sized pieces

1 bunch flat-leaf parsley (about 200 g on the stalk), most of the stalks discarded, coarsely chopped

½ bunch mint (about 100 g on the stalk), leaves only, coarsely chopped

½ bunch purslane (about 100 g on the stalk), leaves only

1 medium pita bread, split open, toasted in a hot oven, broken into bite-sized pieces

Sea salt

FOR THE DRESSING

3 tablespoons (33 g) sumac

6 tablespoons extra virgin olive oil

1. To make the salad: Put the lettuce, sliced scallions, sliced cucumbers, chopped tomatoes, chopped parsley, chopped mint, and purslane in a large mixing bowl and mix well.

2. To make the dressing and salad: Mix the sumac and olive oil in a medium mixing bowl. Add the broken pita and toss until the bread pieces are evenly coated. Add the bread to the salad ingredients and mix well. Taste before you add any salt—sometimes sumac is mixed with salt. Add salt if needed and serve immediately before the bread starts going soggy.

Feryal Osseyran's fattüsh with makdüss, at Yasmine Charafeddine's in Meshref

CHICORY SALAD WITH KISHK
SALATET HINDBEH MA' KISHK

A very interesting salad that belongs to the Druze community in the Shouf. I had never had chicory raw until the day Alaa al-Koukash, a caterer from a Druze village near Aley, organized a tasting of Druze dishes for me at the home of my friends Janine and Tony Mamari at their behest. Later, I told my novelist friend Rabih Alameddine, who is also Druze, about it, and he said it was one of his favorite salads. It may be Rabih's favorite, but to be honest, it is an acquired taste, mainly because of the addition of kishk (page 7), which again I had never had raw.

SERVES 4 TO 6

1 bunch chicory (about 400 g), most of the bottom discarded, washed, dried, cut into thin strips

1 medium red onion (about 150 g), peeled, finely chopped

2 medium tomatoes (about 250 g), diced into small cubes

½ cup (65 g) kishk (page 7)

2 tablespoons (30 ml) wine vinegar

⅓ cup (80 ml) extra virgin olive oil

Sea salt

Put the sliced chicory, chopped onion, cubed tomatoes, kishk, vinegar, and olive oil in a large mixing bowl and mix well. Taste before adding any salt because kishk is already salted and you may not need any. Let sit for about 5 minutes for the kishk to absorb the vinegar, oil, and juices from the tomato. Serve as a side with grilled meat or as part of a mezze spread.

Tomato and cucumber stall in the souks of Tripoli

PURSLANE, TOMATO, AND ARMENIAN CUCUMBER SALAD
SALATET BA'LEH MA' BANADÜRAH WA ME'TEH

Late spring and early summer is the season for both purslane and Armenian cucumbers (*me'teh* in Arabic), and this is when you will find them in Middle Eastern grocery stores. In fact, purslane is becoming trendy these days, and you may also find it in specialty stores or at farmers markets. It has an intriguing earthy taste, but the succulent leaves bruise easily, and you need to store and handle them with care. Armenian cucumbers are drier and crunchier than Persian, with a slightly furry, ridged skin. The color is pale green, while the shape is long, thin, and kind of curly. I prefer them over regular cucumbers, mainly because they are less watery and work really well with purslane. Here, I give a simple sumac seasoning, but you can also use the lemon juice and oil dressing (page 80) with or without garlic.

SERVES 4

FOR THE SALAD

2 medium Armenian cucumbers (about 200 g), thinly sliced

1 bunch scallions (100 g), trimmed, thinly sliced

8 firm ripe cherry tomatoes (about 200 g), quartered

2 bunches purslane (about 400 g on the stalk), leaves only, washed carefully, dried

FOR THE DRESSING

1 tablespoon sumac

3 tablespoons (45 ml) extra virgin olive oil

Sea salt

1. To make the salad: Put the sliced cucumbers, scallions, and tomatoes in a salad bowl. Add the purslane and gently mix well.

2. To make the dressing and finish the salad: Mix the sumac with the olive oil and pour over the salad ingredients. Toss lightly together and taste before adding any salt—sometimes sumac is mixed with salt. Add some if needed and gently mix again. Serve immediately.

ARUGULA SALAD
SALATET JARJIR

Salatet jarjir is one of my favorite salads and a very simple one to prepare. I normally use organic prepacked wild arugula and organic cherry plum tomatoes. Depending on the size of the tomatoes, I either cut them in half if very small or in quarters if medium to large. If I am in Sicily, I skip the search for organic because there are great cherry tomatoes at the farmers market where I normally shop and often they are organic, but because the certification is so complicated, most farmers do without.

SERVES 4

10½ ounces (300 g) wild organic arugula, washed, spun dry

8 firm ripe cherry plum tomatoes (about 200 g), quartered

Juice of ½ lemon, or to taste

⅓ cup (80 ml) extra virgin olive oil

Sea salt

Put the arugula and tomatoes in a salad bowl. Add the lemon juice and olive oil and season with salt to taste. Toss lightly. Taste and adjust the seasoning if needed. Serve immediately.

Vegetable and herb stall in the souks of Tripoli

SALATET MALFÜF
CABBAGE SALAD

Another of my favorites, this is a salad that is traditionally served with mujaddarah (page 261) but is also good on its own or with grilled meat or poultry. When in London, I try to source Lebanese flat cabbage from my local Middle Eastern grocery store to prepare it. Otherwise, I use spring pointed cabbage, which is not as tender but very good all the same, especially when it's organic.

SERVES 4

1 pointed spring cabbage (about 600 g)

2 medium firm tomatoes (250 g), diced into ½-inch (1¼ cm) cubes

Lemon and Garlic Dressing (page 80)

1. Discard any damaged outer leaves of the cabbage and cut into quarters lengthwise. Cut off and discard the core, then thinly slice the cabbage across. Transfer to a salad bowl. Add the tomatoes and mix lightly.

2. Add the dressing to the salad and mix well. Taste and adjust the seasoning if needed. Serve immediately.

Cabbage for sale in the souks of Tripoli

SALATET FÜL AKHDAR

FRESH FAVA BEAN SALAD

A seasonal spring salad that is best when the fava beans are still young with a tender skin. If you cannot find them young, use the same amount of podded beans and prepare as below. You can use frozen fava beans, in which case you can vary the dressing by using the tahini sauce (page 77). You can also omit the garlic in the dressing if you prefer.

SERVES 4

2 pounds 4 ounces (1 kg) young tender fresh fava beans in the pod, topped, tailed, stringed if needed

Sea salt

Lemon and Garlic Dressing (page 80)

1. Cut the beans on an angle into medium-sized pieces, about 2 inches (5 cm) long. Rinse under cold water, drain, and put in a medium pot. Barely cover with water and add salt. Place over medium-high heat and bring to a boil. Reduce the heat to medium and let bubble gently, uncovered, for 10 to 15 minutes, until the beans are tender.

2. Drain, then plunge into ice-cold water to keep them from cooking further and keep their bright green color. Drain and spread on a clean kitchen towel to dry.

3. Put the cooked fava beans in a salad bowl and add the dressing. Toss lightly together. Serve warm, at room temperature, or slightly chilled.

BUTTER BEAN SALAD

SALATET FASSÜLYAH

A hearty mountain salad that is even more delicious when the beans are in season in the summer. You can also make it with chickpeas, in which case it is known as balilah, a typical breakfast dish available at specialty fül and hommus places. If you are using chickpeas, crush them lightly as you mix them with the seasoning, and you can omit the garlic in the dressing if you prefer.

SERVES 4

1⅔ cups (250 g) dried butter beans, soaked overnight in plenty of cold water with 1 teaspoon baking soda

or

3⅓ cups (500 g) fresh butter beans

Lemon and Garlic Dressing (page 80)

Sea salt

A few sprigs flat-leaf parsley, washed, dried, stalks discarded, finely chopped

A few scallions, trimmed, to serve on the side

1. If you are using dried beans, drain and rinse the soaked beans under cold water. Put in a medium pot and cover well with water. Place over medium-high heat and bring to a boil. Reduce the heat to medium-low and let bubble gently for 1 hour, partially covered, or until the beans are very soft but not mushy.

2. If you are using fresh butter beans, you don't need to soak them. Simply boil for 20 to 25 minutes, until tender. Drain and put in a salad bowl.

3. Add the dressing to the beans and mix well. Taste, and add salt if needed. Garnish with the chopped parsley and serve warm or at room temperature with the trimmed scallions and good bread.

THE PRIEST'S SALAD
SALATET EL-RAHEB

I am not sure why this salad is named after a priest, unless it is because it is vegetarian, making it a perfect Friday or Lenten dish, when faithful Christians abstain from eating meat. There seems to be some sort of connection between eggplants and clergy for both Muslims and Christians, as there is also a Turkish eggplant and tomato dish called imam bayildi, supposedly because an imam fainted when he had it, although the story is a myth according to Nevin Halici, the grande dame of Turkish cooking. Anyhow, this salad makes for a fresher way of serving grilled eggplants, and a perfect addition to a mezze spread, particularly on a hot summer day.

SERVES 4

3 large eggplants (about 900 g)

3 medium firm ripe tomatoes (about 375 g), seeded, diced into ½-inch (1¼ cm) cubes

1 bunch scallions (about 100 g), trimmed, thinly sliced

Lemon and Garlic Dressing (page 80)

Fresh mint leaves for garnish

1. Preheat the oven to 450°F (220°C).

2. Prick the eggplants in several places with the point of a knife to stop them from bursting during grilling. Place over a gas fire and turn over until you have charred most of the skin—starting the eggplants on a gas fire gives them the smoky flavor so typical of this salad and finishing them in the oven avoids the mess of flying charred skin, which will happen if you let them cook completely over a gas fire. Transfer onto a nonstick baking sheet or one lined with parchment paper. Roast in the preheated oven for 35 to 45 minutes, until the eggplants have completely softened. Transfer onto a cutting board and cut in half lengthwise. Scoop the flesh out with a spoon and let drain in a colander for about 15 minutes to get rid of any excess liquid.

3. Cut the eggplants lengthwise into long thick strips, then across to have chunky bite-sized pieces. Arrange in a neat layer on a serving platter. Drain the diced tomatoes and spread over the eggplant. Scatter the sliced scallions over the tomatoes and garnish with mint leaves.

4. Prepare the Lemon and Garlic Dressing, adding fresh crushed mint, and put it in a sauceboat—you can omit the garlic if you prefer. It is best to let each diner season and mix their own salad helping on the plate, as it will not be very pretty if you premix it—for the photograph, we cut the grilled eggplants and tomatoes in chunks and gently mixed everything with the dressing. Serve at room temperature, or slightly chilled, with good bread.

YOGURT AND CUCUMBER SALAD

LABAN MA' KHYAR

An essential accompaniment to kibbeh bil-saniyeh (page 160), this is best prepared with thick Greek-style yogurt and Persian or Armenian cucumbers, which are less watery than the large ones. If you are going to use large cucumbers, peel and seed them before using.

SERVES 4

2 cups (500 g) plain full-fat Greek-style yogurt

1½ tablespoons dried mint

Sea salt

3 to 4 Persian cucumbers (about 300 g), quartered lengthwise, thinly sliced

1 clove garlic, peeled, minced to a fine paste

Put the yogurt in a salad bowl. Add the dried mint and salt to taste and mix well. Let sit for 15 minutes to rehydrate the dried mint. Then add the sliced cucumbers and crushed garlic. Mix again. Taste and adjust the seasoning if needed. Serve slightly chilled, or at room temperature with kibbeh bil-saniyeh (page 160), or with grilled lamb, or as part of a mezze spread.

In the souks of Tripoli

SWISS CHARD STALKS IN TAHINI SAUCE

DLÜ' EL-SILE' BIL-TARATOR

This salad is often prepared alongside Stuffed Swiss Chard Leaves (page 204) in order to use up the stalks. And if you have the patience, you can also prepare Swiss Chard Fatayer (page 41) for a Swiss chard degustation. The colors on the table will be pretty. The lime green stalks showing through the pale cream sauce will set off nicely against the dark green rolled leaves and golden fatayer. You will also have a nice contrast in both flavors and textures. There is one drawback, and that is the time it takes to prepare all three. So, make sure to allocate at least three hours, if not longer, to prepare the three dishes. Also, it is interesting to note that Swiss chard (silver beet) may look like succulent giant spinach, but it is not related botanically. The same tahini sauce used here is also perfect with fried or roasted cauliflower as well as baked beets, to name a few. Most home cooks will boil beets, but I prefer to bake them so they are not watery (see page 70).

SERVES 4

2 pounds 4 ounces (1 kg) Swiss chard

Sea salt

Tarator (page 77)

A few flat-leaf parsley or mint leaves for garnish

1. Cut the stalks off the Swiss chard, trim the dirty bottom ends, and pull out any tough strings. Wash, dry, and cut the stalks across on an angle into 1-inch (2½ cm) pieces. Bring a pot of water to a boil over medium-high heat. When the water starts bubbling, add salt the way you would for pasta, then add the stalks and reduce the heat to medium. Let bubble gently for 5 to 10 minutes, until done to your liking, less time for al dente, longer for a softer bite.

2. During that time, you can prepare the tarator. Once done, drain the stalks in a colander and let cool a little, then gently fold into the tahini sauce until thoroughly coated. Transfer to a serving dish. Garnish with parsley or mint leaves and serve warm or at room temperature.

COLOCASIA (TARO) IN TAHINI SAUCE
'EL'ASS BIL-TARATOR

Colocasia was once the potato of the Romans, but for us, it is another prized seasonal vegetable, a large brown root vegetable with a purple stem that appears in markets and at greengrocers in late summer and early fall. You need to peel it first, then either fry or boil it before using—it tends to be slimy if not prepared properly, hence the precooking before finishing it with the sauce. If Seville oranges are not in season, squeeze the juice of tangerines, oranges, grapefruit, and lemons and use the mixture in the tahini sauce.

SERVES 4

FOR THE SALAD

½ cup (100 g) dried chickpeas, soaked overnight in plenty of water with ¼ teaspoon baking soda

3 tablespoons (45 ml) extra virgin olive oil

1 medium onion (about 150 g), peeled, thinly sliced into wedges

1 pound 2 ounces (500 g) Colocasia, peeled, diced into medium chunks

FOR THE TAHINI SAUCE

⅔ cup (160 ml) tahini

Juice of 2 Seville oranges, or to taste

1 clove garlic, peeled, minced to a fine paste

Sea salt

FOR THE GARNISH

A few sprigs flat-leaf parsley, stalks discarded, finely chopped

or

toasted Mediterranean pine nuts

1. Drain the chickpeas and rinse under cold water. Spread on a clean kitchen towel. Cover with another towel and gently press on them with a rolling pin to split in half and loosen the skins. Discard the skins. Set aside.

2. Put the olive oil and onion in a deep, wide sauté pan and place over medium heat. As soon as the oil starts sizzling around the onion, reduce the heat to medium-low and cook, stirring regularly, until soft and golden, 10 to 15 minutes. Add the Colocasia and cook, stirring regularly, for a few minutes. Add the peeled, split chickpeas, then barely cover with water and bring to a boil. Let bubble for 20 to 30 minutes, until both the chickpeas and Colocasia are done and there is hardly any water left in the pot.

3. To prepare the tahini sauce: Put the tahini in a small mixing bowl, then gradually and alternately add the citrus juice and ½ cup (125 ml) water. The tahini will first thicken before it starts loosening. Keep stirring until the sauce has the consistency of heavy cream. Add the minced garlic and salt to taste and mix again.

4. Add the tahini sauce to the Colocasia and chickpeas and gently mix it in, being mindful not to crush either. Let bubble gently, carefully stirring every now and then, until you see a little oil (called *srijeh* in Arabic) float to the surface, a sign that the tahini sauce is ready—if the sauce becomes too thick, add a little water. Take the Colocasia mixture off the heat. Cover with a kitchen towel and let cool. Serve at room temperature, garnished with the chopped parsley or toasted pine nuts.

Selling fresh chickpeas on the road

FRESH THYME SALAD

SALATET ZA'TAR

We often went up to Rechmaya, my maternal grandmother's village in the Shouf Mountains, in the summer, and whenever I saw her taking the garden knives out of the kitchen table's drawer and unhooking the straw baskets hanging in the entrance hall, I knew that she and my mother were preparing to go foraging, in particular for wild thyme. The mountain slopes around the family home were covered with wild thyme bushes, and summer was the time to pick and dry it to make za'tar— *za'tar* is the Arabic word for both thyme and the dried mixture made of it together with sumac and sesame seeds. We also eat za'tar fresh, although the one used fresh is *Thymbra spicata*, a different cultivated variety with long, thin smooth leaves. That said, many people also make a salad with the furry leaf kind known as *zobe'* in Arabic. Both are also used to make a filling for fatayer (page 41). You will find fresh za'tar in Middle Eastern grocery stores throughout the summer. The secret here is to dress the salad at the very last minute so the arugula does not go limp, and the surest way to keep the salad crisp for longer is to dress it with only sumac and olive oil and without any lemon juice.

SERVES 4 TO 6

9 ounces fresh thyme (250 g on the stalk), leaves only

3½ ounces (100 g) wild arugula

1 medium Spanish onion (about 150 g), peeled, very finely chopped

2 teaspoons sumac, or to taste

3 tablespoons (45 ml) extra virgin olive oil

Sea salt

Mix the thyme, arugula, and onion in a salad bowl. Sprinkle the sumac all over and add the olive oil. Mix well. Taste to see if you need any salt— some sumac has added salt, so tasting the salad before adding it is a good idea. Adjust the seasoning if needed. Serve immediately.

At Moussa Ibrahim's mat'haneh in Dibbine

CHICKPEA, CUCUMBER, AND PARSLEY SALAD

SIFF

I often complain about tabbüleh having become a generic term for all kinds of salads that have nothing to do with the classic, but while researching this book, I realized that even in Lebanon, there are several variations, with this one hailing from Rachaya al-Wadi, a beautiful town all the way down south, famous for its pottery. If you use fresh chickpeas when in season at the beginning of summer, the salad will be a lot more interesting even if it is not exactly how it is traditionally prepared. You can use the fresh chickpeas either raw or blanched before splitting them in half. If you are going to blanch them, be sure to plunge them in ice water once done to keep their bright green color. Then all you need to do is drain and dry them before using. You can also vary the recipe below by using fresh or frozen peeled fava beans. Again, be sure to dry them well before adding to the other ingredients.

SERVES 4 TO 6

FOR THE SALAD

2 cups (300 g) cooked chickpeas, coarsely chopped

5 Persian or Armenian cucumbers (about 350 g), peeled in strips, diced into small cubes

1 bunch flat-leaf parsley (about 200 g on the stalk), washed, dried, most of the stalks discarded, finely chopped

1 medium red onion (about 150 g), peeled, finely chopped

FOR THE DRESSING

2 cloves garlic, peeled, minced to a fine paste

Juice of 1 lemon, or to taste

½ cup (125 ml) extra virgin olive oil

1 teaspoon ground dry za'tar (the plain dried herb, not the mix)

1 teaspoon sumac

Sea salt

1. Put the salad ingredients in a large bowl. Mix well.

2. Mix the ingredients for the dressing in a smaller bowl, then add to the salad ingredients. Mix well. Taste and adjust the seasoning if needed. Serve immediately.

Sunday is barbecue day all over Lebanon, or at least it used to be. Long ago, when my grandmother was still alive and before my uncles got married, they were in charge of preparing the fire in the *man'al*, as it is known in Arabic, a light metal rectangular box on short or long legs. They would take it out onto the balcony, together with a bag of charcoal, which they dumped into the man'al. They then lit the coals and waited until they became hot embers before they started grilling. In the meantime, my grandmother, mother, and aunt would have threaded whatever meat we were having that day onto long metal skewers. Sometimes it would be chunks of lamb as well as kafta (page 110); other times, it would be chicken wings and/or pieces (pages 108 and 107). Occasionally, we would have fish, although this was rare. And during fig season, we would feast on tiny little birds, known as *becfigues* in French and *asafir* in Arabic (page 114). My uncles hunted them in the mountains early in the morning and brought them home for my grandmother, mother, and aunt to pluck and gut, which took a fairly long time given how tiny and fragile they are. Once cleaned, they seasoned them with salt then threaded them onto the skewers. When it was asafir on the BBQ, my grandmother insisted on manning the grill even if it was a man's job. I guess she did not trust her sons to grill them right! But before she crouched in front of the grill, she would have dressed the table with a couple of salads and dips as well as fried potatoes and eggplants together with what we call the "decoration of the table" or *zinet el-tawleh* in Arabic, which consisted of olives, crudités, fresh mint, trimmed scallions, pickles, cheese, and nuts.

As soon as the grilled meat was ready, we would all sit around the table to enjoy what was for many families a typical Sunday lunch. My grandmother always interspersed the lamb meat with dainty pieces of tail fat and pearl onions. The chicken skewers were left plain. Occasionally, she grilled quails, in which case she butterflied them before marinating and grilling. As for the chicken wings, she threaded them on two slightly spaced skewers to keep them from swiveling around. It was a particularly joyous day with us children fighting over who would fan the fire. After lunch, my uncles would put LPs on the record player and they would take turns to dance with my beautiful aunt, who was an avid dancer. We children would fool around them, sometimes making them trip, and when we did, we got a scolding and were shooed away, but we didn't leave them alone for too long. We always used metal skewers, but you can use wooden or bamboo ones, in which case be sure to soak them in water for thirty minutes before using so they don't burn during grilling.

CHICKEN KEBABS

SHISH TAWÜ'

One of our most popular kebabs that is always served with tüm (page 76). You can use both white and dark meat here. It is important not to over-grill, bearing in mind that chicken cannot be rare. The marinade is the same as that for chicken wings; it is also the same for poussins or quails, except that you need to butterfly these. I normally do my grilling in a hot oven, threading the pieces onto metal skewers and roasting for 20 to 30 minutes, turning them over and basting with any leftover marinade halfway through.

SERVES 4

FOR THE GARLIC MARINADE

8 large cloves garlic, peeled, minced to a fine paste

2 tablespoons (30 ml) extra virgin olive oil

Juice of 1 lemon, or to taste

¼ teaspoon ground cinnamon

½ teaspoon ground allspice

¼ teaspoon seven-spice mixture (page 19)

¼ teaspoon finely ground black pepper

½ teaspoon Aleppo pepper

Sea salt

TO FINISH

1 large pita bread, split at the seams to have two layers

1 pound 12 ounces (800 g) boneless chicken meat (white and/or dark), cut into medium chunks, preferably from a free-range organic chicken

Tüm (page 76)

1. Put the minced garlic in a large mixing bowl and add the rest of the marinade ingredients. Mix well, then add the chicken pieces. Toss into the marinade to coat well. Let sit for a couple of hours in the refrigerator.

2. Prepare a charcoal fire if you have an outside barbecue. Otherwise, turn your broiler or oven on to maximum heat.

3. Thread the marinated chicken equally onto 8 wooden or metal skewers, leaving a little space in between to allow for even cooking.

4. Place one layer of pita bread over the other, rough-side up, on a plate by the heat—you will use the bread to soak up the juices of the grilled chicken during cooking. Grill for 5 minutes on each side, or until completely done but not dried up. Take a few skewers at a time and place on the pita. Fold over and press on the skewers, so the bread soaks up the cooking juices.

5. Once the meat is done, wrap the bread around the skewers to keep the kebabs hot. Serve with tüm, a salad, and more bread on the side.

BARBECUED CHICKEN WINGS

JAWANEH D'JEJ MESHWIYEH

An essential part of our mezze, the wings in this recipe are always cut into two pieces, one fat drumstick-like part and the other flat. The tip end is discarded. I try to buy organic wings, and I choose them not too large. As I don't have a barbecue, I roast them in the oven at a high enough heat so the edges crisp up as if they were grilled on a live fire. Of course, the slightly charred flavor is not there, but they cook more evenly than under the broiler and they are still extremely moreish. These make a delightful quick lunch, served alongside a salad or a dip. And, of course, they are perfect as part of a mezze spread, served with tüm (page 76).

SERVES 4

Marinade for chicken kebabs (page 107)

12 small free-range organic chicken wings (about 800 g)

1. Put the ingredients for the marinade in a large mixing bowl and mix well. Add the chicken wings and mix well so all the wings are evenly coated with the marinade. Let sit for a couple of hours in the refrigerator, stirring every now and then.

2. Prepare a barbecue fire if you have one, or preheat your broiler to the maximum, or your oven to 450°F (220°C).

3. If you are barbecuing or broiling the wings: Grill for 10 to 15 minutes on each side, until crisp and charred in some places but still moist inside.

4. If you are roasting them in the oven: Roast for about 30 minutes, until they are crisp and completely done. Serve hot with tüm and pita bread.

KAFTA

Kafta is a mixture of ground meat, chopped parsley, and onion that is normally prepared by the butcher albeit under the watchful eye of the home cook, who will choose his/her cut before asking the butcher to grind it—any self-respecting home cook will never buy preground to assure that it is not mixed with too much fat or offcuts. Also, preground meat has a higher fat content and is often not from prime cuts. Instead, ask your butcher to trim the meat you need (either from the leg or shoulder) of most of the fat and skin before asking to grind it for you. You can then chop the herbs and onions at home to mix with the ground meat before seasoning the whole to your taste. I remember always wanting to go with my mother to get kafta because I was fascinated by our butcher's expert handling of his large knife as he chopped the herbs and onion before mixing them with the ground meat, first with the knife and then with his hands. It is unlikely that any Western butcher will offer this service, so it is up to you to make kafta. Before I bought a meat grinder, I used the food processor to grind my meat, but it ended up too smooth and I now prefer to use the fine disk of the grinder so the meat retains a slight texture.

SERVES 4

2 medium onions (about 300 g), peeled, quartered

½ bunch flat-leaf parsley (about 100 g on the stalk), washed, dried, most of the bottom stalks discarded

1 pound 7 ounces (600 g) lean lamb from the leg or shoulder, finely ground

½ teaspoon ground cinnamon

½ teaspoon ground allspice

¼ teaspoon finely ground black pepper

Sea salt

1. Put the onions and parsley in the food processor and process until very finely chopped. Transfer to a large mixing bowl.

2. Add the ground meat together with the cinnamon, allspice, pepper, and salt to taste and mix, preferably with your hands, until well blended. Taste and adjust the seasoning if needed—if you are not keen on tasting raw meat, sear a little in a hot pan to check the seasoning. Serve raw (kaftah nayeh) with pita bread.

3. You can also shape the kafta into patties to sear in a hot pan and serve either in a bun or with a salad. Or divide the kafta into 4 equal pieces and wrap each along a flat metal skewer to barbecue or grill for 2 to 3 minutes on each side under a hot broiler.

LAMB KEBABS

LAHM MESHWI

Long before the economic crisis, and even before that the civil war that began in the mid 1970s and ended in the early '90s, marking fifteen years of interconfessional strife that led to much destruction and killing, almost all Lebanese families could afford lamb kebabs as part of their Sunday grill. Sadly, this is no longer the case. Meat, and in particular lamb, has become affordable only to those with means, a group that is dwindling by the day. Many make these kebabs with beef nowadays because it is relatively cheaper, but I only use lamb because I prefer the texture and taste. And if I am in fat tail country, I will intersperse the kebabs with bits of tail fat to add juice to both the bread and meat. The fat from around the kidneys is the closest to tail fat, and you can, if you want, use it as a substitute. You can also intersperse the meat with pearl onions and/or cherry tomatoes before grilling.

SERVES 4

Marinade for chicken kebabs (page 107)

TO FINISH

1 pound 12 ounces (800 g) lean lamb from the leg or fillet, cut into bite-sized chunks

1 large pita bread, split at the seams into two layers

3½ ounces (100 g) tail fat if you can get it, cut into small pieces

14 to 16 pearl onions, peeled

1. Put the ingredients for the marinade in a mixing bowl large enough to eventually hold the meat and mix well. Add the meat and mix again. Let sit for a couple of hours in the refrigerator, turning the meat every now and then.

2. Prepare a charcoal fire in your barbecue if you have one, or preheat your broiler to maximum.

3. Just before you are ready to grill the meat, place one layer of pita, rough-side up, over the other on a plate by the heat—you will use the bread to soak up the juices from the grilled kebabs.

4. Thread the meat onto 8 skewers, inserting a piece of fat, if you are using it, and a pearl onion in between every two pieces. Grill for about 3 minutes on each side, until done to your liking. As you are grilling the meat, take a few skewers at a time off the heat and place in the middle of the pita. Fold over and press on the meat; do this a couple of times during grilling to let the bread soak up the juices. Serve immediately wrapped in the pita.

SHAWARMA

Shawarma is one of the most famous street foods in the world, once found at practically every corner, though now less so. The shawarma of the Lebanese and Syrian immigrants in Mexico is the inspiration behind the Mexicans' taco al pastor, whereas the Turkish doner kebab, which is basically shawarma, gave the Brits their late-night kebab sandwich. Shawarma is a large, fat kebab, made with lamb or chicken and grilled rotating against a vertical fire—the word comes from the Turkish *cevirme*, meaning to turn or rotate. The meat is sliced into wide, thin pieces, marinated overnight, and skewered onto a long, heavy, standing skewer in the shape of a cone with a little metal disk fixed on the bottom to stop the meat from sliding all the way down. Interspersed between the layers are slices of tail fat, or skin if it is chicken. The skewer is then fixed in front of a vertical grill and left to rotate against a moderate heat for 2 to 3 hours, until the meat is cooked through. As the meat cooks, the fat melts down the length of the kebab, basting it and keeping it moist. The vendor starts slicing the outer layer as soon as it crisps up and he has takers, piling the thin slivers onto pita bread. He then garnishes it with sliced tomatoes, onions, pickles, herbs, and tahini sauce if it is lamb or tüm if it is chicken. He rolls the bread tightly over the filling, half wraps the roll in paper, and hands it to the customer to eat on the go. Shawarma is not usually prepared at home, but I learned a simple, delectable version from Ramez, my Lebanese butcher in London, which is the recipe below.

SERVES 4 TO 6

- 1 pound 12 ounces (800 g) lamb from the shoulder, skinned and most of the fat removed, thinly sliced into long strips
- 2 medium onions (about 300 g), peeled, thinly sliced into wedges
- Juice of 1 lemon, or to taste
- ¼ cup (60 ml) extra virgin olive oil
- ¼ teaspoon ground cinnamon
- ½ teaspoon ground allspice or seven-spice mixture (page 19)
- A few sprigs fresh thyme, leaves only
- Sea salt
- Finely ground black pepper
- 2 or 3 medium round pita breads, opened at the seam into two layers

FOR THE TAHINI SAUCE

- ½ cup (125 ml) tahini
- Juice of 1 lemon, or to taste
- 1 clove garlic, peeled, minced to a fine paste
- Sea salt

FOR THE GARNISH

- 4 to 6 small tomatoes (about 600 g), thinly sliced
- 1 medium red onion (about 150 g), peeled, very thinly sliced into wedges
- 4 to 6 gherkins, thinly sliced lengthwise
- Handful finely chopped mint
- Handful finely chopped flat-leaf parsley

1. Put the meat in a large mixing bowl. Add the onions, lemon juice, olive oil, cinnamon, allspice, and thyme, season with salt and pepper to taste, and mix well. Place in the fridge and leave to marinate for 2 to 4 hours, stirring occasionally.

2. Meanwhile, make the tahini sauce. Put the tahini in a small mixing bowl and gradually whisk in the lemon juice, alternating it with just over ⅓ cup (90 ml) water. Taste from time to time to make sure you are getting the right balance of tartness while keeping the consistency like that of creamy yogurt. The tahini will first thicken to a purée-like consistency before thinning again. If you decide to use less lemon juice, make up for the loss of liquid by adding a little more water or vice versa. Add the crushed garlic and a little salt. Taste and adjust the seasoning if necessary. When the meat is ready, place a large frying pan over medium-high heat. When the pan is very hot, add the meat and sauté for a couple of minutes, or until done to your liking. Take off the heat.

3. Lay the pita rough-side up on your work surface and arrange equal quantities of meat down the middle of each. Divide the garnish ingredients equally among the meat and drizzle over as much tahini sauce as you would like, bearing in mind that too much will make the bread soggy. Roll each sandwich tightly, wrap the bottom half in a paper napkin, and serve immediately.

BECFIGUES

Asafir

These tiny birds are an endangered species now, and their consumption is totally frowned upon. Regardless, they remain a prized seasonal delicacy, with a couple of restaurants in Bhamdoun, a summer resort east of Beirut, specializing in them. The birds start showing up in the summer when figs are in season (hence their French name, which means "pecking at figs"), and once they were plentiful, with men going out to hunt them with small-caliber shotguns. If you drove in the mountains or the Bekaa Valley during the season, you would spot the hunters from the braces of feathered birds hanging on their side mirrors. In those days, you could have easily bitten onto one or more of the metal pellets stuck in their tiny bodies. Sadly, these days people mostly coat the branches of the fig trees with glue so the birds get stuck as they land to feed on the fruit, after which they net and kill them. I still occasionally succumb to the temptation of enjoying them, particularly at Halim, which has been specializing in asafir in Bhamdoun for decades, but much less now that I am aware of the cruel way the birds are caught.

I never had any qualms about eating them when I was young because my maternal uncles hunted them, and as soon as they brought them home, my grandmother, mother, and aunt would set about plucking them, very carefully, especially when it came to their tiny heads, which is the juiciest bit. They then gutted and seasoned them with just salt before going out onto the balcony, where my uncles had already prepared a barbecue fire, for my grandmother to grill them. And because they had a lot of fat on their tiny bodies, she would pick up the skewers every few seconds to press them into the pita she had already prepared to allow the fatty juices to soak into the bread. We ate them whole, bones and all, and it was one of our absolute summer delights. My siblings and I would bicker over who would get the juiciest bits of pita to wrap around the little bodies. My mother, who was never a mother hen but rather a regal albeit loving disciplinarian, made sure she got at least one juicy bite.

There is a tradition of eating similar tiny birds in Hong Kong. Maybe they are the same ones we now have, as I often hear that ours are no longer local but imported from China. Despite the fact that they are endangered and are no longer acceptable as a delicacy to be enjoyed when the fig season is upon us, I thought I would write about them given how intrinsic they are to our culinary traditions.

Asafir on the grill at Halim, Bhamdoun

Holding the counter at Halim, Bhamdoun

Bil-zeyt means "cooked in olive oil," a term that covers a whole range of mostly vegan dishes that are particularly meaningful to the Christian community, who refrain from eating meat on Fridays, because it is the day of the passion of Christ. They also fast during the forty days of Lent that lead to Easter Sunday, which means that Christians have many days in the year where they shun meat. As a result, they have devised a repertoire of dishes with either vegetables or legumes cooked in extra virgin olive oil. Some are cooked in a tomato sauce, while others are prepared with lemon juice or other flavorings.

That is not to say that Muslims and Druze don't also share these dishes, but for them, the bil-zeyt dishes are served as part of a mezze spread or as side dishes to accompany meat, poultry, or fish.

As for the olive oil, it is always extra virgin and often sourced from a relative, a friend, or a friend of a friend who has his/her own olive groves. The network of people we can rely on for müneh (page 2) is quite large, starting with the extended family, on to friends and neighbors. And despite the fifteen-year civil war that pitted confessions and communities against each other and saw more than 150,000 people killed, there is still a real feeling of cooperative spirit in the country, across the religious divide. And there are now great müneh stores where you can buy excellent olive oil (again from the store owner's personal network), together with all kinds of preserves made by village women, either in their home or in communal kitchens that often start out financed by NGOs before being taken over by local cooperatives.

Just harvested olives in Kfarmatta

FAVA BEANS AND SWISS CHARD WITH CILANTRO

FÜL BIL-SIL'

Fava beans are one of our prized spring vegetables. We prepare them in different ways, both with and without meat. This recipe belongs to Beirut's large Sunni Muslim community. I found it in my friend Tarfa Salam's family recipe book. Her family was, and still is, a prominent political dynasty, and Tarfa's uncle served four times as prime minister. She told me that her mother occasionally used spinach instead of Swiss chard. The taste and texture is different, but the result just as delicious. I personally prefer Swiss chard, as the dish ends up less watery. Of course, if you blanch the spinach beforehand and squeeze it dry, you will not have any excess liquid. Regardless, I still prefer the earthy flavor of the chard. You can also vary it by using a wild green of your choice.

SERVES 6

¼ cup (60 ml) extra virgin olive oil

2 medium onions (about 300 g), peeled, finely chopped

4 cloves garlic, peeled, minced to a fine paste

1 pound 12 ounces (800 g) Swiss chard, stalks trimmed, peeled of any stringy bits and diced, leaves shredded into thin strips

10½ ounces (300 g) baby fava beans, fresh or frozen

Sea salt

1 bunch cilantro (about 200 g on the stalk), washed, dried, most of the bottom stalks discarded, finely chopped

Juice of 1 lemon, or to taste

1. Put the olive oil and onions in a pot large enough to eventually hold the fava beans and Swiss chard and place over medium heat. As soon as the oil starts sizzling around the onions, reduce the heat to medium-low and cook, stirring regularly, until soft and golden, 10 to 15 minutes. Add the minced garlic and sauté for another couple of minutes, then add the diced Swiss chard stalks and the fava beans. Add ½ cup (125 ml) water and salt to taste. Mix well. Cover the pot and simmer for 10 minutes.

2. Add the Swiss chard leaves and cilantro. Mix well. Put the lid back on and simmer for 10 more minutes. Add the lemon juice and mix again. Simmer, covered, for a couple more minutes, or until the vegetables are tender and there is no excess liquid. Taste and adjust the seasoning if needed. Take off the heat and let cool. Serve at room temperature.

GREEN BEANS IN TOMATO SAUCE
LÜBYEH BIL-ZEYT

My mother and grandmother often prepared lübyeh bil-zeyt for Friday lunch, a day when they abstained from eating meat. And they served it on pita bread, which I loved. They tore the pita open at the seams and laid one half, rough-side up, on each plate. They then spread enough beans and tomato sauce on each half and served it with trimmed spring onions or quartered regular onions that they had presoaked in water to take away some of the sharpness. We ate with our hands, using torn pieces of pita from the other half or the dry edges to scoop up the beans, and with each mouthful, we took a bite of onion and sucked a garlic clove out of its skin. When we finished eating the beans, we lined a few pieces of onion down the middle of the tomato-soaked bread and rolled it up to eat like a wrap. It is still one of my favorite food memories, and I never fail to have or serve this dish the way they did. It was also the first dish I ever cooked.

SERVES 4

⅓ cup (80 ml) extra virgin olive oil

1 medium onion (about 150 g), peeled, finely chopped

8 to 12 large cloves garlic, unpeeled

1 pound 4 ounces (500 g) green beans (preferably the flat variety), topped, tailed, stringed if needed, cut across on an angle into 2-inch (5 cm) pieces

Sea salt

5 medium ripe tomatoes (about 625 g), peeled, coarsely chopped, or 2 (14-ounce/400 g) cans peeled Italian tomatoes, drained

1. Put the olive oil, onion, and garlic in a pot large enough to eventually hold the beans and tomatoes and place over medium heat. As soon as the oil starts sizzling around the onion, reduce the heat to medium-low and cook, stirring every now and then, until soft and golden, 10 to 15 minutes.

2. Rinse the green beans under cold water and add to the pot. Sprinkle with a generous pinch of salt and cook, stirring, for about 5 minutes, until the beans are evenly coated with oil and have turned a glossy green. Add the tomatoes and more salt to taste and mix well. Increase the heat to medium-high. Cover the pot and let bubble rather energetically for about 15 minutes, stirring every now and then. Reduce the heat to medium-low and let bubble gently for another 5 to 10 minutes, until the tomato sauce has thickened and the beans are done to your liking. Serve warm or at room temperature on or with pita bread.

EGGPLANT IN TOMATO SAUCE
MÜSSA'A'A

In Arabic, *müssa'a'a* means "cooled down," and I guess this dish is called thus because it is served at room temperature. Below, I give the classic version from the mountains, which typically contains split chickpeas. I personally don't like their slight crunch—somehow, they do not soften enough in the time it takes for the dish to be ready—and I prepare it without. However, my mother insisted on using them, saying that the dish is not right without. She may be right, as I have to admit that her version is more interesting. If I make it in the summer, I use fresh tomatoes whenever I can find tasty ripe ones. The rest of the year, I use canned tomatoes, which I drain and cook down a little before adding to the eggplant.

SERVES 4 TO 6

12 small Japanese eggplants, or 2 large ones (about 600 g)

Vegetable oil for frying

¼ cup (60 ml) extra virgin olive oil

2 medium onions (about 300 g), peeled, thinly sliced into wedges

4 cloves garlic, peeled, thinly sliced

1 pound 12 ounces (800 g) ripe fresh tomatoes, peeled, coarsely chopped, or 3 (14-ounce/ 400 g) cans cherry tomatoes, drained

Sea salt

1. If the eggplants have long stalks, shorten them to about ½ inch (1¼ cm) and trim away the husks that cap the top. Peel a thin strip of skin, about ½ inch (1 ¼ cm) wide, the full length of the eggplant. Leave an equal strip of skin unpeeled, then peel another strip and continue until you have a striped eggplant. Prepare the rest of the eggplants the same way. Peel large eggplants in wider strips and quarter them lengthwise.

2. Fill a wide frying pan with enough vegetable oil to deep-fry the eggplant and place over medium heat. When the oil is hot—test by dipping a piece of bread; if the oil immediately bubbles around it, it is ready—fry the eggplants until soft and golden all over. Remove with a slotted spoon and place on a wire rack placed over a baking sheet to drain off any excess oil. (If you don't like the idea of frying, you can generously brush the eggplants with olive oil and roast in a hot oven, preheated to 450°F [220°C], for about 30 minutes, until soft and golden.)

3. Put the olive oil and onions in a deep sauté pan that is wide enough to eventually hold the eggplants in one layer and place over medium heat. As soon as the oil sizzles around the onions, reduce the heat to medium-low and cook, stirring regularly, until the onions are soft and golden, 10 to 15 minutes. Add the garlic and cook, stirring, for a couple more minutes. Add the tomatoes and season with salt to taste. Increase the heat to medium. Cover the pan and bring to a boil. Let bubble gently for about 15 minutes, until the sauce has thickened somewhat.

4. Carefully arrange the eggplants in one layer in the sauce. Add more salt if necessary, cover again, and let bubble gently for 15 to 20 minutes, until the eggplants are completely soft and the tomato sauce has thickened with no excess liquid. If the sauce is too runny, take off the lid and increase the heat to medium-high. Let bubble a little more vigorously for a few more minutes, until all the excess liquid has evaporated. Let the eggplants cool, then gently transfer to a serving dish. Spoon the sauce in between to show off the striped effect on the eggplants. Serve at room temperature.

Müssa'a'a at Sumy Hokayem's

LEBANESE "PARMIGIANA"

MAGHMÜR

Here is an interesting dish from Deir Intar, a southern village that is rather famous for its bulgur wheat dishes and, in particular, the red müjaddarah (page 260). I like to describe maghmür as the Lebanese version of Parmigiana because it kind of looks like it and is similar except that there is no cheese and, instead, plenty of chickpeas, which makes it a supremely healthy vegan dish. That is, if you grill the eggplant instead of frying it, which is what I do. I brush the slices with olive oil before grilling. I also add more olive oil at the very end of cooking, after I take the dish out of the oven.

SERVES 4 TO 6

5 large eggplants (about 1¼ kg)

½ cup (125 ml) extra virgin olive oil, plus extra to brush the eggplant slices and drizzle over the maghmür

Sea salt

3 medium onions (about 450 g), peeled, thinly sliced into wedges

4 large firm ripe tomatoes (about 800 g), diced into small cubes, or 3 (14-ounce/400 g) cans peeled Italian tomatoes, drained, finely chopped

Just under 2 cups cooked chickpeas (about 300 g), cut in half

1. Preheat the oven to 450°F (220°C).

2. Peel the eggplants in strips and slice lengthwise into medium-thick slices. Brush the slices with olive oil on both sides and sprinkle with salt. Lay on a nonstick baking sheet, or one lined with parchment paper, and bake in the oven for about 15 minutes on each side, until soft and golden all over with slightly crisp edges.

3. While the eggplants are baking, put the olive oil and onions in a large frying pan and place over medium-high heat. When the oil starts sizzling around the onions, reduce the heat to medium-low and cook, stirring regularly, until soft and golden, 10 to 15 minutes. Add the tomatoes and let bubble for 10 to 15 minutes, until reduced but still having a fresh color. Add the chickpeas and salt to taste. Take off the heat and set aside.

4. Take a deep enough nonstick baking dish measuring 8 x 12½ inches (20 x 32 cm) and line the bottom with a layer of eggplant. Spread half the onion/tomato/chickpea sauce over it and cover with another layer of roasted eggplant. Spread the other half of the sauce and cover with the remaining eggplant slices. Drizzle with a little olive oil and bake in the preheated oven for 20 to 25 minutes, until the sides are slightly crisp and the sauce has thickened. Take out of the oven and drizzle with a little more olive oil if you feel like it. Serve at room temperature as part of a mezze spread or summer buffet, or as a vegetarian meal with good bread.

OKRA IN TOMATO SAUCE
BAMYEH BIL-ZEYT

Most Lebanese cooks will only use tiny okra, for this or any other okra dish. However, they are not so easy to source in the West. If you can't find small fresh okra, use dried ones (see page 6), which you need to soak overnight in hot water to rehydrate before draining, drying, and using, as with fresh ones. Or use frozen okra, which you can find in Middle Eastern grocery stores. They are a good and simple alternative, and all you need to do is let them thaw before drying and using.

SERVES 4 TO 6

1 pound 5 ounces (600 g) fresh okra

Just over ⅓ cup (100 ml) vegetable oil

3 tablespoons (45 ml) extra virgin olive oil

1 medium onion (about 150 g), peeled, thinly sliced into wedges

5 large cloves garlic, peeled, minced to a fine paste

¼ bunch cilantro (50 g on the stalk), washed, dried, most of the bottom stalks discarded, coarsely chopped

5 medium ripe tomatoes (about 625 g), peeled, coarsely chopped, or 2 (14-ounce/400 g) cans peeled Italian tomatoes, drained, finely chopped

Sea salt

1. Shave off the stem end of the okra, following the slant to end up with a smooth, unbroken pointed top—the reason why you don't want to cut into the okra is to avoid the release of the mucilaginous substance that is so typical of this vegetable. Rinse under cold water. Drain and spread on a kitchen towel. Cover with another towel and pat dry.

2. Pour the vegetable oil into a large frying pan and place over medium heat. When the oil is hot—test by dipping in a piece of bread; if the oil immediately bubbles around it, it is ready—sauté the okra for about 2 minutes, in two or three batches, until bright green and slightly crisp. Do not let them brown. Frying the okra first seals it and helps stop it from getting slimy. Remove with a slotted spoon and spread over a double layer of paper towel to drain off any excess oil.

3. Put the olive oil and onion in a pot large enough to eventually hold both the okra and tomatoes and place over medium heat. When the oil starts sizzling around the onion, reduce the heat to medium-low and cook, stirring occasionally, until soft and golden, 10 to 15 minutes. Add the minced garlic and chopped cilantro and sauté for a couple minutes, or until the aroma rises. Add the tomatoes. Increase the heat to medium and bring to a boil. Let bubble for 5 minutes.

4. Add the okra. Cover the pan and let bubble gently for 20 minutes, or until the okra is cooked through and the tomato sauce has thickened. Take off the heat. Remove the lid and cover with a clean kitchen towel. Let cool, then transfer to a serving platter. Serve at room temperature.

ZUCCHINI IN A MINTY TOMATO SAUCE

MÜTABBA'AT KÜSSA

The best zucchini to use here are the pale green ones, which are the only ones we use in the home country; and the smaller, the better, so you can cut them in half or quarters lengthwise rather than slicing across. It makes for a prettier presentation, especially if you choose ones that are more or less the same size. If you can't source the pale zucchini, use mini dark green ones, which you can leave whole.

Once the dish is ready, arrange the halved zucchini in a rosette shape, cut-side up, on the serving platter and spoon the tomato sauce in between. If you have quartered them, then arrange them in a jumble.

SERVES 4

1 pound 5 ounces (600 g) small pale green or mini dark green zucchini

3 tablespoons (45 ml) extra virgin olive oil

2 medium onions (about 300 g), peeled, thinly sliced into wedges

3 cloves garlic, thinly sliced

5 medium ripe tomatoes (about 625 g), peeled, diced into small cubes, or 2 (14-ounce/400 g) cans peeled Italian tomatoes, drained, finely chopped

Sea salt

1 tablespoon ground dried mint

1. Cut off and discard the stem ends of the zucchini and shave off the bottom brown skins. Rinse under cold water and cut the small pale green zucchini in half lengthwise (if using mini dark green ones, keep whole).

2. Put the olive oil and sliced onions into a wide pot large enough to eventually hold both the zucchini and tomatoes. Place over medium heat. Once the oil starts sizzling around the onions, reduce the heat to medium-low and cook, stirring every now and then, until soft and golden, 10 to 15 minutes. Add the garlic and cook, stirring, for a couple more minutes, then add the zucchini. Mix well. Cover the pan and cook for 5 minutes, stirring occasionally.

3. Add the tomatoes and salt to taste. Put the lid back on. Increase the heat to medium-high and let bubble for 15 minutes, or until the zucchini have softened but are not mushy. Carefully stir in the dried mint and cook uncovered for another 5 minutes, or until the mint has rehydrated and the sauce has thickened. Cover with a kitchen towel and let cool to serve at room temperature.

COOKED IN EXTRA VIRGIN OLIVE OIL

CHICORY IN OLIVE OIL
HINDBEH BIL-ZEYT

Winter is when you find chicory in Middle Eastern grocery stores. Italians also love it, and you can try your luck looking for it at an Italian greengrocer or deli where they have fresh produce. You can use the same recipe with any wild greens that are not too tough or too bitter. We call them sli' (page 22). Most rural home cooks will go foraging for them in the spring and fall, and ambulant greengrocers will pick them when in season to sell from carts or vans. You can also prepare this recipe with the ever-fashionable kale, although you need to cook the kale longer.

SERVES 4 TO 6

2 pounds 4 ounces (1 kg) chicory (or a wild green of your choice)

Sea salt

Just over ⅓ cup (100 ml) extra virgin olive oil

4 medium onions (about 600 g), peeled, thinly sliced into wedges

Sea salt

Lemon wedges for garnish

1. Wash and drain the chicory (or whatever green you are using) and chop into 2-inch (5 cm) strips. Put in a large pot and cover with boiling water. Season with salt and place over high heat. Bring to a boil and let bubble for 3 to 5 minutes, depending on the green that you are using. Drain and let cool.

2. Put the olive oil and onions in a large frying pan and place over medium heat. As soon as the oil starts sizzling around the onions, reduce the heat to medium-low and cook, stirring regularly, until golden brown, 25 to 30 minutes—be careful not to let the onions burn. Take off the heat. With a slotted spoon, remove three-quarters of the onions into a sieve to drain off any excess oil. Shake every now and then to keep the onions crisp. Keep the rest of the onions in the pan.

3. Take handfuls of the greens and squeeze as dry as you can. Pull the clumps apart to undo any leaves that are stuck together. Add to the fried onions. Mix well and return the pan to medium heat. Sauté for a few minutes, stirring regularly, until the greens are well blended with the oil and onions. Taste and adjust the salt if needed. Transfer to a serving platter. Let cool, then garnish with the crisp onions. Arrange the lemon wedges all around and serve at room temperature with pita bread.

ARTICHOKES AND POTATOES IN OLIVE OIL

ARD EL-SHAWKEH BIL-ZEYT

If I am in Lebanon during artichoke season, I always stop by greengrocers to watch them being prepared. They usually sit outside their stores to peel the artichokes and, as they do, piles of artichoke leaves form all around them. They normally do this to order, but some will also do it to sell prepared artichokes, packed in plastic bags and floating in acidulated water. Frozen hearts are a good enough substitute for fresh ones, especially considering the time saved. Try to cut the potatoes and artichokes into more or less equal pieces for a nicer presentation and more even cooking.

SERVES 4 TO 6

2/3 cup (160 ml) extra virgin olive oil

1 pound (450 g) new potatoes, cut into wedges

2 medium onions (about 300 g), peeled, thinly sliced into wedges

1 pound 9 ounces (650 g) artichoke hearts, cut into medium "triangles" more or less the same size as the potato wedges

3/4 teaspoon ground allspice

Sea salt

Juice of 1 lemon, or to taste

A few sprigs flat-leaf parsley, washed, dried, most of the bottom stalks discarded, finely chopped, for garnish

1. Put the olive oil in a deep, wide sauté pan large enough to eventually hold both potatoes and artichokes and place over medium heat. When the oil is hot—test by dipping in a piece of bread; if the oil immediately bubbles around it, it is ready—add the potatoes and fry, turning them over to color evenly, until crisp and golden. Remove onto a plate and set aside.

2. Add the onions to the pan and fry, stirring regularly, until soft and golden, 10 to 15 minutes. Add the artichoke hearts and mix well. Sprinkle with the allspice and mix again. Add 1 cup (250 ml) water and salt to taste. Cover the pan and reduce the heat to medium-low. Let bubble gently for 15 minutes, or until the artichoke hearts are done and the liquid is reduced to a glossy sauce. Add the lemon juice and mix well. Let cool.

3. Return the potatoes to the pan and mix well. Taste and adjust the seasoning if needed. Transfer to a serving dish. Sprinkle the chopped parsley all over and serve warm or at room temperature.

DESERT TRUFFLES WITH CILANTRO

KAMA BIL-KIZBRAH

Desert truffles are totally unlike European ones, both black and white. For one, they are not fragrant and are more like Jerusalem artichokes than proper truffles. This said, they do grow underground like the precious truffles of Italy and France, but in the desert (hence the name) rather than in the woods. And they are used as a vegetable rather than as a garnish. Regardless, they are incredibly prized, because they are very seasonal, starting to appear in February after the heavy rains, and because they are somewhat rare. Some years they are plentiful and others not so. Because we don't have a desert, those used by us come from Syria or the Arabian Gulf. As you can imagine, they are very sandy and need thorough cleaning, which is not so easy if they are small and knobby. Using a brush while keeping them under running water makes the job easier. Sometimes they are very spongy and not so good. Try to choose fairly smooth and firm ones for best results.

SERVES 4

- ¼ cup (60 ml) extra virgin olive oil
- 1 pound 2 ounces (500 g) desert truffles (see page 21), brushed clean, rinsed under cold water, dried, cut into bite-sized chunks
- Sea salt
- Freshly ground black pepper
- 2 large cloves garlic, peeled, minced into a fine paste
- ¼ bunch flat-leaf parsley (50 g on the stalk), washed, dried, most of the bottom stalks discarded, finely chopped
- ¼ bunch cilantro (50 g on the stalk), washed, dried, most of the bottom stalks discarded, finely chopped

1. Put the olive oil in a deep, wide sauté pan and place over medium heat. When the oil is hot—test by dipping in a piece of bread; if the oil bubbles around it, it is ready—add the desert truffles. Season with salt and pepper to taste and sauté until crisp and golden and just done, kind of al dente.

2. Add the garlic, parsley, and cilantro and mix well. Cook, stirring, for a couple of minutes, then taste and adjust the seasoning if needed. Transfer to a serving platter and serve hot, warm, or at room temperature.

ZUCCHINI FRITTATAS
EJJET KÜSSA

These are a perfect example of the ingeniousness of our cooks, who have a complete no-waste policy and use every scrap they can of whatever food they are preparing. In the case of stuffed zucchini (page 187), they save the pulp extracted while coring the zucchini and use it to make the frittatas below or the spread on page 72. Because these omelets are made quite thin, they are perfect wrapped in pita together with fresh mint leaves and thinly sliced tomatoes, even thinly sliced cucumber. You can also use them to make toasted sandwiches, lining the toast with the fresh mint and tomato and cucumber slices before adding the omelets, unless you prefer your sandwich plain.

MAKES 8 MEDIUM FRITTATAS

- 12 free-range organic eggs, beaten
- ¼ cup (31 g) unbleached all-purpose flour
- 1 teaspoon ground cinnamon
- 1 teaspoon ground allspice
- ½ teaspoon finely ground black pepper
- 8 cloves garlic, peeled, minced to a fine paste
- Pulp from pale green zucchini (see page 188; about 650 g), very finely chopped, squeezed very dry
- 2 bunches scallions (200 g), trimmed, thinly sliced
- 1 bunch flat-leaf parsley (200 g on the stalk), washed, dried, most of the bottom stalks discarded, finely chopped
- Sea salt
- Extra virgin olive oil for brushing the frying pan

1. Put the beaten eggs in a large mixing bowl and add the flour, cinnamon, allspice, and pepper. Mix well. Add the garlic, zucchini pulp, scallions, and parsley. Add salt to taste and mix well.

2. Brush a medium nonstick frying pan with a little olive oil and place over medium heat. When the pan is hot, add one-eighth of the frittata mixture and spread all over the pan. Cook for 2 to 3 minutes, until golden on the bottom and fairly dry on top. Flip over and cook for another minute or so. Remove onto a plate and wipe the pan clean. Brush with a little more oil and make the second frittata. Repeat until you have used up all the egg mixture and have made 8 frittatas. Serve warm or at room temperature with good bread and a salad of your choice.

Yogurt is an essential part of our diet, and there is hardly a home cook who doesn't have some in the refrigerator. We enjoy it strained as labneh, usually for breakfast or light dinner. I still remember how my grandmother and aunt would make a 'arüss (literally meaning "bride," but actually describing a wrap) labneh for dinner—their main meal was at lunch, and they ate lightly in the evening. The most common "bride" is one made with labneh, cucumber, fresh mint, olives, and tomatoes. My grandmother first mixed the labneh with extra virgin olive oil and a little salt, then spread it across the bread. She then lined the vegetables, herbs, and olives, which she had pitted, down the center before rolling the bread tightly around them. She always bought large pita, and she would cut the "bride" in two, with one half for her and the other for my aunt who never married and lived with her.

Labneh is not our only way with yogurt. We also cook it as a sauce for meat, eggs, and stuffed vegetables, and we use it as a topping in fatteh, a layered dish of toasted or fried bread, with meat, legumes, or vegetables. We also serve it as a side with grain dishes or stuffed vegetables, to name a few common uses.

When cooking yogurt, you need to stabilize it so it doesn't curdle. Some do this with cornstarch, while others use eggs. I belong to the latter camp because it makes for a silkier, more delicate sauce. I am told that you don't need to stabilize goat's yogurt, but I find that it curdles regardless. The trick for a smooth sauce is to bring the yogurt to a very gentle boil over medium-low heat before turning the heat right down for a bare simmer as you finish the dish with whatever garnish you have chosen.

Chickpea fatteh at El Soussi, Beirut

LAMB FATTEH
FATTET GHANAM

Fatteh is a dish made in layers with many variations, both regional and personal. The word means "crumble" in Arabic, and I am guessing it is called thus because one layer is made up of broken pieces of toasted or fried bread. Traditionally, the bread was laid on the bottom, but today's modern versions have the toasted bread either piled on top or arranged around the yogurt so it stays crisp longer. The bread can be cut into long, thin strips, and as it fries, it curls up, or it can be cut into squares and fried or toasted to be arranged in a ring all around the yogurt. Both make for a very pretty presentation and a nice contrast in textures between the crunchy bread, the velvety yogurt (some people add a couple tablespoons of tahini to give the yogurt extra body), and the more substantial meat, vegetable, or legume layer. I sometimes use the toasted pita whole and layer the ingredients on top. However, I now arrange the bread all around the yogurt, which I learned to do from the lovely Yasmine Charafeddine, an exquisite cook who very generously hosted me and Dalia (who took the location photographs and Yasmine's photo on page 133) at two spectacular lunches. I think it was at the second one that she served the fava bean fatteh (page 139), which I had never had before.

The garnish is normally toasted Mediterranean pine nuts, but hardly anyone uses these nowadays because they have become so expensive. Instead, both restaurant chefs and home cooks use toasted slivered almonds or cashews, or Chinese pine nuts. I still use Mediterranean pine nuts regardless of the increased cost because their crunch is softer, not to mention their more delicate taste.

The recipe here is for lamb, which you can easily replace with chicken. As for the chickpeas, I no longer cook mine. Instead, I buy them precooked in glass jars, preserved in only salt and water. All I have to do then is rinse them well before using. You can of course cook your own, but be sure to add baking soda to the soaking water to soften them and shorten their cooking time. If you prefer chicken to lamb, replace the shanks in the recipe below with a whole organic chicken weighing about 3 pounds 6 ounces (1½ kg) and follow the same instructions as below. For a vegetarian version, omit the meat and use double the amount of chickpeas to have fattet hommus, a classic breakfast version. You can imitate the fried bread effect by brushing the rough side of your pita with extra virgin olive oil and toasting in a hot oven until golden brown all over.

SERVES 4

¾ cup (150 g) dried chickpeas, soaked in plenty of cold water with ½ teaspoon baking soda, or 2 cups (300 g) cooked chickpeas, rinsed under cold water

4 lamb shanks (about 1¼ kg)

1 cinnamon stick

1 tablespoon coarse sea salt

1 large pita bread, split open at the seams

3 tablespoons (45 g) unsalted butter

⅓ cup (50 g) Mediterranean pine nuts

2 large cloves garlic, peeled, minced to a fine paste

3 cups (750 g) plain full-fat yogurt

1. If using dried chickpeas: Drain and rinse the chickpeas under cold water. Put in a large pot and cover well with water. Place over medium heat and bring to a boil. Partially cover the pan, reduce the heat to medium-low, and let bubble gently for 1 hour, or until tender.

2. Put the shanks in a separate pot. Add 1¼ quarts (1¼ liters) water and place over medium-high heat. As the water is about to boil, skim the surface clean. Add the cinnamon stick and salt. Reduce the heat to medium-low and cover the pot. Let bubble gently for 45 minutes to 1 hour, until the meat is very tender and falling off the bone. Remove the shanks onto a cutting board. Take the meat off the bone and trim and discard any fat, skin, and bones. Cut lengthwise into medium pieces. Strain the stock into a clean saucepan. Return the boned meat to the broth together with the drained chickpeas when done, or add the precooked ones. Keep hot.

3. While the chickpeas and meat are cooking, toast the bread in a hot oven or under the broiler until golden brown. Let cool. Some cooks like to fry the bread, while others brush it with extra virgin olive oil before toasting.

4. Melt the butter in a small frying pan and sauté the pine nuts, stirring constantly, until golden brown. Remove with a slotted spoon onto a double layer of paper towel to drain off any excess fat—you can also do what most cooks do, which is to toast the pine nuts at the last minute and pour both nuts and butter over the yogurt. I personally don't like seeing the white velvety yogurt smeared with the browned butter instead of being neatly dotted with the nuts.

5. Add the crushed garlic to the yogurt. Add salt to taste and mix well. Break the toasted bread into bite-sized pieces. Set aside.

6. Using a slotted spoon, scoop both meat and chickpeas out of the stock and spread over a serving platter. Sprinkle the meat and chickpeas with a few tablespoons of stock and spoon the yogurt all over. Garnish with the toasted pine nuts and arrange the toasted bread all around the edges. Serve immediately.

STUFFED EGGPLANT FATTEH
FATTET MAKDÜSS

I first had this fatteh in Syria, where they don't use tomato sauce. This recipe, which seems to be from the south, comes from Joumana Hazim, whose cooking I used to covet while watching her daughter Lynn's video clips on Instagram. When I saw Lynn's post of her mother's fattet makdüss, I shamelessly invited myself and Dalia to see how it is made, taste it of course, and take photos. It was as delicious as I had expected it to be, and we also got to taste Joumana's vegetarian stuffed eggplants, which she had made the day before. She uses pomegranate molasses in her stuffing rather than the plain sumac my mother used. I also had a plain version of eggplant fatteh at my friend Nayla Audi's home, where the eggplants (2 large ones, each weighing about 7 ounces/300 g) are peeled and diced into medium-sized cubes, then deep-fried until golden all over before being layered like in lamb fatteh (see page 135), although without chickpeas and with a little fresh mint.

SERVES 4 TO 6

Joumana Hazim in her kitchen making fattet makdüss

FOR THE EGGPLANTS

About 20 small Japanese eggplants (about 1 kg)

Vegetable oil for frying

FOR THE STUFFING

6 tablespoons (90 g) unsalted butter

½ cup (75 g) pine nuts

1 medium onion (about 150 g), peeled, very finely chopped

1 pound 6 ounces (500 g) lean ground lamb

½ teaspoon ground cinnamon

¾ teaspoon ground allspice

¼ teaspoon finely ground black pepper

Sea salt

FOR THE TOMATO SAUCE

Tomato sauce for Kibbé Balls in Tomato Sauce (page 174)

FOR THE YOGURT TOPPING

Yogurt topping for Fava Bean Fatteh (page 139)

TO FINISH

Vegetable oil for frying

⅓ cup (50 g) Mediterranean pine nuts, toasted in a little butter until golden brown

1 medium pita bread, split open at the seams, toasted in a hot oven until golden brown, broken into bite-sized pieces

1. To prepare the eggplants: Trim and core the eggplants as instructed on page 190. Put to soak in cold water.

2. To prepare the stuffing: Put the butter in a large frying pan and place over medium heat. When the butter is melted, add the pine nuts and toast, stirring continuously, until golden brown. Remove with a slotted spoon onto a double layer of paper towel. Set aside. Add the onion and sauté, stirring regularly, until soft and golden, about 10 minutes. Add the meat to the pan and cook, breaking up any lumps, until completely done and there is no excess liquid in the pan. Take off the heat and season with the cinnamon, allspice, and pepper. Return the pine nuts to the pan. Add salt to taste and mix well. Taste and adjust the seasoning if needed. Let cool while you prepare the tomato sauce. Transfer the tomato sauce to a pot large enough to hold the eggplants.

3. Prepare the yogurt topping.

4. To finish: Drain and rinse the eggplants, then stuff them with the cooled meat and pine nut stuffing—here you can pack them fully, as there is no rice that needs room to expand. Pour a little vegetable oil into a large frying pan and place over medium heat. Fry the stuffed eggplants until soft and wrinkled but not completely done, about 10 minutes, turning them over halfway through. Remove with a slotted spoon and drop into the tomato sauce, preferably in one layer. Place over medium heat. As soon as the tomato sauce starts bubbling, reduce the heat to low and simmer for about 45 minutes, until the eggplants are completely cooked through and the sauce has thickened.

5. Transfer the eggplants to a slightly deep serving platter. Spoon the yogurt all over, but letting an eggplant show here and there. Arrange the toasted bread all around the yogurt and scatter the toasted pine nuts all over. Serve immediately.

FAVA BEAN FATTEH
FATTEH BIL-FÜL EL-AKHDAR

The first time I tasted this version of fatteh was when my lovely new friend Yasmine Charafeddine, with Feryal Osseyran (her daughter's mother-in-law and the owner of the boutique Feryal in Beirut, where they sell all the different müneh), had prepared several specialties for me to try. I immediately fell in love with Yasmine's fatteh, not only because it was a perfect spring dish with the addition of the fava beans to the meat, but also because the meat was braised with onions rather than boiled, which made it a lot tastier even if a little heavier. For me, it was a great addition to the fatteh repertoire, one of my favorite groups of dishes. The only drawback is that you can only prepare it in early spring, when fava beans are still young and tender, making it possible to cook them in their skin. This said, Yasmine prepares a batch in season that she freezes so she can serve the dish all year round. You can of course omit the meat for a vegetarian version, which I think was Yasmine's that day.

SERVES 4 TO 6

FOR THE MEAT

⅓ cup (80 ml) extra virgin olive oil

2 medium onions (about 300 g), peeled, thinly sliced into wedges

1 pound 10½ ounces (750 g) lamb meat from the shoulder, or veal from the ribs, diced into bite-sized chunks

Freshly ground black pepper

Sea salt

FOR THE FAVA BEANS

⅓ cup (80 ml) extra virgin olive oil

2 medium onions (about 300 g), peeled, thinly sliced into wedges

2 pounds 4 ounces (1 kg) young tender fava beans, trimmed, stringed if needed, cut on an angle into 2-inch (5 cm) pieces

Sea salt

FOR THE YOGURT TOPPING

2 cups (500 g) plain full-fat yogurt

1 tablespoon tahini

1 clove garlic, peeled, minced to a fine paste

Juice of ½ lemon, or to taste

Sea salt

FOR THE CILANTRO GARNISH

2 tablespoons (30 g) unsalted butter

4 to 6 cloves garlic, peeled, minced to a fine paste

1 bunch cilantro (about 200 g on the stalk), washed, dried, most of the stalks discarded, finely chopped

TO FINISH

1 medium pita bread, opened at the seams, toasted in the oven until golden, broken into bite-sized pieces

⅓ cup (50 g) Mediterranean pine nuts, sautéed in a little butter until golden brown

YOGURT DISHES

1. To prepare the meat: Put the olive oil and onions in a medium pot and place over medium heat. As soon as the oil starts sizzling around the onions, reduce the heat to medium-low and cook, stirring every now and then, until soft and golden, 10 to 15 minutes. Add the meat. Increase the heat back to medium and cook, stirring, until the meat is browned all over. Add 1 cup (250 ml) water and pepper and salt to taste and let bubble gently for about 1 hour, stirring regularly, until the water is reduced to a silky sauce and the meat is completely done. Taste and adjust the seasoning if needed.

2. To prepare the fava beans: While the meat is cooking, put the olive oil and onions in a wide, deep sauté pan and place over medium heat. As soon as the oil starts sizzling around the onions, reduce the heat to medium-low and cook, stirring every now and then, until soft and golden, 10 to 15 minutes. Add the fava beans and salt to taste and stir until the fava beans are well blended with the onions. Add 1¾ cups (415 ml) water and cook, stirring occasionally, for 30 minutes, or until the water is completely reduced and the beans are done to your liking. Add the meat to the fava beans and mix well. Taste and adjust the seasoning if needed. Keep hot.

3. To prepare the yogurt topping: While the meat and fava beans are cooking, put the yogurt, tahini, garlic, and lemon juice in a large mixing bowl. Mix well, then add salt to taste and mix again. Taste and adjust the seasoning if needed.

4. To prepare the cilantro garnish: Put the butter in a medium frying pan and place over medium heat. When the butter has melted, add the minced garlic and chopped cilantro and sauté for a couple of minutes, or until the herbs have wilted and the aroma has risen. Keep warm.

5. To serve: Transfer the fava beans and meat to a serving platter and spread evenly. Ladle the yogurt all over, leaving the center exposed to show the fava beans and meat. Arrange the toasted bread all around the yogurt. Drizzle the cilantro and garlic in a circle an inch or so inside from the bread. Scatter the toasted nuts all over and serve immediately.

Yasmine Charafeddine's fatteh

COOKED YOGURT SAUCE

LABAN MATBÜKH

Cooking with yogurt may seem unfamiliar to Western cooks, but it is very common for us. Here is the basic sauce, that you can flavor with cilantro or mint depending on what you are using it with. In some regions, they leave the yogurt plain, which I find rather boring. Both cow's and sheep's yogurt curdle if cooked without a stabilizer, which can be egg or cornstarch—I prefer to use egg for a more refined sauce. Also, you cannot leave the sauce for a minute while it is cooking because you need to stir it all the time. Goat's yogurt, on the other hand, does not need to be stabilized, although I am always anxious about it curdling and I treat it the same way as the others. The taste of our goat's yogurt is stronger and slightly more sour than both cow's and sheep's yogurt, which is not necessarily the case in the West. If you are going to flavor the yogurt with dried mint rather than cilantro, prepare it the same way.

MAKES ABOUT 1 QUART (1 LITER)

2 tablespoons (30 g) unsalted butter

½ bunch cilantro (100 g on the stalk), washed, dried, most of the stalks discarded, finely chopped, or 3 tablespoons dried mint

4 large cloves garlic, peeled, minced to a fine paste

1 quart (1 kg) plain full-fat yogurt

1 free-range organic egg, whisked

1. Put the butter in a medium frying pan and place over medium heat. When the butter has melted, add the cilantro and garlic and sauté for a couple of minutes, or until the herbs have wilted and the aroma has risen. Take off the heat and set aside.

2. Put the yogurt in a large pot and add the whisked egg. Mix well and place over medium heat. Bring to a boil, stirring constantly so the yogurt does not curdle. Reduce the heat to low and simmer for 3 minutes, still stirring.

3. Depending on what dish you are preparing, you will be adding the garlic and cilantro or mint at the very end.

LAMB IN YOGURT SAUCE
LABAN EMMOH

The Arabic name of this dish means "the yogurt of his mother," and this charming name is because the meat is cooked in yogurt that would have been made with ewe's milk, which is from the mother of the lamb. Apart from the evocative name, it is a refreshing way to eat meat, and in one exciting seasonal variation, akküb is added (page 23). The Latin name of akküb is *Gundelia tournefortii*. It is an edible thistle that is like artichoke but a lot spinier. You can buy akküb prepared when it is in season in springtime, mostly in rural areas or in the mountains where foragers harvest it. They peel off most of the spiny bits and sell it off their vans or carts. Many also harvest it to sell to greengrocers. Regardless of them taking the trouble to peel it, you will still need to spend a fair amount of time getting rid of the spiny bits they missed until you get to the smooth core. If you are going to use it here, prepare about 1 pound 2 ounces (500 g) akküb by trimming all the spiny bits and blanching it in salted water before adding to the meat and yogurt. Drain it well before adding at the same time as the lamb and onions.

SERVES 4 TO 6

4 lamb shanks (about 1¼ kg)

Coarse sea salt

16 pearl onions (about 400 g), peeled

Cooked Yogurt Sauce (page 142), with adjustments (see below)

1. Put the shanks in a large pot. Add 1½ quarts (1½ liters) water and place over medium heat. Bring to a boil, and as the water is about to bubble, skim the surface clean. Season with salt, then cover the pot and let bubble gently for 50 minutes. Add the pearl onions and simmer for 10 more minutes, or until the meat is done and the onions are slightly underdone.

2. Remove the shanks and onions from the stock. Put the onions in a bowl and the shanks on your work surface to take the meat off the bone, discarding any fat and skin. Cut the meat into medium-sized pieces. Put in the bowl with the onions. Cover with plastic wrap and keep warm. You can, if you want to, strain the stock and reserve it for another use.

3. Prepare the yogurt sauce as instructed on page 142, but don't add the cilantro and garlic until after you have added the meat and onions. Add the meat and onions and let bubble gently, still carefully stirring, for another 3 to 5 minutes, until both the meat and onions are hot. Add the cilantro and garlic and mix well. Serve hot with plain rice or vermicelli rice (page 263).

STUFFED ZUCCHINI IN YOGURT SAUCE

ABLAMAH BIL-LABAN

You can stuff the zucchini here with either meat and rice, as below, or with double the amount of meat and pine nut stuffing (page 201). However, instead of adding cilantro, use dried mint. Many cooks sauté the zucchini in a little butter before adding it to the yogurt sauce. I prefer boiling it because the skin of the zucchini remains smooth and a nice color instead of crinkling up as it fries, not to mention changing to a darker color.

SERVES 4 TO 6

20 small pale green zucchini (about 1¼ kg), trimmed, cored (see page 188)

Cooked Yogurt Sauce (page 142), with adjustments (see below)

FOR THE STUFFING

⅔ cup (125 g) Egyptian, Calasparra, or bomba rice

7 ounces (200 g) lean ground lamb

¼ teaspoon ground cinnamon

½ teaspoon ground allspice

¼ teaspoon finely ground black pepper

Sea salt

1. Prepare the zucchini and let soak in cold water.

2. To prepare the stuffing: Rinse the rice under cold water, drain, and put in a large mixing bowl. Add the ground meat and 2 to 3 tablespoons water. Season with the cinnamon, allspice, pepper, and salt to taste and mix well, preferably with your hands to better blend the ingredients. Dip your finger in the stuffing and taste for salt; or, if you are reluctant to taste raw meat, make a small patty and sear it in a small pan to make sure it is well seasoned.

3. Drain the zucchini and stuff them three-quarters full—you need to leave a little space for the rice to expand. If you are going to use the meat and pine nut stuffing, you can fill the zucchini to the top.

4. Arrange the zucchini with the open end slightly raised in a saucepan where they will fit snugly half-standing. Add 2 cups (500 ml) water. Cover the pan and place over medium-high heat. Bring to a boil, then reduce the heat to medium-low and let bubble gently for 25 minutes.

5. Prepare the yogurt sauce and add the mint and garlic mixture. Turn down the heat to low. Carefully remove the nearly cooked zucchini from the pan with a slotted spoon and gently fold it into the yogurt sauce. Simmer, uncovered, for 10 more minutes, very gently stirring the sauce every now and then so you don't break the zucchini. Taste and adjust the seasoning if needed. Take off the heat and let sit for a few minutes, then gently transfer to a shallow serving bowl. Serve immediately. If you stuffed the zucchini with the meat and pine nut stuffing, serve with plain rice or vermicelli rice (page 263).

FAVA BEANS AND LAMB IN YOGURT
FIST'IYEH

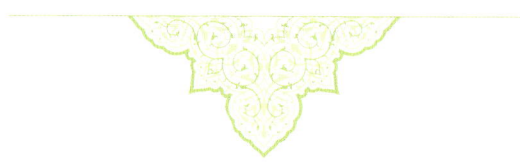

This dish is from Saida, but you also find it in other regions. It was completely new to me when I had it with my friend Jacquot Ayoub, who has been instrumental in giving me both information and recipes for this book. She also very kindly introduced me to other home cooks for me to talk to about regional dishes. I was quite taken by this recipe and have had two versions. Jacquot's is made with goat's yogurt stabilized with cornstarch. She also uses a chicken stock cube to add acidity, but I prefer it without. I also prefer to stabilize yogurt with an egg. However, the main difference between Jacquot's version and that of Feryal Osseyran, another friend, who sells müneh at her boutique of the same name, is that Jacquot uses the fava beans whole with their tender skins, whereas Feryal uses peeled fava beans, making her version more subtle, and whiter, because the peeled beans sink into the yogurt. I like both, and here I give Jacquot's version, but if you want to make Feryal's version, blanch and peel 2 pounds 12 ounces (1 kg) mature podded fava beans (about 1 pound 11 ounces/700 g peeled) and only add them at the very end after having added the meat to the yogurt sauce, then simmer for 5 minutes or so.

SERVES 4 TO 6

FOR THE MEAT

3 lamb shanks (about 950 g)

1 small carrot

1 small onion (about 100 g), peeled

2 bay leaves

1 cinnamon stick

Coarse sea salt

FOR THE FAVA BEANS

⅓ cup (80 ml) extra virgin olive oil or 5 tablespoons unsalted butter

2 medium onions (about 300 g), peeled, finely chopped

2 pounds 4 ounces (1 kg) young tender fava beans, topped, tailed, strings removed, cut across on a diagonal into 2-inch (5 cm) pieces

Sea salt

4 large cloves garlic, peeled, minced to a fine paste

½ bunch cilantro (about 100 g on the stalk), washed, dried, most of the bottom stalks discarded

Cooked Yogurt Sauce (page 142), with adjustments (see below)

1. To cook the meat: Put the lamb shanks in a large pot and cover with water. Place over medium-high heat and bring to a boil. Remove the shanks onto a plate. Drain the water and wipe the pot clean. Return the shanks to the pot and add 1 quart (1 liter) fresh water. Add the carrot, onion, bay leaves, and cinnamon stick and return to the heat. Bring to a boil, then season with salt. Reduce the heat to medium-low and let bubble gently for 45 minutes to 1 hour, until the meat is done and falling off the bone. Remove the shanks onto a cutting board. Take the meat off the bone and trim and discard any fat and skin. Cut into medium pieces and transfer to a bowl. Cover with plastic wrap and set aside. Strain the broth and set aside.

2. To prepare the fava beans: Put the olive oil and onions in a pot large enough to eventually hold the fava beans, meat, and yogurt sauce, and place over medium heat. As soon as the onions start sizzling, turn down the heat to medium-low and cook, stirring regularly, until soft and golden, 10 to 15 minutes. Add the fava beans and sprinkle with a little salt. Sauté for a few minutes, then add the meat and strained broth. Let bubble gently for 30 minutes, or until the beans are done. Add the cilantro and garlic and take off the heat until you are ready to add the yogurt sauce.

3. Prepare the yogurt sauce as instructed on page 142, but leave it plain. Add it to the meat and fava beans and return the pot to medium-low heat. Stir constantly until everything is well blended, making sure the sauce is not too runny. Taste and adjust the seasoning if needed. Transfer to a shallow serving bowl. Serve hot with plain rice or vermicelli rice (page 263).

TINY MEAT DUMPLINGS IN YOGURT SAUCE

SHISH BARAK

The first mention of shish barak is in a fifteenth-century Syrian cookery book, *Kitab al-Tibakhah* (*The Book of Cookery*), written by Ibn al-Mabrad or Ibn al-Mubarrad, a legal scholar from Damascus. In that book, the name of the dish is spelled *shushbarak*, and the instructions are to take ground meat and stuff it in dough rolled out like cut tutmaj (unfilled dough cooked in yogurt). The dumplings are cooked before being covered with yogurt seasoned with garlic and mint. This ancient recipe is closer to Turkish manti, where the yogurt is not cooked but poured over the dumplings, whereas in our version, the yogurt is first cooked and the dumplings can be either simmered in it, or first boiled or baked, then dropped in. I learned from my mother to cook the dumplings directly in the yogurt sauce. Some like to also add kibbé balls (page 162), but I prefer not to. For one, making the dumplings is hard enough work without adding the making of kibbé balls. I also don't think that the tastes or even textures complement each other. The dumplings are very delicate, whereas the kibbé balls are more substantial.

SERVES 4 TO 6

FOR THE DOUGH

1½ cups (185 g) unbleached all-purpose flour, plus extra for kneading and rolling out

Pinch fine sea salt

FOR THE STUFFING

1 small onion (about 100 g), peeled, very finely chopped

Pinch ground cinnamon

¼ teaspoon ground allspice

⅛ teaspoon finely ground black pepper

Sea salt

5 ounces (150 g) lean ground lamb

Cooked Yogurt Sauce (page 142), with adjustments (see below)

1. To make the dough: Mix the flour and salt in a large mixing bowl. Make a well in the center and gradually add ½ cup (125 ml) water, bringing in the flour as you go along. Knead until you have a rough ball of dough, then remove onto a lightly floured work surface and knead for a few minutes. Shape into a ball. Invert the bowl over the dough and let sit for 15 minutes—this will hydrate the dough and reduce kneading time. Knead for a couple more minutes, or until you have a smooth, malleable dough. Cover with a damp cloth and let rest while you prepare the stuffing.

2. To make the stuffing: Put the onion in a medium mixing bowl. Sprinkle with the cinnamon, allspice, pepper, and salt to taste and firmly rub the seasonings into the onion with your fingers to soften it. Add the ground meat and mix well. Taste and adjust the seasoning if needed—if you are not keen on tasting raw meat, sear a little in a hot pan and taste it.

3. Lightly dust a large freezer-proof platter with flour and have on hand to put the dumplings on it.

4. Divide the dough into two. Shape each into a ball, then flatten one slightly. Lightly dip both sides in flour, shake the excess off, and roll out into a large circle, about 1/10 inch (2 mm) thick. Use a 2-inch/5 cm round pastry cutter to cut out as many circles as you can, starting from the very edge and working your way round the outside first, then inside. Pick up the cutouts and knead together. Shape into a ball and let rest while you make the first batch of dumplings.

5. Turn the circles of dough over, then lift one and lay it on the fingers of one hand. Place ¼ teaspoon stuffing in the middle and fold the dough over the filling, aligning the edges to form a half circle. With your free thumb and index finger, pinch the edges tightly into a thin flat wedge, then fold to make the ends meet. Pinch the ends tightly together and stand the curled dumpling onto the floured platter, with the thin flat wedge up—it should look like a tortellino with a narrower uncurled rim. Finish making the dumplings and arranging them neatly on the platter until you have used up both dough and filling.

6. Put the dumplings in the freezer to firm them up while you prepare the yogurt sauce—or you can freeze them for later use; they actually freeze very well. If you are doing this, wait until they are completely frozen before packing them in a freezer bag so they don't lose their shape.

7. Prepare the yogurt sauce following the instructions on page 142, but do not add the cilantro and garlic until after you have dropped in the dumplings. Take the dumplings out of the freezer and carefully drop them into the simmering yogurt. Bring back to a simmer, then add the cilantro and garlic mixture. Simmer, carefully stirring, for 5 more minutes, or until the dumplings are done. Serve hot, with or without plain rice or vermicelli rice (page 263).

ZINKOL

A dish from the west Bekaa, which I first tasted at the summer home of Shirine Abdallah, who had very kindly invited me, Dalia (who took all the photos in Lebanon), and Jacquot Ayoub (who has been one of my most dedicated friends in finding me regional specialties and people in various places to talk to while researching this book). In fact, it was Jacquot who got us invited to Shirine's lunch, where I finally got to taste zinkol. I had first read about it in the late chef Ramzi's book on the culinary heritage of Lebanon. The version I tasted at Shirine's differs from the recipe given in chef Ramzi's book, which I have adapted here, in that the yogurt was not cooked, just the bulgur wheat balls.

SERVES 6 TO 8

FOR THE BULGUR WHEAT BALLS

1 cup (125 g) unbleached all-purpose flour

1 teaspoon fine sea salt

Just under 2 cups (350 g) fine bulgur wheat, rinsed under cold water, drained

FOR THE YOGURT SAUCE

3 pounds 6 ounces (1½ kg) plain goat's yogurt

1 large free-range organic egg

2 tablespoons (12 g) dried mint

Fine sea salt

1. To make the zinkol balls: Put the flour and salt in a large mixing bowl and mix well. Add the bulgur wheat and mix until you have a workable paste. If it's too crumbly, add a little water. Make tiny balls the size of a medium marble. Set on a large baking sheet and place in the refrigerator.

2. For the yogurt sauce: Put the yogurt and egg in a pot large enough to eventually hold the zinkol balls and mix well—you may need to add ½ to 1 cup (125 to 250 ml) water if the yogurt is too thick. Place over medium heat and bring to a very gentle bubble while stirring constantly. Turn down the heat to medium-low. Drop the zinkol balls into the hot yogurt and keep stirring while bringing the yogurt back to a very gentle simmer—be careful not to break the balls. Add the dried mint and salt to taste and keep stirring for a couple of minutes. By then, the bulgur wheat balls should be done, but taste one to make sure they are. Take off the heat and transfer to soup bowls. Serve hot, warm, or chilled.

Goats frolicking in the west Bekaa

KIBBÉ

Kibbé is one of our most festive dishes that can be prepared in many different ways. In fact, I could have dedicated this whole book to it. Instead, I will focus on the most typical versions and those that are most representative of their region.

You can basically divide kibbé into four categories: raw (or *nayeh* in Arabic), baked, grilled or fried, and poached. The raw versions are at their most interesting in the south, while the baked or grilled versions are specific to the north. As for poached or fried kibbé, they are always shaped into balls and can be stuffed or not, and they are pretty universal. There are also fake versions (or *hileh* in Arabic), that is, made without meat and belonging mostly to the Christian community because of all the days in the year that they have to abstain from eating meat but still feel like having kibbé.

Once upon a time, the meat for kibbé was pounded by hand to produce a silky pink paste that is quite unlike what a machine can do. Cooks in the mountains used a large stone mortar and a wooden pestle to do this, whereas in the south, they used a flat marble slab. I can still picture my mother and grandmother pounding the meat for kibbé in our kitchen. On those days, they started by pulling the large stone mortar and massive wooden pestle out of the corner where they lived to place them in the middle of the room. They then set one low stool on either side for them to sit facing each other. My grandmother usually brought the meat with her, having asked her butcher to bone and trim a whole leg of lamb before cutting it into medium chunks. They put the meat on a large tray next to the mortar. They picked a few pieces and dropped them in the mortar and started the pounding. My grandmother took the lead by grabbing the pestle to beat down on the meat. When she got tired, she handed the pestle to my mother, who carried on the beating down on the meat. When they had pulverized the first batch into an impossibly smooth, silky paste, they scooped it out onto a plate, covered it, and put it straight into the refrigerator. In the beginning, the sound was dull because the pestle only hit the meat, but as the meat got smashed, the pestle started to go through it to hit the stone. It was then that the sound got louder and louder. I was mesmerized by

My late mother making kibbé, Ballouneh

both their energy and their working in sync, as if they knew when exactly to take over, not to mention the astonishing transformation of the chunky bits of red meat into a velvety pink mass that I couldn't wait to taste. And when the sound got really loud, I knew that the meat was near being entirely minced, meaning I could have a taste.

My mother was very strict. She didn't allow us to taste anything in the kitchen, always admonishing me and my siblings to wait until we sat down at the table. Fortunately, my grandmother was more laid-back, and she would stealthily pick up some nayeh with her beautiful long fingers to dip in a little salt and slip into my mouth with a cheeky smile on her face.

The large mortar and pestle are long gone now, as are my grandmother and recently my mother, sadly; and hardly anyone grinds meat this way nowadays. That said, some home cooks like to show off the traditional way, although they no longer start from scratch. They buy the meat already coarsely ground to finish at home in the mortar and pestle.

On a recent trip to the south to visit my friend Rami Zurayk's aunt and taste her frakeh, she had done just that. She had ordered the meat already ground from her butcher but had prepared her own frakeh mixture (page 180). She tipped the ground meat onto her flat marble slab and started pounding it with a pestle that looked like a hammer (unlike ours, which was vertical) to make it smoother. She then flattened it with her hands and spread the frakeh mixture all over before starting to mix it, again with her hands. Even there, as a guest, I was unable to wait for her to serve it and asked for a taste right off the slab. And like my grandmother, she was happy to pinch off a little with her fingers to place in my mouth.

Since then, I have tasted many versions of frakeh, with the last made by my lovely new friend Nadine Souheil, who added her own pepper paste to the mixture, which gave it a delightful reddish color and a mild spicy kick. Her version has now become my favorite, although I still love the other less spicy ones. As with all countries with a deep-rooted food culture, the variations on dishes from the same region and from family to family are endless. And the same goes for kibbé.

GOAT TARTARE
KIBBET ME'ZEH NAYEH

This goat version of kibbé nayeh is a specialty of the north. It is on the menu of most traditional restaurants in mountain villages such as Z'gharta and Ehden, and you will also be offered it in homes up north, where cooks will have asked their butcher to grind their cut of choice through the fine disk of the meat grinder two or three times before taking it home and finishing it to their taste. Goat meat is leaner than lamb, and as a result, the raw kibbé has a more vibrant pink color with a finer, less fatty texture. It is an essential part of our mezze, and for you to have it at home, you need to buy the freshest, leanest meat and have your butcher trim it of all ligaments and any other chewy bits. Also prepare it at the very last minute so the color doesn't turn gray because of oxidization. You can avoid this by adding a little pepper paste and laying plastic wrap right on the meat to avoid contact with air, which is what oxidizes the meat. The top of the leg is ideal for nayeh, and, hopefully, your butcher will be kind enough to bone, trim, and grind the meat for you. You can also invest in a meat grinder like I did so you can do it yourself.

SERVES 4 TO 6

Sea salt

1 pound 2 ounces (500 g) goat meat from the leg, skinned, most of the fat trimmed, finely ground

1 small Spanish onion (about 100 g), peeled, grated against the fine side of the grater

2 teaspoons ground cinnamon

2 teaspoons ground allspice

½ teaspoon finely ground white pepper

¾ cup (125 g) fine bulgur wheat

Sprigs of basil or mint for garnish

1. Put some iced water in a medium bowl. Add a little salt and stir until the salt is dissolved. You will need this to dip your hand into every now and then as you mix the meat with the bulgur wheat.

2. Grind the meat in a meat grinder if you are doing it yourself, using the fine disk and passing the meat twice through it; otherwise, ask your butcher to do it for you, making sure he takes as much fat off the meat as he can. Do not buy preground; it will be too fatty and not so nice, either raw or cooked.

3. Transfer the meat to a large bowl. Add the onion, cinnamon, allspice, pepper, and salt to taste.

4. Rinse the bulgur wheat in two or three changes of cold water, drain well, and add to the meat. Mix well with your hand, dipping it every now and then in the salted water to moisten both your hand and the kibbé. Knead until you have a smooth mixture.

5. Taste and adjust the seasoning if needed. Transfer to a serving platter and shape into a thick disk if the platter is round or an oval if the platter is that shape. Use the back of a spoon to make indents inside the edges in one, two, or three rows depending on how wide your platter is. Drizzle a little olive oil in the dips and garnish with sprigs of basil or mint. Serve immediately.

STRETCHED KIBBÉ
KIBBEH MAMDŪDEH

Here is a very interesting variation on the kibbé "pie" (page 160), which I discovered in Ehden, a Christian village up in the mountains, east of Tripoli. Once very beautiful, excessive development has somewhat blighted it, like most of the country's mountain villages following the tragic fifteen-year civil war, when people took refuge there away from the embattled cities. Regardless, Ehden is still charming, not least because most of its inhabitants, who leave it in winter to go to the relative warmth of Z'gharta, a village farther down and more to the west, and who still prepare most of their food and müneh (page 2) the traditional way. In this version, home cooks prepare and shape the kibbé at home, spreading it over beautiful round aluminum baking trays, then carry it to their local communal oven to bake there. Dalia and I spent a morning in the one run by the Zakhia family, who have manned it for three generations; and while Dalia was taking pictures, I talked to Elias Zakhia, who was on duty that day; Peter, whose kibbé was a regular "pie"; and Rita, whose mamdüdeh was delicious. She graciously gave us a taste. They had both brought their kibbé to be baked there. The typical design is for the "pie" to be cut into squares, with each square slashed three times or indented with the tip of a tablespoon to have three curved lines in the center. The recipe below is Rita's. She had actually cut hers in triangles, scoring each in long thin lines. And her secret is to use what seems like an excessive amount of olive oil (or ghee for some families). The kibbé looked as if it was swimming in it, but she assured us that the fat would eventually be absorbed. Still, if you think the amount is too much, just pour out some once the kibbé is done.

SERVES 6 TO 8

Sea salt

½ cup (125 ml) extra virgin olive oil, plus extra to brush the pie dish

1 pound 2 ounces (500 g) lean ground lamb from the leg

Scant 2⅓ cups (400 g) fine bulgur wheat

1 tablespoon seven-spice mixture (page 19)

1. Have a small bowl of cold salted water at hand to wet your hands while you are mixing the kibbé. Preheat the oven to 450°F (220°C). Brush a 10½-inch (26 cm) diameter pie dish with a little olive oil or use nonstick.

2. Put the meat, bulgur wheat, and seven-spice mixture in a large mixing bowl. Add salt to taste and knead the kibbé following the instructions on page 160. Once done, instead of dividing the kibbé in two to make the "pie," line the pie dish with the whole mixture. Level the top with your wet fingers, then cut the kibbé into medium-sized squares. Slash the middle of each square with three short diagonal lines.

3. Pour the olive oil all over and bake in the preheated oven for 10 to 15 minutes. You want the top to be crisp but the inside still moist. Serve hot with Yogurt and Cucumber Salad (page 96) or a simple mixed salad as a light meal, or simply as a snack.

Peter holding the kibbé he had brought for Elias Zakhia to bake for him, plus other kibbés brought by other clients

The kibbé trays baking in Elias's oven

KIBBÉ "PIE"

KIBBEH BIL-SANIYEH

It is very difficult to pinpoint which dish is absolutely Lebanese without it also being Syrian, Palestinian, or Jordanian, or even Turkish for that matter. Of course, each version will be slightly different, even sometimes very different, but if there is one version that can be claimed as our national dish, it would be this one. It is one of our most elegant dishes, prepared as much for large family gatherings as for special occasions or simply to impress guests. I often make this kibbé and freeze it before cooking so I can serve it at very short notice; and if there are any leftovers, I can freeze them again. I normally use clarified butter to dot over the kibbé because it doesn't have any of the milk solids that tend to spoil the presentation. Alternatively, you can melt the butter and pour it over the kibbé before baking, leaving the milk solids in the pan. This is also known as kibbé mütabba'a up in Z'gharta.

SERVES 4 TO 6

FOR THE STUFFING

- 6 tablespoons (90 g) unsalted butter
- Heaping ⅓ cup (60 g) Mediterranean pine nuts
- 3 large onions (about 600 g), peeled, finely chopped
- 7 ounces (200 g) lean ground lamb
- 2 tablespoons (30 ml) pomegranate molasses
- 2 teaspoons ground cinnamon
- 2 teaspoons ground allspice
- ½ teaspoon finely ground black pepper
- Sea salt

1. To prepare the stuffing: Melt the butter in a large frying pan over medium heat and toast the pine nuts, stirring constantly, until golden brown. Make sure you don't burn them—they will turn from golden brown to dark brown very quickly. Remove with a slotted spoon onto a double layer of paper towel.

2. Add the onions to the pan and fry in the same butter, stirring regularly, until soft golden, 10 to 15 minutes. Add the meat and cook, breaking up any lumps, until it loses all traces of pink. Take off the heat and add the pomegranate molasses. Season with the cinnamon, allspice, pepper, and salt to taste and stir in the pine nuts. Mix well. Taste and adjust the seasoning if needed. Set aside.

3. To prepare the kibbé: Prepare a bowl of cold lightly salted water to have at hand for mixing and shaping the kibbé. Put the lamb, bulgur wheat, and onion in a large mixing bowl. Add the cinnamon, allspice, pepper, and salt to taste. Mix with your hands, adding a little salted water every now and then, until you have a malleable paste. Taste and adjust the seasoning if needed—if you are not keen on tasting raw meat, sear a little in a small pan and taste to make sure it is well seasoned.

4. Brush a 10½-inch (26 cm) diameter pie dish with a little melted butter or use nonstick. Preheat the oven to 450°F (220°C).

FOR THE KIBBÉ

Sea salt

1 pound 2 ounces (500 g) lamb from the leg, trimmed of any skin, fat, and sinewy bits, finely ground

1 cup (200 g) fine bulgur wheat

1 small onion (about 100 g), peeled, finely grated

2 teaspoons ground cinnamon

2 teaspoons ground allspice

½ teaspoon finely ground black pepper

5 knobs clarified butter or ghee to dot over the kibbé before baking

5. Finishing and serving: Divide the kibbé into two equal parts. Moisten your hands in the salted water and pinch off a handful from one half. Flatten it between your palms, to a thickness of about ½ inch (1¼ cm), and place on the bottom of the pie dish starting from one edge. Smooth it down evenly with your fingers, pinch off another handful from the same piece, then flatten and lay it next to the first piece, slightly overlapping it. Dip your fingers in water and smooth the pieces together until the seam disappears—be sure to connect the pieces well so they do not come apart during baking. Continue the above process until you have covered the bottom of the dish with the first half of the kibbé. Go over the whole layer with moistened fingers to even it out.

6. Spread the stuffing evenly over the kibbé and lay the other half over the stuffing in the same way. You may find the top layer a little more difficult, as you will be laying it over the loose stuffing instead of the smooth surface of the pie dish, but you will soon get the hang of it.

7. Carefully cut the kibbé into quarters, then, with a small, pointed knife, make shallow incisions to draw a different geometric pattern across each quarter. The "decoration" work is time-consuming, and you can skip it without affecting the taste, but the presentation will not be so attractive, nor will it look traditional—most cooks make a diamond pattern across the kibbé, but my mother's family is more artistic! After you finish "decorating" the kibbé, press one finger down the middle to make a hole. Put a knob of clarified butter over the hole and one over each quarter.

8. Bake in the preheated oven for 10 to 15 minutes, until the kibbé has shrunk slightly and is just done. Remove from the oven and let sit for a few minutes, then cut into triangles and transfer to a round serving platter. Serve hot with Yogurt and Cucumber Salad (page 96).

KIBBÉ BALLS

KIBBEH 'RASS

Kibbé balls are either fried to serve as part of a mezze spread, with drinks or simply as a snack; or they are poached in a sauce such as yogurt (labniyeh, page 163), tahini (arnabiyeh, page 165), or kishk (bil-kishk, page 170) to name a few, and served as a main dish with or without rice. My mother would manage to make 20 balls with the amounts below, but I am not as adept at thinning out the kibbé shell and sometimes manage 15, sometimes a little more, although never as many as 20! In any case, if you haven't made them before, you will need a little practice. The secret here is to moisten your hands while shaping the balls so the kibbé mixture doesn't stick. Many home cooks nowadays order them premade from a good caterer or home cook they know and only prepare the sauce at home. I like to make my own, which I often freeze so I only have to make the sauce, or fry them on the day I plan to serve them.

MAKES 15 TO 20 TO SERVE 6 TO 8

Half the amount of stuffing for Kibbé "Pie" (page 160)

Half the amount of kibbé for Kibbé "Pie" (page 160)

Small bowl of lightly salted water

Vegetable oil for frying

1. Prepare the stuffing and kibbé as indicated on page 160. Divide the kibbé into 15 to 20 balls, each the size of a large walnut.

2. Lightly moisten your hands in the salted water and place one ball in the cup of your hand. Use the index finger of your other hand to burrow a hole into the ball while rotating it on your palm to make the hollowing out easier and more even. You should end up with a kibbé shell that looks like a topless egg, with sides about ¼-inch (5 mm) thick. Be careful not to go through the bottom or sides. If you do, mend the break with your moistened finger or press the kibbé into a ball and start again.

3. Put 1½ teaspoons stuffing inside the shell and pinch the open edges shut with your fingers. Cup your free fingers over the filled kibbé ball and gently shape into an ovoid ball with slightly pointed ends. Put the finished ball on a baking sheet and continue making the kibbé balls until you have finished both meat and stuffing. Put these in the freezer so they harden a little and do not lose their shape in the handling before frying or poaching—if you are going to freeze them for later, wait until completely frozen before bagging them.

4. Heat enough vegetable oil in a large frying pan to deep-fry the kibbé balls—dip in a piece of bread; if the oil immediately bubbles around it, it is ready. Delicately drop in as many balls as will fit comfortably in the pan and fry, turning them over, until evenly browned, 3 to 4 minutes. Remove with a slotted spoon and put to drain onto a wire rack or several layers of paper towel. Serve hot or warm.

KIBBÉ BALLS IN YOGURT SAUCE

KIBBEH 'RASS BIL-LABAN

You will need soup bowls to serve this kibbé, also known as kibbeh labniyeh, because the yogurt sauce is the consistency of heavy cream, perhaps a little thicker, and a deep bowl will make scooping the sauce with each bite of kibbé easier. This dish is normally served with vermicelli rice (page 263), but I don't, as I think it is too much. Some families make the sauce plain without any herbs, but I find it too bland and prefer to add the mint and garlic mixture for more flavor.

SERVES 6 TO 8

Kibbé Balls (page 162)

Cooked Yogurt Sauce (page 142), with adjustments (see below)

Sea salt

1. Prepare the kibbé balls and put in the freezer while you prepare the yogurt sauce.

2. Prepare the yogurt sauce, adding the mint and garlic mixture after you drop in the kibbé balls.

3. Once the yogurt has started bubbling, gently drop in the barely frozen kibbé balls. Reduce the heat to medium-low and simmer for 5 minutes, stirring carefully so as not to break the kibbé balls. Add the mint and garlic mixture and simmer for 3 more minutes.

4. Transfer to a serving bowl and serve immediately. You can reheat it, but as with all dishes cooked in yogurt, be careful not to let the yogurt curdle when reheating. First gently shake the pan from side to side to mix the whey that has separated back into the yogurt. Then place over medium-low heat uncovered and simmer until hot, gently stirring every now and then.

KIBBÉ IN CITRUSY TAHINI SAUCE
KIBBEH ARNABIYEH

Two communities claim this kibbé as theirs: the Sunnis of Saida and the Greek Orthodox of Beirut. And, of course, each prepares it differently. In Saida, the sauce is dark because it is made with caramelized onions, whereas the Beiruti Orthodox version is pale because they poach whole pearl onions in the sauce rather than slice and caramelize them first. Also, because Saida and the whole southern coast are famous for their citrus, southerners use the juice of seven different citrus in the tahini sauce, while Beirutis only use the juice of Seville oranges, which are available in January. As a result, many cooks freeze the juice to use through the year. Some also add boned pieces of lamb shank together with the kibbé balls. I personally only use kibbé balls, but I alternate between the southern and Beiruti version depending on my mood and how much time I have—caramelizing the onions adds more time. I also don't add chickpeas to the sauce, as I think it's substantial enough without.

I am giving the Saida version here. If you want to make the Beiruti version, use an equivalent amount of pearl onions. Peel and sauté them whole in a little vegetable oil until lightly golden and almost tender, then drop into the sauce together with the kibbé balls and finish as below.

You can also make a vegetarian version by replacing the meat and kibbé balls with 1 pound 2 ounces (500 g) peeled Colocasia (page 98), once the potato of the Romans. Rinse the Colocasia under cold water and pat dry before cutting into medium chunks. Shallow-fry in vegetable oil until golden all over before dropping into the bubbling tahini sauce at the very end once you see the oil rising. Cook for 10 minutes, or until tender. One word of advice, though: Be sure to allocate enough time to prepare this recipe. Getting the oil to rise in the tahini sauce (which is called *srijeh* in Arabic) will take close to an hour, not to mention the time it takes to make the kibbé balls and caramelize the onion if you are going to make the Saida version. I add lemon juice to my sauce, but some cooks are totally against it and only use the juice of different oranges and tangerines, saying the taste is more subtle. If you want to follow their example, simply omit the lemons and replace with 1 extra orange and 1 clementine.

SERVES 6 TO 8

Kibbé Balls
(page 162)

⅓ cup Mediterranean pine nuts (50 g), sautéed in a little butter until golden brown, for garnish

FOR THE TAHINI SAUCE

½ cup (125 ml) vegetable oil

4 large onions (about 800 g), peeled, thinly sliced into wedges

2 cups (500 ml) tahini

Juice of 8 to 10 Seville oranges

Juice of 2 oranges

Juice of 2 blood oranges

Juice of 6 tangerines

Juice of 4 clementines

Juice of 1 grapefruit

Juice of 2 lemons (optional)

Sea salt

2 cups (300 g) cooked chickpeas (optional)

1. Prepare the kibbé balls and put them in the freezer while you prepare the sauce.

2. To make the tahini sauce: Put the vegetable oil and onions in a large frying pan and place over medium heat. As soon as the oil starts sizzling around the onions, reduce the heat to medium-low and cook, stirring regularly, until soft and golden brown, 30 to 45 minutes. Let the onions cool a little, then add a little water and process with a handheld blender until completely smooth.

3. Pour the tahini into a large mixing bowl and gradually add the citrus juices, stirring all the time—you should have 3½ to 4 cups (750 ml to 1 liter) juice. The mixture will thicken first before starting to dilute. Taste the sauce two-thirds of the way through so you can adjust the tartness to your taste. If you decide to use less citrus juice, add a little water to make up for the lost liquid. Add salt to taste. You should end up with a runny sauce that has the consistency of heavy cream.

4. Pour the tahini sauce into a pot large enough to eventually hold the kibbé balls and chickpeas (if you are using them) and place over medium heat. Bring to a boil, stirring constantly, and let bubble for a couple of minutes. Add the blended onions—at this stage you can strain the onions into the sauce for a very smooth texture or add as is and strain the sauce later for a perfectly smooth texture. Continue stirring very regularly until the sauce thickens somewhat and a little oil rises to the surface. This will take about an hour, and you will need to add a little water every now and then as the sauce thickens to bring it back to a thick although not dense consistency. Taste and adjust the tartness to your taste.

5. To finish: Remove the kibbé balls from the freezer and gently drop them into the tahini sauce together with the cooked chickpeas (if you are using them). Bring back to a very gentle bubble and simmer for about 10 minutes, very carefully stirring every now and then so as not to break the kibbé balls or mash up the chickpeas. Taste and adjust the seasoning if needed. Transfer to a serving bowl. Garnish with the toasted pine nuts and serve hot with vermicelli rice (page 263).

GRILLED KIBBÉ DISKS
KIBBEH MESHWIYEH

A typical kibbé from the north that I have had with different fillings, from simply seasoned fat tail, to labneh and herbs, to meat, onions, and pine nuts, to name a few. There is a special wooden mold to shape the kibbé that looks like a wide inverted cup with a rounded bottom. If you don't have one or can't get it, simply make the disks in a medium wide, shallow teacup. Some people make the balls completely round by lining two cups with the mixture then sealing them together like you would with an Easter egg, while others mold only the top part and leave the bottom flat, which is what I suggest here. Before I got my wooden mold, I used my mise en place kitchen glass bowls—the size I went for was 7½ x 1½ inches (9 x 4 cm), but use whatever bowl you have on hand that is fairly shallow. Just make sure they are not too big, as you want each to make an individual serving.

MAKES 6

Grilled kibbé at the Attiehs', Beino

FOR THE MEAT AND NUT FILLING

Stuffing for Kibbé "Pie" (page 160)

FOR THE LABNEH FILLING

1 medium onion (about 150 g), peeled, finely chopped

3½ ounces (100 g) tail or kidney fat, finely chopped

1 cup (250 g) labneh

1 cup (150 g) walnut pieces, coarsely chopped

A few sprigs flat-leaf parsley, washed, dried, most of the bottom stalks discarded, finely chopped

1 teaspoon seven-spice mixture (page 19)

Freshly ground pepper

Sea salt

FOR THE TAIL FAT FILLING

2 tablespoons (30 g) unsalted butter

1 medium onion (about 150 g), peeled, finely chopped

10½ ounces (300 g) tail fat, minced through the medium coarse disk of a meat grinder

A few sprigs basil, leaves only, finely chopped

1 cup (150 g) walnut pieces, coarsely chopped

1 teaspoon seven-spice mixture (page 19)

1 teaspoon Aleppo pepper

Freshly ground black pepper

Sea salt

Kibbé mixture for Kibbé "Pie" (page 160)

Melted unsalted butter to brush the kibbé disks

1. If you are going to stuff the disks with the meat and nut filling, follow the instructions on page 160. Taste and adjust the seasoning if needed.

2. If you are going to stuff the disks with the labneh filling, mix the onion, tail or kidney fat, labneh, walnuts, parsley, seven-spice, and salt and pepper to taste. Taste and adjust the seasoning if needed. Set aside.

3. If you are going to make the tail fat filling, mix the butter, onion, tail fat, basil, walnuts, seven-spice, Aleppo pepper, and black pepper and salt to taste. Taste and adjust the seasoning if needed—if you don't want to taste the filling raw, put a tablespoon in a small frying pan, sauté over high heat for a minute or so, then taste and adjust the seasoning as needed.

4. Prepare the kibbé as instructed on page 160.

5. I now make the disks using the special wooden mold that comes in two parts, both with a handle. The top part is like a shallow cup measuring 3¼ x 1½ inches (8 x 4 cm) with the round bottom tray part wider so you can invert the cup over it to seal both parts of the kibbé together. Making these disks is fiddly, but here is how I do it using a tortilla press for the flat bottom part and my hands for the round top part. I prepare 24 squares of parchment paper to cover the tortilla press with a bit of overhang and have a roll of plastic wrap on hand for the cup part. I also have a bowl of lightly salted water on hand to shape the kibbé.

6. Line a nonstick baking sheet with parchment paper just to be on the safe side and have ready to place the kibbé disks on it. Preheat the oven to 450ºF (220ºC).

7. Pinch off a piece of kibbé and roll it into a ball the size of a walnut. Place on a piece of parchment paper on the tortilla press. Flatten it slightly, cover with another piece of parchment paper, and press down to flatten. Don't press too hard, as you don't want the disk of kibbé to be too thin. Spread a piece of plastic wrap on your work surface and pinch off a piece of kibbé twice as large as that for the flat disk. Place on the plastic wrap and with slightly wet fingers spread it into a disk that is about 5 inches (12½ cm) wide. Gently lift the plastic wrap and place in the cup so the flattened kibbé covers the whole cup with a bit of overhang. Gently press on the kibbé to line the cup evenly. Discard any overhang back into the kibbé bowl, then fill the cup of kibbé with the filling of your choice. Let rest while you transfer the kibbé on parchment paper to the "tray" part of the mold. Quickly invert the cup part of the kibbé over the disk and press down to seal the two parts. With the back of a knife, discard any overhang into the kibbé bowl. Gently lift off the wooden cup mold and slide the parchment paper off the "tray" part. Peel off the paper and gently place on the baking sheet. Peel off the plastic wrap and make the other kibbé disks the same way.

8. Brush the kibbé disks with melted butter and bake in the preheated oven for about 15 minutes, until slightly crisp. Serve hot with Yogurt and Cucumber Salad (page 96) if filled with meat and nuts, or fat tail, or a salad if filled with labneh.

Grilled kibbé on the street in Tripoli

FAKE KIBBÉ IN KISHK SAUCE
KIBBEH HILEH BIL-KISHK

The word *hileh* means "ruse" in Arabic, and this kibbé was given this name because it looks like it's made with meat but is prepared without. As a result, it is slightly paler in color. For such a small country, it is amusing that many dishes are named differently depending on the region. This kibbé is also described as *kizzebeh*, meaning "lying," or *hazineh*, meaning "sad." It has to be a Christian specialty given how most abstain from eating meat during the forty days of Lent as well as on Fridays. I guess they also devised the other vegetarian versions so they can still enjoy kibbé even when they can't eat meat. That said, you do find these versions in Muslim communities as well, so my theory may not hold.

SERVES 4

FOR THE STUFFING

- 4 tablespoons (60 g) unsalted butter
- 2 tablespoons (25 g) Mediterranean pine nuts
- 1 medium onion (about 150 g), peeled, finely chopped
- ⅓ cup (50 g) walnuts, coarsely chopped
- ¼ teaspoon ground cinnamon
- ½ teaspoon ground allspice
- ⅛ teaspoon finely ground black pepper
- Sea salt
- 1 teaspoon pomegranate molasses

FOR THE KIBBÉ

- Sea salt
- 1 small onion (about 100 g), peeled, finely grated
- 1 cup (200 g) fine bulgur wheat
- Just under ⅓ cup (50 g) unbleached all-purpose flour
- ¼ teaspoon ground cinnamon
- ½ teaspoon ground allspice
- ⅛ teaspoon finely ground black pepper

FOR THE SAUCE

- 2 tablespoons (30 g) unsalted butter
- 2 cups (250 g) kishk (page 7)

1. To prepare the stuffing: Put the butter in a large frying pan and place over medium heat. Add the pine nuts and fry, stirring constantly, until golden brown. Remove with a slotted spoon onto a double layer of paper towel to drain off any excess fat.

2. Add the chopped onion and cook in the same butter, stirring every now and then, until soft and golden, 10 to 15 minutes. Add the chopped walnuts and cook for a few more minutes, stirring regularly. Season with the cinnamon, allspice, pepper, and salt to taste. Add the pomegranate molasses and pine nuts and stir for another minute or so. Taste and adjust the seasoning if needed. Take off the heat and set aside.

3. Prepare a bowl of cold lightly salted water to have at hand for when you are mixing and shaping the kibbé.

4. To prepare the kibbé: Put the grated onion in a mixing bowl. Rinse the bulgur wheat under cold water and add to the onion. Add the flour. Season with the cinnamon, allspice, pepper, and salt to taste. Mix well, using your hand and dipping it every now and then in the salted water to moisten both your hand and the kibbé. Mix until you have a malleable mixture. Let sit for a while. It will feel a little firm, but you will be able to work it as you dip your hands in water to shape the balls.

5. To make the kibbé balls: Follow the same instructions as for meat kibbé balls (page 162) and put the balls in the freezer.

6. To prepare the kishk sauce: Put the butter in a pot large enough to eventually hold the kibbé balls and place over medium heat. When the butter has melted, add the kishk and stir for a minute or two. Gradually add 2 quarts (2 liters) water, about 1 cup (250 ml) at a time, stirring all the time to make sure the sauce is smooth and has no lumps. Bring to a boil, stirring constantly, then reduce the heat to low. Taste before adding any salt, as kishk is already salted. If there is a need, add a little salt, but only after you add the kibbé balls. Simmer for a couple of minutes, or until the sauce is like a thin porridge.

7. Take the kibbé balls out of the freezer and gently drop them into the sauce. Bring back to a boil and simmer for 5 minutes, carefully stirring every now and then so as not to split the kibbé balls. Serve very hot in soup bowls to eat with a spoon.

VEGETARIAN GRILLED KIBBÉ DISKS
BOU EMNEH

A very interesting vegetarian take on grilled kibbé that I discovered in Beino, courtesy of Nahla Attieh's aunt Mona (see page 343). The name is a little confusing, and some pronounce it as *bwebneh*, while others pronounce it as written above, which means either the father of Amina or the father of the one who is faithful. It also goes by another name, *jermash*. Either way, it is a great vegetarian take on regular kibbeh meshwiyeh (page 167). The shell is made with fine bulgur wheat and flour, while the stuffing is simply caramelized onions, seasoned with pomegranate molasses, to which I have added coarsely chopped walnuts for a little texture. These make great picnic food, as they are just as delicious at room temperature.

SERVES 4 TO 6

FOR THE STUFFING

¼ cup (60 ml) extra virgin olive oil

3 medium onions (about 450 g), peeled, thinly sliced into wedges

1½ tablespoons pomegranate molasses

⅓ cup (50 g) coarsely chopped walnuts

Sea salt

Kibbé for Kibbeh Hileh bil-Kishk (page 170)

1. To prepare the stuffing: Put the olive oil and onions in a large frying pan and place over medium heat. As soon as the oil starts sizzling around the onions, reduce the heat to medium-low and cook, stirring regularly, until the onions are soft and lightly golden brown, 15 to 20 minutes. Add the pomegranate molasses and walnuts. Season with salt to taste and stir until all the ingredients are well blended. Take off the heat and let cool.

2. Preheat the oven to 450°F (220°C) or prepare a barbecue fire.

3. Prepare the kibbé as per the instructions on page 170 and divide into 12 equal pieces. Roll each into a ball, more or less the size of a walnut, then using a tortilla press, place a ball between two pieces of parchment paper and flatten in the press to have a disk about 4 inches (10 cm) in diameter. Divide the filling equally among 6 disks, placing it in the middle of each. Brush the edges with water, then lay a disk each over the filling to have 6 kibbé disks. Lightly press on the edges to seal, then carefully transfer to a nonstick baking sheet, or one lined with parchment paper or a silicone mat. Bake in the preheated oven for 10 to 15 minutes, until the edges are slightly crisp and the kibbé is just done. Traditionally they are grilled over the barbecue for 5 to 10 minutes on each side. Serve hot, warm, or at room temperature.

CHICKPEA KIBBÉ

KIBBET HOMMUS

Another interesting vegetarian variation from the north, where the meat is replaced with chickpeas. There are two ways of preparing this kibbé. One is plain, with the mixture spread over the baking dish and baked, again drenched in olive oil like with mamdüdeh (page 158); or with a layer of caramelized onions spread over the bottom of the baking dish before covering with the kibbé mixture. The contrast between the crisp kibbé and the melting onions is quite irresistible. I got this recipe from Emily Finianos, a lovely lady in Ehden who sells spices from a shop near the gorgeous Karaz hotel, where I had spent the night and which sadly burned down soon after. Emily's recipe is without caramelized onions, but if you want to add them, which I prefer, simply cook 3 medium onions (about 450 g), sliced into thin wedges, in ½ cup (125 ml) extra virgin olive oil, stirring regularly, until soft and lightly golden, 10 to 15 minutes. Spread the caramelized onions over the bottom of the baking dish before laying the kibbé mixture on top.

SERVES 4 TO 6

⅓ cup dried chickpeas (75 g), soaked overnight in plenty of cold water and ½ teaspoon baking soda

¼ cup (60 ml) extra virgin olive oil, plus extra to brush the pie dish

Just under 1 cup (175 g) fine bulgur wheat

½ cup (60 g) unbleached all-purpose flour

1 teaspoon ka'k spice mixture (page 50)

Sea salt

1. Drain the chickpeas, rinse under cold water, then spread on a clean kitchen towel. Cover with another towel and gently press on them with a rolling pin, going back and forth in order to split them in half and loosen the skin without crushing them. Uncover and peel. Discard the skins. If there are still some that are whole, cover and press on them again to split and loosen the skin. Rinse and drain. Set aside.

2. Prepare a bowl of cold lightly salted water to moisten your hands as well as the kibbé so it is easier to spread in the pie dish. Brush an 12¼-inch (26 cm) pie dish with a little olive oil or use nonstick.

3. Preheat the oven to 450°F (220°C).

4. Rinse the bulgur wheat under cold water. Drain and put in a large mixing bowl. Add the flour and split chickpeas together with the ka'k spice mixture. Season with salt to taste. Knead until you have a mixture that holds together—it may feel a little firm, but it will become more malleable as you wet your hands to flatten the kibbé to lay in the baking dish.

5. Spread the mixture in the pie dish. Make deep cuts, although not all the way to the bottom, to have 4 triangles, then cut each triangle in half lengthwise, again not all the way to the bottom. Pour the olive oil all over. Bake in the preheated oven for 25 to 30 minutes, or until crisp and golden all over. Serve hot, either as a snack or as a light meal with a mixed salad.

KIBBÉ BALLS IN TOMATO SAUCE
'RASS KIBBEH BIL-BANADÜRA

This is another recipe that I had never had until I had lunch at my friend Sumy Hokayem's beautiful country house, east from Batroun up north, where she served this dish along many others. Some I was familiar with, while others, like this one, were new to me. I love the way the tomato sauce somewhat lightens and freshens the kibbé balls. It is a wonderful way to serve it, with or without rice. When tomatoes are in season, I make the sauce with fresh ones, otherwise I use canned plum tomatoes. If you like your sauce to be really intense, add 1 or 2 tablespoons tomato paste after it starts bubbling.

SERVES 4 TO 6

Kibbé Balls (page 162)

FOR THE TOMATO SAUCE

⅓ cup (80 ml) extra virgin olive oil

2 medium onions (about 300 g), peeled, finely chopped

7 large ripe tomatoes (about 1½ kg), peeled, seeded, finely chopped, or 5 (14-ounce/400 g) cans peeled Italian tomatoes, drained, finely chopped

Freshly ground black pepper

Sea salt

1. Prepare the kibbé balls following the instructions on page 162. Arrange on a baking sheet and keep in the freezer while you prepare the tomato sauce.

2. To prepare the tomato sauce: Put the olive oil and onions in a pot large enough to hold both the tomatoes and the kibbé balls and place over medium heat. As soon as the oil starts sizzling around the onions, reduce the heat to medium-low and cook, stirring every now and then, until soft and golden, 10 to 15 minutes. Add the tomatoes and let bubble gently, again stirring occasionally, for about 1 hour, until the sauce is concentrated but not too thick. Season with salt and pepper to taste.

3. Drop the kibbé balls into the sauce and let bubble gently for about 15 minutes, until the kibbé balls are done. Stir every now and then but very carefully, so as not to break the kibbé balls. Serve plain or with vermicelli rice (page 263).

PUMPKIN KIBBÉ
KIBBET LA'TEEN

Also known as *kibbé haziné* (meaning "sad"), because it is vegetarian and, as such, consumed during Lent and on Fridays, both sad times for Christians. You can make this kibbé into a pie as described below or shape it into balls following the instructions on page 162.

SERVES 4 TO 6

FOR THE STUFFING

7 ounces (200 g) baby spinach or Swiss chard, coarsely chopped

Sea salt

Just over ⅓ cup (90 ml) extra virgin olive oil, plus extra to brush the baking dish

3 medium onions (about 450 g), peeled, thinly sliced into wedges

½ cup (75 g) cooked chickpeas, rinsed if preserved in brine, cut in half

⅓ cup (50 g) walnut pieces, coarsely chopped

1 teaspoon ground allspice

½ teaspoon seven-spice mixture (page 19)

½ teaspoon ground cinnamon

⅛ teaspoon finely ground black pepper

1½ to 2 tablespoons pomegranate molasses

FOR THE KIBBÉ

2 pounds 4 ounces (1 kg) peeled butternut squash, cut into medium chunks

1 medium potato (about 200 g), peeled, cut into medium chunks

1 medium onion (about 150 g), peeled, finely grated

Just under 2 cups (350 g) fine bulgur wheat

1 tablespoon unbleached all-purpose flour

1 teaspoon ground allspice

½ teaspoon seven-spice mixture (page 19)

½ teaspoon ground cinnamon

⅛ teaspoon finely ground black pepper

Sea salt

1. To prepare the stuffing: Put the greens in a large mixing bowl and sprinkle with a little salt. Rub with your hands until very wilted. Squeeze very dry, then loosen the leaves. Set aside.

2. Put the olive oil and onions in a large frying pan and place over medium heat. Once the oil starts sizzling around the onions, reduce the heat to medium-low and cook, stirring regularly, until soft and golden, 10 to 15 minutes. Add the chickpeas. Mix well and cook for a couple more minutes. Add the chopped walnuts and greens. Season with the allspice, seven-spice, cinnamon, pepper, and salt to taste. Add the pomegranate molasses and mix well. Take off the heat. Taste and adjust the seasoning if needed. Cover with a clean kitchen towel and let cool.

3. To prepare the kibbé: Put the butternut squash pieces in the top part of a steamer, add water to the bottom part, and place over high heat. When the water comes to a boil, reduce the heat to medium and steam for 15 to 20 minutes, until very soft. Remove the squash and transfer to a large mixing bowl and mash with a masher or a fork. Cover with a clean kitchen cloth and set aside.

4. While the squash is steaming, boil the potato until very soft. Drain and mash.

5. Prepare a bowl of slightly salted cold water and have at hand for when you mix and shape the kibbé.

6. Add the potato mash to the butternut squash. Add the grated onion, bulgur wheat, allspice, seven-spice, cinnamon, pepper, and salt to taste. Mix with your hand until you have a homogenous mixture. Taste and adjust the seasoning if needed.

7. Preheat the oven to 400ºF (200ºC). Brush a 10½-inch (26 cm) diameter pie dish with olive oil or use nonstick.

8. Divide the kibbé into two equal parts. Moisten your hands in the salted water and pinch off a handful of kibbé from one piece. Flatten it between your palms, to a thickness of about ¼ inch (½ cm), and lay on the bottom of the baking dish starting from one edge. Pinch off another handful from the same piece, flatten it, and lay it next to the first piece, slightly overlapping it. Dip your fingers in water and smooth the two pieces together until the seam disappears—be sure to connect the pieces well so they do not come apart during baking. Continue the above process until you have covered the bottom of the pan with the first half of kibbé. Go over the whole layer with moistened fingers to even it out.

9. Spread the stuffing evenly over the kibbé and lay the other half over the stuffing in the same way as above. Spreading the top layer will prove slightly more difficult, as you will be laying it over the loose stuffing rather than a smooth surface, but you will soon get the hang of it.

10. With a small, pointed knife, cut through the kibbé to divide it into quarters. Wipe the knife clean, and make shallow incisions to draw a geometric pattern across each quarter, wiping the knife clean every now and then. The decoration work is time-consuming and can be omitted, or you can make a larger diamond pattern. The taste will not be affected, but the presentation will not be as pretty. After you finish decorating the kibbé, press one finger down the middle to make a dip, then drizzle a little olive oil into the dip and over each quarter.

11. Bake in the preheated oven for 10 to 15 minutes, until the kibbé has shrunk slightly and is just done. Remove from the oven and let sit for a few minutes, then cut into triangles and serve hot or warm with a green salad.

FISH KIBBÉ

KIBBET SAMAK

Tyre was once a thriving Phoenician city-state with colonies all around the Mediterranean, including Sicily and Tunisia, but it is now a charming, sleepy coastal town all the way down south. I was there recently, and was told by locals, including Philip Tabet, who owns and runs a small chain of delightful hotels and whose family is from there, that fish kibbé is a specialty of that city. I was told the same thing up north, where I had it shaped into balls at a restaurant in Anfeh, another seaside town known for its salt flats. Whether fish kibbé is a northern or southern specialty, or both, doesn't really matter. It is a delectable light variation on the meat version. The classic recipe does not have raisins in the filling, but I like the added hint of sweetness. Some cooks spread the filling on the bottom of the pie dish, then lay the kibbé mixture on top. This caramelizes the onion and slightly toasts the nuts, but I prefer the two-layer version, which is what I give below.

SERVES 4

FOR THE FILLING

½ cup (125 ml) extra virgin olive oil, plus extra to brush the baking dish

3 large onions (about 600 g), peeled, thinly sliced into wedges

⅓ cup (50 g) Mediterranean pine nuts

⅓ cup raisins (50 g), soaked in warm water for a couple of hours

Good pinch saffron, soaked in 2 tablespoons (30 ml) water

¼ teaspoon finely ground white pepper

Sea salt

Juice of ½ lemon, or to taste

FOR THE KIBBÉ

¼ bunch cilantro (50 g on the stalk), washed, dried, most of the stalks discarded

1 pound 2 ounces (500 g) boneless, skinless white fish fillets, cut into medium chunks

1 medium onion (about 150 g), peeled, quartered

Grated zest of ½ unwaxed orange

Grated zest of ½ unwaxed lemon

½ teaspoon ground cinnamon

¼ teaspoon finely ground white pepper

Sea salt

¾ cup (150 g) fine bulgur wheat, rinsed under cold water, drained

1. To make the filling: Put the olive oil and onions in a large frying pan and place over medium heat. As soon as the oil start sizzling around the onions, reduce the heat to medium-low and cook, stirring regularly, until soft and golden, 10 to 15 minutes. Add the pine nuts and raisins together with the saffron water and season with the pepper and salt to taste. Stir for a couple more minutes. Take off the heat. Add the lemon juice and mix well. Cover with a clean kitchen towel and let cool.

2. Preheat the oven to 350°F (180°C) and brush a medium round baking dish (about 10½ inches/26 cm) with a little olive oil or use nonstick.

3. To make the kibbé: Put the fish fillets together with the cilantro, quartered onion, orange and lemon zests, cinnamon, pepper, and salt to taste in the food processor and process until you have a smooth mixture. Transfer to a large mixing bowl. (You could use a meat grinder for the fish to have more texture, but you will still need to mince the herbs and onion in the food processor.)

4. Add the drained bulgur wheat to the fish mixture. Mix well—it is best to use your hands so everything is well blended.

5. Divide the fish kibbé in two equal parts, then make and decorate the kibbé following the instructions for kibbeh bil-saniyeh (page 160). Drizzle a little olive oil all over and bake in the preheated oven for 10 to 15 minutes, until just done. Serve hot or warm.

The souks, Tripoli

LENTIL KIBBÉ
KIBBET ADASS

A typical vegetarian version that is as much a southern specialty as an Armenian one. It can be prepared with or without the pepper paste. I like it with, as it gives the kibbé a nice kick and a nice color too.

SERVES 4 TO 6

Just over 1½ cups (250 g) red split lentils

¾ cup (150 g) fine bulgur wheat, rinsed under cold water, drained

3 tablespoons (45 ml) extra virgin olive oil, plus extra to drizzle over the kibbé

1 medium onion (about 150 g), peeled, very finely chopped

2 tablespoons (32 g) mild or hot red pepper paste, depending on your taste

¼ cup (about 25 g) kammüneh (page 18)

Sea salt

Leaves from two gem lettuces

A few sprigs flat-leaf parsley, washed, dried, most of the bottom stalks discarded, finely chopped, for garnish

1. Put the lentils in a large saucepan and add 2½ cups (625 ml) water. Place over medium heat and bring to a boil, then reduce the heat to medium-low and simmer for 30 minutes, or until the lentils are done and mushy and the water has almost completely evaporated. Add the bulgur wheat and mix well. Take off the heat, cover the pan, and let sit while you fry the onions.

2. Put the olive oil and onion in a large frying pan and place over medium heat. When the oil starts sizzling around the onion, reduce the heat to medium-low and cook, stirring regularly, until very soft and golden, 10 to 15 minutes. Add the pepper paste (if you are using it) and mix well.

3. Transfer the lentils and bulgur wheat mixture to a large mixing bowl. Let cool until you can handle the mixture with your hands. Add the onion and its oil together with the kammüneh and salt to taste and, with your hand (wear a glove, as the mixture may dye your hand red), mix until you have a smooth paste. Add a little water if the mixture is too stiff. Taste and adjust the seasoning if needed.

4. Arrange the gem lettuce leaves on a round platter. Pinch off pieces of kibbé and make oval patties, which you then squeeze with your fingers to make deep indents, and place a piece over each lettuce leaf. You can also spread the kibbé on a plate, like with the nayeh (page 157), and make dips with the back of a tablespoon, then drizzle with olive oil. Garnish with the parsley. Serve immediately.

NAYLA'S HERB KIBBÉ

FRAKET NAYLA

Nayla Audi, another great friend in Lebanon, was the one who first introduced me to the cooking of the south. Nayla's late father's family comes from Kfar Rumman, a village all the way down south, and their house is a lovely old square stone structure built around an inner courtyard. The family tomb, where all her relatives are buried, is just outside the courtyard. Sunday lunches in Kfar Rumman were wonderful affairs when her parents were alive, with family and friends gathered around a selection of different kibbés, including the one below, which differs from the regular kibbeh nayeh in that the bulgur wheat is mixed with different herbs and spices before being mixed with the meat to become frakeh. You can also spread the green bulgur wheat mixture over the raw meat to eat together, in which case the dish is called *malseh*, meaning "smoothed." The taste is very different, and I often keep the meat and bulgur wheat mixture separate, so I can decide how much of each I eat together. Whereas people in the north use goat for their nayeh, the rest of the country prefers lamb, occasionally veal.

SERVES 4 TO 6

FOR THE TAHWICHEH (ALSO KNOWN AS FRESH KAMMÜNEH)

- 1 small onion (about 100 g), peeled, quartered
- ¼ bunch (50 g on the stalk) flat-leaf parsley, washed, dried, most of the stalks discarded
- A few sprigs (30 g) fresh marjoram, leaves only, washed, dried
- Small handful basil leaves, washed, dried, plus extra for garnish
- 3 dried rosebuds, petals only
- Zest of ½ unwaxed lemon
- Zest of ½ unwaxed orange
- ½ cup (100 g) fine bulgur wheat
- 1 teaspoon ground cumin
- ¼ teaspoon ground cloves
- 1 teaspoon Aleppo pepper
- Sea salt
- Freshly ground black pepper

FOR THE KIBBÉ

- 10½ ounces (300 g) finely ground lean lamb from the top part of the leg
- Extra virgin olive oil for drizzling over the kibbé

1. Put the onion, parsley, marjoram, basil, and rose petals in a food processor and process until chopped very fine. Transfer to a large mixing bowl. Add the citrus zests and bulgur wheat together with the ground cumin, ground cloves, and Aleppo pepper. Season with salt and pepper to taste and mix well.

2. Put some cold water in a medium bowl. Add a little salt and stir until the salt is dissolved—this lightly salted water is for you to dip your hands in as you mix the meat with the tahwicheh.

3. Add the ground meat to the herby bulgur wheat mixture and mix well, using your hand and dipping it every now and then into the salted water. Divide into 16 pieces. Shape each into an oval patty, then squeeze with your fingers to make deep indentations. Arrange on a serving platter in the shape of a rosette. Pile fresh basil in the middle. Serve immediately, with olive oil for those who would like to drizzle some over their kibbé.

Nadine Souheil making the tahwicheh mixture for frakeh, Burj Rahal

POTATO KIBBÉ
KIBBET BATATA

Another interesting kibbé from the south, this time vegetarian. I fell in love with it when I discovered it at my friend Nayla Audi's house in the south, and if you love the idea of mashed potatoes, you will love this unusual variation that is very different, and very tasty because of the added herbs and spices, not to mention the bulgur wheat.

SERVES 6 TO 8

- 2 pounds 4 ounces (1 kg) potatoes
- Sea salt
- 1 cup (175 g) fine bulgur wheat, rinsed under cold water, drained
- 1 tablespoon kammüneh, or to taste (page 18)
- 2 or 3 scallions, trimmed, very thinly sliced
- A few sprigs fresh mint, leaves only, washed, dried, sliced into thin slivers, plus extra for garnish
- A few sprigs marjoram, leaves only, washed, dried, sliced into thin slivers
- A few sprigs basil, leaves only, washed, dried, sliced into thin slivers
- Extra virgin oil to drizzle over the kibbé

1. Peel the potatoes and cut into big chunks. Put the potatoes in a pot and cover well with water. Place over medium-high heat and bring to a boil. Season with salt and reduce the heat to medium. Cover the pot and let bubble gently for 20 to 25 minutes, until soft enough to mash but not disintegrating. Drain and mash immediately either with a potato masher, a potato ricer, or a mill. Transfer to a large mixing bowl.

2. Add the bulgur wheat and spice mixture and mix well, ideally with your hands so you can blend the ingredients evenly. Add the scallions, mint, marjoram, and basil and mix again. Taste before adding any salt and adjust the seasoning if needed.

3. Transfer to a round or oval serving platter and flatten the kibbé over the plate to about ¾-inch (2 cm) thickness, either indenting the sides with your fingers or flattening them with the back of a pastry spatula. Then, with the back of a tablespoon, make evenly spaced dips in several lines across the kibbé. Drizzle a little olive oil into the dips and garnish with mint. Serve immediately, either on its own, as part of a mezze spread, or as part of a kibbé tasting.

TOMATO KIBBÉ
KIBBET BANADÜRA

Also known as *da'a*, this vegetarian kibbé is the ultimate summer dish when tomatoes are at their best. It is one of the most delicious versions of the southern kibbé repertoire. It can be made as below or with slightly cooked tomatoes and onions, in which case it is called *ghmass* (meaning "dipped"). You can use dry kammüneh (page 18) here, but I prefer it the way my friend Feryal (page 342) makes it, with a mix of dry and fresh herbs. The version with fresh herbs doesn't last as long as the one made with the dry mixture, but it is very moreish. When I crave it outside of summer, I try to buy the best tomatoes I can get, and whizz them with a handheld blender to produce a little juice while retaining enough texture for the kibbé to feel summery. You don't need to rinse the bulgur wheat here because it will absorb all the excess liquid from the tomatoes.

SERVES 4

4 large ripe tomatoes (about 800 g), peeled, very finely chopped

1 medium onion (about 150 g), finely grated, or 2 to 3 scallions, trimmed, very thinly sliced

1 small red chili, trimmed, seeded, very finely chopped

A few sprigs fresh mint, leaves only, washed, dried, sliced into thin slivers, plus extra for garnish

A few sprigs marjoram, leaves only, washed, dried, sliced into thin slivers

A few sprigs basil, leaves only, washed, dried, sliced into thin slivers

A few sprigs flat-leaf parsley, washed, dried, most of the bottom stalks discarded, very finely chopped

1 cup (200 g) fine bulgur wheat, plus more if needed

1 tablespoon kammüneh (page 18), or to taste

Sea salt

Extra virgin oil to drizzle over the kibbé (you can also add a little to the kibbé)

Sprigs of mint or basil leaves for garnish

1. Put the tomatoes, onion, chili, mint, marjoram, basil, and parsley in a large mixing bowl. Mix well, then add the bulgur wheat and the spice mixture. Add salt to taste and mix well, ideally with your hand so you blend the ingredients evenly. Taste and adjust the seasoning if needed. If the mixture is a little too loose, add a little more bulgur wheat, but remember that it will expand as it soaks up the juices.

2. Transfer to a serving platter, spreading the kibbé to a thickness of ¾ inch (2 cm). Make dips or waves here and there and drizzle olive oil into the dips. Garnish with fresh mint or basil and serve immediately, either on its own, as part of a mezze spread, or as part of a kibbé tasting.

STUFFED VEGETABLES

Stuffed vegetables is one of my favorite groups of dishes, and one I always used to ask my mother to prepare for me when I visited her in the home country, although that was before she reached her nineties! There are four different stuffings you can use with almost any vegetable that takes your fancy. The vegetarian version is served as part of a mezze spread, or during the days when Christians abstain from eating meat, while the meat-based versions, made with rice, or rice and tomatoes, or simply pine nuts (some add onions, but I don't in most cases) are served as a main course. Of course, within these four basic stuffings there are variations, both regional and personal.

The vegetarian stuffing can be made with added split chickpeas, and it can be seasoned with only sumac and lemon juice like I do, or with pomegranate molasses, which adds an intriguing sweet-savory note. The meat stuffings also vary. The meat and rice can be very lemony or left rather bland, and the sauce can be tomatoes. Some add mint and garlic to the cooking juices, but only for some vegetables, whereas others don't. I will give as many of the variations as I can without being repetitive, although the recipes will on the whole follow my personal preference. Apart from peppers and tomatoes, all the other vegetables will take a fair amount of preparation before they are ready to be stuffed, so be sure to allow enough time when you decide to make any of the following recipes.

Sami, my favorite greengrocer in Batroun, helping me with my shopping for the samkeh harrah lunch I cooked at Cathy Chami's

VEGETARIAN STUFFED ZUCCHINI
MEHSHI KOUSSA BIL-ZEYT

The classic stuffing here is made with added chickpeas that are peeled and split in half. I personally find that they never seem to cook enough in the time it takes for the stuffed vegetables to be ready and, long ago, I convinced my mother to stop adding them. From then on, we always made these without. Conversely, while testing the recipe again, I found that the soft crunch of the chickpeas was rather pleasing and a nice contrast to the velvety rice stuffing, so I decided to add them again. Not many but enough to make the stuffing more interesting, and more typical of the one used in the mountains of Lebanon where my mother came from. In both north and south, they add pomegranate molasses for a headier flavor that reminds me of the Iranian stuffed vine leaves that are cooked with pomegranate molasses. Joumana Hazim, who gave me the recipe for fattet makdüss (page 137), adds pomegranate molasses when she makes her vegetarian stuffed eggplants, while my friend Mona Zaatari adds it to her stuffed cabbage leaves, which she lets caramelize on the bottom to give some rolls a partial crispiness. You will find Mona's recipe on page 196, and if you use eggplants, the dish will come very close to Joumana's version. You can also use the stuffing below with vine or cabbage leaves, Swiss chard, eggplant, bell peppers, tomatoes, or even potatoes (see page 202).

SERVES 6 TO 8

30 medium pale green zucchini (about 1½ kg)

FOR THE STUFFING

½ cup (60 g) dried chickpeas, soaked overnight in plenty of cold water with ¼ teaspoon baking soda

¾ cup (150 g) Egyptian, Calasparra, or bomba rice

3 medium firm ripe tomatoes (about 375 g), diced into ¼-inch (5 mm) cubes

½ bunch scallions (about 50 g), trimmed, thinly sliced

½ bunch flat-leaf parsley (about 100 g on the stalk), washed, dried, most of the bottom stalks discarded, chopped medium-fine

¼ bunch mint (about 50 g on the stalk), leaves only, washed, dried, chopped medium-fine

Juice of 1 large lemon, or to taste

⅔ cup (160 ml) extra virgin olive oil

Heaping 2 tablespoons (30 g) sumac

¼ teaspoon ground cinnamon

½ teaspoon ground allspice

¼ teaspoon finely ground black pepper

Sea salt

FOR THE BOTTOM OF THE PAN

2 large ripe tomatoes (400 g), sliced into medium-thick disks

1. To core the zucchini: Cut off and discard the stem ends of the zucchini and shave off the bottom brown skins.

2. Place one zucchini in the palm of your hand with the cut top facing you. Cup your fingers firmly around it and insert a long vegetable corer (page 23), which you can find in well-stocked Middle Eastern grocery stores, into the cut top about ¼ inch (2 to 3 mm) inside the skin, or as close to the edge as possible, and push it halfway down. Take it out and insert the corer again next to the first cut and repeat until you have cut a rosette all around the inside. Twist the corer inside the zucchini to loosen the pulp and pull out the first piece. Slide it off the corer into a bowl (you will save the pulp to use in the recipes on pages 198 and 201), then insert again and start scraping the sides and bottom of the zucchini, going all the way around the inside, to remove as much pulp as possible—do this as gently and carefully as you can, gradually extracting the pulp so as not to split the top or pierce the sides or bottom. You should be left with ¼-inch (2 to 3 mm) thick "walls." Drop the cored zucchini into a bowl of cold water, filling the inside. Finish coring the remaining zucchini. Let them soak while you prepare the stuffing.

3. To prepare the stuffing: Drain and rinse the chickpeas. Spread over a clean kitchen towel. Cover with another towel and gently press down on them with a rolling pin to split in half and loosen their skin. Peel and discard the skins. Rinse again under cold water, drain, and transfer to a large mixing bowl.

4. Rinse the rice under cold water, drain, and add to the split chickpeas. Add the tomatoes, scallions, parsley, and mint. Mix well, then add the lemon juice, olive oil, sumac, cinnamon, allspice, and pepper. Add salt to taste and mix again. The stuffing will look like tabbüleh—in fact, my mother often would use leftover tabbüleh to make vegetarian stuffed vegetables—except that it would be with rice rather than bulgur wheat. Taste and adjust the seasoning if needed.

5. Line the bottom of a large pot where you can arrange the zucchini snugly half-standing with the tomato slices.

6. To stuff the zucchini: Drain the zucchini well, then take one and hold it upright by cupping your hand around it. Pick up a little filling with the other hand and, with your finger, gently push it inside the zucchini. Every now and then shake the zucchini down to make sure the filling is well inside it. Only fill up to three-quarters of the zucchini, so as to leave enough space for the rice to expand, and do not press down on the filling with your finger. Put the filled zucchini in the pot with the open end slightly raised.

7. Continue filling and arranging the zucchini, first around the side of the pot, then on the inside—they should all fit comfortably half-standing in one layer—until you have finished both zucchini and stuffing. If you have

a little stuffing left, cook it separately in one and a half times its volume of water and serve on the side.

8. Pour a little water into the empty bowl and swirl it around to collect the last bits of stuffing. Pour over the zucchini to half cover them. Add salt to taste, bearing in mind that the stuffing is already seasoned. Cover the pot and place over medium-high heat. Bring to a boil, then reduce the heat to medium and let bubble gently for 45 minutes to 1 hour, until both zucchini and stuffing are done. Two-thirds of the way through, taste the sauce and add more salt if needed. At this stage, you can drizzle in a little olive oil to make the sauce richer.

9. Let the zucchini sit covered until completely cooled before serving. The best way to remove the fairly soft zucchini intact is to use your fingers. Gently pull away one zucchini at a time before sliding a flattish spoon underneath and lifting it to lay on a round serving platter. Arrange in the shape of a rosette either in one or two slightly overlapping layers, then ladle some of the cooking juices all over and serve as part of a mezze spread, a summer buffet, or a vegetarian main course.

Sheikh Hadi at al-Hassad, in Aley, with the spectacular breakfast he had prepared for us

STUFFED VEGETABLES

MEATY STUFFED EGGPLANTS

MEHSHI BATINJAN BIL-LAHMEH

Here I am using the meat, rice, and tomato stuffing with eggplants, but you can also use it with zucchini, marrow, peppers, tomatoes, potatoes, carrots, and vine or cabbage leaves. The amount of stuffing varies according to the vegetable you use. If you plan on serving a selection of stuffed vegetables, cook the eggplants on their own, whereas you can mix the zucchini with vine leaves, the marrow with cabbage leaves, and the tomatoes with peppers, carrots, and potatoes. In fact, whatever takes your fancy except for the eggplants, which have a slightly bitter taste and are best cooked separately.

SERVES 4 TO 6

About 20 small Japanese eggplants (about 2 pounds 4 ounces/1 kg)

FOR THE STUFFING

½ cup (100 g) white Egyptian, Calasparra, or bomba rice

5 ounces (150 g) lean ground lamb

2 medium ripe tomatoes (about 250 g), diced into ¼-inch (5 mm) cubes

¼ teaspoon ground cinnamon

½ teaspoon ground allspice

½ teaspoon finely ground black pepper

Sea salt

TO FINISH

2 large ripe tomatoes (about 400 g), sliced into medium-thick disks

3 or 4 lamb bones (optional)

2 cups (500 g) plain full-fat yogurt to serve on the side

1. To core the eggplants: Cut off and discard the stem ends of the eggplants and remove any husks capping the skin. You can core them in either one of two ways. One will allow you to extract most of the pulp in one piece so you can cook it in the same pot and serve on the side, while the other is to core them as you would zucchini (see page 188), in which case the pulp will break up and be too messy to use.

2. To extract the pulp in one piece: Take one eggplant and start pinching the skin on the fat part between your thumb and index fingers to pull it away from the pulp. Push the loose skin around to the firm side and continue pinching all the way around the fat part before moving upward to about ½ inch (1¼ cm) or a little more short of the top, then as far down as you can. By then, the skin will be mostly detached from the pulp except at the top and possibly at the bottom.

3. Insert the corer into the cut top, as close to the edge as possible, about ⅛ inch (2 to 3 mm) inside the skin, and gently push it in until it meets no resistance. Take out, insert again next to the first incision, and repeat until you have cut a rosette all around the inside. Squeeze the bottom end of the eggplant with your fingers to detach the skin from the pulp and slowly squeeze out the pulp. Do this gently; if not, the top will split. Put the pulp on a plate and scrape the inside and bottom of the eggplant with the corer, again gently and carefully so as not to pierce the skin, to remove the last bits of pulp, leaving a shell that is about ⅛ inch (2 to 3 mm) thick. Plunge the cored eggplant into a bowl of cold water and let the inside fill with water. Core the rest of the eggplants and let soak while you prepare the stuffing.

4. To extract the pulp in pieces: Follow the instructions for coring zucchini on page 188.

5. To make the stuffing: Rinse the rice under cold water, drain, and put it in a large mixing bowl. Add the meat and tomatoes. Season with the cinnamon, allspice, pepper, and salt to taste and mix, preferably with your hand, to blend the ingredients well. Taste and adjust the seasoning if needed.

6. Line a large pot with the tomato slices, the eggplant pulp, and the bones, if you are using them—they make the sauce richer.

7. Stuff and cook the eggplants following the instructions for the zucchini (page 188). Serve hot with the yogurt as well as the sauce and pulp on the side.

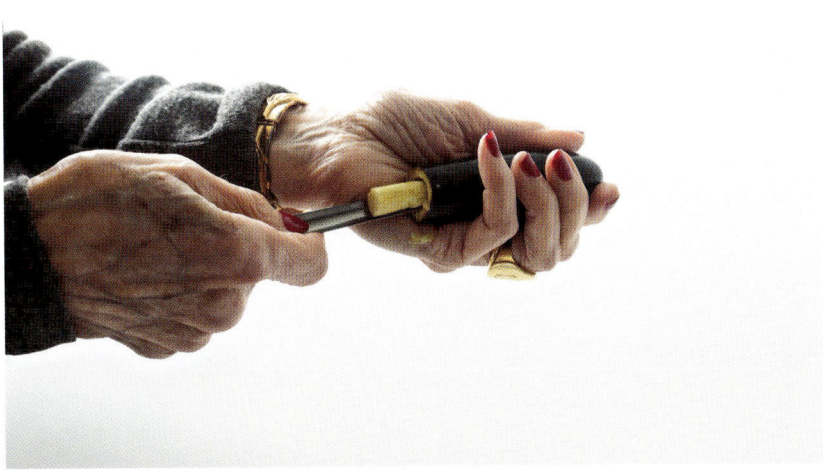

My late mother coring eggplant to get the inside in one piece

STUFFED MARROW

MEHSHI ARE'

Are' is a type of slightly furry marrow from the *Cucurbitaceae* family that we pick fairly small and use in mehshi, which means "stuffed" in Arabic. The term *mehshi* is used for all stuffed vegetables followed by the name of the vegetable used. You will find marrows in Middle Eastern grocery stores in spring and summer when they are in season. However, make sure to pick them all more or less the same size. Also, buy those that are a lovely uniform pale green color, which means they are very fresh. You can use zucchini here, but both taste and texture will be different. Marrows are firmer and ever so slightly bitter. As for getting rid of the furry skin, you can either grate it off the way we do traditionally or peel it. Both grating and peeling and coring are a bit of a hassle, but they are definitely worth the trouble. This stuffing is also good with cabbage, zucchini, eggplant, peppers, and tomatoes. If you are using cabbage, finish the same way as below with the garlic, mint, and lemon juice mixture.

SERVES 4 TO 6

6 medium marrows (about 1 kg)

Meat, rice, and tomato stuffing (page 190)

Sea salt

FOR THE POT

6 lamb chops

4 medium ripe tomatoes (about 500 g), sliced into medium-thick disks

TO FINISH

7 large cloves garlic, peeled, minced to a fine paste

Heaping 1 tablespoon crushed dried mint

Juice of 1½ lemons, or to taste

2 tablespoons (30 ml) extra virgin olive oil

Sea salt

2 cups (500 g) plain full-fat Greek-style yogurt to serve on the side

1. Cut off and discard the stem end of the marrows, leaving most of the narrow top end on. Slice off a little of the bottom to create enough of an opening to core and stuff the marrows. Peel or grate the skin, then core the marrow from the wide bottom end, leaving about ⅛-inch (2 to 3 mm) thick "walls." The best way to do this is to place the marrow in the palm of your hand with the cut bottom facing you. Cup your fingers around it, and holding it firmly, insert a long vegetable corer (page 23), which you can find in well-stocked Middle Eastern grocery stores, into the cut top as close to the edge as possible, about ⅛ inch (2 to 3 mm) inside the skin, and push as far down as you can. Take out and insert again, next to the first cut, and repeat until you have cut a rosette all around the inside. Twist

the corer inside the marrow to loosen the cut pulp and pull out the first piece. Slide it off the corer and insert again, then, with a circular motion, scrape the sides and bottom to remove as much pulp as possible. Do this gently and carefully, gradually extracting the pulp; otherwise you will split the top or pierce the sides or bottom of the marrow. Plunge the cored marrow in a bowl of cold water where you have added a little lemon juice and lemon pieces to stop it from oxidizing and fill the inside with water. Finish coring the marrows and let soak while you prepare the stuffing.

2. Mix all the ingredients for the stuffing in a large mixing bowl and add salt to taste. Taste and adjust the seasoning if needed.

3. Line the bottom of a large pot with the lamb chops and spread the sliced tomatoes all over.

4. Fill each marrow up to a little more than three-quarters with the stuffing—you need to leave space for the rice to expand during cooking, and pack the marrows snugly over the lamb chops and tomatoes, raising the open ends slightly.

5. Swirl some water inside the empty stuffing bowl to collect the last bits of stuffing and pour over the marrows to half cover. Add salt to taste, bearing in mind that the stuffing is already seasoned. Cover the pot and place over medium-high heat. Bring to a boil, then reduce the heat to medium and let bubble somewhat energetically for 40 minutes. Check the water level to make sure the marrows are not drying up.

6. While the marrows are cooking, mix the minced garlic with the dried mint, lemon juice, and olive oil in a small mixing bowl and add salt to taste. Set aside.

7. When the 40 minutes are up, stir the garlic and mint mixture into the cooking juices. You will have to tilt the pot to bring up enough juice to the surface. Taste and adjust the salt if necessary. Cook for another 10 minutes.

8. Take off the heat and let sit, covered, for about 10 minutes, then gently transfer to a serving platter. Serve hot with the sauce and a bowl of yogurt on the side.

STUFFED MARROWS IN TOMATO SAUCE WITH OKRA

MEHSHI ARE' MA BAMIYEH

Here is another version of stuffed marrows, which I discovered thanks to my friend Jacquot Ayoub, whose late cook used to prepare this dish, and until I started researching this book, I had never seen it, nor tasted it, nor even known about it. Even my late mother, who was a fount of knowledge for all things culinary in the country, didn't know about it. According to the late chef Ramzi, who documented the food of Lebanon in a massive volume, *Le Patrimoine Culinaire du Liban* (*The Culinary Heritage of Lebanon*), it is from Hasbaya. His tome was published in 2002, and it is a precious source I often refer to, to both learn about regional food and double check the recipes I was given, even if his are somewhat vague and may be difficult to follow if you are unfamiliar with the cuisine, but if you are not, you can adapt them. That said, the recipe below comes from Jacquot.

SERVES 4 TO 6

- 8 medium marrows (about 1¼ kg)
- Lemon for the soaking water
- Vegetable oil to sauté the okra
- Freshly ground black pepper

FOR THE STUFFING

- 4 tablespoons (60 g) unsalted butter
- ⅔ cup (100 g) Mediterranean pine nuts
- 9 ounces (250 g) lean ground lamb from the shoulder
- ½ cup (100 g) cooked chickpeas, cut in half
- Sea salt

FOR THE SAUCE

- 4 tablespoons (60 g) unsalted butter
- 2 medium onions (about 300 g), peeled, thinly sliced into wedges
- 4 large cloves garlic, peeled, minced to a fine paste
- 9 ounces (250 g), lean lamb from the shoulder, diced into bite-sized chunks
- 2 tablespoons (30 ml) pomegranate molasses
- ½ bunch cilantro (about 100 g on the stalk), washed, dried, most of the bottom stalks discarded, finely chopped
- 5 large ripe tomatoes (about 1 kg), peeled, diced into small cubes
- 1 tablespoon tomato paste
- 1 pound 2 ounces (500 g) okra, washed, dried, top peeled as described on page 125

1. Peel, core and soak the marrows in lemony water following the instructions on page 192.

2. To make the stuffing: Put the butter in a large frying pan and place over medium heat. When the butter is melted, add the pine nuts and sauté, stirring constantly, until golden brown. Remove with a slotted spoon into

a bowl. Add the ground meat to the pan and cook, breaking up any lumps, until it is no longer pink. Add the chickpeas and mix well. Return the pine nuts to the pan and mix again. Season with salt to taste and set aside.

3. To make the sauce: Put the butter in a pot large enough to eventually hold the okra, meat, tomatoes, and marrows and place over medium heat. Add the onions and cook, stirring occasionally, until soft and golden, 10 to 15 minutes. Add the minced garlic and cook, stirring, for a couple of minutes, then add the meat. Sauté until the meat is browned all over. Add the pomegranate molasses and mix well, then add the cilantro. Sauté for a couple of minutes. Add the diced tomatoes and the tomato paste and let bubble gently for 15 minutes.

4. While the sauce is cooking, drain the marrows and fill them with the stuffing—here you do not need to worry about leaving space for expansion. In a large frying pan, sauté the okra in a little vegetable oil for a couple of minutes to seal and turn them bright green.

5. Add the sautéed okra to the sauce, together with pepper to taste. Then carefully arrange the stuffed marrows in between. Cover the pot and let bubble gently for 30 to 45 minutes, until both okra and marrows are done to your liking—I like to keep my vegetables just done and not let them get too soft. The sauce should have thickened somehow without becoming dry. Serve hot with vermicelli rice (page 263).

STUFFED CABBAGE LEAVES
MEHSHI MALFÜF

The best cabbage to use here is the flat one, which is what we all use in the home country. You can find them in Middle Eastern grocery stores, sometimes even in farmers markets. The leaves are larger and more tender. You need to handle them gently, both as you detach them from the core when raw so they don't break, and after you blanch them so they don't tear.

SERVES 4 TO 6

1 small flat white cabbage (about 1 kg)

FOR THE STUFFING

½ cup (100 g) white Egyptian, Calasparra, or bomba rice

5 ounces (150 g) lean ground lamb

2 medium ripe tomatoes (about 250 g), diced into ¼-inch (5 mm) cubes

¼ teaspoon ground cinnamon

½ teaspoon ground allspice

½ teaspoon finely ground black pepper

Sea salt

TO FINISH AND FOR THE POT

7 large cloves garlic, peeled and minced to a fine paste

Heaping 1 tablespoon crushed dried mint

Juice of 1½ lemons, or to taste

2 tablespoons (30 ml) extra virgin olive oil

Sea salt

2 cups (500 g) plain full-fat Greek-style yogurt to serve on the side

1. To prepare the cabbage leaves: Cut into the cabbage leaves as close to and all around the core so you can gently detach them one by one—be sure not to break them in the process. Reserve the damaged outer leaves to line the bottom of the pot. Divide the leaves into piles. Set aside.

2. Fill a large pot with water and place over high heat. Bring to a boil. Plunge the first pile of leaves, one by one, into the boiling water and blanch for a minute or so, until the leaves have softened enough to roll but are not mushy. Remove with a slotted spoon into a colander, still being careful not to damage them. Finish the remaining leaves the same way.

3. Take one blanched leaf and, depending on its size, keep whole, slicing off the back of the spine without breaking into it; or cut across in two, either side of the spine. Reserve the spines for the bottom of the pot. Lay the leaf on your work surface, glossy-side down. Prepare the rest of the leaves in the same way and arrange in neat piles.

4. Line the bottom of a large pot with the cabbage leaves and spines and tomato slices.

5. Put all the ingredients for the stuffing in a medium mixing bowl and mix well.

6. Lay one cabbage leaf on your cutting board, glossy-side down with the cut side nearest to you. Spread ½ to 1½ teaspoons stuffing depending on the size of the leaf in a thin raised horizontal line across the leaf, about ½ inch (1¼ cm) inside the edge nearest to you and the same distance from the sides. Roll flatly and fairly loosely so as to leave enough space for the rice to expand during cooking. Lift and place, seam-side down, onto the tomatoes in the pot.

7. Continue filling, rolling, and arranging the leaves, side by side, doing one layer at a time, until you have finished both leaves and stuffing—if you have any stuffing left over, cook in a small saucepan with one and a half times its volume in water. Simmer for 10 to 15 minutes and serve on the side. If you have any leftover leaves, use them to cover the rolled ones.

8. Swirl some water inside the empty stuffing bowl to collect the last bits of stuffing and pour over the stuffed leaves until you have half covered them. Add salt to taste, remembering that the stuffing is already seasoned, and place an overturned heatproof plate over the leaves to stop them from unrolling during cooking. Cover the pot and place over medium-high heat. Bring to a boil, then reduce the heat to medium and let bubble somewhat energetically for 30 minutes.

9. While the cabbage rolls are cooking, mix the minced garlic, dried mint, lemon juice, and olive oil in a small mixing bowl (see page 192). Add salt to taste.

10. When the cooking time is up, uncover the pot and tilt it slightly to bring up the cooking juices. Stir in the garlic and mint mixture, then reduce the heat to medium and continue cooking, covered, for another 20 minutes. Taste and add more salt if needed. Take off the heat and let sit for about 10 minutes, then gently transfer the cabbage rolls onto a serving platter. Serve hot with some sauce and yogurt on the side.

JENNY GEBARA'S AUNT'S STUFFED ZUCCHINI AND VINE LEAVES WITH A WHOLE CHICKEN

MEHSHI AMMET JENNY GEBARA: WARA' ENAB WA KOUSSA MA DJEJEH

This is an extraordinary recipe that I discovered while visiting my friend Zelfa Hourani in Marja'yün, a southern town, not far from the border. That day, Zelfa's friend Jenny Gebara was also visiting, and, as we discussed regional recipes, she told me about her aunt Claire's recipe for stuffed vegetables, where she cooks zucchini and vine leaves together with a whole stuffed chicken. Claire prepared it every Sunday. Jenny explained that the stuffed vine leaves were prepared ahead and kept in the freezer to reduce the workload on the day. So do not prepare this dish on a whim. It is time-consuming even if you have stuffed vine leaves in the freezer. That said, it is definitely worth making, as it is one of the most impressive dishes I came across during my research. And the poached chicken comes out very silky, quite unlike a regular poached one.

SERVES 6 TO 8

FOR THE STUFFED CHICKEN

4 tablespoons (60 g) unsalted butter

½ cup (75 g) Mediterranean pine nuts

½ cup (75 g) blanched almond halves

5 ounces (150 g) lean ground lamb

1¼ cups (250 g) Egyptian, Calasparra, or bomba rice, soaked in cold water for 1 hour

½ teaspoon ground cinnamon

1. To prepare the stuffed chicken: Melt the butter in a large saucepan over medium heat and sauté the pine nuts, stirring constantly, until golden brown. Remove with a slotted spoon onto a double layer of paper towel. Sauté the almond halves in the same butter until they turn the same color, then remove to drain onto a double layer of paper towel. Then add the ground meat and cook, breaking up any lumps, until it loses all traces of pink. Drain the rice and add to the meat together with half of the toasted pine nuts and almonds—you will use the rest for garnish. Mix well. Season with the cinnamon, allspice, pepper, and salt to taste. Sauté for a couple of minutes until the rice is glossy, then take off the heat and set aside. Taste and adjust the seasoning if needed.

2. Once the rice mixture has cooled, use half of it to stuff the chicken. Sew the opening tight and truss the chicken, then rub it with the softened butter. Wrap tightly with cheesecloth. Then, with a metal skewer, poke the chicken in a few places to allow the cooking broth to get inside. Set aside.

3. To prepare the vegetable stuffing: Drain the rice and put it in a large mixing bowl. Add the ground meat together with about ¼ cup (60 ml) water. Season with the cinnamon, allspice, black pepper, and salt to taste and mix well. Taste and adjust the seasoning if needed—if you are not

LEBANON

½ teaspoon ground allspice

¼ teaspoon finely ground black pepper

Sea salt

1 free-range organic chicken (about 1½ kg)

Softened butter for rubbing the chicken

FOR THE VEGETABLE STUFFING

2 cups (400 g) Egyptian, Calasparra, or bomba rice, soaked in cold water for 1 hour

1 pound 5 ounces (600 g) lean ground lamb

½ teaspoon ground cinnamon

¾ teaspoon ground allspice

½ teaspoon finely ground black pepper

Sea salt

20 smallish (about 1½ kg) pale green zucchini

7 ounces (200 g) vine leaves, preserved in brine or vacuum-packed

FOR THE BOTTOM OF THE POT

1 to 2 lemons, peeled, thinly sliced

1 large potato, thinly sliced

TO FINISH

Juice of 6 to 8 lemons, or to taste

keen on tasting raw meat, just dip your finger in the stuffing and lick it to make sure you have added enough salt.

4. To core and stuff the zucchini, follow the instructions on page 187.

5. Line a large 8-quart (8 liter) pot with the lemon slices first, then the potato slices.

6. To prepare the vine leaves: Rinse the vine leaves under cold water to get rid of the saltiness of the brine and cut off and discard any stems. Line up two or three on your work surface, glossy-side down with the stem end nearest to you, and, depending on the size of the leaf, arrange ½ to 1½ teaspoons stuffing in a thin raised line across the top of the leaves, about ½ inch (1¼ cm) away from the top and sides. Fold the sides over the stuffing, tapering them toward the bottom, and fold the top edge over the filling, then roll neatly but fairly loosely to leave enough space for the rice to expand during cooking. Place seam-side down over the potato slices, starting from the edge. Continue filling, rolling, and arranging the vine leaves, side by side, until you have covered most of the potato, leaving enough space in the center for the chicken. Put the wrapped chicken over the sliced potatoes, and continue filling and rolling the vine leaves, arranging them all around the chicken and over the first layer, until you have finished the leaves and stuffing.

7. Arrange the stuffed zucchini half-standing all around the chicken. Add enough water to just under the top of the chicken and add half of the lemon juice. Sprinkle with a little salt and place the pot over medium-high heat. Cover and bring to a boil. Let bubble rather energetically for about 30 minutes. Uncover the pot and taste the broth for salt. Adjust the salt if needed. Add the remaining lemon juice and cover the pot again. Reduce the heat to medium and let bubble gently for another 15 to 30 minutes, until everything is done. You may want to take out one zucchini to taste for doneness. Take off the heat and let sit for 15 minutes.

8. While the chicken and stuffed vegetables are resting, put the remaining rice stuffing in a small pot. Add just under 1 cup (250 ml) water and place over medium heat. Cook for 10 to 15 minutes, until just done.

9. Jenny's aunt unwraps the chicken and cuts it in half, to show the rice stuffing. She serves it on one platter, with the reserved toasted nuts scattered all over. Then she serves the stuffed vegetables on separate platters with the yogurt on the side. I unwrap the chicken like she does, but I serve it whole together with the vine leaves on one platter, the rice on another platter, garnished with the reserved toasted nuts, and the zucchini on a separate platter with the yogurt on the side. Whichever way you like to serve this dish, you are sure to impress your guests, as it is a real show-stopper, not to mention that it is also absolutely delectable!

STUFFED ZUCCHINI IN YOGURT SAUCE

ABLAMAH

Some people in the south cook these stuffed zucchini in a tomato sauce rather than in yogurt, but I find the yogurt version more sophisticated. If you want to cook the zucchini in tomato sauce, use 3 (14-ounce/400 g) cans of chopped tomatoes, season with a little cinnamon, allspice, and black pepper, and cook the stuffed zucchini directly in the tomato sauce for at least 45 minutes—you may have to add a little water if the sauce thickens too much. You can also use the meat and rice stuffing (page 145) instead of just meat and pine nuts with the yogurt sauce. If you do, cook the zucchini for longer to allow for the uncooked rice inside to soften before dropping in the yogurt. Also, make sure to fill the zucchini up to only three-quarters to leave enough space for the rice to expand.

SERVES 4

20 smallish pale green zucchini (1½ kg), trimmed and cored as per the instructions on page 188

Cooked Yogurt Sauce (page 142), with adjustments (see below)

FOR THE STUFFING

4 tablespoons (60 g) unsalted butter

½ cup (75 g) Mediterranean pine nuts

5 ounces (150 g) ground lean lamb

¼ teaspoon ground cinnamon

½ teaspoon ground allspice

¼ teaspoon finely ground black pepper

Salt

1. To make the stuffing: Melt the butter in a medium frying pan over medium heat and sauté the pine nuts in it, constantly stirring so they color evenly, until golden brown. Remove with a slotted spoon and put onto a double layer of paper towel to drain.

2. Cook the ground meat in the same butter until it loses all traces of pink, breaking up any lumps. Remove from the heat and season with the cinnamon, allspice, pepper, and salt to taste. Add the toasted pine nuts and mix well. Taste and adjust the salt if needed. Let cool.

3. Drain the zucchini, making sure you empty the water inside, and stuff them following the instructions on page 188. Here you do not need to leave any room, as there is no rice in the stuffing. Arrange the zucchini half-standing in a saucepan where they will fit comfortably. Add water until just below the open ends and place over medium-high heat. Bring to a boil, then reduce the heat to medium-low. Place the lid over the pan and let bubble gently for 25 minutes. Some cooks fry them, but it browns the skin and crinkles it, and I prefer to boil them.

4. While the zucchini are cooking, prepare the yogurt sauce (page 142) using dried mint instead of cilantro.

5. Carefully transfer the zucchini from the pan to a shallow bowl, and once the yogurt is gently bubbling, add them to the pot. Let bubble gently until the zucchini are tender but not mushy, about 10 minutes. Gently stir the yogurt during that time, being careful not to the break the zucchini. Serve hot with or without vermicelli rice (page 263).

VEGETARIAN STUFFED EGGPLANTS

BATINJEN MEHSHI ATE'

Traditionally this stuffing has added split chickpeas (about ⅓ cup/50 g) for the quantities below. They are soaked overnight with a little baking soda to shorten their cooking time, then split in half by spreading over a kitchen towel, covering them with another, and slightly pressing on them with a rolling pin to split them and loosen their skin so it is easier to peel them. A variation from the south is to leave out the lemon juice and increase the amount of sumac to 3 tablespoons. This recipe is for stuffed eggplants, but you can use the same stuffing with zucchini (2 pounds 13 ounces/1¼ kg), vine leaves (about 7 ounces/200 g preserved ones), or Swiss chard (2 pounds 4 ounces/1 kg), which you need to trim and discard the stalks, before blanching and rolling like vine leaves. Bell peppers (about 8 red or yellow ones, each weighing 5 ounces/about 150 g) and even tomatoes are also great with this stuffing. And if you want to add pomegranate molasses, like Joumana Hazim does, add ¼ cup (60 ml) to the stuffing and ¼ cup (60 ml), or to taste, pomegranate molasses to the cooking water.

SERVES 4 TO 6

FOR THE STUFFING AND EGGPLANT

¾ cup (150 g) white Egyptian, Calasparra, or bomba rice

3 medium firm red tomatoes (about 375 g), diced into ¼-inch (5 mm) cubes

½ bunch scallions (about 50 g), trimmed, thinly sliced

½ bunch flat-leaf parsley (about 100 g on the stalk) washed, dried, most of the stalks discarded, chopped medium-fine

¼ bunch mint (about 50 g on the stalk), leaves only, washed, dried, chopped medium-fine

Heaping 2 tablespoons (30 g) sumac

¼ teaspoon ground cinnamon

½ teaspoon ground allspice

¼ teaspoon finely ground black pepper

Sea salt to taste

Juice of 1 large lemon, or to taste

½ cup plus 1½ tablespoons (150 ml) extra virgin olive oil

24 small Japanese eggplants (each about 50 g)

TO FINISH

2 large tomatoes (about 400 g), sliced into medium-thick disks

Cores of the eggplants

Sea salt

1. Rinse the rice under cold water. Drain and put in a large mixing bowl. Add the remaining stuffing ingredients and mix well—the stuffing should look like a salad. Taste and adjust the seasoning if needed.

2. Core the eggplants as instructed on page 190. Plunge the cored eggplants in a bowl of cold water, filling the inside. Stuff the same way as with the meat and rice recipe (page 190).

3. Line a pot large enough to hold the eggplants half-standing with the tomato slices and eggplant cores (that is, if you have taken them out in one piece) and snugly arrange the stuffed eggplants. Add water to half cover the eggplants. Add salt to taste, bearing in mind that the stuffing is already seasoned, and place over medium-high heat. Bring to a boil, then reduce the heat to medium-low and let bubble gently for about 1 hour, until the eggplants are soft and the rice inside is done—check the water and add a little if it's drying up. Take off the heat and cover with a clean kitchen towel. Let cool. Serve at room temperature as part of a mezze spread or summer buffet or as a vegetarian main course.

Joumana Hazim's vegetarian stuffed eggplants

STUFFED SWISS CHARD LEAVES
MEHSHI SILLE'

Possibly my favorite of all the vegetarian stuffed vegetables. I love the silky texture of the Swiss chard, which is very different from that of vine leaves or cabbage leaves, and I find the contrast between the tart stuffing and the earthy taste of the chard irresistible. This recipe works equally well with vine leaves (7 ounces/200 g) and cabbage leaves (1 small flat cabbage weighing about 2 pounds 4 ounces/1 kg). My friend Mona Zaatari adds pomegranate molasses to her filling for cabbage leaves. She also lets the bottom caramelize, which makes for a supremely moreish dish with some of the leaves melting and crisp in parts. Whenever we eat at her place in Saida, down south, and she has this dish on the menu, we polish it off before anything else. For her version, add ¼ cup (60 ml) pomegranate molasses to the stuffing and another ¼ cup (60 ml) to the cooking water. Otherwise prepare as below.

SERVES 4

2 pounds 4 ounces (1 kg) Swiss chard

Vegetarian Stuffed Eggplants stuffing (page 202)

2 large ripe tomatoes (about 400 g), sliced into medium-thick disks

Sea salt

1. Cut off the stalks of the Swiss chard leaves and divide each leaf into three pieces by first cutting across the top third, taking where the spine becomes thin and pliable as the dividing line. Then slice off and remove the thick spine, leaving two more pieces of chard leaf. The cut pieces should make rolls 3 to 4¾ inches (8 to 12 cm) long. Some leaves are too small to cut in three, in which case, divide in two, again taking the place where the spine becomes thin as the dividing line. Shave off the backs of any particularly thick parts of spine without breaking the leaf. Reserve the stalks and the stems to line the bottom of the pot—if the stalks are in very good condition, use them to make a salad (page 97). Wash the cut leaves in cold water and arrange them, smooth-side down, in neat layers inside a colander. Gently run boiling water over them to soften them.

2. Line the bottom of a large pot with the tomato slices. Rinse the reserved stalks and stems and spread over the tomatoes.

3. Prepare the vegetarian stuffing following the instructions on page 202.

4. Then take one leaf and lay it, smooth-side down, on your work surface with the cut side nearest to you and the veins running away from you. Spread 1 teaspoon stuffing (or more depending on the size of the leaf) in a long, thin, slightly raised line, the thickness of your little finger, about ½

inch (1¼ cm) inside the edge nearest to you and the same distance from the side edges. Fold the narrow strip of leaf over the stuffing and roll into a flat, fairly loosely packed roll so the rice has enough room to expand. Flatten the empty edges, lift the rolled leaf, and carefully lay over the stems in the pot, seam-side down.

5. Continue stuffing, rolling, and arranging the stuffed leaves side by side, doing one layer at a time until you have finished both leaves and stuffing. If you have any stuffing left over, put it in a small pan, cover it with water, and cook over low heat to serve on the side. Use the leftover leaves, if any, to cover the rolled ones.

6. Pour enough water into the pot to barely cover the stuffed leaves and add salt to taste, bearing in mind that the stuffing is already seasoned. Cover the leaves with an overturned heatproof plate to stop them from unrolling during cooking, put the lid on the pan, and place over medium-high heat. Bring to a boil, then reduce the heat to medium and let bubble gently for 45 minutes. Two-thirds of the way through cooking, taste the cooking liquid to check the salt and add more if needed.

7. When the 45 minutes are up, it is a good idea to taste a rolled leaf to make sure the rice is done. If it is cooked through, remove the pot from the heat. Remove the lid and cover with a clean kitchen towel. Let cool before delicately transferring the rolls onto a serving platter (I usually pick up the rolled leaves with my fingers to keep them intact; if you don't like using your fingers, use two flattish spoons for the longest leaves). Ladle some of the sauce into a sauceboat and serve on the side.

STUFFED VINE LEAVES WITH LAMB CHOPS
MEHSHI WARA ENAB MA KASTALETTAH

Ideally, you should prepare this dish with fresh vine leaves, but these are only available in late spring/early summer. Many cooks freeze them to use all year round, and they come out pretty well and definitely taste better than those preserved in brine. You can also buy vacuum-packed ones, which are the next best. However, if your only option is those preserved in brine, be sparing with the salt, as they remain salty even after rinsing under cold water. The time you need to prepare this dish will depend largely on the speed with which you roll the leaves. A practiced cook will fill and roll the amount given below in an hour, even less, whereas a novice cook will spend nearly twice as long. In Tripoli, the country's second-largest city, in the north, they make them tiny, less than half the size of your little finger, while elsewhere, they are a regular size but never as fat or hard as those you see in delis in the West. I was fortunate enough to be invited to lunch at my friends Mona and Misbah Ahdab's in Tripoli specifically to taste the tiny stuffed leaves. Nawal, their cook, had prepared them, but Mona's mother had arranged them in the pot with stuffed intestines, lamb, and bones on the bottom and tiny stuffed zucchini on top. The pot was put over very low heat and left to cook overnight. When it was time to serve the dish, Nawal took the zucchini and some of the cooking juices out before overturning the pot to have a fabulous looking "cake" of the tiniest and most delectable stuffed vine leaves. One of the most delicious versions of stuffed vine leaves that I have ever had.

SERVES 4

Mona and Misbah Ahdab's stuffed vine leaves

8 thin lamb chops (about 600 g), most of the fat trimmed and discarded

Sea salt

1 cinnamon stick

7 ounces (200 g) medium-sized fresh or preserved vine leaves

Meat and rice stuffing (page 145)

Juice of 1 lemon, or to taste

2 cups (500 g) plain full-fat Greek-style yogurt

1. Put the lamb chops in a pan, cover with water, and place over medium heat. As the water is about to boil, skim the surface clean, then add a little salt and the cinnamon stick. Cover the pan and boil for 5 minutes. Lift the chops out of the pan and onto a plate. Set aside.

2. Prepare the meat and rice stuffing following the instructions on page 145. Then choose a pot with straight sides that is large enough to arrange the lamb chops in a tight, even layer over the bottom.

3. Put the vine leaves (fresh or preserved) in a colander and run boiling water over them. This will soften them and make them easier to roll. If you are using preserved vine leaves, rinse them under cold water first, at least a couple of times, to get rid of the briny taste.

4. Take two or three vine leaves and cut away the stem, if any, then line them on your work surface, glossy-side down with the stem end nearest to you. Arrange from ½ to 1½ teaspoons stuffing (depending on the size of the leaf) in a thin raised line across the top of the leaves, about ¾ inch (2 cm) away from the tip of the stem and again the same distance short of either side—the line should be thinner than your little finger, about ½ inch (1¼ cm). Fold the sides over the filling, in a line that slightly tapers toward the bottom, then fold over the top and roll neatly but fairly loosely to leave enough space for the rice to expand during cooking. Place the rolled vine leaves, seam-side down, on the lamb chops, starting from the edge of the pan. Continue filling, rolling, and arranging the vine leaves, side by side, doing one layer at a time, until you have finished them. If you have any leftover stuffing, put it in a small pan, add one and a half times the amount of water, and cook for 10 to 15 minutes to serve on the side.

5. Pour enough water over the rolled leaves to barely cover them. Add salt to taste, bearing in mind that the stuffing is already seasoned. Lay an overturned heatproof plate over the leaves to stop them from unrolling during cooking. Cover the pot and place over medium-high heat. Bring to a boil, then reduce the heat to medium and let bubble gently for about 50 minutes. Add the lemon juice and cook for another 10 minutes.

6. Once the leaves are done, turn off the heat and let sit, covered, for about 10 minutes.

7. Wearing heatproof mitts, first pour out any cooking juices into a bowl while holding the leaves back with the plate covering them. Then remove the plate and cover the pot with the inside of a big, round, flat serving platter. Slowly slide the pan over the edge of your work surface, then, holding the plate firmly against the pot with one hand, place the other hand underneath the pot. Lift the pot and quickly turn it upside down. Slide the platter back onto your work surface and slowly lift the pot off to uncover a cake of vine leaves topped with juicy lamb chops. Serve hot with yogurt.

8. Alternatively, you can spoon the rolled leaves out, a few at a time, and arrange in neat layers onto a serving platter, then arrange the lamb chops on top or all around. Baste with some of the cooking juices and serve hot with yogurt on the side.

THE LORD OF STUFFED VEGETABLES
SHEIKH EL-MEHSHI

Possibly the most elegant of all stuffed vegetables, hence the name. There are two ways of preparing this dish: the elegant way, which I give below, or a relatively faster way, using larger eggplants and building the dish in layers. I prefer my version, but if you want to make the faster layered version, use 3 large eggplants (each about 9 ounces/250 g); peel them in stripes before slicing lengthwise and frying until soft and golden; then layer with double the amount of stuffing and the same amount of tomato sauce and bake as instructed below. There is also an interesting variation from the north where the tomato sauce is replaced with a yogurt one. The recipe remains the same except for using yogurt and cooking it over the stovetop instead of in the oven. If you are going to use yogurt instead of tomatoes, arrange the stuffed eggplants in a deep, wide sauté pan that will hold them in one layer. Prepare the cooked yogurt sauce (page 142), and use 3 tablespoons dried mint instead of cilantro. Mix the mint and garlic into the cooked yogurt before pouring over the eggplants. Simmer over low heat for about 10 minutes—it is cooked on the stovetop because the yogurt will curdle in the oven even when stabilized. Gently shake the pan every now and then during cooking to make sure the yogurt doesn't curdle.

SERVES 4

FOR THE STUFFING

6 tablespoons (90 g) unsalted butter

⅓ cup (50 g) Mediterranean pine nuts

5 ounces (150 g) lean ground lamb

½ teaspoon ground allspice

¼ teaspoon ground cinnamon

¼ teaspoon finely ground black pepper

Sea salt

1. Preheat the oven to 350°F (180°C).

2. To make the stuffing: Put the butter in a large frying pan and place over medium heat. When the butter has melted, add the pine nuts and fry, stirring constantly, until golden brown. Remove with a slotted spoon onto a double layer of paper towel.

3. Add the meat and cook, stirring to break up the lumps, until it loses all traces of pink. Take off the heat. Season with the allspice, cinnamon, pepper, and salt to taste. Add the toasted pine nuts and mix well. Taste and adjust the seasoning if needed.

4. To prepare the eggplants: Trim the stems of the eggplants back to about ½ inch (1¼ cm) above the calyxes (caps). Peel the eggplants lengthwise, leaving strips of skin about ½ inch (1¼ cm) wide.

5. Pour 2 inches (5 cm) vegetable oil into a large deep frying pan and place over medium heat—test the heat by dipping in a piece of bread; if the oil immediately bubbles around it, it is ready. Fry the eggplants until golden all over. Remove with a slotted spoon onto several layers of paper towel to drain off any excess oil.

FOR THE EGGPLANTS

12 Japanese eggplants, each about 4 inches (10 cm) long (50 g)

Vegetable oil for frying

FOR THE TOMATO SAUCE

2 (14-ounce/400 g) cans peeled plum tomatoes, drained, finely chopped

¼ teaspoon ground allspice

¼ teaspoon ground cinnamon

⅛ teaspoon finely ground black pepper

Sea salt

6. Take one eggplant and, with a small knife, slit it lengthwise down the middle and no more than halfway into the flesh—the peeled section will cut more easily. Gently pry the eggplant open and press on the flesh inside to form a pocket in which you will put 1 tablespoon stuffing. Place in a deep oven-to-table baking dish and fill the rest of the eggplants in the same way. If there is any leftover stuffing, spread it on the bottom of the dish between the eggplants.

7. To make the tomato sauce: Season the chopped tomatoes with the allspice, cinnamon, black pepper, and salt to taste and spread evenly in the baking dish, in between the eggplants. Bake in the preheated oven for 40 minutes, or until most of the excess juice from the tomato sauce has evaporated. Serve hot with or without vermicelli rice (page 263).

FISH

The whole of Lebanon lies alongside the Mediterranean, and until not so long ago, we had an abundance of fish in the sea. No longer, sadly, even if many of our restaurants pretend to serve local fish when it is more often than not imported. However, even when fish was plentiful, we didn't have a whole lot of elaborate fish recipes in our culinary repertoire, mainly because people value it so much that they prefer to have it plain, either fried or grilled, or baked under salt and served with tarator (page 77) or simply with excellent extra virgin olive oil and lemon juice.

It was left to the few Sunni families (until recently the main Muslim sect in Lebanon), who were the undisputed lords of the coast for centuries, to devise the few fancy fish dishes we have, which are normally reserved for large family gatherings or celebrations.

Fish is expensive, and as such, not really daily fare, especially when prepared in an elaborate way. In this chapter, I give the most interesting recipes, including variations on one of our most famous fish dishes, samkeh harrah or spicy fish.

Stuffing the fish for Samkeh Harrah 2 (page 216), Batroun

BAKED FISH WITH A TRIPOLITAN TAHINI CILANTRO SAUCE

SAMKEH MA TARATOR TRABÜLSI

A very interesting and simple sauce that is a specialty of Tripoli, a city that has kept its Ottoman character far more than the capital. The cooked tahini sauce is flavored with cilantro and garlic, and it is served with plain baked or grilled fish, and even if it is traditionally specifically a fish sauce, you can easily use it with grilled vegetables, meat, or chicken. In the recipe below, I suggest baking the fish, but you can also grill it if you prefer.

SERVES 4

1 lemon, sliced across into medium-thin disks

Sea bass or bream weighing about 4½ pounds (2 kg), gutted, rinsed, patted dry, at room temperature

Sea salt

⅓ cup (80 ml) extra virgin olive oil

8 large cloves garlic, peeled, minced to a fine paste

½ bunch cilantro (about 100 g on the stalk), washed, dried, most of the stalks discarded, finely chopped

¾ cup (180 ml) tahini

Juice of 2 lemons, or to taste

1. Preheat the oven to 450°F (220°C). Arrange the lemon slices in a long line down the middle of a nonstick baking dish, or one lined with parchment paper.

2. Season the fish with salt inside and out and place over the lemon slices. Bake in the preheated oven for 25 minutes, or until just done—this timing is for a fish brought to room temperature. If the fish is straight out of the refrigerator, it will take a little longer. Take the fish out of the oven and let rest while you finish the sauce.

3. To make the tahini sauce: Put the olive oil, garlic, and cilantro in a large frying pan and place over medium heat. Stir until the cilantro is wilted and the garlic is softened. Take off the heat.

4. Put the tahini and lemon juice in a medium mixing bowl. Stir the juice into the tahini—the tahini will thicken at first, but do not worry, this is perfectly normal; it will start becoming creamy again as you add just under ½ cup (100 ml) water. Mix well. The sauce should have the consistency of heavy cream. Add the tahini sauce to the cilantro and garlic and return to the heat. Mix well and let bubble gently, stirring regularly, until you see a little oil rising to the surface—this is called *srijeh* in Arabic. (You may need to add a little water if the sauce becomes too thick.) Transfer to a serving bowl. Cover with a kitchen towel and set aside.

5. Transfer the fish, whole, to a serving platter. Put the sauce in a sauce boat to serve on the side, or peel the skin off, fillet the fish, and serve covered with the sauce—serving the fish whole makes for a more impressive presentation. Serve at room temperature.

SPICY FISH IN TAHINI SAUCE

SAMKEH HARRAH 1

Samkeh harrah is a specialty of the north, and this recipe comes from one of my favorite restaurants in Tripoli, Lebanon's second-largest city, with a mostly Sunni population. There are many variations to this dish. In Tripoli's old port, known as al-Mina, there are stalls that specialize in making samkeh harrah sandwiches (page 220). Their sauce is spicier than the one in the recipe below.

SERVES 4 TO 6

1 large sea bream or sea bass (about 2 kg), scaled, gutted, rinsed, patted dry

Sea salt

FOR THE SAUCE

4 tablespoons (60 g) unsalted butter

⅓ cup (50 g) Mediterranean pine nuts

⅔ cup (100 g) walnuts

1 cup (250 ml) tahini

6 to 8 cloves garlic, peeled, minced to a fine paste

Juice of 3 lemons, or to taste

Vegetable oil for frying

1 lemon, thinly sliced across into disks

⅓ cup (80 ml) extra virgin olive oil

2 medium onions (about 300 g), peeled, finely chopped

1 medium red Romano pepper, trimmed, seeded, finely chopped

½ bunch cilantro (100 g on the stalk), washed, dried, most of the bottom stalks discarded, finely chopped

1 tablespoon ground coriander

1 teaspoon Aleppo pepper

½ teaspoon ground cumin

1. Rub the fish with salt inside and out. Preheat the oven to 425°F (220°C).

2. Put the butter in a small frying pan and place over medium heat. When the butter has melted, add the pine nuts and fry, stirring constantly, until golden brown. Remove with a slotted spoon onto a double layer of paper towel. Spread the walnuts on a nonstick baking sheet, or one lined with parchment paper or a silicone mat, and toast in the preheated oven for 5 to 6 minutes, until crisp. Let the walnuts cool, then coarsely chop.

3. Put the tahini in a large mixing bowl and add the garlic. Add the lemon juice and start mixing it in. You will notice the tahini thickening at first, but do not worry, it will eventually thin out as you add the water. Slowly add ¾ cup (180 ml) water, stirring all the time, until you have a sauce the consistency of heavy cream. Set the tahini sauce aside.

4. Arrange the lemon slices in a line down the middle of a nonstick pan, or one lined with parchment paper or a silicone mat, and place the fish over the lemon slices. Bake in the preheated oven for about 25 minutes, until just done—this timing is for a fish brought to room temperature. Take the fish out of the oven and let rest while you finish the spicy tahini sauce.

5. Add the olive oil, onions, and Romano pepper to a large sauté pan and place over medium heat. Sauté until the onions are golden and the pepper is completely softened, 10 to 15 minutes. Add the cilantro and stir until wilted. Add the chopped walnuts, coriander, Aleppo pepper, cumin, and salt to taste. Add the tahini sauce and let bubble gently, stirring regularly, until you see a little oil (called *srijeh*) rise to the surface—you may have to add a little water if the sauce thickens too much.

6. Peel the skin off the fish and transfer the fish to a serving platter. Pour the sauce all over and garnish with the toasted pine nuts. Serve immediately.

Cityscape, Tripoli

STUFFED SPICY FISH

SAMKEH HARRAH 2

Here's another way with samkeh harrah that I learned from my mother. She was Maronite, and both her mother's and father's family come from the mountains, but she always lived in Beirut before she married my father, in the Christian part. Once married, she moved to the Muslim part in West Beirut, and I assume she learned this dish from one of our neighbors. This version is particularly delectable, and because it is served at room temperature, it is ideal for summer, either as part of a buffet spread or simply as a main course. You can use one large fish, two medium ones, or four individual ones, and depending on what is available at your fishmonger, you can prepare it with sea bass, sea bream, gray mullet, grouper, John Dory, or even pike, which, despite being a freshwater fish, has a delicate, firm white flesh that makes it ideal for this stuffing.

SERVES 4

1 large fish (about 2 kg), scaled, gutted, rinsed, patted dry

Sea salt

FOR THE STUFFING

½ cup (75 g) Mediterranean pine nuts

½ cup (75 g) walnuts, medium coarsely ground

10 large cloves garlic, peeled, minced into a fine paste

2 bunches cilantro (400 g on the stalk), washed, dried, most of the stalks discarded, finely chopped

1 medium onion (about 150 g), peeled, finely chopped

1 medium tomato (about 125 g), diced into ¼-inch (5 mm) cubes

⅔ cup (160 ml) extra virgin olive oil

Juice of 2 lemons, or to taste

1 teaspoon ground coriander

1 teaspoon ground cumin

½ teaspoon cayenne pepper

¼ teaspoon coarsely ground black pepper

Sea salt

FOR THE GARNISH

8 small ripe firm tomatoes (about 800 g), tops sliced off, seeds removed, turned over to drain any excess liquid—eventually you will fill them with the stuffing

1. Rub the fish dry with a little salt inside and out.

2. Put the pine nuts and walnuts in a large mixing bowl. Add the garlic, cilantro, onion, and chopped tomato. Add the olive oil and lemon juice, then season with the coriander, cumin, cayenne, black pepper, and salt to taste. Mix well. Taste and adjust the seasoning if needed. Set aside.

3. Preheat the oven to 350ºF (180ºC).

4. Put as much stuffing as you can inside the fish and flap the sides shut. Fill the tomatoes with the remaining stuffing. Then take a large nonstick baking dish, or one lined with parchment paper or a silicone mat, and lay the fish on it. Arrange the filled tomatoes around the fish and wrap any leftover stuffing in aluminum foil. Place on the same baking dish or a separate one. Bake in the preheated oven for 30 to 35 minutes, until the fish and tomatoes are just done. Remove from the oven and let cool, then transfer to a serving platter, arranging the filled tomatoes around the fish. Serve at room temperature.

My Samkeh Harrah 2 at Cathy Chami's house in Batroun

STEWED SPICY FISH

SAMKEH HARRAH 3

Here is yet another way with samkeh harrah, probably the simplest of them all. It was everyone's favorite when I recently did a samkeh harrah tasting for my friends in Batroun, which surprised me given how simple it is compared to the other versions. I am not sure if this version is also from Tripoli. If not, it certainly is from somewhere along the coast, as it wasn't until recently that mountain people indulged in eating fish. Traditionally, this is served with rice, but you can also serve it with very good crusty bread; and if you feel like giving it a summery touch, you can add a smattering of diced tomatoes to lift the color of the sauce and freshen it.

SERVES 4

- 2 pounds 4 ounces (1 kg) white sea fish fillets
- Vegetable oil for frying
- ⅔ cup (160 ml) extra virgin olive oil
- 4 medium onions (about 600 g), peeled, finely chopped
- 10 large cloves garlic, peeled, minced into a fine paste
- 2 bunches cilantro (400 g on the stalk), washed, dried, most of the stalks discarded, finely chopped
- 1 teaspoon ground cumin
- ½ teaspoon ground coriander
- ½ teaspoon cayenne pepper
- 1¼ cups (310 ml) lemon juice, or to taste
- Sea salt
- Freshly ground black pepper

1. Pat the fish fillets dry with paper towels. Pour enough vegetable oil into a large nonstick frying pan to shallow-fry the fish and place over medium heat. When the oil is hot—test the heat by dipping a piece of bread in it; if the oil immediately bubbles around it, it is ready—put as many fish fillets, skin-side down, as will fit comfortably in the pan and fry for a couple of minutes, or until the skin is crisp. Remove with a slotted spoon onto a rack.

2. Put the olive oil and chopped onions in a deep, wide sauté pan and place over medium heat. Cook, stirring regularly, until the onions are soft and golden, 10 to 15 minutes. Add the minced garlic and stir for another minute or so. Add the cilantro. Season with the cumin, coriander, and cayenne and stir for a couple of minutes, until the cilantro is wilted. Add the lemon juice and salt and pepper to taste and bring to a boil. Let the sauce bubble for about 5 minutes. Reduce the heat to medium-low and arrange the fish in the sauce. Cover the pan and simmer for 5 minutes, or until the fish is just done and the sauce has thickened somewhat. Taste and adjust the seasoning if needed. Serve warm or at room temperature, with or without plain rice.

FRIED FISH

Samak Me'li

When we go out to any one of the fish restaurants by the sea, we always order some fried fish as part of our selection. Depending on the catch of the day, it will be either tiny red mullets or whitebait, which we call *bizri*. There is no need for a recipe here. All you need to do is season some flour with salt and pepper, then dip the fish in the flour (if it's red mullet) or put the whole lot (if it is whitebait) in a plastic bag together with the seasoned flour and shake the bag until all the fish are well coated. Then heat some vegetable oil in a deep frying pan over medium heat—to test the heat, dip a piece of bread in the oil; if it immediately bubbles around it, it is ready—and when the oil is ready, drop in the fish. It will only take a few minutes for the fish to become crisp and golden, at which point, remove it with a slotted spoon onto a wire rack to drain off any excess oil. Serve immediately with tarator (page 77). In the restaurants, they will also serve fried pita bread, which is scrumptious but not the healthiest way to have bread!

SPICY FISH WRAP

ARÜSS SAMKEH HARRAH

There aren't very many places where you can have fish on the street unless you are in the Mina (fishing port) in Tripoli, where small fishing boats are moored just below the pavement. Across the road and slightly set back is a cluster of gorgeous old houses, sadly falling into ruin. And not too far from there, you will find a row of modest-looking cafés where you can enjoy two of the best sandwiches in the country: samkeh harrah (spicy fish) and akhtabüt (octopus). Both are prepared more or less the same way, except the sauce for the fish has tahini and that for the octopus doesn't. I was given the recipe below by Maher Jaber, the third-generation owner of Mat'am Jaber (restaurant Jaber). If you want to make the sandwich with octopus, sauté the cilantro and garlic with all the seasonings as described below and add lemon juice to taste. Once cooled, mix with boiled, chopped octopus. Make the sandwich with the same garnish. At Jaber, they use gray mullet, but you can also use cod fillet, or any other white sea fish that takes your fancy.

SERVES 4

- 2 pounds 4 ounces (1 kg) cod fillets, or your choice of fish
- 3 tablespoons (45 ml) extra virgin olive oil
- 4 cloves garlic, peeled, minced to a fine paste
- ½ bunch cilantro (about 100 g on the stalk), washed, dried, most of the stalks discarded, finely chopped
- ½ teaspoon ground coriander
- ½ teaspoon ground cumin
- ½ teaspoon crushed red pepper flakes
- Tarator (page 77), with adjustments (see below)
- Sea salt

FOR THE SANDWICHES

- 4 medium pita breads, opened at the seam to have 8 layers
- Garlic sauce (page 76)
- 1 medium tomato (about 125 g), thinly sliced
- 1 cup (75 g) shredded lettuce, or to taste
- Sea salt

1. Preheat the oven to 350°F (180°C).

2. Lay the cod fillets, skin-side down, on a wire rack over a baking sheet. Bake the fish for 15 to 20 minutes, until just done—this timing is for a fish brought to room temperature. You do not want to overcook the fish or it will be rubbery. Let cool. Flake into small pieces. Cover and set aside.

3. Put the olive oil, garlic, cilantro, and coriander in a medium frying pan and place over medium heat. Cook, stirring all the time, until the smell rises. Then add the cumin and red pepper flakes. Mix well and take off the heat. Set aside.

4. Make the tarator using ½ cup (125 ml) water and omitting the garlic. Pour into a small saucepan. Place over medium heat and bring to a boil, stirring regularly. Reduce the heat to medium-low and let bubble gently, stirring every now and then, until a little oil (known as *srijeh*) rises to the surface. Add the sautéed cilantro and simmer for a few more minutes. Take off the heat. Cover with a clean kitchen towel and let cool.

5. Drain any excess liquid from the fish and add it to the tahini sauce. Mix well. Taste and add salt if needed.

6. Lay two layers of pita, one on top of the other, rough-side up, and spread a little garlic sauce down the middle, then spoon a generous amount of the fish mixture over the garlic sauce. Add a little tomato and lettuce and sprinkle with a little salt. Roll the bread over the filling and place the wrap in a preheated sandwich press to crisp it up a little. Half-wrap the sandwich in paper and serve immediately. If you don't have a sandwich/panini press at home, you can create the same effect by lightly toasting the sandwich in a frying pan.

FISH IN TAHINI SAUCE

SAMAK BIL-TAHINEH

I still remember how my grandmother and aunt prepared this dish, using whole individual fish, which they first deep-fried, then finished in the sauce. Using whole fish rather than fillets, as I suggest, is tastier and the sauce is more intense, but it makes for messy eating, as you will be picking the fish off the bone while covered in sauce. They did this with their hands, which was even messier than using a fork. You may lose a little intensity preparing this dish with fillets, but eating it will be easier!

SERVES 4

¾ cup plus 1 tablespoon (200 ml) tahini

Juice of 2 to 3 lemons, or to taste

2 pounds 4 ounces (1 kg) white sea fish fillets

Vegetable oil for frying

3 large onions (about 600 g), peeled, thinly sliced into wedges

Sea salt

2 to 3 tablespoons Mediterranean pine nuts, toasted in a little butter until golden brown for garnish

1. Pour the tahini into a large mixing bowl. Add the lemon juice and start mixing it in. You will notice the tahini seizing up instead of diluting, but do not worry, it will eventually thin down and become creamy as you gradually add 1½ cups (375 ml) water. Keep stirring until you have a pale sauce that has the consistency of heavy cream. If you use less lemon juice, make up for the reduction in liquid by adding more water.

2. Pat the fish fillets dry with paper towels. Pour vegetable oil into a large nonstick frying pan to a depth of about ½ inch (1¼ cm) and place over medium heat. When the oil is hot—test by dipping a piece of bread into it; if the oil immediately bubbles around it, it is ready—slide the fish fillets in, skin-side down, and cook for a couple of minutes to crisp up the skin. Remove onto a plate and set aside.

3. Fry the onions, stirring regularly, in the same oil as the fish until soft and golden, 10 to 15 minutes. Remove with a slotted spoon and drop into the tahini sauce. Add salt to taste and mix well. Pour out whatever vegetable oil remains in the pan and wipe it clean. Add the tahini sauce and place over medium heat. Let the sauce bubble until it darkens slightly and a little oil rises to the surface—this is called *srijeh*. Then slip the fish fillets into the tahini and onion sauce, spooning a little sauce over the top to coat them evenly, and let bubble gently until the fish is just done. It won't be more than a few minutes depending on the thickness of your fillets. Serve warm or at room temperature, garnished with the toasted pine nuts.

HUDA'S FISH "RISOTTO"
HUDA'S SAYYADIYEH

Sayyadiyeh is one of our most festive fish dishes, and this version, which is my friend Huda Baroudi's, is particularly so, with its three different sauces and the addition of fennel, orange slices, and saffron to the fish. In the classic version, we finish cooking the fish with the rice, but Huda prefers to cook it separately to avoid overdoing it. I also prefer her way. In fact, I sometimes go one step further and roast a whole fish instead of using fillets, which she bakes en papillote. Huda also adds sautéed shrimp to the rice, but you can skip this step given how many elements there are to the dish. In her version, the rice is golden brown because it is cooked in a broth made with caramelized onions. However, most people in the south cook the rice with turmeric for a golden version. My mother's sayyadiyeh was also golden brown, but her version is a lot simpler. She also used short-grain rice, whereas Huda uses basmati, which makes for a fluffier rice. One thing is for sure, you will need a fair amount of time to prepare Huda's sayyadiyeh, so make sure to start well ahead of when you need to serve it.

SERVES 4 TO 6

Huda Baroudi's sayyadiyeh, with sauce and tomato salad, Beirut

FOR THE SAFFRON WATER

3 good pinches saffron threads

2/3 cup (160 ml) water

FOR THE CARAMELIZED ONIONS

1 cup (250 ml) extra virgin olive oil, plus extra for brushing the aluminum foil and sautéing the shrimp

7 large onions (about 1¼ kg), peeled, sliced into thin wedges

2½ cups (500 g) basmati rice

2 tablespoons (30 g) coarse sea salt

FOR THE FISH BROTH

¼ cup (60 ml) extra virgin olive oil

Fish heads and bones from the filleted sea bass

Shrimp heads and shells from the peeled shrimp

1 small onion (about 100 g), peeled

1 tablespoon ground turmeric

1½ teaspoons ground cumin

10 cardamom pods, slightly crushed

10 black peppercorns

1 cinnamon stick

Coarse sea salt

FOR THE TAJEN SAUCE

¾ cup (180 ml) tahini

Juice of 4 Seville oranges, squeezed by hand to avoid bitterness

Juice of 2 oranges (plus 4 if Seville oranges are not available)

Juice of 1 small grapefruit

Juice of 5 tangerines

Juice of 3 clementines

Juice of 1 lemon (if no Seville oranges)

Sea salt

¼ cup (60 ml) extra virgin olive oil

2 large onions (about 400 g), peeled, finely chopped

FOR THE PARSLEY TARATOR

Tarator (page 77)

A few sprigs parsley, washed, dried, most of the stalks discarded, finely chopped

FOR THE PINE NUT GARNISH

3 tablespoons (45 g) unsalted butter

⅓ cup (50 g) Mediterranean pine nuts

FOR THE FISH

2 fennel bulbs, trimmed, thinly sliced into wedges

2 oranges, quartered lengthwise, sliced into thin triangles

¼ cup (60 ml) extra virgin olive oil

Sea salt

Freshly ground black pepper

4 whole sea bass or 4 sea breams (each about 750 g), filleted, heads and bones reserved for the broth

FOR THE SHRIMP GARNISH

2 tablespoons (30 ml) extra virgin olive oil

8 large shrimp, peeled, heads and shells reserved for the broth

A little of the fish fennel garnish

---

1. To make the saffron water: Put the saffron and water in a small bowl and let infuse.

2. To make the caramelized onions: Put the olive oil and onions in a large frying pan and place over medium-high heat. As soon as the oil starts sizzling around the onions, reduce the heat to medium-low and fry the onions, stirring regularly, until dark brown but not burned, 45 minutes to 1 hour—the color is important, as they will eventually color the fish broth, which will give the rice a rich golden brown color. Transfer to a large pot and add 2 quarts (2 liters) water. Return to the heat and let bubble gently for 45 minutes, or until the broth is dark brown. Strain and set aside the broth, discarding the onions. Strain.

3. In a bowl, soak the rice in water at room temperature and stir in the coarse sea salt.

4. To make the fish broth: Put the olive oil, fish heads, bones, shrimp debris, and onion in a large pot. Add the turmeric, cumin, cardamom, peppercorns, and a little coarse sea salt and place over medium-high heat. Sauté for about 5 minutes, then add the strained onion broth. Bring to a boil. Reduce the heat to medium-low and let bubble gently for 45 minutes to 1 hour. Strain the broth. Let the fish debris cool a little, then take any meat off the heads and bones to later add to the rice. Measure 3 cups (750 ml) broth to cook the rice in and pour the rest into a saucepan to make one of the sauces. Place over medium heat and let bubble until reduced to a somewhat thick, dark sauce. Keep hot.

5. To make the tajen sauce: Put the tahini in a large mixing bowl and add the citrus juices—you should have at least 3 cups (750 ml). Mix well— you will notice the tahini thickening at first, but do not worry, it will start loosening as you keep stirring and incorporating more liquid. Add salt to taste and mix again. The sauce should have the consistency of heavy cream. Add more citrus juice if it's still too thick, but taste before to make sure it is not too tart, otherwise add water. Put the olive oil and chopped onions in a large saucepan and place over medium heat. Fry the onions, stirring every now and then, until soft and golden, about 10 to 15 minutes. Add a little water to the onions and, with the help of a handheld blender, liquidize them. Add the tahini sauce and bring to a boil, stirring constantly. Reduce the heat to medium-low and let bubble gently, stirring every now and then, until the color of the tahini darkens somewhat and you see a little oil rising to the surface, 25 to 30 minutes. Stir in ¼ cup (60 ml) saffron water, then take off the heat and keep hot.

6. To make the tarator: Prepare the tarator as indicated on page 77. Add the chopped parsley and mix well. Transfer to a serving bowl, cover, and set aside.

7. To make the pine nut garnish: Melt the butter in a small frying pan over medium heat. Add the pine nuts and sauté, stirring constantly, until golden brown. Remove with a slotted spoon onto several layers of paper towel to drain off the excess butter. Set aside.

8. Preheat the oven to 450°F (220°C).

9. To make the rice: Drain the rice and put it in a large pot. Add the reserved broth and loose fish meat and place over medium heat. As soon as the broth starts bubbling, reduce the heat to medium-low. Add ¼ cup (60 ml) saffron water and wrap the lid in a kitchen cloth. Cover the pot with the wrapped lid and simmer for 10 minutes. Take off the heat and let sit while you roast the fish.

10. To roast the fish: Put the fennel and orange slices in a bowl. Add the remaining saffron water and the olive oil. Season with salt and pepper to taste and mix well. Prepare 8 aluminum foil sheets to bake the fish fillets en papillote. Brush each with a little olive oil. Then lay a fish fillet over each sheet. Season with a little salt and pepper. Top with a little of

Top left: In the kitchen with Huda Baroudi; *Top right:* Arranging the fish fillets on the foil; *Bottom left:* Pouring a little saffron water on the fish fillets; *Bottom right:* The final dish with the rice for the sayyadiyeh and the sautéed shrimp

the fennel mixture. Loosely wrap the foil around the fish, leaving enough space at the top, and transfer to a baking sheet. Roast in the preheated oven for 10 to 12 minutes. Remove from the oven. Open up a little of the foil to release the steam and let rest while you sauté the shrimp.

11. To make the shrimp garnish: Put the olive oil in a medium frying pan. Add what remains of the fennel and orange mixture and place over medium-high heat. As soon as the oil starts sizzling around the fennel, shake the pan and cook for 3 to 5 minutes, until the fennel crisps up around the edges. Then add the shrimp and cook for 1 minute on each side. Take off the heat.

12. To serve: Open the aluminum foil papillotes and gently transfer the fish fillets and their garnish onto a serving platter. Transfer the rice onto another large platter. Arrange the shrimp all around the rice and garnish with the toasted pine nuts. Put the sauces in three separate sauceboats and serve immediately with the fish and the rice. Huda always serves a tomato salad with her sayyadiyeh.

SQUID IN INK SAUCE
HABBAR BIL-HIBR

A dish that you find with slight variations all around the Mediterranean. In Sicily, they slice the squid and use it as a pasta sauce, whereas we serve it as part of a mezze spread or as a light main course together with rice.

SERVES 4 TO 6

- ⅓ cup (80 ml) extra virgin olive oil
- 1 medium onion (about 150 g), peeled, thinly sliced into wedges
- 1 large garlic clove, peeled, minced into a fine paste
- 1 tablespoon double tomato concentrate
- 2 pounds 4 ounces (1 kg) squid, ink sacs removed and kept in a small bowl, rinsed under cold water, legs separated from body, cut into bite-sized dice
- 1 bay leaf
- Sea salt
- Freshly ground black pepper
- Juice of 1 lemon, or to taste
- 2 or 3 extra packs squid ink

1. Put the olive oil in a wide sauté pan. Add the onion and place over medium heat. As soon as the oil starts to sizzle around the onion, reduce the heat to medium-low and cook, stirring regularly, until soft and golden, 10 to 15 minutes. Add the minced garlic and cook, stirring, for a minute or so.

2. Add the squid and mix well. Barely cover with water and increase the heat back to medium. Add the bay leaf and season with salt and pepper to taste. Add the squid ink and bring to a boil. Let bubble for 5 minutes, then reduce the heat to medium-low and simmer for about 45 minutes, until the sauce has thickened and the squid is completely done. Let cool. Serve warm or at room temperature, with good crusty bread or with rice.

FISH BAKED IN SALT

Samak Meshwi bil-Melh

There was a wonderful seaside restaurant just past Jounieh called Chez Sami, where they baked fish in salt to perfection. Again, there is no need for a real recipe here. Just choose a beautiful sea bass, sea bream, or grouper weighing about 4 pounds 8 ounces (2 kg) to serve 4 to 6 people. Make a bed of coarse sea salt, mixed with a little water to make it stick together once baked, in a baking dish large enough to hold the fish. Lay the fish over the salt and cover with more salt mixed with a little water, packing it tightly over the fish—some mix the salt with egg white to make it stick. Bake in an oven preheated to 450°F (220°C) for 30 minutes. Let sit for a few minutes once out of the oven, then break the salt with a knife and push it away from the fish. Peel the skin off, lift the fillets, and serve with extra virgin olive oil and lemon juice or tarator (page 77).

I still remember when chicken was precious and reserved for Christmas or other celebratory meals, and of course large family gatherings where the atmosphere was always festive. We usually stuffed it with rice mixed with ground meat and toasted nuts and either poached or roasted it and served it with more rice on the side. We also grilled it, of course, to serve with what apparently is now the world's most popular sauce/dip, tüm, an amazing pure garlic "mayonnaise" that is an essential accompaniment to chicken, although we also eat it with fresh tomatoes or French fries.

We don't have a tradition of frying chicken like in other countries, but we are very keen on grilling it and eating all parts of it, from the wings to the liver and heart. As for the rest of the chicken to be grilled, we either dice it into fleshy cubes for shish tawü' (page 107) or butterfly it if it is small, such as poussins. We also serve it with moghrabiyeh (large couscous, page 233), mülükhiyeh (page 237), or frikeh (page 235).

It is now mostly mass farmed and, as a result, has become daily fare given how widely available it is. What is not so easily available is proper organic, free-range farm chicken because most of the production is in the hands of big companies, with the most famous being Hawa. Anyhow, I only buy organic chicken, and I suggest you do the same.

Moghrabiyeh sandwich in the making at Dabboussi, in the souks of Tripoli

SPICED LEBANESE "COUSCOUS"
MOGHRABIYEH

Moghrabiyeh means North African in Arabic, and I assume that these pasta-like balls are called this because they are basically the same as large-grain couscous, which in Morocco is called *m'hammssa*. You can buy moghrabiyeh fresh or dried and cook it pretty much like pasta. At Dabboussi, the famous moghrabiyeh specialist in Tripoli, whose stall is in the Ottoman souks, he serves it as a sandwich mixed with chickpeas and pearl onions and wrapped in pita; he also serves it on pita together with pickles for those who want to have it sitting down (he has a few tables at the back of his stall). Mr. Dabboussi himself is always at the front, manning a large griddle where he keeps the moghrabiyeh, pearl onions, and chickpeas hot. His is without meat. One day, when I was ordering my plate of moghrabiyeh, I asked if his was fresh and he explained that he makes it in a large factory outside the town. During Ramadan, he stops serving it in the stall because everyone is fasting during the day, and instead, he sells the steamed grain, together with the required amount of boiled onions, chickpeas, and spices, for people to take home and finish to their taste. His stall is heaving with buyers during that month, all wanting moghrabiyeh, a favorite for breaking the fast. The taste of fresh moghrabiyeh is different and finer than that of the dried. However, you can only buy it dried in the West, and often it is sold wrongly labeled as Israeli couscous, when it is not.

SERVES 4

FOR THE POUSSINS

2 poussins (about 1½ kg)

1 cheesecloth parcel in which you put a few cardamom pods, peppercorns, a cinnamon stick, and a couple of bay leaves

1 medium onion (about 150 g), peeled

Coarse sea salt

1. Put the poussins in a medium pot. Add 1½ quarts (1½ liters) water, together with the spice parcel and onion, and place over medium-high heat. Bring to a boil. Just as the water is about to bubble, skim the surface clean. Then add 1 tablespoon coarse sea salt. Reduce the heat to medium-low and let bubble gently for 30 minutes. Turn off the heat and let sit for 15 minutes, then carefully cut each poussin in half and cover with aluminum foil so as not to let them dry. Keep hot.

2. While the poussins are cooking, put some water in a medium pot and place over medium heat. Bring to a boil, then add salt as you would for pasta. Add the dried moghrabiyeh and let bubble for 10 minutes, stirring every now and then so it does not stick to the bottom of the pot. If you are using fresh moghrabiyeh, boil for 2 to 3 minutes. Drain and set aside.

FOR THE MOGHRABIYEH

2⅔ cups (400 g) moghrabiyeh

5 tablespoons (75 g) unsalted butter

2 tablespoons (30 ml) vegetable oil

3 medium onions (about 450 g), peeled, thinly sliced into wedges

1 tablespoon unbleached all-purpose flour

1½ to 2 cups (375 to 500 ml) strained poussin stock

1½ cups (250 g) cooked chickpeas

½ teaspoon ground cinnamon

2 teaspoons moghrabiyeh spice mixture

¼ teaspoon finely ground black pepper

Slivered pistachios for garnish

3. Put the butter in a deep, wide sauté pan and place over medium heat. When the butter has melted, add the oil and onions, and as soon as the fat starts sizzling around the onions, reduce the heat to medium-low and cook, stirring regularly, until soft and golden, 10 to 15 minutes. Stir in the flour, then the stock, and continue stirring until you have a thickish sauce. Add the moghrabiyeh and chickpeas together with the cinnamon, spice mixture, and pepper and carefully stir while letting the sauce bubble and thicken a little more. Let bubble, stirring every now and then, until the moghrabiyeh is done to your liking—I like it al dente—and the sauce is thick but not dry, a little like for a risotto. Transfer to a shallow bowl. Arrange the poussins over the moghrabiyeh. Garnish with slivered pistachios and serve hot.

CHICKEN WITH ROASTED GREEN WHEAT

DJEJ ALA FRIKEH

Frikeh is mostly produced in the south, where farmers harvest the wheat still green and roast it in the fields by setting fires to large bales of just-harvested wheat before threshing it to separate the chaff from the grain. They then dry it in the sun before coarsely cracking it. Some farmers leave the wheat whole, but I prefer it cracked because it takes less time to cook and the taste is smokier. Moussa Ibrahim, who has a wonderful spice and müneh shop in Dibbine, down south, that was recently bombed during the two-plus months of conflict between Hezbollah and Israel, invented a metal contraption that looks like a large cylindrical metal cage where he puts the just-harvested green wheat before rotating it over a fire. The machine both burns the grain and threshes it, allowing Moussa to produce more frikeh in the short time when the wheat is still green. Moussa then picks the charred wheat and lets it dry in the sun before cracking it. Frikeh has a delightful, addictive smoky flavor, and unlike bulgur wheat, it keeps a nice firm bite after cooking, perhaps because the wheat is not parboiled. You can find it in Middle Eastern grocery stores, either loose or prepacked. The greener it is, with slightly charred bits, the better it will be.

SERVES 4

- 1 medium free-range organic chicken (about 1½ kg)
- 1 medium onion (about 150 g), peeled
- 1 medium cinnamon stick
- 1 tablespoon coarse sea salt

FOR THE FRIKEH

- 2 tablespoons (30 g) unsalted butter
- Heaping 1 cup (200 g) frikeh
- ½ teaspoon ground cinnamon
- ½ teaspoon ground allspice
- ⅛ teaspoon finely ground black pepper
- Sea salt
- ⅓ cup (50 g) Mediterranean pine nuts, toasted in a little butter until golden brown, for garnish
- 2 cups (500 g) plain full-fat Greek-style yogurt to serve on the side

1. Put the chicken in a large pot. Add 2 quarts (2 liters) water and place over medium-high heat. Bring to a boil. Just as the water is about to bubble, skim the surface clean, then add the onion, cinnamon stick, and salt. Reduce the heat to medium-low, cover the pot, and let bubble gently for 45 minutes to 1 hour, until the chicken is done.

2. About 30 minutes before the chicken is ready, remove 2½ cups (625 ml) of the chicken stock for cooking the frikeh (the chicken will go on cooking with the stock left in the pot).

3. Put the butter in a medium pot and place over medium heat. When the butter has melted, add the frikeh and stir until well coated. Add the chicken stock. Season with the cinnamon, allspice, and pepper and bring to a boil. Taste for salt and add more if needed. Reduce the heat to low and simmer for 25 minutes, or a little longer, until the frikeh is done and the stock is fully absorbed—this cooking time is for cracked frikeh. Take off the heat, wrap the lid with a clean kitchen towel, and place it back on the pot. Let sit while you prepare the chicken.

4. Transfer the chicken onto a cutting board and cut into 8 pieces. You can keep the skin on, as I do, or remove it depending on your preference. Transfer the frikeh to a serving platter. Arrange the chicken pieces on top or all around. Scatter the toasted pine nuts all over and serve immediately, with yogurt on the side.

Hard at work in Moussa Ibrahim's mat'haneh in Dibbine

JEW'S MALLOW

MÜLÜKHIYEH

Mülükhiyeh (*Corchorus olitorius*) is a seasonal green that appears in markets and at greengrocers throughout the summer. The plant is native to Egypt and India, and it has large leaves with strange little whiskers where they join the stalk. For a long time, I had a particular aversion to it. It is still one of my least favorite dishes, which is odd given how everyone simply loves it and can't wait for it to be in season. Some make it with lamb, others with chicken, and some with both. Whether you prepare it with one kind of meat or both, it remains a composite dish made up of layers starting with toasted bread, then rice, then meat, all covered with mülükhiyeh. My mother would serve it with an onion and vinegar dressing on the side, but many prefer to keep it plain.

I still remember my young summer days, which I spent lazing at the St. George beach, where they had a very good restaurant with a daily plat du jour on the menu. Mülükhiyeh was their most popular dish, and on that day, the restaurant would quickly fill up with both beachgoers and those coming especially to eat it. I disliked the slimy texture of the green "soup," and while everyone tucked in, I stayed on my chaise longue by the pool, enjoying the emptiness around me and the sunshine of course. Later, my mother taught me how to get rid of most of the "slime" by first picking the leaves neatly off the stalk, just under the funny whiskers—the stem is where the slimy substance lurks—and by adding lemon juice to the broth just before dropping in the mülükhiyeh, then letting it boil for just a couple of minutes.

Mülükhiyeh was once considered an aphrodisiac, and as such, it was forbidden by the Fatimid ruler of Egypt, al-Hakim bi Amr Allah. He ruled for twenty-five years at the end of the tenth and the beginning of the eleventh centuries, and because the Druze view al-Hakim as an almost divine authority, they continue to observe the ban and most Druze do not eat it to this day.

SERVES 6 TO 8

1 medium free-range organic chicken (about 1½ kg)

2 medium onions (about 300 g), peeled

1 medium cinnamon stick

1 tablespoon coarse sea salt

2 medium pita breads, split open at the seam, toasted until golden brown, broken into bite-sized pieces

Plain rice or vermicelli rice (page 263)

FOR THE MÜLÜKHIYEH

7 ounces (200 g) fresh mülükhiyeh leaves (about 600 g on the stalk), or 3½ ounces (100 g) dried leaves, or 1 pound 2 ounces (½ kg) frozen

Just under 1 stick (100 g) unsalted butter

12 large cloves garlic, peeled, minced to a fine paste

1 bunch cilantro (200 g on the stalk), washed, dried, most of the stalks discarded, finely chopped

½ teaspoon ground coriander

Juice of 2 lemons, or to taste

½ teaspoon ground cinnamon

1 teaspoon ground allspice

½ teaspoon finely ground black pepper

Sea salt

FOR THE DRESSING

½ cup (125 ml) red wine vinegar

1 medium red onion (about 150 g), peeled, very finely chopped

1. Put the chicken in a large pot and add 2 quarts (2 liters) water. Place over medium-high heat and bring to a boil. As the water is about to start bubbling, skim the surface clean. Then add the onions, cinnamon stick, and salt to taste. Reduce the heat to medium and let bubble gently for 45 minutes to 1 hour, until the chicken is done.

2. If you are using dried mülükhiyeh: Crumble the leaves with your hands, discarding any stalks.

3. If you are using frozen mülükhiyeh: Take out of the freezer about an hour before you are ready to add it to the broth. The sauce made with dried leaves will taste different from that prepared with frozen, and both will be different, and not as good as with fresh leaves.

4. If you are using fresh mülükhiyeh: Pick the leaves cleanly off the stalks. Wash and spin dry in a salad spinner, then spread on clean kitchen towels to let dry completely, turning them over every now and then. You need to chop the leaves in very fine slivers, and the best way to do this is in small batches. Roll a handful of leaves together. Then hold down onto the cutting board, and with a razor-sharp knife, slice into 1/10-inch (1 to 2 mm) strips, basically a chiffonade. Put in a bowl and cover with a clean kitchen towel. Set aside—you can also drop the leaves whole into the stock as they do in the south, a good time-saving alternative and just as delicious.

5. Melt the butter in a large frying pan over medium heat. Add the minced garlic and cilantro together with the ground coriander and sauté for a minute or so, until the cilantro is wilted, without letting it brown. Take off the heat and set aside.

6. Take the boiled onions out of the chicken stock and mash into a purée. Add to the cilantro and garlic mixture.

7. Remove the chicken from the pot. Discard the cinnamon stick, then measure 1¼ quarts (1¼ liters) chicken stock and strain into a clean pot. Place over medium heat and bring to a boil. Add the lemon juice. Then drop in the chopped (or whole) mülükhiyeh and season with the cinnamon, pepper, and salt to taste. Bring back to a boil. Add the cilantro mixture. If you are using dried leaves, boil for 8 to 10 minutes, and only a couple of minutes if using fresh or frozen. In the case of the latter, time it only after it has come back to a boil. Do not boil any longer, otherwise the mülükhiyeh will sink in the broth instead of staying suspended in it.

8. Pour the vinegar into a small serving bowl. Add the chopped onion and set aside. Bone the chicken and tear the meat into bite-sized pieces. Transfer to a serving dish and keep hot.

9. Put the toasted bread in another serving dish, and the rice in another, and pour the mülükhiyeh into a soup tureen. Serve immediately.

10. The way to build your mülükhiyeh plate is to first spread a little toasted bread—soup plates are best here. Then spoon as much rice as you like over the bread and scatter a few pieces of chicken on top. Cover generously with mülükhiyeh and spoon as much of the onion and vinegar sauce as you prefer all over—you can leave it out, but it gives the dish a real kick. Eat with a spoon, making sure you scoop a little of each element in the same bite.

CHICKEN AND WHOLE WHEAT "PORRIDGE"

H'RISSEH ALA DJEJ

The history of this dish goes back to the times of the Abbasid Caliphs, who reigned for centuries over a large Muslim empire from Baghdad, their capital. The origins of h'risseh are reputed to go back to the sixth century, during the reign of the Persian king Khosrow. The Muslims discovered it when they conquered Persia, and as with tharid (page 72), it became a favorite of the Prophet's. You can make it with either chicken or lamb, and both Christians and Muslims prepare it to give out as an alms dish, to poor and rich alike. Christians make it in huge quantities on August 15 (the day of the assumption of the Virgin Mary) in front of their churches to distribute to the faithful, whereas Shia Muslims prepare it on Ashura, the tenth day of the month of Muharram, to mark the martyrdom of Hussein bin Ali, the Prophet's grandson. If you walk along the route of the Ashura commemorative march (*massirah* in Arabic), you will see huge pots of h'risseh cooking over wood or gas fire, ready to be given out to anyone wanting it.

Whether you make it with chicken or lamb, it is best to cook the meat on the bone, then take it out to bone it and return to the pot to finish cooking it with the grain. Both are then beaten until the mixture resembles a thick porridge. Cooking the meat on the bone may mean a little more work, but you will end up with a more flavorful dish.

SERVES 4

1 medium free-range organic chicken (about 1½ kg), or 1 small shoulder of lamb, skinned, trimmed of most fatty bits

2 cups (about 350 g) hulled wheat (or barley), soaked overnight

1 medium cinnamon stick

½ teaspoon ground allspice

¼ teaspoon finely ground white pepper

Sea salt

Just under 1 stick (100 g) unsalted butter

1. Put the chicken or lamb in a large pot. Add 2 quarts (2 liters) water and place over high heat. Bring to a boil, and as the water is about to start bubbling, skim the surface clean. Add the wheat together with the cinnamon stick and reduce the heat to medium-low. Cover the pot and let bubble gently for about 1 hour, until the meat is done.

2. Lift the meat and cinnamon stick out of the pot. Reduce the heat to low and let the wheat simmer while you are boning the meat. Discard the skin (if you are using a chicken) and shred the meat into small pieces. Return to the pot. Cover and continue simmering until the wheat is cooked, 20 to 30 more minutes, stirring regularly, so the mixture does not stick to the bottom of the pot. If you find it is too dry, add a little water, though not too much, as the end result should be like a thick-textured porridge.

3. Transfer the pot to your smallest burner and turn the heat to very low. Season with the allspice, white pepper, and salt to taste, then start beating the mixture with a heavy wooden spatula or spoon, cutting into the meat to break it into thin filaments. It needs to practically disintegrate into the wheat so you have a homogeneous textured thick porridge-like mixture. You can also use a handheld blender, but you'll need a fairly powerful one. Take off the heat and keep covered.

4. Put the butter in a small frying pan and place over medium heat. Cook until browned without letting it burn. Add to the h'risseh and mix well. Taste and adjust the seasoning if needed. Serve hot.

Stirring h'risseh during the massira of Ashura, Dahiyeh, Beirut

ROAST CHICKEN WITH RICE AND NUTS

DJEJ BIL-FURN MA REZZ WA MUKASSARAT

This was one of our most festive dishes, at a time when chickens were still considered precious. That said, we still prepare this dish for large family gatherings, special occasions, and even Christmas or Eid, depending on the communities. There are slight regional variations, but the dish is pretty universal. In Marja'yün, a charming southern town, they use roosters (also known as capons and often their own) because they are bigger than chickens and less dry than turkey. They also cook the stuffed chicken together with stuffed vegetables (page 198) or they roast it like in the recipe below. The same meat and nut rice is also served with roast lamb.

SERVES 4

Extra virgin olive oil

Sea salt

1 medium free-range organic chicken (about 1½ kg)

Ground allspice

2 tablespoons (30 ml) pomegranate molasses (optional)

FOR THE RICE

1½ cups (300 g) Egyptian, Calasparra, or bomba rice, soaked in cold water for 30 minutes

4 tablespoons (60 g) unsalted butter

½ cup (75 g) Mediterranean pine nuts

½ cup (75 g) blanched almonds

5 ounces (150 g) lean ground lamb

½ teaspoon ground cinnamon

½ teaspoon ground allspice

¼ teaspoon finely ground black pepper

Sea salt

1¾ cups (450 ml) chicken stock or water

2 cups (500 g) plain full-fat Greek-style yogurt to serve on the side

1. Preheat the oven to 450°F (220°C). Brush a baking dish with a little olive oil and add ⅓ cup (80 ml) water and a little salt.

2. To prepare the stuffing: Drain the rice and put it in a large mixing bowl. Melt the butter in a large saucepan over medium heat and sauté the pine nuts, stirring constantly, until golden brown. Remove the pine nuts with a slotted spoon onto a double layer of paper towel. Sauté the almonds in the same butter, also until golden brown, and remove onto paper towels. Cook the meat in the same butter until it loses all traces of pink, breaking up any lumps. Add to the rice and mix well. Add three-quarters of the toasted nuts, the cinnamon, allspice, pepper, and salt to taste and mix again until all the ingredients are well blended.

3. Rub the chicken with allspice and half fill with the rice mixture. Place in the baking dish and roast for about 1 hour, until the chicken is golden all over and done. Start basting the chicken after the first 20 minutes with

the water in the dish, and continue to do so at 20-minute intervals, adding a little water if it's drying up. This should keep the chicken moist and give you a light sauce to serve with the rice. Fifteen minutes before the chicken is ready, dilute the pomegranate molasses (if you are using it) with a little water and add to the basting juices to give the sauce an intriguing sweet and sour flavor.

4. Halfway through roasting the chicken, start cooking the remaining rice stuffing. Put it in a medium pot and add one and half times the volume in water. Add more salt if needed and place over medium heat. Bring to a boil, then reduce the heat to low and cover the pot. Simmer for 10 to 15 minutes, until the liquid is absorbed and the rice is done. Wrap the lid with a clean kitchen towel and cover the pot. Let sit until the chicken is ready.

5. Take the chicken out of the oven and let sit for 5 to 10 minutes, then transfer to a large serving platter—you will carve it at the table and serve the meat with a little of the stuffing and a little of the cooked rice, which you will be serving on another platter, garnished with the reserved nuts. Serve immediately with yogurt on the side.

OFFAL

FRIED CHICKEN LIVERS

ASBETT DJEJ ME'LIYEH

A classic that you can season with either garlic and lemon juice or pomegranate molasses diluted in a little water. I like both versions but always make sure to cook the livers until just pink so they don't become rubbery. The preparation is simple and quick, and they are lovely served on their own, to eat with pita bread, or piled over a bed of seasoned salad leaves. At Em Sherif Deli in Beirut, they use mar'ü' bread to make mini wraps filled with deliciously tender chicken livers. The recipe below is for the garlic and lemon juice version. If you like the idea of pomegranate molasses, dilute 1 to 2 tablespoons molasses with a little water and deglaze the pan as you would with the garlic/lemon juice mixture.

SERVES 4

3 tablespoons (45 ml) extra virgin olive oil

1 pound 2 ounces (500 g) chicken livers, preferably from free-range organic chickens

½ teaspoon ground allspice

¼ teaspoon finely ground black pepper

Sea salt

3 cloves garlic, peeled, minced to a fine paste

Juice of 1 lemon, or to taste

1 tablespoon finely chopped cilantro or flat-leaf parsley for garnish

Put the olive oil in a large frying pan and place over medium heat. Check if the oil is hot by dipping a piece of bread in it; if the oil immediately sizzles around it, it is ready. Arrange the chicken livers in the pan in an even layer and cook for 2 to 3 minutes. Turn over and cook for another couple of minutes, until done to your liking. Season with the allspice, pepper, and salt to taste, then add the minced garlic and lemon juice. Shake the pan for a minute or so to emulsify the sauce. Take off the heat. Garnish with the chopped cilantro or parsley and serve immediately with good bread.

RAW LAMB'S LIVER

Asbeh Sawdah Nayeh

Raw lamb's liver is one of our great delicacies, and it is often served for breakfast, especially in the mountains for large family gatherings or honored guests. The liver needs to be extremely fresh, practically warm out of a freshly slaughtered lamb, which may horrify some, but it is definitely worth a try, even if the taste is slightly gamy. We eat it wrapped in pita with fresh mint, seasoned with a selection of different spices neatly arranged in tiny piles on a dish alongside the liver. The liver is cut into bite-sized pieces and served with tiny pieces of raw fat from the sheep's tail (*liyeh*).

You make the bites by first laying one or two mint leaves on a torn piece of pita, then the liver, which you pick up with a fork and dip in salt then each of the spices on the plate. You then nestle a tiny piece of tail fat against the liver before wrapping the bread over them and popping the luscious bite into your mouth. I don't really remember when I started eating raw liver, but it had to be from when I first could chew, given that Lebanese children eat the same foods as adults. When we were children, my mother or grandmother made us the bites. Until my beautiful mother left us, I used to ask her to make me the raw liver bites when we went to my favorite restaurant, Al'at el-Rümiyeh, not far from where she lived in Ballouneh. The restaurant owners rear and slaughter their own lambs, and as a result, the liver there is always very fresh, as are all their nayeh (raw) dishes. They serve the liver diced into small cubes surrounded with the freshest mint with the ground spices (cinnamon, allspice, seven-spice mixture, cayenne pepper, black pepper, sumac, and salt) arranged in neat little piles on a plate next to it. Because we often went there just the two of us, we never finished the liver, so my mother would take it home to sauté the next day in a little butter before deglazing the pan with a little pomegranate molasses. There is no need for a recipe either way, especially because I doubt you can find very fresh lamb's liver in the West to safely have it raw. If you are keen to taste it, you will need to wait until you get to a country where you know it will come from a freshly slaughtered sheep, and preferably a fat tail one.

LAMB'S SWEETBREADS

H'LEYWAT GHANAM

A favorite of my mother's, which she always ordered when we went out to eat. Sweetbreads have a very delicate texture, and when grilled, they get crisp on the outside but remain creamy on the inside, which makes them supremely moreish. They are the glands that form around the neck and heart of an animal, and the older the animal is, the fatter they get, which makes them ideal for threading onto skewers and grilling. However, you need to be careful not to overcook them, because they will quickly turn rubbery. I always soak them in several changes of water before cooking to get rid of any excess blood. Then I blanch them before grilling over a very hot fire to get charred bits on the outside without overcooking the inside.

SERVES 4 TO 6

Sea salt

1 pound 7 ounces (600 g) lamb's sweetbreads, soaked in several changes of cold water to get rid of any excess blood, cut into bite-sized chunks

Freshly ground black pepper

Melted butter to brush the sweetbreads while grilling

Lemon wedges to serve on the side for those wanting to squeeze a little over the sweetbreads

1. Prepare a charcoal fire about half an hour before you are ready to grill; or preheat your broiler to maximum.

2. Bring a large pot of water to a boil. Add salt like you would with pasta. Drain the sweetbreads and drop into the boiling water. Blanch for a couple of minutes. Drain and spread on paper towels to dry them.

3. Season the sweetbreads with salt and pepper to taste and thread equally onto 6 skewers. Grill for a couple of minutes on each side, until just done—brush with melted butter as they are grilling. I personally like them just underdone so as not to lose the melting texture, but if you like your meat completely done, leave on the fire for 1 to 2 minutes longer. Serve immediately with the lemon wedges.

SHEEP'S TESTICLES
BEYD GHANAM

The idea of eating sheep's testicles may put off some, but I can assure you that they are exquisite and considered a delicacy throughout the country. The thick skin coating them needs to be peeled off, but your butcher will do this before cutting them into bite-sized chunks—I prefer to quarter them lengthwise so I can better control the cooking time. The classic way to prepare these is to sauté them in butter before deglazing the pan with lemon juice mixed with minced garlic, but you can also grill them like with sweetbreads (page 248). I often omit the garlic for a more subtle flavor and only ever have them grilled in a restaurant, because they have charcoal grills and I don't. I also make a point to ask that they do not overcook them, as the texture is very delicate and can be ruined if overdone.

SERVES 4 TO 6

2 to 3 tablespoons (30 to 45 g) unsalted butter

4 sheep's testicles, peeled, each cut lengthwise into 4 wedges, or cut into bite-sized chunks

Sea salt

2 cloves garlic, peeled, minced to a fine paste

Juice of ½ lemon, or to taste

Melt the butter in a large frying pan over medium heat. When the butter is melted and starts foaming, add the testicles. Season with salt to taste and fry for a couple of minutes on each side, or until slightly crisp and golden. While the testicles are cooking, mix the garlic with the lemon juice. Add at the very end and shake the pan for a minute or so to emulsify with the butter. Serve hot with pita bread.

STUFFED TRIPE AND INTESTINES

GHAMMEH

I like to think that making this elaborate dish is a little like dressmaking. You need the same tools of the trade: scissors, thread, and a needle. I had never cooked it before I prepared it for a blog post several years ago, but I had watched my mother make it many times and I just followed what she did from memory. I cut up the tripe the same way, in good-sized well-shaped pieces that were neither too small nor too large so I could have nice, manageable parcels once the tripe was stuffed and cooked. Mine were a little smaller than my mother's, but it may be because sheep in England are slaughtered at a younger age than in the home country. It is also easier to source intestines there. Also, all the butchers there know how to clean both the tripe and intestines so that you buy them relatively clean. You still need to wash them again at home, in several changes of lightly soapy water, before rinsing well to get rid of the gamy taste. The recipe here is for both tripe and intestines. If you can't find the latter, either halve the quantities for the stuffing and use one stomach or keep as is and prepare two tripes. We add trotters to the cooking broth to make it richer, so ask your butcher to get you some and singe them before cleaning well to get rid of any remaining hairy bits.

SERVES 6 TO 8

FOR THE STUFFING

1 cup (200 g) dried chickpeas, soaked overnight in plenty of cold water with ½ teaspoon baking soda, plus 1 teaspoon baking soda to rub the chickpeas

2¼ cups (450 g) Egyptian, Calasparra, or bomba rice

2 (14-ounce/400 g) cans peeled Italian tomatoes, drained, coarsely chopped

3 medium onions (about 450 g), peeled, very finely chopped

1 pound 2 ounces (500 g) lean ground lamb

2 teaspoons seven-spice mixture (or allspice)

½ teaspoon finely ground black pepper

½ teaspoon ground cinnamon

Sea salt

TO FINISH

4 trotters, singed, washed

1 medium cinnamon stick

1 sheep's tripe, washed, rinsed, cut into pieces half the size of a letter-size paper (you should have 6 to 7 pieces)

1 full intestine, stripped of part of its fat, washed the same way as the tripe, left whole

FOR THE BROTH TO SERVE ON THE SIDE

1 whole head garlic, peeled, minced to a fine paste

Juice of 2 lemons, or to taste

Stuffed intestines at Sumy Hokayem's

1. Drain and rinse the chickpeas, then rub with the baking soda. Let sit for 15 to 20 minutes, then rinse well under cold water. The purpose of this operation is to soften the chickpeas further and as a result shorten their cooking time.

2. Rinse the rice under cold water, drain, and put in a large mixing bowl. Add the tomatoes, onions, lamb, seven-spice, black pepper, cinnamon, and salt to taste and mix well. Taste—if you don't like tasting raw meat, cook a little in a small pan—and adjust the seasoning if needed.

3. Put the trotters in a large pot. Cover well with water and place over medium-high heat. As the water is about to come to a boil, skim the surface clean, then add the cinnamon stick. Cover and cook for 1 to 1½ hours.

4. Fold the pieces of tripe, keeping the smooth side inside, and sew one and a half sides of each to create pouches. Fill these with the stuffing, making sure they are only three-quarters full. The rice will expand during cooking, and you need to leave enough space for it to fill the pouches without bursting the seams. Sew the open ends shut and set aside.

5. Now start filling the intestine. This is quite fiddly, especially when you get to the thin end.

6. Take one end of the intestine and invert a short length. Push a little stuffing into it with your finger. As you are doing this, more of the intestine will pull up for you to fill. Again, you want to fill the intestine loosely to allow space for the rice to expand. Tie each end of the intestine securely with a thread and rinse again—if you have a meat grinder with a sausage-making attachment, you can use it to fill the intestines, using the wide funnel because of the chickpeas.

7. Add the stuffed tripe and intestines to the trotters. Add more water to cover if needed. Season with salt and put the lid back on. Cook for 2 to 2½ hours, until tender. Serve very hot with some of the broth on the side which you will have seasoned with the minced garlic and lemon juice.

BRAISED SPLEEN

T'HAL

This is one of my all-time favorites. Before my late mother reached the venerable age of ninety, I used to give her a list of dishes to prepare for me whenever I visited, and t'hal was always on that list, as was ghammeh (page 250). Sadly she is no longer with us and it is now my turn to prepare this dish, having written down all her recipes in my first book. I also used to often surprise her with recipes she was not familiar with. Anyhow, the texture of spleen is incredibly soft and melting, and the taste of the thick, dark tart sauce is so moreish that my mouth waters just thinking of it.

SERVES 4 TO 6

2 heads garlic (about 18 to 20 cloves), peeled, minced to a fine paste

½ bunch cilantro (about 100 g on the stalk), washed, dried, most of the stalks discarded, finely chopped

1 teaspoon ground coriander

⅛ teaspoon cayenne pepper

Sea salt

1 cow's spleen

3 tablespoons (45 ml) extra virgin olive oil

½ teaspoon seven-spice mixture (page 19)

Scant ¼ teaspoon ground cinnamon

⅓ cup (80 ml) red wine vinegar

⅓ cup (80 ml) lemon juice

1. Mix the minced garlic and chopped cilantro in a medium mixing bowl. Add the ground coriander, cayenne, and salt to taste. Mix well and set aside.

2. Remove any loose skin or fat from the spleen and cut across in two equal pieces. Slide your knife inside the flesh, at the thickest part of the spleen, and make long slits. Fill these with as much garlic/cilantro mixture as you can, using your finger to push it in.

3. Put the olive oil in a large pot and place over medium-high heat. When the oil is hot—test by dipping a piece of bread; if the oil immediately bubbles around it, it is ready—add the spleen and brown on both sides for a total of 15 minutes, or until crisp and browned all over.

4. Add the seven-spice mixture, cinnamon, and salt to taste together with half the vinegar and half the lemon juice. Reduce the heat to medium-low, cover the pot, and simmer for a few minutes. As the sauce reduces and thickens, add more lemon juice and vinegar, a little at a time, until you have used up both, turning the spleen regularly. This should take 15 to 20 minutes.

5. Reduce the heat to very low and simmer for another 20 to 30 minutes, checking on the sauce to make sure it is not becoming too dry. If it is, add a little water, although not too much, as you want a very concentrated sauce. Take off the heat. Let cool to serve warm or at room temperature.

LAMB'S TONGUE SALAD
SALATET LSENET

I can never bite into a lamb's tongue without feeling for a short, surreal moment as if I am biting into a human tongue. Human and lamb tongues are more or less the same size, and the texture of the skin is fairly similar, perhaps a little coarser, not that I can tell from experience. Still, this sensation has never put me off eating tongue, both lamb's and ox, and I hope you will enjoy this salad as much as we do in the home country.

SERVES 4 TO 6

8 lamb's tongues (about 750 g)

Half the peel of 1 lemon

1 medium cinnamon stick

1½ teaspoons sea salt

A few gem lettuce leaves to make a bed for the tongues

A few sprigs flat-leaf parsley, washed, dried, most of the stalks discarded, finely chopped

FOR THE DRESSING

1 or 2 cloves garlic, peeled, minced to a fine paste

Juice of 1 lemon, or to taste

⅓ cup (80 ml) extra virgin olive oil

Sea salt

1. Put the tongues to soak for a couple of hours in several changes of cold water to get rid of any excess blood. Drain and rinse well. Put in a large pot. Cover with water (about 3 cups/750 ml) and place over medium-high heat. As the water is about to boil, skim the surface clean. Add the lemon peel, cinnamon stick, and salt. Reduce the heat to medium-low and let bubble gently for 1½ hours, or until the tongues are tender.

2. While the tongues are cooking, prepare the dressing by mixing the garlic, lemon juice, olive oil, and salt to taste in a small mixing bowl.

3. When the tongues are done, leave them in the broth until cool enough to handle. Then take them out, one by one, pat dry with paper towels, and peel and trim off any excess fat. Cut in half lengthwise. Arrange the lettuce leaves on a serving platter, then arrange the tongue halves, cut-side up, over the lettuce. Drizzle the dressing all over. Scatter the chopped parsley all over. Serve immediately as part of a mezze spread or light main course.

OX TONGUE STEW

ROSTO

I always thought that this dish had its inspiration in French cooking; and when I looked up the classic French recipe, my suspicion grew stronger. It must have been during the French protectorate that the Lebanese came across French ox tongue in tomato sauce and, given their taste for all things foreign, they must have adopted it, tweaking it to make it their own by adding allspice, cinnamon, and black pepper. Then they must have skipped fresh tomatoes in favor of tomato paste; and, finally, they replaced the cornichons and capers with potatoes and garlic to produce a spicier, headier sauce. All this is rather convoluted conjecture, of course, but it makes for a fairly credible story.

SERVES 6 TO 8

1 ox tongue (about 1¼ kg)

2 medium cinnamon sticks

3 medium onions (about 450 g), 1 left whole, the other 2 quartered

Sea salt

¼ teaspoon ground cinnamon

2 teaspoons seven-spice mixture (page 19)

½ teaspoon finely ground black pepper

20 cloves garlic, peeled

4 tablespoons (60 g) unsalted butter

2 tablespoons (30 ml) sunflower oil

1 (5-ounce/150 g) can tomato paste

3 pounds 6 ounces (1½ kg) medium potatoes, peeled, quartered

1. Soak the ox tongue for a couple of hours in several changes of cold water to get rid of any excess blood. Drain and rinse well. Put in a large pot. Add 1 cinnamon stick, the whole onion, and a little salt. Place over medium heat and bring to a boil. As the water is about to boil, skim the surface clean. Then reduce the heat to medium-low and let bubble gently for 1 hour. Remove the tongue and peel off the thick skin while still hot. If you wait, the skin will not come off so easily.

2. Make 10 slits all over the tongue. Then mix the ground cinnamon, seven-spice, and pepper with a little salt to taste. Dip half the garlic into the spice mixture and insert into the slits.

3. Put the butter and oil in a large pot and place over medium-high heat. Add the peeled tongue and brown on all sides. Remove onto a plate. Add the quartered onions and garlic to the pan. Sauté for 10 to 15 minutes, until softened and lightly golden. Return the tongue to the pot and strain enough broth over it to cover.

4. Add the other cinnamon stick and salt to taste and let bubble for 1 hour. Remove the cinnamon stick and add the tomato paste together with the potatoes and what remains of the spices. Reduce the heat to medium and let bubble fairly gently for another 20 minutes, or until the potatoes are done and the sauce has thickened. Serve very hot with plain rice or just good crusty bread.

GRAINS AND LEGUMES

If bread is our main staple, grains and legumes are next. There is hardly a meal without one or the other. Bulgur wheat is the preferred grain of rural communities of all confessions; in the old days, many rural folk grew their own wheat to make their bulgur wheat. They harvested, threshed, and parboiled the wheat before drying it in the sun and sending it to the local mill to be ground into fine and coarse grades to last the household until the next harvest.

As for legumes, chickpeas rule the roost. Lentils are also very popular, as are beans. They are often combined with fresh vegetables in delightful vegetarian or even vegan dishes. I could have actually devoted this whole book to grains and legumes recipes given the many variations I have come across. Instead, I have chosen to include the most interesting ones together with classics.

Sumy's müjaddarat fassüliah

CRANBERRY BEANS AND BULGUR WHEAT "RISOTTO"

MÜJADDARAT FASSÜLIAH

I lived in Lebanon for twenty-one years before leaving for London. Since then, I have been going back regularly for the last fifty-plus years, but it is only when I started researching this book that I discovered this delectable version of müjaddarah, made with Vermont cranberry beans instead of lentils and left very moist, a little like Italian risotto. It takes its brown color from the caramelized onions, and it is only found in the north where the beans are grown. Sumy Hokayem and her brother Gaby Daher, who introduced me to the dish, told me that it is not so easy to buy the small reddish beans, as they are grown and sold only in the north. Fortunately, I had no problem sourcing Vermont cranberry beans in London when I tested the recipe, which is Sumy's, although those grown in Lebanon are smaller in size. Müjaddarah is often served with raw onion on the side because the crunch and slight heat of the onion is a perfect counterpoint to the soft, mellow müjaddarah.

SERVES 4 TO 6

½ cup (125 ml) extra virgin olive oil, plus extra for serving

3 large onions (about 600 g), peeled, thinly sliced into wedges

2 cups (400 g) Vermont cranberry beans, soaked overnight in plenty of water—they will rehydrate more than double in size

1 cup (175 g) coarse bulgur wheat

Sea salt

Freshly ground black pepper

A couple quartered raw onions, soaked in cold water, to serve on the side

1. Put the olive oil and onions in a pot that is large enough to eventually hold both the beans and bulgur wheat and place over medium-high heat. As soon as the oil starts sizzling around the onions, lower the heat to medium-low and cook, stirring regularly, until golden brown, 25 to 30 minutes. Do not let the onions burn. They have a tendency to quickly turn from golden brown to burned, so watch them carefully toward the end.

2. Drain the beans and add to the caramelized onions. Add 1½ quarts (1½ liters) water and place over medium-high heat. Bring to a boil, then lower the heat to medium-low and let bubble gently for 40 minutes.

3. When the beans are ready, add the bulgur wheat. Season with salt and pepper to taste and let bubble for another 20 minutes, or until both beans and bulgur wheat are done but the mixture is still very moist, a little like risotto. If you think it is too dry, add a little boiling water, and if it's too wet, increase the heat and let bubble more strongly to allow the excess liquid to evaporate. Serve hot or warm, drizzled with very good extra virgin olive oil, pita bread, and the raw onions.

RED MÜJADDARAH

MÜJADDARAH HAMRA

This müjaddarah is described as red not because it is made with red lentils but rather because the onions are fried until dark brown, but not burned, in order to color the liquid in which the lentils and bulgur wheat are cooked. This recipe is from the south, and in particular from Deir Intar, a village that is famous for it.

SERVES 4 TO 6

3 cups (525 g) dried brown lentils, soaked in plenty of cold water for 30 minutes

¾ cup (180 ml) extra virgin olive oil

3 large onions (about 600 g), peeled, finely chopped

Just over 1 cup (200 g) coarse bulgur wheat

Sea salt

1. Drain the lentils and put them in a medium pot. Add 1½ quarts (1½ liters) water and place over medium heat. Bring to a boil, then reduce the heat to medium-low and let bubble gently for 20 minutes.

2. While the lentils are cooking, put the olive oil and chopped onions in a large frying pan and place over medium heat. As soon as the oil starts sizzling around the onions, reduce the heat to medium-low and cook, stirring regularly, until the onions have turned dark brown, 35 to 45 minutes—be sure not to let them burn, which they will do very quickly in the end if you don't watch them carefully.

3. Add the bulgur wheat to the lentils together with the onions and their oil. Mix well and season with salt to taste. Cook for another 15 minutes, or until the liquid is fully absorbed and the lentils are cooked through. Serve hot, warm, or at room temperature.

SILKY MÜJADDARAH

MÜJADDARAH M'SAFFAYEH

Also known as *bahriyah* (meaning "maritime") in the south, this version of müjaddarah is a typical Friday Lenten meal for Christians. M'saffayeh means "drained" in Arabic, and it is called thus because it is practically a purée, although not as smooth—the lentils are processed before the rice and fried onions are added. It is traditionally served at room temperature alongside a cabbage salad, trimmed raw onions, and pita bread. In the south, people prefer to flavor müjaddarah with cumin rather than cinnamon. Besides being a typical vegetarian meal, it is also one that housewives prepare when they do a deep spring clean, removing the carpets to bare the cool tiled floors for the hot summer months. They prepare the müjaddarah early in the morning and let it cool while they carry out their chores, one of which is draping the carpets over the balcony railings and beating them with a bamboo carpet beater. I remember it as a really fun time with neighbors talking to each other across balconies while beating the dust out of their Persian rugs.

SERVES 4

1 cup (200 g) dried brown lentils, rinsed and soaked in cold water for 30 minutes

⅓ cup (80 ml) extra virgin olive oil

2 medium onions (about 300 g), peeled, thinly sliced into wedges

⅛ cup (25 g) short-grain white rice

½ teaspoon ground cinnamon

½ teaspoon ground allspice

¼ teaspoon finely ground black pepper

Sea salt

1. Put the lentils in a pot and add 2 quarts (2 liters) water. Place over medium heat and bring to a boil. Give the lentils a good stir, then reduce the heat to medium-low and let bubble gently for about 1 hour, until the lentils are very tender and the water is reduced by two-thirds.

2. Put the olive oil and onions in a large frying pan and place over medium heat. When the oil starts sizzling around the onions, reduce the heat to medium-low and cook, stirring regularly, until soft and transparent, 10 to 15 minutes. Remove half the onions with a slotted spoon and reserve on a plate. Continue cooking the rest, stirring regularly, until they caramelize and turn a rich golden brown—be careful not to let them burn. Remove with a slotted spoon onto a sieve and shake every now and then to get rid of any excess oil and keep them crisp. Reserve the oil.

3. Rinse the rice under cold water. Drain and set aside.

4. When the lentils are done, use a handheld blender to purée them. Add the soft onions and their frying oil together with the rice. Season with the cinnamon, allspice, pepper, and salt to taste and simmer uncovered for about 20 minutes, stirring regularly, until the rice is completely done and the mixture has thickened, without it drying out. Taste and adjust the seasoning if needed, and immediately pour into a shallow serving bowl or individual soup plates. Let cool, then scatter the caramelized onions all over. Serve at room temperature with your choice of salad.

LENTIL "RISOTTO"
MÜDARDARAH

Müdardarah is basically a dry müjaddarah, with the rice and lentils staying separate and fluffy, a little like a pilaf. You can make it with coarse bulgur wheat like they do in the south, in which case, you may need to add a little more water—coarse bulgur wheat absorbs a little more liquid than rice.

SERVES 4 TO 6

⅔ cup (160 ml) extra virgin olive oil

3 medium onions (about 450 g), peeled, thinly sliced into wedges

¾ cup (150 g) dried brown lentils, soaked in cold water for 30 minutes

¾ cup (150 g) Egyptian, Calasparra, or bomba rice

½ teaspoon ground cinnamon

½ teaspoon ground allspice (or seven-spice mixture, page 19)

½ teaspoon finely ground black pepper

Sea salt

1. Put the olive oil and onions in a large frying pan and place over medium heat. When the oil starts sizzling around the onions, reduce the heat to medium-low and cook, stirring regularly, until they turn a rich golden brown, 25 to 30 minutes—be careful not to let them burn. With a slotted spoon, remove three-quarters of the onions into a sieve and shake every now and then to drain any excess oil and keep them crisp—you will use the crisp onions for garnish and add the remaining ones to the müdardarah. Set aside.

2. Drain and rinse the lentils. Put in a medium pot and add 3 cups (750 ml) water. Place the pot over medium heat and bring to a boil. Then reduce the heat to medium-low, give the lentils a good stir, and cover the pot. Let bubble gently for 15 minutes, or until the lentils are nearly done.

3. Rinse the rice under cold water and add to the lentils. Season with the cinnamon, allspice, pepper, and salt to taste and bring back to a boil. Add the onions left in the pan together with their oil. Cover and simmer for another 10 to 15 minutes. Turn off the heat. Wrap the lid with a clean kitchen towel and put back over the pot. Let sit for 10 minutes. Then carefully stir the lentils and rice to fluff them up. Transfer to a serving platter. Scatter the caramelized onions all over the top and serve hot or warm.

VERMICELLI RICE

REZZ BIL-SH'AYRIYEH

A slight variation on plain rice, here vermicelli is toasted and cooked with the rice. This version is normally served with meats cooked in yogurt or tahini sauce, but I like to also serve it with dawüd basha. To make it plain rice, simply omit the vermicelli and prepare as below.

SERVES 6

2 tablespoons (30 g) unsalted butter

2 to 3 tablespoons (30 g) vermicelli, broken into approx. 1-inch- (2½ cm) long pieces

1 cup (200 g) bomba or Calasparra rice

Sea salt

1. Rinse the rice in several changes of cold water, drain, and set aside.

2. Melt the butter in a saucepan over medium heat. Add the vermicelli and cook, stirring constantly, until the vermicelli is golden brown—it needs to be very dark, although not burned, so that it doesn't lose its color while cooking with the rice. Add the rice and mix well.

3. Add 1⅔ cups (410 ml) water and salt to taste. Bring to a boil. Then reduce the heat to low, cover the pan, and simmer for 15 minutes, or until the rice is cooked through and the water is absorbed. Wrap the lid with a clean kitchen towel. Replace over the pan and let sit for 5 minutes. Serve hot.

Lunch with friends at Jnaynit al-Khawaja in Beirut, going clockwise from the empty chair: Gaby Daher, Hania Rayess Boustani, who was hosting, Mona Ahdab, Christophe Gollut, Carole Ghosn, Huda Baroudi; to my left: Renata Zeidan, Denise Makari Safa, and Misbah Ahdab; and Dalis Khamissy behind the camera!

FALAFEL

The most important tip I can give you to produce falafel that are perfectly crisp on the outside and moist and fluffy on the inside is to grind the legumes in a meat grinder and not a food processor. I learned this from my friend Mohammed Antabli, once the chef/owner of Al Waha restaurant in London, which was my favorite place for Lebanese food when he still had it. I used to process my legumes in a food processor, but he used a meat grinder for a lighter, slightly textured fritter. In Lebanon, most falafel makers use a mixture of dried chickpeas and peeled fava beans. I use only chickpeas. Both versions are good, but the latter is crisper on the outside and fluffier inside. You can shape falafel by hand as instructed below or you can use a special mold, which has a spring platelet that ejects the molded falafel into the hot oil. And if you are planning to make sandwiches instead of serving the falafel as part of a mezze spread, use medium-sized pita (I like to use one layer, but the norm is to use two, one on top of the other, rough side up—the pita we use is much thinner than the supermarket ones in the West, and we split it in two layers and put one over the other before wrapping around the filling), and make sure to have parsley, tomatoes, and pickles on hand. Arrange the falafel down the middle of the rough side of the pita, slightly flattening them, then line as much of the salad and pickle garnish as you want before drizzling tarator all over. Wrap the bread tightly around the whole, half wrap with a table napkin, and serve immediately.

SERVES 4 TO 6

- Just under 2 cups (300 g) dried chickpeas, soaked overnight in plenty of water with 1 teaspoon baking soda
- 5 large cloves garlic, peeled, minced to a fine paste
- 1 small onion (about 100 g), peeled, grated over the fine part of the grater
- ¼ bunch cilantro (50 g on the stalk), washed, dried, most of the bottom stalks discarded, very finely chopped
- 1 teaspoon ground cumin
- 1 teaspoon ground allspice (or seven-spice mixture)
- ¼ teaspoon finely ground black pepper
- ⅛ teaspoon cayenne pepper
- Sea salt
- ½ teaspoon baking soda
- Vegetable oil for frying the falafels

1. Drain and rinse the chickpeas. Mince in a meat grinder through the fine disk. Transfer to a large mixing bowl. Add the garlic, onion, and cilantro and mix well.

2. If you don't have a meat grinder, process in a food processor together with the garlic, onion, and cilantro until you have a medium-fine paste. Transfer the mixture to a bowl.

3. Add the cumin, allspice, black pepper, cayenne, and salt to taste and mix well. Taste and adjust the seasoning if needed. Add the baking soda and mix again. Cover and let rest in the refrigerator for about 30 minutes.

4. Pinch off a little falafel mixture and shape it between the palms of your hands into a small ball, just under the size of a golf ball. Flatten it slightly, place on a plate, and continue making the falafel balls until you have used up all the mixture. You should end up with 20 to 25 falafels.

5. Pour enough vegetable oil in a large, deep frying pan to deep-fry the falafel and place over medium heat. When the oil is hot—dip in a piece of bread; if the oil immediately bubbles around it, it is ready—drop as many balls as will fit comfortably. Fry for 3 to 4 minutes, stirring every now and then, until golden brown and crisp all over. Remove with a slotted spoon onto several layers of paper towel or a wire rack to drain off the excess oil. Serve hot or warm with tarator (page 77), or make into a sandwich as described above.

Just fried falafel in Beirut

GREEN BULGUR WHEAT "RISOTTO"

MAFRÜKEH

Another interesting dish from Deir Intar, down south, where the bulgur wheat is cooked with greens and a tomato sauce. Again, I had never come across it before, having only had bulgur wheat cooked in a fresh tomato sauce. However, the addition of scallions and herbs here makes for a fresher and more intriguing combination. Also, it is served like tabbüleh and is scooped with fresh vine leaves when in season or raw cabbage leaves, a kind of cooked tabbüleh, as it were.

SERVES 4 TO 6

- ⅓ cup (80 ml) extra virgin olive oil
- 1½ cups (250 g) coarse bulgur wheat, soaked in cold water for 30 minutes
- 1 bunch scallions (about 100 g), trimmed, sliced fairly thin
- 1 bunch flat-leaf parsley (about 200 g on the stalk), washed, dried, most of the stalks discarded, finely chopped
- ¾ bunch mint (about 150 g on the stalk), leaves only, washed, dried, finely chopped
- ½ cup tomato paste, diluted in 3 cups (750 ml) water
- Sea salt
- Fresh vine leaves or cabbage leaves to scoop the mafrükeh

Put the olive oil in a medium wide pot and place over medium heat. Drain the bulgur wheat and add to the pot. Stir for a couple of minutes, then add the scallions, parsley, and mint. Mix well, then add the diluted tomato paste. Season with salt to taste. Cover the pan and let bubble for 10 to 15 minutes, until the bulgur wheat has absorbed all the liquid and is done. Wrap the lid with a clean kitchen towel and put back on the pot. Let cool. Serve at room temperature with either vine leaves if they are in season or cabbage leaves.

GREEN BEANS, BULGUR WHEAT, AND CHICKPEAS

MADFÜNEH

A great bulgur wheat dish where the wheat is cooked with green beans and chickpeas in a fresh tomato sauce. Most of these interesting bulgur wheat dishes seem to come from the south, and this one is no different, hailing from the southern town of Rashaya. It is a definite winner, combining all the nutrition you need in a vegetarian/vegan dish that is utterly delicious.

SERVES 4 TO 6

- ¼ cup (60 ml) extra virgin olive oil
- 1 medium onion (about 150 g), peeled, thinly sliced into wedges
- 3 cloves garlic, peeled, minced to a fine paste
- 1 pound (450 g) French green beans, trimmed, cut on an angle into medium pieces
- Sea salt
- 6 medium tomatoes (about 750 g), diced into small cubes
- ½ teaspoon ground cinnamon
- 1 teaspoon ground cumin
- Heaping 1 cup (200 g) coarse bulgur wheat, soaked in cold water for 30 minutes, drained
- 1 cup (175 g) cooked chickpeas
- Freshly ground black pepper
- Trimmed scallions to serve on the side

1. Put the olive oil and onion in a deep, wide sauté pan—having a wider surface will avoid mushing the beans and chickpeas—and place over medium heat. When the oil starts sizzling around the onion, reduce the heat to medium-low and cook, stirring regularly, until golden, 10 to 15 minutes. Add the minced garlic and cook, stirring, for a couple more minutes.

2. Add the green beans and salt to taste and cook, stirring, for another couple of minutes, or until the green beans are glossy green and well coated with oil.

3. Add the tomatoes, together with the cinnamon and cumin and more salt to taste. Cover the pot and let the tomatoes bubble for 10 minutes, stirring every now and then.

4. Add the bulgur wheat to the pot together with the chickpeas and black pepper to taste. Mix well and add ½ cup (125 ml) water. Cover the pot and cook for 10 to 15 minutes, until the liquid is completely absorbed and everything is done to your liking. Taste and adjust the seasoning if needed. Wrap the lid with a clean kitchen towel and put back on the pot. Let sit for 10 minutes or so to fluff up the bulgur wheat. Serve hot or warm with trimmed scallions.

MARSHÜSHEH 1

The first time I had marshüsheh was in 2023, at the home of Sumy Hokayem, who had very kindly invited Dalia and me to a spectacular lunch in her country house above Batroun, to introduce me to regional dishes. Marshüsheh was one of them, prepared by her sister, Fadia. Apparently, it is a specialty of Zawiyah, a northern region extending from Zgharta to Ehden. Sumy's sister's version is different from a recipe I found in Chef Ramzi's book, where it is made with cannellini beans, wild greens, and coarse bulgur wheat (page 273). Fadia's version below is simply made with cabbage, onions, and bulgur wheat.

SERVES 4 TO 6

¼ cup (60 ml) extra virgin olive oil

2 medium onions (about 300 g), peeled, finely chopped

5 cloves garlic, peeled, minced into a fine paste

1 tablespoon ground turmeric

1 teaspoon paprika

1 teaspoon seven-spice mixture (page 19)

1 teaspoon Aleppo pepper

1 pointed cabbage, trimmed, very thinly shredded

1 cup (175 g) coarse bulgur wheat, rinsed under cold water, drained

Sea salt

1. Put the olive oil and onions in a deep, wide sauté pan and place over medium heat. As soon as the oil starts sizzling around the onions, reduce the heat to medium-low and cook, stirring every now and then, until soft and golden, 10 to 15 minutes. Add the garlic and cook, stirring, for a minute or so, then add the turmeric, paprika, seven-spice, and Aleppo pepper. Mix well, then add the cabbage and mix again.

2. Cover the pan and cook the cabbage for about 5 minutes, then uncover the pan and add ½ cup (125 ml) water together with the bulgur wheat and salt to taste. Mix well. Cover the pan and cook for 15 minutes. By then the cabbage should have cooked completely and the bulgur wheat should have softened and absorbed all the water. Taste and adjust the seasoning if needed. Serve warm or at room temperature.

CANNELLINI BEANS, BULGUR WHEAT, AND GREENS

MARSHÜSHEH 2

A completely different dish from Fadia's (page 272), but just as delicious, and which I adapted from one in Chef Ramzi's tome on regional Lebanese cuisine (page 194). He places the recipe in the village of Andaket or 'and'et (the way we pronounce it). The only common ingredient in the two versions is bulgur wheat, otherwise the recipes are very different. Sli' can be a mixture of foraged greens or simply one of them. I will leave it to you to choose which green to use, and when I don't have foraged greens, I use chicory (hindbeh) or a mixture of parsley, scallions, and Swiss chard or just rainbow Swiss chard. You can also use kale, but it takes longer to soften.

SERVES 4 TO 6

2 cups (300 g) dried cannellini beans, soaked overnight in plenty of cold water with ½ teaspoon baking soda

1 pound 2 ounces (500 g) sli' (page 22) or the green of your choice, washed, dried, finely shredded

1 cup (175 g) coarse bulgur wheat, rinsed under cold water, drained

Sea salt

½ cup (125 ml) extra virgin olive oil, plus extra for those who want to drizzle more over the finished dish

Juice of 1 lemon, or to taste

1. Drain and rinse the cannellini beans and put in a wide, deep sauté pan. Add 1 quart (1 liter) water. Place over medium-high heat and bring to a boil. Then reduce the heat to medium-low and partly cover the pan. Let bubble gently for 30 to 40 minutes, until almost done.

2. Add the greens, cover the pan, and let wilt, then mix with the beans. Then add the bulgur wheat and mix well. Cook for another 15 minutes, then add salt to taste. By then, there should not be any excess liquid in the pan. If the mixture is still wet, uncover the pan, increase the heat, and let bubble while stirring every now and then until all the excess liquid has been absorbed. Take off the heat. Add the olive oil and lemon juice and mix well. Taste and adjust the seasoning if needed. Transfer to a serving platter and serve warm or at room temperature.

WARM BULGUR WHEAT AND KISHK SALAD

OMEISHEH

This is an ancient and rather fascinating recipe that is typical of the cooking of the Druze community in the Shouf region. I got it from Alaa al-Koukash, a caterer from Azüniyeh in Aley Directorate. My friends Janine and Tony Mamari had invited Alaa via Ghada Hmaidan, Janine's caregiver/companion, to prepare a selection of Druze dishes in their home in Beirut for me to taste. Most of the dishes Alaa had prepared that day included bulgur wheat, which is pretty much a staple of rural communities. I was intrigued by this dish because it had kishk (page 7) as a salad ingredient rather than a base for a thick soup or a flatbread topping. In fact, Alaa also used kishk in another salad (page 88). He insisted that omeisheh is a specialty of his village, but the Food Heritage site places it in Rashaya. Whether it belongs to one or the other, it remains a southern specialty, and there is no reason it cannot belong to both villages. The only drawback to making this recipe in the West is that there is no substitute for kishk, and you may have difficulty sourcing it, even in Middle Eastern grocery stores in the UK or the US. I always bring back a stock from the home country and store it in the freezer, where it keeps brilliantly for as long as I need it.

SERVES 4

¼ cup (60 ml) extra virgin olive oil

2 medium onions (about 300 g), peeled, finely chopped

1 teaspoon ground caraway

1 cup (175 g) fine bulgur wheat, rinsed under cold water, drained

1½ cups (185 g) kishk (page 7)

Sea salt

Grilled onions or scallions to serve on the side

1. Put the olive oil and chopped onions in a large, deep sauté pan and place over medium heat. As soon as the oil starts sizzling around the onions, reduce the heat to medium-low. Add the caraway and cook until the onions are soft and golden, 10 to 15 minutes.

2. Add the bulgur wheat together with 1 cup (250 ml) water. Mix well, then add the kishk. Mix again and keep stirring until all the ingredients are well blended and you have a kind of soft, crumbly mixture. Taste before adding any salt—kishk is already salted.

3. Transfer to a shallow serving bowl and serve warm with grilled onions or scallions.

CHICKPEAS, LAMB, AND BULGUR WHEAT
BURGHUL BI-DFINEH

Burghul bi-dfineh is one of those hearty dishes that is particularly suited to cold weather. I remember my mother making it in winter, with pork meat and skin. She also used bones for a richer broth, while in Muslim communities, they make it with lamb. My family is Christian, and in my youth, it was much easier to buy pork meat from butchers in west Beirut, but it is almost impossible now. There are specialty pork butchers in predominantly Christian villages, such as Ehden up north, where I found one. You can also prepare this dish with rice, once the preserve of rich city dwellers when rice was a luxury item—the recipe doesn't change. My mother always presoaked the chickpeas and cooked them with the meat, whereas I use precooked chickpeas preserved in water and salt and packed in glass jars. The Spanish brands are those I prefer, and I first rinse the chickpeas before adding them toward the end so as not to let them go mushy. I also prefer to make this dish with lamb shanks rather than pork.

SERVES 4

4 tablespoons (60 g) unsalted butter

4 lamb shanks (about 1¼ kg)

1 medium onion (about 150 g), peeled, finely chopped

1 cinnamon stick

1½ cups (250 g) coarse bulgur wheat, soaked in cold water for 30 minutes, drained

1½ cups (250 g) cooked chickpeas

½ teaspoon ground cinnamon

1 teaspoon ground allspice

¼ teaspoon finely ground black pepper

Sea salt

1. Melt the butter in a large, wide pot over medium heat and brown the shanks. Remove the shanks onto a plate, then add the chopped onion and cook, stirring regularly, until soft and translucent, 10 to 15 minutes. Return the shanks to the pan. Add 3 cups (750 ml) water together with the cinnamon stick. Cover the pot and let bubble gently for 1 hour, or until the meat is tender, practically falling off the bone.

2. Remove the shanks from the pot and take the meat off the bones once they are cool enough to handle. Trim away any skin and fat and tear into medium pieces. Discard the bones. Remove the cinnamon stick, then add the bulgur wheat and cooked chickpeas to the pot together with the meat. Season with the cinnamon allspice, pepper, and salt to taste. Reduce the heat to low and simmer for 15 to 20 minutes, until the bulgur wheat has absorbed all the liquid and is done—check halfway through to see if it is getting too dry, in which case add a little boiling water. Wrap the lid with a clean kitchen towel. Place it back on the pot and let sit for a few minutes. We usually serve this dish with yogurt on the side.

STEWS AND BRAISES

Of all the dishes in our repertoire, these are the ones most associated with daily family meals. When I lived in Beirut, my mother often made one or two for lunch, and we loved them because they were both comforting and totally moreish. They are the quintessence of what a simple Lebanese family meal is, easy to prepare and always served with rice, a salad or two, and the "decoration of the table" (see page 106), followed by fruit rather than dessert.

My favorite is the citrusy peas and carrot stew, but I also liked my mother's simple tomato one, which we ate with pita, dipped in the stew until very wet, before scooping a little more and enjoying with a wedge of raw onion. Her potato stew with ground meat was also a favorite. I often make one or the other to freeze in individual portions so I can have a quick hearty lunch when I am working at home and want something more substantial than a salad or cold cuts but don't feel like preparing it. Most of these stews and braises are cooked in a tomato sauce, but there are a couple that are not, which makes for an interesting change.

Having breakfast at El Soussi, Beirut

CITRUSY PEAS, CARROTS, AND MEAT STEW

YAKHNET BAZELLA WA JAZAR

The traditional way to make this stew is to cook the peas with the carrots once the meat is done, but I don't like it when the peas soften too much or, worse, when they turn yellow, which happens if they are cooked covered. So, I use frozen peas, which I defrost with boiling water. I do this in two steps. I first add boiling water to simply defrost them. I then drain it immediately and add more boiling water, which I leave for a couple of minutes, just to heat the peas. I then drain the water and let them sit until I am ready to add them at the very end so they keep their vibrant green color. This stew has an intriguing taste of orange and lemon peel, which works perfectly with the carrots and peas.

SERVES 4

- 8 medium ripe tomatoes (about 1 kg), diced into small cubes, or 3 (14-ounce/400 g) cans peeled Italian tomatoes, drained, finely chopped
- Just under ½ stick (50 g) unsalted butter
- 1 medium onion (about 150 g), peeled, finely chopped
- 14 ounces (400 g) trimmed lamb from the shoulder, cut into bite-sized pieces
- 3 medium carrots (about 300 g) peeled, sliced into ¼-inch (5 mm) disks (you can also use mini carrots, which you can leave whole)
- Peel of 1 small unwaxed orange, preferably cut in one piece
- Peel of ½ unwaxed lemon, preferably cut in one piece
- ½ teaspoon ground cinnamon
- ½ teaspoon ground allspice
- ¼ teaspoon finely ground black pepper
- Sea salt
- 1 pound 2 ounces (500 g) frozen petits pois, defrosted with boiling water, then warmed through with more boiling water, drained

1. Put the tomatoes in a large saucepan and place over medium-high heat. Let bubble for 10 to 15 minutes to get rid of some of the excess liquid.

2. Melt the butter in a large pot over medium heat. Add the onion and cook, stirring regularly, until soft and golden, 10 to 15 minutes. Add the meat and cook, stirring, until browned. Add the carrots and mix well. Reduce the heat to low, cover the pan, and cook for 5 minutes, stirring occasionally.

3. Add the tomatoes together with the orange and lemon peel. Season with the cinnamon, allspice, pepper, and salt to taste. Cover the pot and increase the heat to medium. Bring to a boil, then let bubble gently for 15 to 20 minutes. Discard both peels, then add the peas. Cook for another couple of minutes, uncovered, or until the vegetables and meat are done and the tomato sauce has thickened. Serve hot with plain rice or vermicelli rice (page 263).

MEATBALLS IN A LEMONY SAUCE

DAWÜD BASHA

Dawüd Basha was the name of the Ottoman empire's first mütasariff (governor), who was sent to Lebanon in 1861 to help reunite the people of the province after their second bout of serious sectarian fighting (we were then part of the empire). He proved to be a wise and honest governor, and I guess this dish was either created for him or named after him to honor his wise and just rule. You can vary here by cooking the meatballs in a tomato sauce, in which case leave out the flour, water, and lemon juice. Then, once you have toasted the pine nuts and cooked the onions and meat, set them aside. Add 4 large ripe tomatoes (about 800 g), peeled and coarsely chopped, or an equivalent weight of drained Italian canned tomatoes, and let bubble uncovered for 20 minutes, or until the tomatoes have lost most of their excess liquid. Return the onions to the pot. Cover the pan and simmer for 15 minutes, before adding the meatballs and pine nuts and letting simmer uncovered for another couple of minutes.

SERVES 6 TO 8

FOR THE MEATBALLS

1 medium onion (about 150 g), peeled, grated over the fine side of the grater

1 pound 12 ounces (800 g) lean finely ground lamb

Ground cinnamon, allspice, finely ground black pepper, and sea salt

2 to 3 tablespoons soda water

TO FINISH

Just under 1 stick (100 g) unsalted butter

½ cup (75 g) Mediterranean pine nuts

3 medium onions (about 450 g), peeled, thinly sliced into wedges

1½ teaspoons unbleached all-purpose flour

¼ teaspoon ground cinnamon

½ teaspoon ground allspice

¼ teaspoon seven-spice mixture (page 19)

¼ teaspoon finely ground black pepper

Sea salt

Juice of 1 lemon, or to taste

1. Put the grated onion in a large mixing bowl and add the meat. Season with a little cinnamon, allspice, pepper, and salt to give the meatballs some flavor, bearing in mind that the main seasoning will be in the sauce. Add the soda water and mix well, preferably with your hand so as to blend everything well—the soda water will lighten the meatballs. Shape into medium-sized meatballs and arrange on a small baking sheet. Refrigerate while you prepare the rest of the ingredients.

2. Put half the butter in a wide, deep sauté pan and place over medium heat. Toast the pine nuts, stirring constantly, until golden brown. Remove onto a plate and add the onions to the pan. Cook, stirring regularly, until soft and golden, 10 to 15 minutes. Remove onto a separate plate, then brown the meatballs, still in the same butter, and transfer to a separate plate.

3. Put the rest of the butter in the pan, wait until it starts foaming, then stir in the flour. Add 1 cup (250 ml) water and season with the cinnamon, allspice, seven-spice, pepper, and salt to taste. Increase the heat to medium-high, let the sauce start bubbling, then return the onions to the pan. As soon as the sauce starts bubbling again and thickening, add the meatballs. Let bubble for a few minutes, then add the lemon juice. Let bubble for a couple more minutes. Taste and adjust the seasoning if needed. Add the pine nuts and mix well. Transfer to a shallow serving bowl and serve immediately with plain rice or vermicelli rice (page 263).

GREEN BEANS AND MEAT IN A TOMATO SAUCE

LÜBYEH BIL-LAHMEH

The perfect green beans to use here are the flat ones, which we call *badriyeh*, while the flat ones that I buy in the supermarket in London are much longer and wider and labeled *helda*. You can of course use French beans, but they are very fine and cook quicker, so if you do use them, be sure to reduce the tomato sauce before adding them.

SERVES 4

1 pound 2 ounces (500 g) green beans, topped, tailed, stringed if needed

4 tablespoons (60 g) unsalted butter

2 medium onions (about 300 g), peeled, thinly sliced into wedges

10½ ounces (300 g) trimmed lamb from the shoulder, cut into bite-sized pieces

Sea salt

4 medium ripe tomatoes (about 500 g), peeled, finely chopped, or 2 (14-ounce/400 g) cans peeled Italian plum tomatoes, drained, finely chopped

1 teaspoon ground cinnamon

1 teaspoon ground allspice

¼ teaspoon finely ground black pepper

1. Rinse the green beans under cold water. Set aside.

2. Melt the butter in a large pot over medium heat and add the onions. Cook until soft and translucent, 5 to 10 minutes. Add the meat and brown, stirring regularly, for about 5 minutes. Then add the beans. Sprinkle with a little salt and mix well. Cover the pot and cook for 5 minutes, stirring the beans every now and then.

3. Add the tomatoes. Season with the cinnamon, allspice, pepper, and more salt to taste and bring to a boil. Then cover the pot and let bubble gently for 15 to 20 minutes, until both the beans and meat are done. If the tomato sauce is not thick enough, uncover the pot and increase the heat. Let bubble energetically, stirring every now and then, until the excess liquid has evaporated. Taste and adjust the seasoning if needed. Serve hot with plain rice or vermicelli rice (page 263).

OKRA AND MEAT STEW

BAMYEH BIL-LAHMEH

Most of the okra you find in the West is rather large, whereas those we use are much smaller, less than half the size of your small finger. It is a prized seasonal vegetable, and we cook it in myriad ways, both with and without meat. The most important step in preparing okra is the way you peel the stalk off. You need to do this without cutting into the okra so as not to let the mucilaginous substance that is so typical of this vegetable come out. We also sauté it in vegetable oil before cooking it, again to seal it. You can use frozen okra, which is even smaller, or dried, which you need to rehydrate first. Whether prepared with or without meat, it is almost always paired with cilantro and garlic.

SERVES 4

- 1 pound 5 ounces (600 g) okra
- Vegetable oil for frying
- 2 tablespoons (30 g) unsalted butter
- 1 medium onion (about 150 g), peeled, thinly sliced into wedges
- 14 ounces (400 g) lamb from the shoulder, cut into bite-sized pieces
- 7 large cloves garlic, peeled, minced into a fine paste
- ½ bunch cilantro (about 100 g on the stalk), washed, dried, most of the stalks discarded, finely chopped
- ¼ teaspoon ground coriander
- Sea salt
- 8 medium ripe tomatoes (1 kg), peeled, finely chopped, or 3 (14-ounce/400 g) cans peeled Italian plum tomatoes, drained, finely chopped
- ¼ teaspoon ground cinnamon
- ½ teaspoon ground allspice
- ¼ teaspoon finely ground black pepper

1. Prepare and fry the okra following the instructions on page 125.

2. Put the butter in a large pot and place over medium heat. When the butter is melted, add the onion and cook, stirring regularly, until soft and golden, 10 to 15 minutes. Add the meat and stir to brown all over. Add the minced garlic, together with the cilantro and ground coriander and a pinch of salt. Sauté for a minute or so, until the cilantro has wilted.

3. Add the tomatoes. Season with the cinnamon, allspice, pepper, and salt to taste and bring to a boil. Cover the pot and let bubble gently for 15 minutes. Add the sautéed okra and bring back to a boil. Reduce the heat to medium-low and let bubble gently, covered, for 15 minutes, or until the okra is done and the tomato sauce has thickened. Taste and adjust the seasoning if needed. Serve hot with vermicelli rice (page 263).

SPINACH, CILANTRO, AND MEAT STEW

S'BANEGH BIL-LAHMEH

You can easily make this dish vegetarian, and it will remain just as delicious—all you need to do is omit the meat and prepare as below. You can also vary the ground meat by using bite-sized pieces of meat. My mother used to say it is tastier with ground meat. I beg to differ as I am not so keen on ground meat unless it is in kibbé, stuffings, or meatballs, but as it is her recipe, I am using ground meat!

SERVES 4

4 tablespoons (60 g) unsalted butter

1 medium onion (about 150 g), peeled, finely chopped

½ teaspoon ground coriander

9 ounces (250 g) ground lean lamb

5 cloves garlic, peeled, minced to a fine paste

½ bunch cilantro (about 100 g on the stalk), bottom stalks discarded, finely chopped

2 pounds 4 ounces (1 kg) spinach, washed, drained, dried, shredded into thin strips

Sea salt

Juice of 1 lemon, or to taste

¼ teaspoon finely ground black pepper

1. Put the butter in a large pot and place over medium-low heat. Once the butter has melted, add the onion and ground coriander and cook, stirring regularly, until soft and golden, 10 to 15 minutes. Add the meat and cook, breaking up any lumps, until all traces of pink have disappeared.

2. Add the minced garlic and cilantro. Mix well, then add the spinach. Add salt to taste and mix again. Cover the pot and cook for a couple of minutes, or until the spinach has wilted, then uncover the pot and mix well. Place the lid back on and cook over medium heat for 10 minutes. If the spinach has released too much water, uncover the pot and increase the heat to let bubble energetically until most of the excess liquid has evaporated. Add the lemon juice and cook, stirring, for another couple of minutes. Taste and adjust the seasoning if needed. Serve hot with plain rice or vermicelli rice (page 263).

LAMB SHANKS IN VINEGAR

LAHM BIL-KHALL

A specialty of Beino, a picturesque town in Akkar, the country's most northern region. It is very important to use a good vinegar here because it is the main flavoring, and you want it rather mellow but with a lot of flavor. I use an organic apple cider vinegar rather than one made with wine; you can also use champagne vinegar or simply an apple one like the one used in the home country. Again, this dish was new to me, and it was my friend Jacquot (page 341) who first mentioned it. Then I met Nahla Attieh, whose family is from Beino, on social media, and she very kindly invited me to her Aunt Mona and her husband, Elias's, home in Beino to see how the dish is made, and to taste it of course. It was the most wonderful morning—it took me back to those long-ago days when I lived in Lebanon and enjoyed many similar mornings at my mother's relatives in Rechmaya, where family and friends gathered over coffee and delicious nibbles on the balcony while the cooks were busy in the kitchen preparing all kinds of delightful dishes for our meals. The "building" of lahm bil-khall is amazing. Therese, Mona's cook, had all the ingredients already prepared. She first put an impressive amount of ghee in the pot before spreading a first layer of pearl onions. She then added the meat that she had previously boiled, then fried. She covered the meat with a layer of peeled carrots and another of zucchini. And, finally, a few heads of garlic. As she was about to cover the pot, Mona said that they sometimes added quince when it was in season. I liked the idea—we don't have a tradition of cooking fruit with meat, but Beino is very near the border with Syria, which may explain the combination. Anyhow, Therese said they had quince in the freezer and asked if she should add some. I nodded enthusiastically, and she did. She added water and covered the pot. We then had to wait until the dish was done. It took a couple of hours before she was ready to add the vinegar and another hour or so before it was done. You can prepare this dish with the onions left whole or sliced. Slicing them will make the sauce richer, as they melt into the vinegar, whereas leaving them whole makes for a prettier presentation.

Once the dish was ready, we moved to another beautiful house in Beino, where Denise Safa, our hostess, had organized an enchanting lunch in her garden with many friends who had come from Beirut to taste the local specialties. We had Nahla's aunt's lahm bil-khall, always served with flat disks of grilled kibbé, and her Bou Emneh (page 172), as well as many other delightful dishes that Denise's cook had prepared—if you want to serve it with grilled kibbé, make the kibbé for Kibbeh bil-Saniyeh (page 160); divide it into 12 pieces and flatten each in a tortilla press, if you have one, into 4-inch (10 cm) disks, which you can grill under your broiler or on your barbecue. The finish to the meal was a spectacular display of sweets from Hallab, the foremost sweets maker of Tripoli. Denise had asked them to also send a couple of waiters so they could prepare and serve the sweets.

SERVES 4

FOR THE MEAT

4 lamb shanks, (about 1¼ kg)

1 cinnamon stick

1 small onion (about 100 g), peeled

Sea salt

TO FINISH

1 stick (120 g) unsalted butter or ghee

1 tablespoon vegetable oil

3 medium onions (about 450 g), peeled, thinly sliced into wedges, or the same amount pearl onions, peeled

1 tablespoon unbleached all-purpose flour

2 to 3 heads garlic, left whole, trimmed of extra skin and dirty root ends

1 cup (250 ml) red wine vinegar or apple cider vinegar

1 pound (450 g) Chanteney or baby carrots, trimmed, brushed clean

1 pound (450 g) pale green zucchini, trimmed, cut in half lengthwise, sliced across on a diagonal

Sea salt

Freshly ground black pepper

1. Put the shanks in a large pot. Cover with water and place over medium-high heat. As soon as the water is about to boil, skim the surface clean. Then add the cinnamon stick and onion. Add salt to taste and cover the pan. Reduce the heat to medium-low and let bubble gently for about 1 hour, until the meat is done and practically falling off the bone. At this stage, you can leave the shanks as they are or take the meat off the bone and trim it of skin and fat. Set aside.

2. Put the butter and vegetable oil in a large deep sauté pan and place over medium heat. When the butter has melted, add the onions and cook, stirring regularly, until soft and golden, 10 to 15 minutes—if you are using pearl onions, stir for a few minutes. Stir in the flour, then add the garlic, vinegar, and 1 cup (250 ml) water. Mix well. Return the meat to the pan. Add the carrots and reduce the heat to medium-low. Cover the pan and let bubble gently for 10 minutes, or until the sauce has thickened a little.

3. Add the zucchini. Season with salt and pepper to taste and let bubble for another 20 to 30 minutes, until the meat is very tender and practically falling off the bone and the vegetables are just done. You may need to add a little water or vinegar or both if the sauce is becoming too thick. By then, the sauce should be fairly thick and silky. Serve hot with plain rice or vermicelli rice (page 263).

Mona and Elias Attieh's lahm bil-khall

CANNELLINI BEAN AND MEAT STEW

FASSÜLYAH BIL-LAHMEH

Traditionally, this dish is made with only tomato paste and with pork in Christian communities and lamb in Muslim ones. I have changed it slightly by using a combination of fresh tomatoes and paste and olive oil instead of butter. I also make mine with lamb regardless of the fact that my mother always made it with pork until it became less readily available. Here, I am using fresh beans, which are plentiful in late spring, early summer. They are quicker to cook than dried beans with none of the overnight soaking, turning this into a seasonal dish rather than an all-year one.

SERVES 4

¼ cup (60 ml) extra virgin olive oil

1 large onion (about 200 g), peeled, sliced into medium-thin wedges

1 pound 2 ounces (500 g) boned lamb from the shanks, cut lengthwise into medium pieces

2 or 3 bones from the lamb (optional)

1 teaspoon ground cinnamon

1 teaspoon ground allspice

½ teaspoon finely ground black pepper

¼ teaspoon ground nutmeg

Sea salt

4 large tomatoes (about 800 g), peeled, finely chopped, or 2 (14-ounce/400 g) cans peeled Italian tomatoes, finely chopped

2 tablespoons (30 ml) tomato paste

2½ cups (500 g) fresh cannellini or haricot beans

1. Put the olive oil and onion in a large pot and place over medium heat. As soon as the oil starts sizzling around the onion, reduce the heat to medium-low and cook, stirring occasionally, until soft and golden, 10 to 15 minutes. Add the bones (if you are using them) and the meat and sauté until they lose all traces of pink. Add 1½ cups (375 ml) water, together with the cinnamon, allspice, pepper, nutmeg, and salt to taste. Cover the pot and bring to a boil. Increase the heat to medium and let bubble gently for 30 minutes.

2. Add the tomatoes and tomato paste together with 1 cup (250 ml) water and bring back to a boil. Give the whole thing a good stir. Then reduce the heat to medium-low. Cover the pot and cook for another 30 minutes. By that time, both meat and bones (if you have used them) will be almost done.

3. When the time is up, add the beans. Put the lid back on and simmer for 20 to 30 more minutes, until the sauce has thickened and the beans are cooked. Taste, and adjust the seasoning if needed. Remove the bones, if you used them. Serve hot with plain rice or vermicelli rice (page 263).

STEWS AND BRAISES

Sweets are at the heart of our legendary hospitality. Whether it is for special occasions, or regular visits, or simply gentle moments with family and friends, there will always be Turkish coffee and sweets—in the homes of émigrés (the number of Lebanese in the diaspora is as large as those living in the home country), you may also be served maté, originally Argentinian but now very much part of the repertoire in those communities. Most hosts and hostesses will have bowls filled with a selection of long-lasting sweets, such as malban (grape jelly studded with pistachios), chocolates, or nougats, to name a few, dotted around their drawing rooms, ready to serve to those wanting to "sweeten their mouth," a literal translation from Arabic!

We have three main centers for sweets in Lebanon: Beirut, the capital; Saida, down south; and Tripoli, the country's second-largest city, in the north. They all make the classics, such as baklava and k'nafeh, albeit with their own slight variations; and of course they each have their own regional specialties. The most famous of these sweets makers in the north is Hallab, with their Palace of Sweets (Qasr el-Helü), a whole building where they make and serve an amazing selection of sweets. The place is a must if you happen to be there. In Beirut, there is, among many, Amal Bohsali, my favorite. As for the south, the most famous is Al Baba, but there are many small and not so small sweets makers that produce either excellent selections or their own specialties. And even though most of us will buy our sweets from specialty stores, many can be made at home, and I have included recipes for the ones that are easiest to replicate in a home kitchen.

Ma'jü'a "sandwich" at Dabboussi, Tripoli

MA'JÜ'A

This is an interesting sweet from Tripoli that combines cheese with semolina like halawet el-jibn. The method here for ma'jü'a is different, though, as are the final taste and texture. Ma'jü'a is soft and silky, whereas halawet el-jibn is dry and slightly textured. It is rather tricky to prepare, not so much in the step where you are melting the cheese with the fragrant waters but in the way you incorporate it into the dough. At Dabboussi, in the souks of Tripoli, as well as at other vendors, you can see them make it to order. They melt the cheese over a large hot plate before incorporating the wet semolina, using a scraper to first mix the cheese with the fragrant waters then with the semolina dough. They divide the stretchy dough, shape it into disks, and dip it into powdered sugar before stuffing it into the typical Tripoli ka'keh (page 52). Use a large flat, preferably nonstick frying pan. Then, with a plastic baking scraper, first mix the melting cheese with the fragrant waters, then blend it into the wet semolina dough.

SERVES 4 TO 6

2 cups (325 g) semolina

¾ cup (150 g) baker's or superfine sugar

1½ cups (375 ml) organic whole milk

½ cup (125 ml) rose water

½ cup (125 ml) orange blossom water

1 pound 2 ounces (500 g) akkawi cheese, cut into slices, soaked in several changes of cold water to desalt it

1½ cups (180 g) powdered sugar

6 round sesame galettes to make the sandwich, opened at the seam but not completely separated into two layers

1. Put the semolina and superfine sugar in a large mixing bowl and mix well. Gradually add the milk, bringing in the flour and sugar as you go along. Add 2 tablespoons of the rose water and 2 tablespoons of the orange blossom water and knead until you have a loose dough.

2. Drain the cheese and pat dry with paper towels. Put the remaining fragrant waters in a large flat frying pan and place over medium-low heat. Spread the cheese all over the pan and leave over the heat until it starts to melt. Work the cheese in with the fragrant waters with the help of a baking scraper, then add the semolina dough, and still with the baking scraper, start incorporating the melted cheese into the dough by scraping and folding them together, then stretching them against the pan with your scraper. Repeat again and again until the cheese and dough are well blended.

3. Divide into 6 pieces and roll each piece into a ball. Spread the powdered sugar over a large flat platter. Transfer the dough to the powdered sugar and flatten it in the sugar, turning it over until it is just under the size of the sesame galette and is well coated with the powdered sugar. Slide into the sesame galette and serve immediately, which is how they serve it in Tripoli.

CHEESE AND SEMOLINA DESSERT

HALAWET EL-JIBN

A simple sweet to prepare at home that can be served warm or chilled, drizzled with sugar syrup or in rolls, wrapped around clotted cream. Once you have made the sugar syrup and before you start cooking the cheese and semolina mixture, brush a large baking sheet or silicone mat with syrup. Then cook the mixture and pour it onto the baking sheet. Dip a spatula in the syrup and use it to spread the hot mixture into a thin layer, about ½ inch (1¼ cm) thick. Let cool, then cut into 2½-inch (6¼ cm) squares. Spread a tablespoon of clotted cream down the middle of each square before making medium-thin rolls. If the cheese mixture is sticky, dip your fingers in a little syrup to make rolling easier. Arrange the filled rolls on a serving platter and dust with coarsely ground pistachios, or garnish with orange blossom jam.

SERVES 4

Sugar Syrup (page 300)

Just under 1 stick (100 g) unsalted butter

Just under 1 cup (150 g) regular semolina

1 pound 2 ounces (500 g) akkawi (page 22) or cow's milk mozzarella cheese, cut into ¼-inch (½ cm) slices, put to soak in several changes of cold water to desalt it

7 ounces (200 g) ashtah (page 301) or English clotted cream (optional)

2 to 3 tablespoons chopped pistachios or orange blossom jam (optional)

1. Prepare the sugar syrup and measure ⅔ cup (160 ml) to use with the cheese and semolina. Set the rest aside.

2. Put the butter in a medium saucepan and place over medium heat. When it is melted, add the semolina and stir for a few minutes, until the semolina has absorbed all the fat. Add the measured syrup and continue stirring until the mixture is smooth and well blended.

3. Drain the cheese and add to the pan. Stir, scraping the bottom so the cheese does not stick, until the cheese is completely melted and the mixture is a thick, stretchy paste. Spread as explained in the headnote. Then, once cooled, tear into pieces. Pile the pieces in an irregular flattish mound and serve topped with clotted cream and drizzled with sugar syrup. Garnish with chopped pistachios or orange blossom jam (if you are using one of them).

Halawet el-jibn at Helwayat al-Tom, Tripoli

SWEET CHEESE PIE
K'NAFEH BIL-JEBN

Our breakfasts are mostly savory, although we have one quintessential sweet one, k'nafeh, a kind of sweet cheese pie stuffed inside a sesame galette and drenched in sugar syrup that is one of my all-time favorites. It is totally irresistible despite being a thousand calories a bite. If there is such a thing as a sweet sandwich, k'nafeh is one of the greatest. There are two ways of making it, both with "hair" pastry, more commonly known as *kataifi*. The first is to break the kataifi into medium-sized strands before tossing it in a lot of melted butter or ghee and toasting it without letting it color. It is then cooled and ground in a food processor, then sifted through a fine flat sieve until it is like semolina—in fact, many sweets makers use semolina, but you notice the difference, both in taste and texture. The other way, which you mostly find in the south because of its proximity to Palestine, where this version originated, and from Nablus in particular, is to keep the pastry whole but still toss it in a lot of melted butter or ghee. Whether ground, in which case it is called *mafrükeh* (meaning "rubbed"), or kept whole, in which case it is called *k'nafeh nabülsiyeh*, the pastry is spread thickly over a round baking dish, baked until golden, then covered with cheese and baked again until golden brown. Once done, it is overturned and kept hot so the cheese stays melting. You can also cook it over the stove, making sure you turn the baking dish regularly so the pastry colors evenly.

You can eat it as is, drizzled with sugar syrup, or stuffed inside the galette as described above. People usually buy k'nafeh from their favorite sweets maker rather than prepare it at home, even if it is fairly simple to make. All you need to do is source good kataifi—we call it *sha'r*, meaning "hair" in Arabic, because it is like very long, thin strands of hair that are gathered and folded into packs and sold either fresh or frozen and either whole or ground. The cheese you need to use here is part akkawi (page 22) and part tressed hallüm (page 21), but cow's milk mozzarella (fior di latte) is an acceptable substitute.

You often see kataifi these days described as shredded phyllo, but it is not. In fact, the way it is made is mesmerizing, either by hand or in an automated machine. Either way, it is made by dropping very thin strands of batter through tiny holes (by hand with the help of a cup-like implement with a row of narrow funnels on the bottom and by machine through a trough lined with multiple narrow funnels along the bottom) onto a hot metal plate. The batter is dropped in a circular motion and the thin strands sizzle as soon as they come in contact with the heat. They are then immediately gathered in a figure eight and laid on paper or linen towels to be later delivered to the sweets makers who use them in k'nafeh along with sweets such as fayssaliyeh (page 306), borma, or bird's nests.

You can vary the cheese version by using 1 pound (450 g) ashtah (page 301). Bake the pastry by covering it with parchment paper and weighing it down with baking beans, then let it cool before spreading the cream and turning it over. It is served at room temperature and should really be eaten on the day.

SERVES 4 TO 6

Sugar Syrup (page 300)

9 ounces (250 g) kataifi or "hair" pastry

Just under 1 stick (100 g) unsalted butter or same weight ghee, plus extra for brushing the baking dish

14 ounces (about 400 g) akkawi and tressed hallūm cheeses (7 ounces/ 200 g of each), or cow's milk mozzarella cheese, soaked in several changes of water until completely desalted, patted dry with paper towels, coarsely grated

1. Prepare the sugar syrup and let cool. Preheat the oven to 450°F (220°C).

2. Chop the pastry into ½-inch (1¼ cm) pieces. Put the butter in a wide frying pan and place over medium-low heat. As soon as the butter is melted, add the chopped pastry and, with your hands, rub the fat into the pastry until well coated—this will take a few minutes. Stir over the heat to slightly crisp up the pastry without coloring it. Let cool, then process in a food processor to crumble it completely.

3. Generously brush the bottom and sides of an 10½-inch (26 cm) round baking dish with 1½-inch (4 cm) sides with butter or ghee. Sift the crumbled pastry (known as *mafrūkeh*) evenly across the dish and press down with your hands. Bake in the preheated oven for 7 to 8 minutes, until lightly colored.

4. Take the pastry out of the oven and spread the grated cheese evenly all over it. Return to the oven and bake for 15 to 20 more minutes, until the cheese is completely melted and the pastry has become golden brown— turn the dish halfway through to color the pastry evenly. Brush your serving platter with a little syrup and turn over the k'nafeh onto it—the sugar syrup on the plate will keep the cheese from sticking to it. Drizzle a little sugar syrup all over and serve hot—you want the cheese to remain very melty— with more syrup on the side, and with or without ka'k (page 51).

Serving k'nafeh at Yasmine Charafeddine's

SUGAR SYRUP

ATER

The traditional syrup is made with white sugar. As a result, it is colorless, but I like to use natural cane sugar, which means that my syrup looks more like honey with a light golden color. I only use white sugar when I am making white desserts and I need the syrup to be transparent. Fortunately, you can now find organic white sugar; I stock up on it whenever I find it so my refined sugar is at least organic. People in the West often think that baklava is sweetened with honey, but in fact it is sweetened with sugar syrup, which is prepared the same way throughout the country.

MAKES ABOUT 1⅓ CUPS (330 ML)

1¾ cups (350 g) baker's or superfine sugar

2 teaspoons lemon juice

1 tablespoon rose water

1 tablespoon orange blossom water

Put the sugar and ⅔ cup (160 ml) water in a saucepan. Add the lemon juice and place over medium heat. Bring to a boil, stirring occasionally. Let bubble for a few minutes, until the sugar is completely dissolved and the syrup has thickened a little. Take off the heat. Let sit for a couple of minutes, then add the fragrant waters. Let cool before using with any of the recipes calling for sugar syrup.

CLOTTED CREAM
ASHTAH

Ashtah's name comes from the verb *asht* meaning "to strip," because it is basically the thick skin that forms on milk as it simmers over a low flame. The flame is always to one side, so the milk bubbles in one place and, as it does, the skin, which is basically the cream in the milk, is pushed away to the other side, at which point it is skimmed and layered in perforated plastic baskets, to drain off the excess liquid. The milk is put in very wide shallow pans in order to get more skin forming on top. It is not something that cooks attempt at home because there is no shortage of specialty sweets makers selling ashtah back in the home country. But if you have the patience, it is both fun and rewarding to make your own. The slow method that I describe below will take a few hours. If you don't have time, you can make a quick version by boiling milk with either soft white breadcrumbs or semolina to thicken it and make it feel like cream. I give both methods below.

FOR THE SLOW METHOD

MAKES JUST OVER ½ CUP (150 G)

1 quart (1 liter) whole organic milk

1⅓ cups (310 ml) heavy cream

1. Put the milk and cream in a wide, shallow round pan (the widest pan possible for your burner so as to maximize the amount of skin formed) and place over low heat. Bring to a boil, then reduce the heat to very low and simmer for 1½ to 2 hours.

2. Once ready, cover the pan and let it sit undisturbed for 6 to 8 hours, after which, put the pan in the refrigerator and leave it there overnight. Skim the thick skin and put it in an airtight container to use when you need it. As for the leftover liquid, you can use it instead of water when making dough.

FOR THE QUICK METHOD

MAKES ABOUT 2 CUPS (500 G)

3½ ounces (100 g) soft white breadcrumb from inside any good but soft white bread, torn into small pieces

2½ cups (625 ml) half-and-half

Put the breadcrumbs in a medium saucepan and add the half-and-half. Place over medium heat and bring to a boil. Then reduce the heat to low and simmer for 10 minutes, stirring regularly. Take off the heat and let cool completely, then transfer to an airtight container, where it will keep for 3 to 4 days in the refrigerator.

NATEF

Natef is an extraordinary sweet dip made with soap. Not actual soap, mind you, but water that has been boiled with the root of soapwort (shirsh el-halaweh), a plant that contains saponin, thus, soap. The root is boiled for a long time so the water reduces by more than half, by which time it is a murky brown color. However, as you start whisking it, it starts turning into a brilliant white foam. Then sugar syrup is whisked in and the white foam turns glossy, a little like soft meringue. It is a process that remained a mystery until I began an investigation, together with the late Alan Davidson and Helen Saberi, author of *Noshe Djan* (*Afghan Food and Cookery*), to get to the bottom of how this dip was made, and with what exactly—I knew very little about soapwort then. We found out that shirsh el-halaweh (the Arabic name of the dried root) is actually the root of soapwort. In some recipes, I was told to peel the root, or to pulverize it, but I nearly broke my knife and food processor trying to do this. I then went to a Lebanese sweets maker in London, Kamal Mudallal, and asked him to show me how he makes natef, which he very kindly did. Kamal washes the roots before boiling them whole until the water is reduced by three-quarters. He then lets the murky water cool before straining and whisking it into foam (the saponin at work). After that, he whisks in the sugar syrup and the white foam turns into a beautiful glossy soft meringue-like dip that is exclusively served with karabij (page 322) and one of my favorite sweets.

Unfortunately, these days many sweets makers make natef with egg white, which is a definite no-no as far as I am concerned. Even if it is not so easy to source soapwort root in the West, you can use bois de panama (the bark of the Panama tree) instead.

MAKES 1½ QUARTS (1½ LITERS)

2 ounces (60 g) soapwort root

FOR THE SUGAR SYRUP

2 cups (400 g) baker's or superfine sugar

2 teaspoons lemon juice

1 tablespoon rose water

1 tablespoon orange blossom water

1. Rinse the soapwort root under cold water to get rid of any grit, then put it in a small pot. Add 2½ cups (625 ml) water and place over medium-low heat. Bring to a boil—watch carefully, as it will make quite a froth, and you don't want it to boil over. Reduce the heat to low to bring the froth down. Simmer for about 1 hour, until the liquid has reduced to one-quarter of the initial amount, about ⅔ cup (160 ml).

2. While the soapwort is boiling, prepare the sugar syrup. Put the sugar and ½ cup (125 ml) water in a medium saucepan. Add the lemon juice and place over medium heat. Do not whisk it. Wait until the sugar starts melting and gently stir it every now and then. Let bubble for a few minutes, until the sugar is completely dissolved. Take off the heat and add the fragrant waters. Keep warm.

3. Strain the reduced murky liquid into a large mixing bowl and let cool, then use a handheld electric mixer to whisk it. As you are whisking, you will witness a miraculous transformation as the brown liquid turns into a brilliant white foam. Once the liquid is completely transformed into a thick white foam, start slowly adding the warm sugar syrup, still whisking until you have a shiny white mousse. Whisking by hand will not really work unless you are very powerful and very fast; you need a machine and quite a powerful one at that. Let cool, then refrigerate. Serve with karabij (page 322).

BAKLAVA
BA'LAWA

Baklava is a generic term that refers to a whole selection of dainty sweets that are made with either phyllo or "hair" pastry, aka kataifi (see page 298). Kol wa shkor (meaning eat and be thankful) is the name that describes those made with phyllo. They come in different shapes and forms, ranging from fingers to small squares to tiny "baskets," whereas those made with kataifi are known under different names. One is borma (meaning "twisted"), and it describes cylinders where the kataifi is wrapped around pistachios, while ballüriyeh is white, square versions of borma. Kataifi is also used to make tiny bird's nests filled with pistachios. Despite the fact that making baklava at home is fairly simple, most people tend to buy it from their preferred sweets maker. I, on the other hand, like to make my own, mostly with phyllo because it is more readily available. The pros roll out their own phyllo, but store-bought Turkish or Greek phyllo will save you the trouble and it is perfectly acceptable. Here, you can use whichever nuts you prefer. Before Mediterranean pine nuts became expensive (mainly because of a pest infestation that decimated the pine trees), sweets makers also had a pine nut filling in their selection, but now it is either pistachios, cashews, or walnuts.

SERVES 4 TO 6

Borma at Al-Haddad, Tripoli

Half recipe Sugar Syrup (just over ⅔ cup/175 ml, page 300)

FOR THE FILLING

1⅓ cups (200 g) walnuts or pistachios, ground medium coarse

½ cup (100 g) baker's or superfine sugar

¾ teaspoon ground cinnamon

1 tablespoon rose water

1 tablespoon orange blossom water

TO FINISH

1 stick (120 g) unsalted butter, melted

12 sheets of phyllo pastry measuring 7 x 12½ inches (18 x 32 cm)

1. Prepare the sugar syrup and let cool. Preheat the oven to 400°F (200°C).

2. Put the nuts in a medium mixing bowl. Add the sugar, cinnamon, and rose and orange blossom waters and mix well.

3. Take a nonstick baking dish measuring about 7 x 12½ x 1¼ inches deep (18 x 32 x 3 cm) or brush a regular one with melted butter. Spread one sheet of phyllo pastry on the bottom of the baking dish—keep the other sheets covered with plastic wrap then a damp cloth on top to keep them from drying up. Brush with melted butter. Then lay another sheet, brush with melted butter, and another, again brushing with butter until you have six layers of phyllo pastry.

4. Spread the nut filling evenly over the phyllo and cover with six more layers, making sure to brush each with melted butter. Pour any leftover butter over the phyllo and cut into squares or diamonds with sides measuring 2 inches (5 cm).

5. Bake in the preheated oven for 15 to 20 minutes, until crisp and golden all over. Take out of the oven and let sit for a couple of minutes, then pour the syrup all over. Serve at room temperature. This baklawa will keep for a few days stored in an airtight container.

KING FAYSAL'S SWEET
FAYSSALIYEH

These amazing pastries, which are filled with pistachio, are a specialty of Tripoli, our country's second-largest city, in the north. Traditionally, they were fried in ghee and are still made this way at some traditional sweets makers like Al-Haddad, but if you find ghee too heavy, use vegetable oil. They were named after Faysal I, the leader of the great Arab revolt in the First World War, and subsequently the king of Iraq, who visited Tripoli for a festival organized in his honor. The then premier sweets maker of the city, Rafaat al Hallab, created this sweet for the occasion and named it after him. Making the triangles with kataifi is a little fiddly at first, but you will soon get the hang of it.

MAKES 12 PASTRIES TO SERVE 6 TO 12

FOR THE FILLING

1 cup (150 g) whole raw pistachios (not salted)

TO FINISH

14 ounces (400 g) kataifi

Vegetable oil or ghee to bake the fayssaliyeh

Double recipe Sugar Syrup (page 300)

1. Preheat the oven to 450°F (220°C). Spread the pistachios over a nonstick baking sheet and toast in the oven for about 10 minutes. Take out of the oven and let cool while you prepare the kataifi.

2. Divide the kataifi into medium-thick strips measuring 8 x 3 inches (20 x 7½ cm) and arrange on your work surface with the length going away from you. Divide the pistachios equally among the strips, arranging them in a mound about 1 inch (2½ cm) away from the top. Then fold the kataifi over the pistachios to form a triangle, fold again, and again until you have completely encased the pistachios and have medium-sized triangles.

3. Arrange one next to the other on a baking dish that you had previously generously brushed with oil or ghee. Cover with parchment paper, then lay a slightly smaller baking dish over them and weigh it down with baking beans or whatever weight you have that will help flatten them somewhat and keep them from unrolling during frying. Let sit for 3 hours or longer.

4. Pour enough vegetable oil to cover the bottom of a large nonstick frying pan by ½ inch (1¼ cm) and place over medium heat. Place as many pastries as you can in the pan and drizzle more vegetable oil all over them. Fry for 3 to 5 minutes on one side, until golden, then carefully turn over to fry the other side until it is the same color. Remove with a slotted spoon onto the baking dish and pour syrup all over. Fry the next batch in the same way, then remove onto the baking dish. Pour the rest of the syrup all over and let the pastries sit until they have absorbed the syrup, about 30 minutes. Transfer to a serving platter and serve immediately or store in an airtight container, where they will keep for a few days.

ANISEED FRITTERS

MA'CARÜN

Christians prepare ma'carün for Epiphany (Ghtass in Arabic) or the feast of Santa Barbara, which is our Halloween, together with other fritters, such as owwamat (page 309) and zellabya (a kind of long doughnut). They also prepare them for the Assumption of the Virgin (Eid el-Saydeh) on August 15, whereas Muslims have them as one of their essential sweets during the month of Ramadan. The way they are prepared does not vary from one community to the other, and both use aniseed as the predominant flavor.

MAKES 20

Just over 1½ cups (275 g) fine semolina

¼ teaspoon instant (fast-acting) yeast

1 teaspoon ground aniseed

¼ teaspoon ground cinnamon

3 tablespoons (45 ml) vegetable oil, plus more for frying

Double recipe Sugar Syrup (page 300)

1. Put the semolina, yeast, aniseed, and cinnamon in a large mixing bowl and mix well. Add the vegetable oil and, with your fingertips, work it into the dry ingredients until fully incorporated. Add ½ cup plus 2 tablespoons (155 ml) water and knead until you have a firm, elastic dough. Cover with a damp cloth and let sit for 45 minutes.

2. While the dough is resting, prepare the sugar syrup and have on hand to drop in the fritters immediately after they are fried.

3. Divide the dough into 20 equal pieces and shape each into a fat sausage, 2 to 2¾ inches (5 to 7 cm) long. Place the pastry "sausages" against a flat perforated surface, like the bottom of an inverted colander, and with your fingers, press the dough down and roll it toward you to make a knobbly roll. Place, seam-side down, on a platter and continue "stamping" the pastry "sausages" in the same way until you have done them all.

4. Pour enough vegetable oil into a large, deep frying pan to deep-fry the ma'carün and place over medium heat. When the oil is hot—test by dipping a piece of bread; if the oil immediately bubbles around it, it is ready—drop as many ma'carün as will fit comfortably in the pan and fry, turning them over every now and then, until golden brown all over. Remove with a slotted spoon and drop into the sugar syrup. Let them absorb the syrup until the second batch is ready, then lift onto a serving platter and drop in the second batch. Serve at room temperature, soon after they were fried, for maximum crunch.

PELLET FRITTERS

OWWAMAT

Making the batter here is very simple. What is less simple is dropping it in the hot oil in the shape of balls, but even if you don't achieve perfect round shapes, they will still be delicious. This said, be sure to serve them soon after frying before they lose some of their crunch. Again, they are reserved for special occasions, both for Christians and Muslims. You can use the same batter to make m'shabbak (meaning "entangled" in Arabic), which I like to call Jackson Pollock fritters, by piping the batter through a narrow nozzle into the hot oil, making thin squiggly overlapping lines, to achieve a kind of laced rosette. At the sweets makers you find them multicolored, but I never found out how to do this, so I keep mine golden.

SERVES 4

1¼ cups (150 g) unbleached all-purpose flour

¼ teaspoon baking soda

Just under 1¼ cups (300 g) plain full-fat yogurt

Sugar Syrup (page 300)

Vegetable oil for frying

1. Mix the flour and baking soda in a large mixing bowl and make a well in the center. Add the yogurt and whisk until the ingredients are well blended and the batter is smooth. Cover with plastic wrap and let rest for 45 minutes.

2. While the batter is resting, prepare the sugar syrup and have on hand to drop the fritters in once they are fried.

3. Pour enough vegetable oil into a deep frying pan to deep-fry the fritters and place over medium heat. When the oil is hot—test the heat by dipping a piece of bread in it; if the oil immediately bubbles around it, it is ready—dip a rounded dessertspoon in a little oil, scoop as much batter as you can, and drop it in the hot oil. Ideally, the dropped batter will have the shape of a ball, but it is not so easy to master the trick at first and you will need a little practice. Anyhow, drop in as many spoonfuls of batter as will fit comfortably in the pan and fry, stirring to brown them evenly, until they are golden all over.

4. Remove with a slotted spoon and drop into the syrup. Turn a few times, then remove onto a serving platter. Fry the rest of the batter in the same way and drop into the syrup. Serve at room temperature, soon after frying, for maximum crunch.

SEMOLINA CAKE

NAMMÜRAH

A simple and delicious cake that is one of the very few sweets that we prefer to make at home rather than buy from specialty sweets makers. The homemade version is lighter and less cloying than any commercial ones. Be sure to start your preparation well ahead of time, as the cake mixture needs 3 hours' rest, then time to bake before more time to absorb the syrup. I was also told a very interesting little nugget of information by Fadi BouKaram, who is famous on Instagram as Cedrusk. I had posted a picture of nammürah on Instagram, and he commented that in Terboul, the village in the Beqaa where he had spent some time as a child, they made pita sandwiches with nammürah (known as *h'risseh* there, the same as in Syria), either plain or with akkawi cheese (page 22), which they toasted for a quick k'nafeh-like fix. I loved the idea and tried it myself, although I can't say I would be having that sandwich often, but it is a fun idea for leftover nammürah.

SERVES 4

Sugar Syrup (page 300)

FOR THE CAKE

1¼ cups (225 g) regular semolina

Heaping ¼ teaspoon baking soda

¼ cup (50 g) baker's or superfine sugar

Just under 1 stick (100 g) unsalted butter, softened

1½ cups (450 g) plain full-fat yogurt

TO FINISH

1 tablespoon tahini to grease the baking dish

⅓ cup (50 g) blanched almonds

1. Prepare the sugar syrup to have on hand and let cool.

2. Put the semolina, baking soda, and sugar in a large mixing bowl and mix well. Add the softened butter and, with the tips of your fingers, work it in until well blended. Add the yogurt and, with the help of a spatula, mix well. You should end up with a fairly firm batter.

3. Brush a nonstick or regular square baking dish measuring about 8 x 8 x 1½ inches (20 x 20 x 4 cm) or a 10¼ inch (23 cm) round one with the tahini—the syrup cancels the nonstick function, hence the need for a thin coat of tahini or even butter. Pour the batter into it and gently shake the dish to spread the batter evenly across it. Cover with plastic wrap and let rest for 3 hours.

4. Shortly before the resting time is up, preheat the oven to 450°F (220°C). Press blanched almonds at regular intervals, imagining that each will be in the middle of a square or diamond with sides measuring about 2 inches (5 cm), or garnish as in the photograph on the next page. Bake in the preheated oven for 25 to 35 minutes, until golden all over and completely dry inside—test by inserting a skewer in the middle to see if it comes out dry.

5. Remove from the oven and evenly pour the syrup all over. The cake will look as if it is swimming in syrup, but do not be alarmed—it will fully absorb it within half an hour. Transfer the cake onto a serving platter as is or cut into squares. Serve at room temperature or store in an airtight container, where it will keep for a few days.

SWEET WALNUT OR CLOTTED CREAM TRIANGLES

SH'AYBIYATT

These do not go under the umbrella of baklava even if they are fairly similar. Perhaps it is because of their larger size. Anyhow, you can make them with either walnuts or clotted cream (page 301). I personally love the contrast between the crisp pastry and the soft, melting cream.

MAKES 12

Half recipe Sugar Syrup (about ⅔ cup/175 ml, page 300)

FOR THE WALNUT FILLING

½ cup (75 g) walnuts, ground medium fine

1 tablespoon baker's or superfine sugar

¼ teaspoon ground cinnamon

½ teaspoon rose water

½ teaspoon orange blossom water

FOR THE ASHTAH FILLING

6 ounces (175 g) ashtah (page 301)

TO FINISH

4 tablespoons (60 g) unsalted butter, melted

8 sheets phyllo pastry, measuring 11 x 17 inches (28 x 43 cm)

1. Prepare the sugar syrup and let cool.

2. To make the walnut filling: Put the walnuts in a medium mixing bowl. Add the sugar, cinnamon, and rose and orange blossom waters and mix well.

3. Brush a large baking sheet (even if it is nonstick) with melted butter. Preheat the oven to 450°F (220°C).

4. Lay one sheet of phyllo on your work surface—keep the other sheets covered with plastic wrap then a damp cloth on top, as they dry out quickly—and brush with melted butter. Lay another piece over it, brush with butter, and lay another two, brushing each with butter. Cut the layered sheets into 3½-inch (9 cm) squares. Separate one square and spread a heaping teaspoon walnut or ashtah filling in the middle, leaving the edges clear. Fold the pastry over the filling to make a triangle and press on the tip to seal it. Brush the top with butter and place on the baking sheet. Make the remaining triangles in the same way and arrange on the baking sheet until you have finished the first lot of pastry and half the filling. Do the same with the remaining four sheets of phyllo.

5. Bake in the preheated oven for 10 minutes, or until crisp and golden all over. Take out of the oven and let sit for a couple of minutes, then pour the syrup all over. Let cool, then transfer to a serving platter. Serve at room temperature.

THE BREAD OF THE SERAGLIO
AYSH EL-SARAYA

It is rather ironic to give this bread pudding such a grand name when it is made with day-old bread and caramelized sugar syrup. The only rich ingredients are the clotted cream and pistachio nuts. This said, sugar would have been precious in Ottoman times, and perhaps bread too—from the name you know it is an Ottoman sweet, and depending on how you read *seraglio* (harem or Turkish palace), it could have been a cheap dessert for concubines in the harem or a fancy dessert served to the ruling aristocracy. Anyhow, it is now very much part of our sweets repertoire and a great favorite for many.

SERVES 4

FOR THE BASE

14 ounces (400 g) one-day-old white breadcrumbs, crust discarded (bread torn into small pieces)

1¼ cups (250 g) baker's or superfine sugar

1 teaspoon lemon juice

1 tablespoon orange blossom water

1 tablespoon rose water

TO FINISH

12 ounces (350 g) ashtah (page 301)

2 heaping tablespoons (20 g) medium coarsely ground or slivered pistachios, or to taste

Handful of dried rose petals

1. Pack the breadcrumbs into a round serving dish measuring about 8 inches (20 cm) inside.

2. Put the sugar, ¼ cup (60 ml) water, and the lemon juice in a deep frying pan and place over medium heat. Bring to a boil and let bubble, stirring occasionally, for about 15 minutes, until it is a beautiful golden color. Gradually add just over ¾ cup (200 ml) boiling water—this is quite a risky operation, because the syrup will splutter as soon as you add the boiling water, so be sure to do this slowly and keep well away from the splutters.

3. Pour the caramelized syrup all over the bread and press on the bread with the back of a wide spatula to keep it together and let it soak up the syrup. Keep the bread inside the inner rim and tidy up the edges with the wiped spatula. Wipe the edges of the serving dish clean if needed and let cool. Top with the clotted cream. Sprinkle the pistachios and dried rose petals all over and serve immediately, or refrigerate and serve slightly chilled.

CLOTTED CREAM FRITTERS
KELLAGE

A Ramadan sweet par excellence, kellage is sold either fried or raw, as it were. It is made with large round disks of dry pastry that are similar to communion wafers. Both the pastry and the sweet are called kellage, and you should be able to find the wafer-like disks in Middle Eastern stores. The pastry needs to be brushed with milk to soften it so you can wrap it around the creamy filling. During the whole month of Ramadan, which is the most sacred in the Islamic calendar, some sweets makers set up deep frying pans outside their shop to fry enormous quantities of kellage, both for those who are fasting and for those who are not. They also sell it raw, but even though it is good, it doesn't compare to the fried version that I give below.

MAKES 8

Sugar Syrup (page 300)

FOR THE PASTRIES

8 sheets kellage

A small bowl of organic whole milk

7 ounces (200 g) ashtah (page 301)

Vegetable oil for frying

1. Prepare the sugar syrup and have on hand to drop the fritters in after frying, or to drizzle all over them.

2. Lay one kellage sheet on your work surface and brush with milk. Fold the sides of the circle to have a rectangle measuring about 6 x 8 inches (15 x 20 cm), brushing the folds with more milk if they are too dry. Place 1 heaping tablespoon ashtah in the middle, spreading it slightly, then fold over, the long sides first, before the shorter ones, to have a filled rectangle measuring about 2½ x 4 inches (6 x 10 cm). Prepare the rest of the kellage pastries the same way. Set aside.

3. Pour enough vegetable oil into a large, deep frying pan to deep-fry the pastries and place over medium heat. When the oil is hot—test by dipping in a piece of bread; if the oil immediately bubbles around it, it is ready—drop in as many pastries as will fit comfortably in the pan and fry, turning them over regularly, until lightly golden all over. Remove with a slotted spoon and drop into the sugar syrup. Turn over a couple of times, then lift onto a serving platter. You can also remove them onto a mesh grill to drain off any excess oil and to serve drizzled with the syrup. Finish frying and dipping the remaining pastries in the same way. Serve warm or at room temperature, soon after frying, for maximum crunch.

FILLED PANCAKES

ATAYEF

There is a whole group of pancakes that are cooked on one smooth side while the other is left to kind of bubble until it is full of holes, and atayef is one of them. They can be served as they are, filled with ashtah (page 301) with one half of the atayef sealed while the other half is left open to show the cream. Syrup is then drizzled all over. Or they can be filled with walnuts, ashtah, or unsalted cheese, sealed shut into half-moons, and fried before being dipped in syrup. Most people buy the pancakes ready-made from specialty sweets makers, such as Al-Rashidi in Beirut and Helwayat al-Tom in Tripoli, and fill and fry them at home. This said, they are fairly simple to make. You can make them small (about 2¾ inches/7 cm in diameter) or large (about 4 inches/10 cm in diameter). The thickness remains the same, at around ¼ inch (5 mm). When home cooks buy them ready-made, they also buy ashtah at the same time, but they prepare the cheese or walnut filling at home. They are an absolute must during the month of Ramadan and for Eid. Those you will make will not be nearly as perfect as those made by specialists who pass their skill from one generation to the next, but they will be good and easy to work with. If you want to serve the clotted cream–filled ones unfried, all you need to do is to half close the pancake around the cream filling, leaving the top open. You then arrange them on a round serving platter in a rosette with the sealed end on the inside before drizzling syrup all over. The classic garnish is chopped pistachios or orange blossom jam placed over the cream. Sometimes I scatter a few dried rose petals all over. Serve with more syrup on the side for those who want them sweeter.

MAKES 8 SMALL PANCAKES TO SERVE 4 OR 6

FOR THE PANCAKE MIX

1¼ cups (150 g) unbleached all-purpose flour

¾ teaspoon instant (fast-acting) yeast

Pinch fine sea salt

Sugar Syrup (page 300)

FOR THE CREAM FILLING

7 ounces (200 g) ashtah (page 301)

FOR THE WALNUT FILLING

¾ cup (100 g) walnut pieces, ground medium-fine

1 tablespoon baker's or superfine sugar

¼ teaspoon ground cinnamon

¼ teaspoon orange blossom water

FOR THE CHEESE FILLING

5 ounces (150 g) akkawi cheese (page 22) or fior di latte (cow's milk mozzarella), soaked in several changes of cold water to desalt it, patted dry, coarsely grated

Vegetable oil

1. To make the pancakes: Mix the flour, yeast, and salt in a medium mixing bowl and make a well in the center. Gradually add ¾ cup plus 2 tablespoons (220 ml) water, bringing in the flour as you go along, first with a spatula, then with a whisk, until you have a smooth batter. Cover the bowl with plastic wrap and let sit for 1 hour, or until the batter has risen and the surface is bubbly.

2. While the batter is rising, prepare the sugar syrup and filling of your choice—if it is the walnut filling, mix all the ingredients well together. Set aside.

3. Use a nonstick frying pan or brush a regular one with a little vegetable oil. Place over medium heat. When the pan is very hot, measure 1½ heaping tablespoons batter into a ladle and pour into the pan—you need to pour the batter in one go—to have a circle about 4 inches (10 cm) wide by ¼ inch (5 mm) thick. You may have to tilt the pan to spread the batter evenly. Cook on one side for 2 to 3 minutes, until the bottom is golden brown and the top is full of tiny holes and dry. Remove onto parchment paper and finish making the rest of the pancakes the same way.

4. Let the pancakes cool completely before filling. Pick up one and lay it on your hand, smooth-side down. Place 1 tablespoon filling in the middle, then fold the pancake into a half-moon and pinch the edges to seal them shut. Fill the remaining pancakes the same way.

5. Pour enough vegetable oil in a large, deep frying pan to deep-fry the pancakes and place over medium heat. When the oil is hot—test by dipping in a piece of bread; if the oil immediately bubbles around it, it is ready—slide in as many pancakes as will fit comfortably in the pan and fry, turning them over regularly, until crisp and golden brown all over.

6. Remove with a slotted spoon and drop into the syrup. Turn in the syrup a few times until well coated, then, with a slotted spoon, remove onto a serving platter. Serve warm or at room temperature. These are best served soon after frying for maximum crunch.

SEMOLINA CREAM PASTRIES
TAMRIYEH

These delectable pastries have a strong religious association for Greek Orthodox Christians, who prepare them on October 5 to celebrate the day of Mar Metr (Saint Dimitri), while Maronites have them on August 15 during the celebrations for the Assumption of the Virgin (Eid el-Saydeh). In Arabic, *tamriyeh* means "made with dates," a strange name given that they don't have any. Instead, they are made with a very thin freshly made phyllo-like dough—so thin you can read a newspaper through it—wrapped around a thick semolina "custard." Unlike most fried pastries, they are not dipped in sugar syrup but rather dusted with powdered sugar. You can bake them instead of frying, and you can easily skip making the dough and use phyllo instead, which is what I do. It won't be quite the same, but they will be just as good.

SERVES 4

FOR THE FILLING

5 tablespoons regular semolina

2 cups (500 ml) organic whole milk

5 tablespoons (62 g) baker's or superfine sugar

1 tablespoon orange blossom water

TO FINISH

Vegetable oil, if frying

8 sheets phyllo dough (12½ x 7 inches/32 x 18 cm)

1 stick (120 g) unsalted butter, melted

Powdered sugar for dusting the pastries

1. Put the semolina, milk, and sugar in a medium saucepan and place over medium heat. Bring to a boil, stirring constantly. Reduce the heat to low and continue stirring for 5 more minutes. Take off the heat, then add the orange blossom water. Keep stirring the mixture for another minute or so.

2. Pour into a 6-inch (15 cm) square dish, spreading the mixture evenly to about ½ inch (1¼ cm) thick. Let cool completely, then cut into 1½-inch (4 cm) squares to have 16 pieces.

3. Preheat the oven to 450°F (220°C).

4. Take one sheet of phyllo and lay it on your work surface, with the long side going away from you. Brush with the melted butter and cut in half lengthwise. Fold each half in two lengthwise and place a semolina square over each, about 1¾ inches (4 cm) away from the end near you. Fold the sides over the semolina square, then fold the top over. Brush with melted butter and keep folding until you end up with a square fully encasing the semolina "custard." Brush both sides with butter and lay on a nonstick baking sheet, or one lined with parchment paper or a silicone mat. At Jammal, a wonderful seaside restaurant in the north, they make tamriyeh into long thin fingers, and you can do the same by dividing the semolina "custard" into 2½-inch (6 cm) long sticks that are just over ½ inch (1½ cm) wide and rolling the phyllo around them. You will still end up with 16 pieces.

5. Bake in the preheated oven for 12 to 15 minutes, until lightly golden. Remove and let cool slightly on a wire rack. Or put enough oil in a large, deep frying pan to deep fry the pastries and place over medium heat. When the oil is hot—test by dipping in a piece of bread; if the oil immediately bubbles around it, it is ready—fry, turning over regularly until crisp and golden all over. Remove onto a mesh grill to drain off any excess oil. Dust with powdered sugar and serve just warm or at room temperature.

DATE PASTRIES

'RASS BIL-TAMR

This is a group of pastries that many in the West group under the term of ma'mūl that is important to both Christians and Muslims. The former make them for Easter, while the latter consider them essential sweets for Ramadan and Eid. When I lived in Beirut, the days before Easter were full of excitement, mainly because my mother, grandmother, and aunt spent their day in the kitchen making industrial quantities of ma'mūl, 'rass bil-tamr, and ka'k el-eid. My sisters and I kept darting in and out of the kitchen to steal some. And if we were planning to go for an afternoon walk through Hamra (then the Bond Street of Beirut) or the cinema, we would sneak a few more in a bag to take with us. There was always a dramatic moment when my mother would notice our mischief and start exhorting us to save them for Easter—not only to offer to visitors but also to send out to friends and neighbors. However, they were so good freshly baked that we couldn't resist provoking her ire—she was very strict but also very loving and was always happy to feed us, but at the right time. Anyhow, it is important to prepare these with unsweetened dried dates; otherwise they will be too sweet. You can also save yourself the sticky chore of pitting the dates by buying them already pitted. Better still, you can buy prepared date paste that comes in the shape of a cake, although read the label carefully because some press the dates into a cake with the pits and you want to buy those made with already pitted dates. These pastries are shaped in a special mold called *tabe'* in Arabic, meaning "stamp." The traditional ones are carved out of wood, but many are now made of plastic.

MAKES ABOUT 40

FOR THE PASTRY

- 2 cups (350 g) regular semolina
- ⅓ cup (40 g) unbleached all-purpose flour
- ¼ cup (50 g) baker's or superfine sugar
- ¼ teaspoon instant (fast-acting) yeast
- Just under 1½ sticks (150 g) unsalted butter, softened
- 1½ tablespoons rose water
- 1½ tablespoons orange blossom water

FOR THE FILLING

- 12 ounces (350 g) pitted, dried unsweetened dates, or unsweetened dried date paste
- ½ teaspoon ground cinnamon
- 2 tablespoons (30 g) unsalted butter, melted

1. To make the pastry: Put the semolina, flour, sugar, and yeast in a large mixing bowl and mix well. Add the softened butter and, with the tips of your fingers, work it into the mixture until fully incorporated. Add the rose and orange blossom waters and knead until you have a smooth, malleable pastry. Cover with plastic wrap and let rest for 1½ hours.

2. To make the filling: Put the pitted dates, cinnamon, and melted butter in a food processor and blend into a smooth paste—do not let the paste become too fine, as it should retain some texture. Remove to a large mixing bowl—if you are using a prepared paste, it comes in cake form and you will need to work the cinnamon and melted butter in with your hands until you have a malleable mixture.

3. Pinch off a small piece of date paste and shape it into a round disk about 2½ inches (3½ cm) in diameter and ¼ inch (5 mm) thick and put on a baking sheet or platter. Continue making the date disks until you have finished the paste. Cover with plastic wrap and keep on hand to use with the pastries.

4. Preheat the oven to 400°F (200°C).

5. To make the pastries: Pinch off a small piece of pastry and roll it into a ball the size of a walnut. Put on the palm of one hand and, with the fingers of your other hand, flatten evenly into a round disk about ¼ inch (5 mm) thick and 2¾ to 3¼ inches (7 to 8 cm) wide. Place one date disk in the middle and flap the pastry over, pinching the sides tightly together. Remove any excess pastry to end up with a smooth top. The date filling should be wrapped in an even layer of pastry.

6. In case you don't have the special mold for these, you can shape the pastry with your hands to produce a flat round cake about 2 inches (5 cm) in diameter and ½ inch (1¼ cm) thick, or you can use the traditional mold (tabe'). If the latter, gently press the filled cake into the mold, un-pinched-side down, making sure you do not press too hard; otherwise some pastry might stick to the mold. Tap the pastry out onto the tips of your fingers and slide onto a nonstick baking sheet, or one lined with parchment paper. Continue filling and shaping the pastries until you have finished both pastry and date paste. Scrape the inside of the mold every now and then to get rid of any pastry that has stuck inside the grooves. You should end up with about 40 pastries. If you have any leftover filling, have it as a sweet snack; and if you are left with any extra pastry, shape and bake it as dry biscuits.

7. Bake the pastries in the preheated oven for 15 to 18 minutes, until lightly golden. If your oven is not large enough to hold all of them at once, bake one lot after the other. Take out of the oven and let cool, then serve or pack into an airtight container, where they will keep for at least a week.

WALNUT PASTRIES

MA'MÜL BIL-JOZ

Like the date pastries (page 320), these are meaningful to both Muslims and Christians. They can be filled with walnuts (joz) or pistachios (festü'). The walnut-filled ones are round, while the pistachio-filled ones are oval. You can use the same pastry to make karabij, replacing the walnuts with pistachios and shaping them by hand into fingers with slightly rounded ends and a flat bottom. They need to be about 2 inches (5 cm) long and 1 inch (2½ cm) wide. Karabij are not dusted with powdered sugar because they are served with natef (page 302). You can also make your life easier by dividing the dough in two equal pieces to make a "pie" rather than individual pastries. Pinch off a piece from one half and flatten it on the palm of your hand to a thickness of about ½ inch (1¼ cm). Lay on the bottom of a nonstick baking dish (or one lined with parchment paper) measuring 8¼ x 13¾ inches (20½ x 34½ cm). Start from one corner, then smooth the pastry with your hand, before pinching off another piece, flattening and laying it next to the first one, overlapping them slightly so they do not come apart during baking. Repeat until you have covered the bottom of the dish, making sure the dough is spread evenly and thinly. Spread the filling all over and lay the remaining pastry over it, in the same way. This will be a bit more difficult, as you will be doing it over slightly chunky bits of filling rather than a flat surface. Cut into 2-inch (5 cm) squares. Bake and finish as below.

MAKES ABOUT 30

Dough for Date Pastries (page 320)

FOR THE FILLING

1⅛ cups (175 g) walnuts or pistachios

¼ cup (50 g) baker's or superfine sugar

½ teaspoon ground cinnamon

1½ teaspoons rose water

1½ teaspoons orange blossom water

TO FINISH

Powdered sugar

1. Prepare the dough for the date pastries following the instructions on page 318 and let rest for 1½ hours.

2. To prepare the filling: Put the walnuts or pistachios in a food processor and grind until medium-fine. Transfer to a medium mixing bowl. Add the sugar and cinnamon and mix well. Add the rose and orange blossom waters and mix again. The mixture should be slightly sticky so it holds when you are filling the pastries.

3. Preheat the oven to 400°F (200°C).

4. To make the pastries: Pinch off a small piece of pastry and roll it into a ball the size of a walnut. Place on the palm of one hand, cup your hand around it, and with the index finger of the other hand, burrow a hole in it (be careful not to pierce the bottom) while rotating it to make it easier to get even "walls" until you have a shell resembling a topless egg with "walls" that are about ¼ inch (5 mm) thick.

5. Fill the hollowed pastry with a teaspoon of the filling and pinch the open sides shut. Carefully shape the filled dough into a ball and press

it lightly into the ma'mül tabe' (page 23)—if you don't have one, use a conical tea strainer about 2½ inches (6 cm) wide—putting the smooth side on the inside so you get a perfect top. Tap the pastry out onto the tips of your fingers and slide onto a nonstick baking sheet, or one lined with parchment paper or a silicone mat. Scrape the insides of the mold every now and then to get rid of any residue pastry that may have stuck to the grooves. You can also shape the pastries by hand and decorate them by lightly dragging a fork over the top of each, or by pinching all over, at regular intervals with tweezers. Repeat the above process until you have finished both pastry and filling. You should end up with about 30 pastries each measuring approximately 2 inches (5 cm) wide and 1½ inches (3 cm) high.

6. Bake the pastries in the preheated oven for 12 to 15 minutes, until done but without having colored much.

7. Remove the pastries from the oven and let cool, then dust them lightly with powdered sugar. Arrange on a serving platter or pack into an airtight container (in which case leave the sugar dusting until just before serving), where they will keep for at least a week.

EASTER RINGS
KA'K EL-EID

These are made for Easter alongside the ma'mūl (page 322) and 'rass bil-tamr (page 320), or at least they were in our home. My siblings and I loved playing with them when my mother was making them, wearing them around our fingers and trying to eat them off our hands without breaking them. They have an unmistakable, intriguing flavor of mastic and mahlep and a slightly crumbly texture that makes them totally irresistible.

MAKES ABOUT 50

2 cups (250 g) fine semolina

⅛ teaspoon instant (fast-acting) yeast

¼ teaspoon finely ground mastic

⅛ teaspoon ground nutmeg

¼ teaspoon ground mahlep (page 17)

Just under 1 stick (100 g) unsalted butter, or ghee, softened

Heaping ⅓ cup (75 g) baker's or superfine sugar

⅓ cup plus 1½ tablespoons (100 ml) organic whole milk

Unbleached all-purpose flour to dust the bowl

1. Put the semolina, yeast, mastic, nutmeg, and mahlep in a large mixing bowl and mix well. Add the softened butter (or ghee) and, with the tips of your fingers, rub into the semolina until fully incorporated.

2. Put the sugar and milk in a small pitcher and stir until the sugar is completely dissolved. Add the sweetened milk to the semolina and knead until you have a smooth, malleable dough. Shape into a ball and put in a lightly floured bowl. Cover with plastic wrap and let rest for 1½ hours.

3. Preheat the oven to 400°F (200°C).

4. Pinch off a small piece of dough and shape into a ball the size of a small walnut. Roll into a thin sausage about ¼ inch (¾ cm) thick and 4½ inches (11 cm) long. Bring both ends together and press one on top of the other to have a ring about 2 inches (5 cm) in diameter. Gently lift onto a nonstick baking sheet, or one lined with parchment paper or a silicone mat, taking care not to spoil the shape. Continue making and arranging the rings until you have about 50.

5. Bake in the preheated oven for about 10 minutes, until golden. Let cool before serving, or pack into an airtight container, where they will keep for at least a week.

SHORTBREADS

GHRAYBEH

Ghraybeh are dainty, fragrant biscuits that melt in your mouth, a kind of shortbread but even more buttery. You can shape them in three different ways. As described below; in round "cakes" about 2 inches (5 cm) in diameter and ¾ inch (2 cm) thick, with a slightly depressed center where you press an almond or a pistachio; or in diamonds the same thickness as the round "cakes" but with 2-inch (5 cm) sides, and again with a nut pressed in the middle. You can also make these with unbleached flour. The recipe remains the same, but you may have to use a little less of the fragrant waters, 2 tablespoons each.

MAKES ABOUT 36

Just under 1 stick (100 g) unsalted butter, softened

1¼ cups (125 g) powdered sugar

2½ cups (310 g) fine semolina

2½ tablespoons (37 ml) rose water

2½ tablespoons (37 ml) orange blossom water

⅓ cup (50 g) raw pistachios

1. Put the softened butter and powdered sugar in a large mixing bowl and work together with a spatula until you have a creamy, smooth mixture.

2. Gradually add the semolina and work it into the sweet butter until fully incorporated. Then add the rose and orange blossom waters and knead until you have a soft, smooth pastry.

3. Divide the pastry into 36 equal pieces and roll each into a ball the size of a small walnut. Place on a nonstick baking sheet, or one lined with parchment paper or a silicone mat, and press a pistachio in the middle. Continue shaping and garnishing the ghraybeh until you have used up both pastry and nuts. Leave a little space between each, as they will spread during baking. Refrigerate for about 1 hour.

4. Preheat the oven to 325°F (170°C) 20 minutes before the time is up.

5. Bake in the preheated oven for 12 to 15 minutes, until completely done but still very pale in color. Let cool, then serve or store in an airtight container, where they will keep for at least a week.

AL-JARDALI'S SHORTBREADS
SANIÜRAT AL-JARDALI

Named after the family who created this sweet, saniüra is a typical sweet from Saida in the south. The recipe below comes from one of their most famous sweets makers, who actually specializes in k'nafeh. Classic saniüra are made plain and in the shape of diamonds. Sometimes the edges are crinkly, but most of the time they are left straight. I have had them stuffed with a little pistachio, but most of the time, they are left plain. And, like ghraybeh, they simply melt in the mouth.

MAKES ABOUT 40

1⅛ cups (125 g) powdered sugar

⅓ cup (80 g) ghee

¾ cup plus 1 tablespoon (100 g) unbleached all-purpose flour, plus extra for rolling out

1 teaspoon rose water

1. Put the sugar and ghee in a large mixing bowl and mix well. Add the flour and rose water and knead until you have a soft pastry. Let rest for 30 minutes in the refrigerator, then roll out to a thickness of about ¼ inch (½ cm). Cut into diamonds just over 2 inches (5½ cm) long. Carefully transfer, using a baking scraper, to a nonstick baking sheet, or one lined with parchment paper or a silicone mat, and refrigerate again for 30 minutes.

2. Preheat the oven to 325ºF (170ºC).

3. Bake in the preheated oven for 12 minutes, or until done and barely colored. Take out of the oven and let cool, then serve or store in an airtight container, where they will keep for at least a week.

FRAGRANT WHEAT PORRIDGE

AMEH

Also known as *snayniyeh* (meaning "for teeth"), ameh is prepared for a baby's first teeth as well as for Eid el-Barbara (the feast of Saint Barbara), which is our Halloween. In Sicily, they cook wheat for Santa Lucia, and on that day I love giving my friends our Lebanese version, which is obviously different from theirs, which is cooked with cooked wine (vino cotto). I like to have it for breakfast instead of porridge and sometimes prepare a batch ahead and simply reheat what I need in the morning, mix it with sugar and fragrant waters, and top it with the presoaked nuts.

SERVES 4 TO 6

Just under 1½ cups (250 g) hulled wheat, soaked overnight with 1 teaspoon baking soda, plus 1 tablespoon for rubbing into the wheat

1 tablespoon anise seeds, wrapped in cheesecloth

½ cup (75 g) Mediterranean pine nuts, soaked in boiling water, drained and dried just before serving

½ cup (75 g) walnuts, soaked in boiling water and peeled, that is if you have the patience, drained and dried just before serving

½ cup (75 g) blanched almonds, soaked in boiling water, drained and dried just before serving

FOR EACH SERVING

1 tablespoon granulated sugar, or to taste

1 teaspoon rose water

½ teaspoon orange blossom water

1. Drain the wheat and rinse under cold water. Sprinkle with 1 tablespoon baking soda and rub into the wheat. Rinse again. Drain and put in a medium pot. Add 1 quart (1 liter) water together with the anise seed parcel. Place over medium-high heat and bring to a boil. Skim the surface clean if needed, then partially cover the pan and let bubble for 10 minutes. Reduce the heat to medium-low and let bubble gently for 50 more minutes, stirring from time to time and checking on the water so the wheat doesn't dry up. You want to end up with a thin porridge-like mixture with the wheat berries doubled in size but still whole.

2. Once done, take off the heat and discard the anise seed parcel. Serve hot in individual bowls, adding the sugar and fragrant waters to each serving. Mix well, then garnish with as much of the presoaked nuts as you like.

SWEETS

YELLOW "SPONGE" CAKE
S'FÜF

S'füf holds a special place in the heart of Lebanese kids as the ultimate post-school snack. It is one of the very few sweets that is not the preserve of professional sweets makers. It went out of fashion for a while but seems to be back again. You can make it more luxurious by replacing the turmeric with saffron. If you choose to do this, use two or three good pinches of saffron threads. Grind them first, then steep in the rose water for at least half an hour before adding to the cake mix.

SERVES 4 TO 6

Tahini to brush the cake pan, if needed

FOR THE CAKE

2 cups (250 g) unbleached all-purpose flour

1 cup (125 g) fine semolina

2 teaspoons ground turmeric

¼ teaspoon fine sea salt

2 teaspoons baking powder

1¼ cups (250 g) baker's or superfine sugar

⅓ cup (80 ml) extra virgin olive oil

2 tablespoons (30 ml) rose water

FOR THE GARNISH

⅓ cup (50 g) Mediterranean pine nuts or blanched almonds

1. Preheat the oven to 350°F (180°C). Use a nonstick deep cake pan measuring 8 inches (21 cm) in diameter or brush a regular one with a little tahini.

2. Mix the flour, semolina, turmeric, salt, baking powder, and sugar in a large mixing bowl. Add the olive oil and, with a spatula, rub the fat into the dry ingredients until well absorbed.

3. Add the rose water and ⅔ cup (160 ml) water and mix well. Pour the mixture into the cake pan. Scatter the pine nuts or almonds all over and bake in the preheated oven for 50 to 55 minutes, until the cake has risen and is dry inside. Prick the middle with a toothpick or skewer. If it comes out dry, the cake is done.

4. Remove from the oven. Let cool completely, then cut into medium-sized triangles, squares, or diamonds. Serve at room temperature. It will keep for a few days stored in an airtight container.

MEGHLI

Meghli is the classic sweet prepared to celebrate a newborn. *Meghli* means *boiled*, and the name comes from the fact that you need to boil it for a long time, while stirring constantly, to get the right consistency, which is actually like that of a custard but instead of eggs to set it, we use rice flour. The mixture is then poured into individual bowls, and once it is set, it is garnished with presoaked nuts and shredded dried coconut, which I don't use. The meghli is offered to those visiting to congratulate the family, while the rest is sent to relatives, neighbors, and friends to announce the happy event.

I no longer go to the trouble of making meghli from scratch because my friend Jacquot Ayoub (page 341) introduced me to a brilliant prepared mix she buys from Mat'hanet Khoury, a wonderful spice shop in Achrafiyeh, the Christian quarter of Beirut, where they mix the rice flour with the spices and sell the mix with instructions on how much sugar and water to add to make the meghli. Then, all you have to do is let it soak for two hours before boiling for less than half an hour, shorter than if you start from scratch. It was and still is one of my favorite sweets, and I remember enjoying it at the Antabli Fountain in downtown Beirut before it got destroyed in the civil war. Much later, Antabli reopened in Beirut souks, a soulless place that became a ghost town following the huge explosion of August 4, 2020, that devastated half the city and in particular the part nearest to the port but is coming back to life now.

SERVES 6

1 cup (200 g) rice flour

2 tablespoons (5 g) ground caraway

1 tablespoon ground anise

1 tablespoon ground cinnamon

¾ cup (150 g) baker's or superfine sugar

FOR THE GARNISH

½ cup (75 g) Mediterranean pine nuts, soaked overnight in several changes of cold water

½ cup (75 g) walnuts, soaked overnight in several changes of cold water, peeled if you have the patience

½ cup (75 g) unpeeled almonds, soaked overnight in several changes of cold water, drained, peeled, and dried

1. Put the ground rice in a large saucepan. Add 2 quarts (2 liters) water, together with the caraway, anise, cinnamon, and sugar, and let soak for a couple of hours. Place over medium-high heat and bring to a boil, stirring constantly. Keep stirring for 25 minutes. Then reduce the heat to medium-low and let bubble for 25 more minutes, still stirring, until the mixture has thickened. Reduce the heat to low and keep stirring for another 10 minutes, until it becomes quite thick but will still set flat when poured into the one large or several individual bowls.

2. Take off the heat and pour into one large shallow serving bowl or 6 individual ones. Let cool, then garnish with the drained and dried nuts. Serve chilled.

MILK PUDDING
MÜHALLABIYEH

According to Charles Perry, the world's foremost expert on medieval Arab cookery, mühallabiyeh is named after a ninth- or tenth-century aristocrat. It is a wonderfully creamy, eggless "custard" that can be made with either ground rice or cornstarch—I prefer the latter because the texture is more delicate. I also tend to make it a little more wobbly than the classic version and often add saffron to make it more luxurious, even if it is not traditional. This said, saffron is now grown in the Bekaa by two great ecological entrepreneurs, Karl Karam and Jihad Farah, under the brand Safran du Liban, so some of my compatriots will also soon start making mühallabiyeh with local saffron. When I first started writing about the food of my country, more than thirty years ago, most Western chefs as well as many of my friends were unfamiliar with the taste of rose water and orange blossom water; when I served them mühallabiyeh, they felt like they were eating perfume. Fortunately, things have changed since, and both fragrant waters have now entered the mainstream, more or less!

SERVES 4 TO 6

1 quart (1 liter) organic whole milk

¾ cup (150 g) granulated sugar

4 heaping tablespoons (50 g) cornstarch

2 teaspoons rose water

2 teaspoons orange blossom water

¼ teaspoon ground mastic

Slivered pistachios and dried rose petals for garnish

1. Put the milk, sugar, and cornstarch in a large saucepan and whisk together until the sugar has completely dissolved. Place over medium heat and bring to a boil, whisking all the time to avoid any lumps. Then reduce the heat to medium-low and continue whisking for another 10 to 15 minutes, until the mixture has thickened.

2. Remove from the heat. Add the rose and orange blossom waters. Gradually stir in the mastic and immediately pour into one large shallow bowl or 4 to 6 individual ones. Let cool, then refrigerate and serve chilled. Garnish with the pistachios and rose petals just before serving.

REZZ BIL-HALIB

A more substantial take on mühallabiyeh (page 332). It is another favorite. Again, I like to make it a little less thick than the classic version. Be sure to use short-grain white rice, and kind of broken if you can find it, as you want the rice to practically dissolve. In fact, my mother used to sometimes make it with rice flour, but I think it is more interesting made with rice.

SERVES 4 TO 6

½ cup (100 g) short-grain white rice

2½ cups (625 ml) organic whole milk

½ cup (100 g) baker's or superfine sugar

1 tablespoon rose water

1 tablespoon orange blossom water

Slivered pistachios for garnish

1. Rinse the rice under cold water and put it in a large saucepan. Add 1½ cups (375 ml) water and place over medium heat. Bring to a boil, then reduce the heat to low and simmer for 15 minutes, or until the rice has absorbed all the water.

2. Add the milk and increase the heat to medium. Bring back to a boil, stirring occasionally. Cook for 5 minutes, then lower the heat and simmer for another 10 to 15 minutes, stirring the mixture so the rice does not stick.

3. Add the sugar and let bubble for a couple more minutes, still stirring. Remove from the heat. Add the rose and orange blossom waters. Mix well, then pour into 4 to 6 individual bowls or one shallow serving bowl. Serve chilled, garnished with slivered pistachios.

TAHINI RICE PUDDING
MÜFFATA'A

Here is a unique take on rice pudding that is a Sunni specialty from Beirut. It used to be made on the last Wednesday of April, which is the Wednesday of the Prophet Job, together with müdardarah, boiled potatoes, and eggs to eat with or distribute to friends. Apparently, the Prophet Job healed from his painful wounds on Beirut's seashore after dipping himself seven times in the water and rubbing himself with a local plant or flower. On that day, many Sunni Beirutis will go out to picnic along the corniche or by the sea a little higher up, and they will make sure to have müffata'a. I never knew about it when I lived there and only discovered it a few years back when I was researching my book *Feast*, when my friend Ziad Ghorly took me to al-Makari, the most famous müffata'a maker in the city. Mr. Makari very kindly gave me his recipe and advised me not to serve the pudding in either silver or melamine. I am not sure why, but he used to sell it in porcelain plates, and I am guessing people brought back the plates, like you would with milk bottles. Sadly, he is now older and no longer able to stir for hours. Another factor is the economic crisis, so now his sons make it in a central kitchen and sell it in aluminum containers. When I tasted it again recently, I felt that it was not as good as when the old man used to make it, but you can make your own following his recipe below.

SERVES 8 TO 10

1 tablespoon ground turmeric

1¼ cups (250 g) short-grain white rice, rinsed under cold water, soaked for 30 minutes

1 cup (250 g) tahini

2½ cups (500 g) baker's or superfine sugar

½ cup (75 g) Mediterranean pine nuts

Pinch each ground fennel and ground anise

1. Put 3½ cups (875 ml) water in a large pot together with the turmeric and place over high heat. Bring to a boil. Drain the rice and add to the water. Bring the heat down to low and let bubble gently, partly covered, for 30 to 45 minutes, stirring regularly.

2. Put the tahini, sugar, and pine nuts in another pot large enough to eventually hold the cooked rice. When the rice is done, add it together with its liquid, if any, to the tahini. Add the ground fennel and ground anise and place over medium-low heat. Cook, stirring, for 1 hour or so, until the oil from the tahini rises (in Arabic, it is called *srijeh*) and the pudding is very thick—you'll know it is ready when you dip a spatula into the rice then pull it out and no rice drops back into the pot.

3. Spread on one large serving platter or 8 to 10 individual plates, making a groove all around the inside. Serve at room temperature.

FRUIT ICE CREAM
BÜZA ALA FAWAKEH

This recipe is your base to use with almost any fruit you fancy. However, when you are using berries or apricots, you need to add one step and cook them slightly with sugar first to concentrate the flavor and get rid of any excess liquid—a great tip I got from my pastry chef friend Shuna Lydon. If using other fruit, such as bananas and mangoes, simply puree them before adding to the milk and cream. The weight below is your guideline as to the quantity of fruit pulp. Also, our ice cream "cone" is rectangular in shape instead of conical and it is more like a wafer than a biscuit. I used to love watching the ice cream vendor cram it so full of layer after layer of flavors that it bulged at the sides, almost to the breaking point. Having ice cream in these odd-shaped "cones" never fails to conjure up a madeleine moment that takes me back to my teenage years when my sisters and I would go out in the afternoon or early evening for ice cream and walk up and down Hamra, in those days the Bond Street of Beirut. We lived just down from it, not far from the sea, and it was where we went to the movies, to hang out in cafes, or just for a stroll.

SERVES 4

1 cup (250 ml) organic whole milk

1 pound 2 ounces (500 g) fresh fruit pulp

1 cup (200 g) baker's or superfine sugar

1¼ cups (310 ml) crème fraîche or heavy cream

1. Put the milk in a small saucepan and place over medium heat. Bring to a boil—carefully watch toward the end so as not to let it boil over. Take off the heat. Cover with a clean kitchen towel and let cool.

2. If you are using berries or apricots, put them together with the sugar in another saucepan and place over medium heat. Cook, stirring regularly, until the sugar is completely dissolved and the fruit is softened. Let cool, then process with a handheld blender or in a food processor until completely pureed—I strain raspberries, but you don't have to if you don't mind the seeds. If you are making the ice cream with mango or bananas, puree them in a food processor. If you are using figs, peel first, then weigh and cook like the berries for a more concentrated flavor.

3. Transfer the puréed fruit to a large measuring jug, and add the cooled milk and cream, and sugar if you haven't already added it to the fruit. Mix well, then refrigerate, stirring every now and then. Once completely chilled, pour into an ice cream maker and follow the manufacturer's instructions to churn the ice cream. Transfer to a freezer-proof container and put in the freezer, uncovered for the first 15 minutes so the top does not form crystals. Then put the lid on and serve whenever you need to, not forgetting to remove from the freezer about 20 minutes ahead of serving.

MILK ICE CREAM
BÜZA ALA HALIB

This is the base you would use to make pistachio ice cream by adding 1 cup (150 g) raw pistachios, finely ground, to the mix. And now that saffron is grown in the Bekaa Valley by Safran du Liban, I often add it to make saffron ice cream. I grind the saffron in a small mortar, add the rose water, and let it steep for about half an hour before adding to the mixture. The thickening agent in our ice cream is salep, which comes from Turkey or Iran, and is now a protected species and as a result, not so easy to source. You can use cornstarch instead, although salep thickens the ice cream in a different way, giving it a stretchy, chewy texture that extends the pleasure of enjoying it because it takes longer to melt in the mouth. Even if you don't get as much of a chewy, stretchy texture with cornstarch, it is your only option for a substitute. So, don't hesitate to use it. It is the closest you will get to making real büza.

MAKES 1¼ QUARTS (1¼ LITERS)

1 quart (1 liter) organic whole milk, at room temperature

1¼ cups (250 g) baker's or superfine sugar

1 tablespoon salep (or ¼ cup/30 g cornstarch)

1¼ cups (310 ml) crème fraîche or heavy cream

3 tablespoons (45 ml) rose water

½ teaspoon ground mastic

1. If you are going to use salep: Put the milk and sugar in a large saucepan and place over medium-low heat. Give the sugar a good stir with a whisk, then very slowly and gradually add the salep, whisking all the time, so you don't get any lumps—the purer the salep, the less risk there is of the base becoming lumpy. Once you have used up the salep, bring the milk to a boil, whisking constantly. Let the milk bubble gently for at least 10 minutes, still whisking all the time, then for another 10 minutes or so—if you like it thicker, let the milk bubble for longer.

2. If you are going to use cornstarch: Put a little milk in a medium mixing bowl and add the cornstarch. Whisk until completely diluted. Put the rest of the milk and the sugar in a large saucepan and place over medium-low heat. Whisk the milk and cornstarch again, then slowly pour it into the pan while whisking the milk. Keep whisking the milk until it comes to a boil, then let bubble gently for 10 minutes, still whisking all the time.

3. Once the milk has thickened, whisk in the crème fraîche, then the rose water, and, finally, slowly and gradually add the ground mastic without stopping the whisking—if you add the mastic in one go, it will clump up in the hot mixture. You really have to do it very slowly or wait until the mixture has cooled before adding it.

4. Let the mixture cool completely (I like to refrigerate it overnight), then churn the mixture in an ice cream maker following the manufacturer's instructions.

APRICOT LEATHER ICE CREAM
BÜZA ALA AMAR EL-DINN

Amar el-dinn means "moon of the religion," and I am not sure why this name was given to apricot leather. It is possible it has to do with the fact that during Ramadan, apricot leather is diluted in water to make the drink with which to break the fast, but this is only guesswork. Anyhow, the ice cream is exquisitely delicate, with the flavor of the apricot leather enhanced by the orange blossom water with the whole spiked with Mediterranean pine nuts. When it is apricot season, I like to add 2 to 3 fresh apricots (which I pit and blend) to add a little freshness and have orange flecks in the ice cream.

MAKES ABOUT 1¼ QUARTS (1¼ LITERS)

½ cup (75 g) Mediterranean pine nuts

¼ cup (60 ml) orange blossom water

2 cups (500 ml) organic whole milk

10½ ounces (300 g) apricot leather, cut into medium squares

⅓ cup (75 g) baker's or superfine sugar

2 to 3 fresh apricots, when in season (optional)

1¼ cups (310 ml) crème fraîche or heavy cream

1. In a small bowl, put the pine nuts to soak in the orange blossom water to rehydrate them so they are soft to the bite. This will take a bit longer, but they will continue rehydrating in the ice cream mix as it is cooling.

2. Put the milk in a large saucepan. Add the apricot leather and sugar and place over medium-low heat. Use a whisk to stir the apricot leather in the milk as it melts. When the milk is hot but not about to boil and the apricot leather is almost completely dissolved, take it off the heat and use a handheld blender or food processor to completely dissolve the apricot leather, together with the fresh apricots if you are using them. Transfer to a large measuring jug.

3. Add the crème fraîche and stir until well blended. Add the orange blossom water and pine nuts and mix well. Let cool, then refrigerate. Churn in an ice cream maker following the manufacturer's instructions.

ACKNOWLEDGMENTS

My agents, Nicole Aragi in New York and Caspian Dennis in London, who are not only the best-ever agents but also great friends with whom I have long, fun lunches in London, testing my recipes on them.

My publishers, Gabriella Doob at Ecco in New York and first Kitty Stogdon, then Samhita Foria at Bloomsbury in London. It was an absolute pleasure to work with Gabriella on *Feast* and the same on this book, while I never got the chance to work with Kitty because she left before I finished the book, but it was great working with Samhita.

Also at Ecco, Renata De Oliveira, who, like for *Feast*, has again produced a wonderful design; Will Howard, Gabriella's assistant, for always being very helpful; Alicia Gencarelli, my production editor, for being incredibly attentive to every detail; and the same with Leda Scheintaub, my copy editor. While at Bloomsbury, Laura Brodie, the production controller.

My late mother, of course, who, before she left us, I surprised this time by teaching her about some of our food rather than the opposite. Regardless, she was always a fount of knowledge ready to help whenever I needed her to.

Dalia Khamissy, with whom I traveled the country in search of new dishes and interesting people and places to photograph. Despite Dalia not being a food photographer, she accepted to work with me on this book, and I love what she did. I also enjoyed our occasional bickering as we got to know each other better with each photographic excursion. It was great to team again with Kristin Perers for the amazing studio photographs of the recipes, and Claire Ptak for her gorgeous styling, as I had done for *Feast*. Kristin was again assisted by Sophie Levi Bronze and Aloha Bonser-Shaw. As for Claire, she was assisted for the first time by Allegra d'Agostini, and all three were also lovely to work with.

Victoria Allen and everyone else at Props Ltd. for their amazing props; it was the second book we did using their beautiful tableware. Also, Ayse Habibe Kucuk, who lent us some of her beautiful ceramics, and, finally China And Company.

And again, I asked Amy Dencler to test the recipes. It is the third book that Amy tested the recipes for in her American kitchen; her comments were again incredibly helpful, and thanks to her I was able to adjust some of the recipes.

Jacquot Ayoub for having introduced me to, among other recipes, füstü'iyeh, a typical broad bean and meat dish cooked in yogurt from the south. Jacquot is also a fount of knowledge about regional specialties. She also introduced me to many more dishes as well as different parts of the country that I was not familiar with.

Huda Baroudi, with her sister Mona Zaatari, are among my favorite cooks in Lebanon. Mona's kibbeh arnabiyeh (page 165) is my reference for that dish, while Huda's sayyadiyeh (page 224) is my ultimate, even if not entirely classic, version. There are of course other versions of both dishes, but theirs are my favorites. Huda has also been super generous with her home and kitchen, allowing me to use them for both filming and photographing.

Ziad Ghorly, for arranging sumptuous meals at his wonderful grandmother Soussou's, who told me about typical southern dishes and of course gave me a taste of her frakeh, among others. Ziad's uncle Ghazi Ghorly, who took us around Baalbek for the best sfiha. Ziad was also the one to introduce me to müffata'a (page 334).

Ziad Mikati, who sent me and Dalia with his driver, Ibrahim, to one of Tripoli's best ka'k bakeries, Ka'k al-Al'a, where Dalia and I spent an afternoon watching the mesmerizing spectacle of the incredible bakers working in a meticulously synchronized chain to shape and bake, on a daily basis, hundreds of loaves of northern ka'k, a quite different ka'k from those shaped like a handbag that you buy on the streets of Beirut. Ziad and his wife, Mirna, also hosted me at a wonderful lunch at their home in Beirut, where they served Tripoli specialties.

Akram Zaatari, one of our greatest artists, for introducing me to his mother, Nazek, a descendant of the Sufi branch of Tripoli known as Mawlawis, who has provided me with fascinating insights on the Lebanese mawlawi (from *mawla* meaning Sufi lord) culinary traditions.

Hania Rayess Boustani, who was my new best friend for a short while before becoming a firm friend, together with her husband, Naji. She hosted me many times in her lovely homes in Beirut and Aabey, also in Batroun, and introduced me to various friends, each of whom added to my knowledge about different regional dishes, products, or produce. Hania also specializes in giveaways, and every time I see her, I leave with one or more delicacies.

Renata Zeidan, for bringing me from her countryside the best fresh cheese and arisheh. Ghada and Bahjat al-Darwiche, from Dar Zefta, and their gorgeous manager and cook, Zeinab al-Souhail, who in turn introduced me to the baker Sahjouneh in al-Numeyriyeh, who made us delicious mishtah (page 26); and her adorable sister Nadine Souheil Krayani and her charming family, who hosted Dalia and me to wonderful lunches and gave me insights into southern dishes.

Lynn Hazim, who introduced me to her mother, Joumana, who welcomed Dalia and me into her home, despite having never met us, to show me how to make fattet makdüss (page 137).

Gaby Daher and his sister Sumy Hokayem, who both hosted me in their homes, with Sumy introducing me to a few northern specialties, and her sister Fadia, who gave me the recipe for marshüsheh 1 (page 272).

Shirine Abdallah, who received us in her lovely home in the west Bekaa and gave me my first taste of zinkol.

Feryal Osseyran Barakat, her son Kamel, and daughter-in-law Karma. Karma's mother, Yasmine Charafeddine, and her husband, Mohamed, who hosted us to two spectacular lunches in the Charafeddine home in Meshref. Maha Mroue, whom I met at Yasmine's and who told me about the cooking of her village in the south. Feryal also generously shared her recipe for kammüneh (page 18), while Yasmine gave me her recipe for fatteh bil-ful el-akhdar (page 139).

Moussa Ibrahim in Dibbine, who sadly lost his müneh business in both the south and in Beirut as well as part of his home during the Israeli aggression in the fall of 2024. Raji el-Soussi in Beirut, who serves the best-ever breakfast at his eponymous restaurant, and who very kindly gave Dalia free rein to photograph him and his food despite being very busy serving a stream of customers.

Breakfast staff at Dar Alma, who very graciously let us organize our breakfast twice to photograph it.

Jihad Farah and Karl Karam of Safran du Liban, who very generously gave me some of their saffron. Jihad also told me about the various culinary traditions of his village in the north.

Joumana Abu Eid, a beautiful TV presenter and a partner in the gorgeous Karaz hotel in Ehden, who introduced me to their manager Najat el-Kareh, who took us around when we went there in search of kibbé and other dishes. The hotel has sadly burned down since. I was introduced to Joumana by Robert Nakhel, whom I met at a beautiful dinner Nadim Koteich gave for me in Abu Dhabi and saw again at a spectacular lunch at Paula Al-Askari's, also in Abu Dhabi.

Mona and Misbah Ahdab in Tripoli, who very graciously hosted Dalia and me to an exquisite lunch to give me a taste of their cook Nawal's stuffed vine leaves. Hers are absolutely tiny and melting in the mouth because she lets them cook for hours over very low heat—they were the best I have ever had, even better than my mother's! The morning of that lunch, Misbah and Mona had organized for Cheikh Sidawi, who works for them, to take us to see ma'ju'a being made, as well as halawet el-rezz, which I like to describe as the Lebanese mochi. Cheikh was another fount of knowledge for all things culinary from the north. A few months earlier, Misbah had taken us around the souks of Tripoli, and wherever we went with him, he was greeted warmly, which cannot be said of many Lebanese ex–members of parliament. Misbah also brought me the best orange blossom jam I have had in years, which reminded me of those I loved when I lived there—this jam is the garnish of choice for our cream-based sweets.

Anna Ansari, for testing some of the recipes and sending me helpful comments and photos.

Janine and Tony Mamari and their son Reda. Janine and Tony asked Ghada H'maidan Nasr, who works for them, to organize a tasting of Druze dishes (Ghada is from a Druze village) cooked by Alaa al-Koukash, who very kindly gave me his recipes. Also, Rabih Alameddine, whose family is from Aitat in the Shouf, who told me about Alaa's chicory salad with kishk (page 88).

Chef Riad Aboulteif, who introduced me to Sheikh Hadi and Sheikh Amir (whom I call prince because *amir* means "prince" in Arabic), who have the most wonderful müneh shop in Aley called al-Hassad, meaning "the harvester." They prepared the most delectable breakfast (pictured on the cover) for Dalia and me when we visited and gave us free rein to photograph in their shop.

Riad also introduced me to Liliane Ghannam, who runs the cooperative kitchen Matbakh Ors el-Shams in Mükhtara, where cooks bring their ingredients to prepare their müneh (page 2), ranging from tomato paste to pomegranate molasses to makdüss and so on. There is also a saj in one corner of the kitchen for those who want to bake their own bread. On the day we were there, there was a wonderful sheikha (Druze lady) baking bread to order for various people in the village.

Lina Njeim, the cook at Al Fundok in Ma'asser el-Shouf, who introduced me to grilled stuffed intestines. Hers were the most delicious I have ever had.

Cathy Chami, who let me cook a fun samkeh harrah (page 218) lunch in her and her sister's beautiful house in Batroun so Dalia could take pictures.

Rima Husseini and her husband, Ali, in Baalbek, who organized an enchanting lunch with local specialties in their historic hotel Palmyra overlooking the magnificent archeological site.

The Attieh family in Beino, Nahla and her mother, Mani, her aunt Mona and husband, Elias, her great-aunt Renée, and Anita, her cousin. They graciously received us one morning to show us how to make lahm bil-khall (meat braised in vinegar, page 287) as well as taste other typical Beino dishes. Anita also gave me her recipes. Also, Denise Asfar, who later that day hosted a very glamorous lunch in her beautiful home with Nahla's family dishes as well as her own. And, finally, Ruby el-Sha'er and her father, Fayez, who hosted us in the delightful Beino Blue House. Fayez also introduced us to the mayor of Beino, Khalil Kafrouneh, who took us foraging for sli' (page 22), and didn't mind Dalia photographing him. Nahla's aunt's cooks, Nada and Therese, couldn't have been more patient with my questions and with Dalia photographing them. Therese also told us about sli'.

Mickey Jammal, whose seaside restaurant, Jammal, is one of my absolute favorites, both for lunch and breakfast, which he very kindly invited me to last time I was there with Dalia, Huda Baroudi, and her chef daughter, Mariam. Because they are in the north, Mickey has tabüneh bread (page 33) on his menu, which he also uses to make fatayer, a wonderfully fast version of those made with dough (page 36).

Joumana Rizk Yarak and her husband, Fadi Sami Yakub, who hosted me for a delightful lunch in their house up north. Rima Abdelbaki, for information gleaned from the women of her village in the Druze heartland. Youssef Akiki, who invited Dalia and me to lunch at the restaurant he consults for in Batroun; Nada Boulos, who hosted me for a glamourous lunch in Beirut that happened to be on my birthday and gave me a taste of her family's goat nayeh (page 157); Tony Saade, who hosted me and Hania to a fabulous breakfast in Le Montagnou, his hotel in Kfardebian, where he served us the most exquisite stuffed intestines (page 250) that we wolfed down in no time; Gregory Buchakjian; and Karim Chaya, who a few years back gave me my first-ever lot of akküb, which I trimmed further, even if it had been already cleaned, before using it in laban emmoh (page 144).

Ahmad al-Bakkar at Dar el-Amar restaurant in Tripoli, who treated us to a magnificent dinner one evening when the region was hit by a second earthquake, although not as dramatic as the first one that destroyed so much in Turkey and Syria. Georges Chidiac of Chidiac Sweets, who very kindly allowed Dalia to photograph the distillation process of orange blossom water. Zelfa Hourani, who happened to be in Maraja'yün when I was going south and hosted me and Dalia in her charming house there; Zelfa also introduced me to Jenny Gebara, who gave me possibly the most extravagant recipe in this book (page 198). Doris al-Zir, who I met through Dalia and who gave me a booklet about sli', published by the Council of Environment Kobayat.

And so many whom I have not named and whom I encountered on my research: greengrocers, butchers, waiters, and sweets makers, to name a few. Each of whom gave me a tip or two to add to the culinary lore of my home country.

And, finally, I would like to apologize to those I have forgotten to mention. My memory is no longer what it used to be. As a result, I always forget to mention some of those who have helped me in my research despite being careful to take notes as I go along.

INDEX

(Page references in *italics* refer to illustrations.)

A

Abbas Galettes, 50, *50–51*
Abdallah, Shirine, 150, 342
Ablamah, 145, 201–2
Adass bil-Hamüd, 56
Ahdab, Mona and Misbah, 206, *264–65*, 343
akkawi cheese, 22
   see also cheese *for specific recipes*
akküb, 23, 144, 344
Alameddine, Rabih, 88, 343
Al Baba, Saida, 294
Al-Haddad, Tripoli, *304*, 306
al-Hakim bi Amr Allah, 237
al-Hassad, Aley, 189
Al-Jardali's Shortbreads, 326
al-Koukash, Alaa, 88, 274, 343
allspice, 17
almonds, 11, 20, 68, 135
   see also nuts *for specific recipes*
Amal Bohsali, Beirut, 294
Ameh, 327
Aniseed Fritters, 308
Anjar Cheese "Pizza," 46
Antabli, Mohammed, 266
Apricot Leather Ice Cream, 339
Ard el-Shawkeh bil-Zeyt, 129
arisheh, 21
   Curd Cheese Sambüsak, 38, *39*
Artichokes and Potatoes in Olive Oil, 129
arugula:
   Fresh Thyme Salad, 100
   Salad, 90
Arüss Samkeh Harrah, 220–22, *221*
asafir (tiny birds), 114, *114*
Asbeh Sawdah Nayeh, 247, *247*
ash'awan, 22
Ashtah, 301
   Clotted Cream Fritters, 314
   Clotted Cream Triangles, 312
Ashura, Chicken and Whole Wheat "Porridge" for, 240–41, *241*
Assumption of the Virgin. See Eid el-Saydeh
Atayef, 315–16, *317*
Ater, 300
Attieh family, Beino, *167*, 172, 287, *289*, 343–44
Audi, Nayla, 26, 137, 180, 182
awarma, 2, 7, 63
   Awarma (recipe), 15
   Topping (for Mana'ish), 35, *35*
   Winter Tabbüleh, 83
Ayoub, Jacquot, 17, 146, 150, 194, 287, 330, 341
Aysh el-Saraya, 312

B

Baba Ghannüge, 69
Baklava (Ba'lawa), *304*, 304–5
balilah, 93
ballüriyeh, 304
Bamyeh bil-Zeyt, 125
Barbecued Chicken Wings, 108, *109*
Baroudi, Huda, 224, 227, *264–65*, 341–42, 344
becfigues (tiny birds), 114, *114*
Beet Dip, 70, *71*
Beino, dishes from, xiii, *167*, 343–44
   Lamb Shanks in Vinegar (Lahm bil-Khall), 287–88, *289*
   Vegetarian Grilled Kibbé Discs (Bou Emneh), 172
Beyd Ghanam, 249
bil-zeyt ("cooked in olive oil"), 118
   see also olive oil, dishes cooked in
Bissara, 74–75, *75*
borma, *304*, *304*
Bou Emneh, 172
BouKaram, Fadi (Cedrusk), 310
Boustani, Hania Rayess, *264–65*, 342
braises. See stews and braises

breads:
   Sacred (Orban), 48
   of the Seraglio (Aysh el-Saraya), 312
   Sweet Saj (Talami), 47
   see also flatbreads
breakfast:
   chickpea salad (balilah), 93
   Fragrant Wheat Porridge, 327
   Mana'ish with various toppings, 34–35, *35*
   Sweet Cheese Pie, 298–99, *299*
"bride" (wrap with labneh), 134
bulgur wheat, 5–6, 258
   balls, in zinkol, 64–65, 150
   Cannellini Beans, and Greens, 273
   Chickpeas, Lamb and, 275
   and Cranberry Beans "Risotto," 258, *259*
   Green Beans, and Chickpeas, 270, *271*
   and Kishk Salad, Warm, 274
   Marshüsheh, 272
   Mixed Legume and Grain Soup, 57
   Red Müjaddarah, 260
   "Risotto," Green, 268, *269*
   see also kibbé; Tabbüleh
Burghul bi-Dfineh, 275
Butter Bean Salad, 93
buttermilk, 19
Büza ala Amar el-Dinn, 339, *338*
Büza ala Fawakeh, 336
Büza ala Halib, 337

C

cabbage:
   Leaves, Stuffed, 196–97
   Marshüsheh, 272
   Salad, 91
   White Tabbüleh, 84, *85*
cakes:
   Semolina, 310, *311*
   Yellow "Sponge," 328, *329*

cannellini bean(s):
　Bulgur Wheat, and Greens, 273
　and Meat Stew, 290–91, *291*
　Mixed Legume and Grain Soup, 57
　Mixed Legume and Kishk Soup from Mükhtara, 58, *59*
carob molasses, 4
Carrots, Peas, and Meat Stew, Citrusy, 279–80, *280*
Charafeddine, Batoul, 74–75, *75*
Charafeddine, Yasmine, 73, *87*, *133*, *135*, *139*, *342*
cheese, 21–22
　Curd, Sambüsak, *38*, 39
　Filled Pancakes, 315–16, *317*
　Ma'jü'a, *294*, 295
　Pie, Sweet, 298–99, *299*
　"Pizza," Anjar, 46
　and Semolina Dessert, 295, 296, *297*
　Topping (for Mana'ish), *35*, 35
chicken, 232, 235–43
　Jew's Mallow, 237–39
　Kebabs, 107
　Roast, with Rice and Nuts, 242–43, *243*
　with Roasted Green Wheat, 235–36
　Soup of the Feast, 62
　Whole, Stuffed Zucchini and Vine Leaves with, 198–200, *199*
　and Whole Wheat "Porridge," 240–41, *241*
　Wings, Barbecued, 108, *109*
Chicken Livers, Fried, 246
chickpea(s), 258
　Colocasia (Taro) in Tahini Sauce, 98–99
　Cucumber, and Parsley Salad, 102, *103*
　Falafel, 266–67, *267*
　fatteh, *134*
　Green Beans, Bulgur Wheat and, 270, *271*
　Hommus (Hommus bi-Tahini), 68
　Kibbé, 173
　Lamb, and Bulgur Wheat, 275
　Lamb Fatteh, 135–36
　Lebanese "Parmigiana," 124
　Mixed Legume and Grain Soup, 57
　Mixed Legume and Kishk Soup from Mükhtara, 58, *59*
　salad (balilah), served as breakfast, 93

　Spiced Lebanese "Couscous," 233–34, *234*
　Vegetarian Stuffed Zucchini, 187–89
　Winter Tabbüleh, 83
　Zinkol with Verjuice, 64–65
chicory:
　in Olive Oil, 128
　Salad with Kishk, 88
cilantro:
　Desert Truffles with, 129
　Fava Beans and Swiss Chard with, 119
　Spinach, and Meat Stew, 286
　Tahini Sauce, Tripolitan, Baked Fish with, 213
cinnamon, 17
Citadel Bakery's Sesame Galettes, 52–53, *53*
Citrusy Peas, Carrots, and Meat Stew, 279–80, *280*
Citrusy Tahini Sauce, *164*, 165–66
clarified butter, 12
Clotted Cream, 301
　Fritters, 314
　Triangles, Sweet, 312
Colocasia (Taro) in Tahini Sauce, 98–99
communal or cooperative kitchens, 2–3, 14, 28, *31*, 81, 118, 343
concentrates (pantry), 3–5
couscous, Lebanese (moghrabiyeh), 8
　Spiced, 233–34, *234*
Crackers, Olive Oil, 28, *29*
Cranberry Beans and Bulgur Wheat "Risotto," 258, *259*
cucumber:
　Armenian, Purslane, and Tomato Salad, 89
　Chickpea, and Parsley Salad, 102, *103*
　and Yogurt Salad, 96
Curd Cheese Sambüsak, *38*, 39

D

Dabboussi, Tripoli, *232*, 233, *294*, 295
Daher, Gaby, 259, 264–65, *342*
Dar el-Qanün, Olive Oil Crackers (Mallet-el-Smid) from, 28, *29*
darfiyeh, 22
Date Pastries, 320–21
Davidson, Alan, 9, 302
Dawüd Basha, 281–82
"decoration of the table" (zinet el-tawleh), 106, 278
Deir Intar, dishes from:

　Green Bulgur Wheat "Risotto" (Mafrükeh), 268, *269*
　Lebanese "Parmigiana" (Maghmür), 124
　Red Müjaddarah (Müjaddarah Hamra), 260
Desert Truffles with Cilantro, 129
desserts. *See* sweets
dips and spreads, 67–77
　Beet Dip (Mütabbal Shmandar), 70, *71*
　Eggplant Dip (Baba Ghannüge), 69
　Fava Bean and Mülükhiyeh Spread (Bissara), 74–75, *75*
　Garlic Dip (Tüm), 76
　Hommus (Hommus bi-Tahini), 68
　Sumac Eggplant Spread (Tridet el-Batenjan), 73
　Tahini Dip (Tarator), 77
　Zucchini Spread (Tridet el-Küssa), 72
distilled ingredients, 5
Djej ala Frikeh, 235–36
Djej bil-Furn ma Rezz wa Mukassarat, 242–43, *243*
Dlü' el-Sile' bil-Tarator, 97
dried ingredients, 5–12
Druze, xi, xii, 2, *31*, 57, 58, 118, 237, 343, 344
　Chicory Salad with Kishk (Salatet Hindbeh ma' Kishk), 88
　Warm Bulgur Wheat and Kishk Salad (Omeisheh), 274
Dumplings, Tiny Meat, in Yogurt Sauce, 148–49

E

Easter:
　Date Pastries ('Rass bil-Tamr) for, 320–21
　Rings (Ka'k el-Eid), 324
eggplant(s):
　Dip (Baba Ghannüge), 69
　in Extra Virgin Olive Oil, 14
　Lebanese "Parmigiana," 124
　Lord of Stuffed Vegetables, 208–9
　Meaty Stuffed, 190–91
　Priest's Salad, 95, *94*
　Stuffed, Fatteh, *137*, 137–38
　Sumac Spread, 73
　in Tomato Sauce, 122–23, *123*
eggs, in Zucchini Frittatas, 131
Eid al-Adha (Feast of the Sacrifice):

Abbas Galettes (Ka'k al-Abbas) for, 50, 50–51
Date Pastries ('Rass bil-Tamr) for, 320–21
Filled Pancakes (Atayef) for, 315–16, 317
Eid el-Barbara (feast of Saint Barbara):
  Aniseed Fritters (Ma'carün) for, 308
  Fragrant Wheat Porridge (Ameh) for, 327
Eid el-Saydeh (Assumption of the Virgin):
  Aniseed Fritters (Ma'carün) for, 308
  Chicken and Whole Wheat "Porridge" (H'risseh ala Djej) for, 240–41, 241
  Semolina Cream Pastries (Tamriyeh) for, 318, 318–19
Ejjet Küssa, 131
'El'ass bil-Tarator, 98–99
El Soussi, Beirut, 134, 278, 342
Em Sherif Deli, Beirut, 246
Epiphany, Aniseed Fritters (Ma'carün) for, 308

F

Fake Kibbé in Kishk Sauce, 170–71
Falafel, 266–67, 267
falafel scoop, 23
Farah, Jihad, 332, 343
Fassülyah bil-Lahmeh, 290–91, 291
fatayer:
  Dough for, 36, 37
  Strained Yogurt (Fatayer bil-Labneh), 41
  Swiss Chard (Fatayer bil-Sil'), 41
fatteh:
  chickpea, 134
  Fava Bean (Fatteh bil-Fül el-Akhdar), 139–40, 141
  Lamb (Fattet Ghanam), 135–36
  Stuffed Eggplant (Fattet Makdüss), 137, 137–38
Fattüsh, 86, 87
fava bean(s):
  Fatteh, 139–40, 141
  Fresh, Salad, 92
  and Lamb in Yogurt, 146–47
  Mixed Legume and Kishk Soup from Mükhtara, 58, 59
  and Mülükhiyeh Spread, 74–75, 75
  and Swiss Chard with Cilantro, 119

Fayssaliyeh, 306, 307
feta, 21
figs, dried, 9–10
Filled Pancakes, 315–16, 317
fish, 211–29
  Baked, with a Tripolitan Tahini Cilantro Sauce (Samkeh ma Tarator Trabülsi), 213
  Baked in Salt (Samak Meshwi bil-Melh), 229, 229
  Fried (Samak Me'li), 219, 219
  Kibbé (Kibbet Samak), 177–78
  "Risotto," Huda's (Sayyadiyeh), 224, 224–27, 227
  Spicy, in Tahini Sauce (Samkeh Harrah 1), 214–15
  Spicy, Wrap (Arüss Samkeh Harrah), 220–22, 221
  Squid in Ink Sauce (Habbar bil-Hibr), 228
  Stewed Spicy (Samkeh Harrah 3), 218
  Stuffed Spicy (Samkeh Harrah 2), 212, 216–17, 217
  in Tahini Sauce (Samak bil-Tahineh), 223
Fist'iyeh, 146–47
flatbreads, 25–35
  Handkerchief Bread (Mar'ü'), 30–31, 31
  Mana'ish with various toppings, 34–35
  Olive Oil Crackers (Mallet-el-Smid), 28, 29
  Pita (Khobz), 32–33, 33
  from the South (Mishtah), 26–27, 27
  Tabüneh, 33, 33
floral tisane, 11
foraging, 22–23, 128
Fragrant Wheat Porridge, 327
Fraket Nayla, 180–81
fresh essentials (pantry), 19–23
Fried Chicken Livers, 246
Fried Fish, 219, 219
frikeh, 6
  Chicken with Roasted Green Wheat, 235–36
Frittatas, Zucchini, 131
fritters:
  Aniseed, 308
  Clotted Cream, 314
  Pellet, 308, 309
Fruit Ice Cream, 336
Fül bil-Sil', 119

G

galettes:
  Abbas, 50, 50–51

Olive Oil, 49
  Sesame, Citadel Bakery's, 52–53, 53
  sesame, in Ma'jü'a, 294, 295
garlic:
  Dip, 76
  Marinade, 107
Gaspard, Maria, 70
Gebara, Jenny, 198, 344
Ghammeh, 250–52, 251
ghee, 12
Ghosn, Carole, 264–65
Ghraybeh, 325
goat's cheese, 22
goat's yogurt, 134
Goat Tartare, 156, 157
Gollut, Christophe, 264–65
Grain and Mixed Legume Soup, 57
grains and legumes, 257–75
  Cannellini Beans, Bulgur Wheat, and Greens (Marshüsheh 2), 273
  Chickpeas, Lamb, and Bulgur Wheat (Burghul bi-Dfineh), 275
  Cranberry Beans and Bulgur Wheat "Risotto" (Müjaddarat Fassüliah), 258, 259
  Falafel, 266–67, 267
  Green Beans, Bulgur Wheat, and Chickpeas (Madfüneh), 270, 271
  Green Bulgur Wheat "Risotto" (Mafrükeh), 268, 269
  Lentil "Risotto" (Müdardarah), 262
  Marshüsheh, 272–73
  Red Müjaddarah (Müjaddarah Hamra), 260
  Silky Müjaddarah (Müjaddarah m'Saffayeh), 261
  Vermicelli Rice (Rezz bil-Sh'ayriyeh), 263
  Warm Bulgur Wheat and Kishk Salad (Omeisheh), 274
grape molasses, 4
Greek Orthodox Christians, xii, 318
green bean(s):
  Bulgur Wheat, and Chickpeas, 270, 271
  and Meat in a Tomato Sauce, 283
  in Tomato Sauce, 120, 121
  Green Bulgur Wheat "Risotto," 268, 269
green cheese (jibneh khadrah), 21

INDEX   347

greens:
    Cannellini Beans, Bulgur Wheat and, 273
    wild (sli'), 22–23
    wild (sli'), for Chicory in Olive Oil, 128
    see also chicory; Swiss chard
grilled dishes, 105–14
    becfigues, or asafir (tiny birds), 114, *114*
    Chicken Kebabs (Shish Tawü'), 107
    Chicken Wings, Barbecued (Jawaneh d'Jej Meshwiyeh), 108, *109*
    Kafta, 110
    Kibbé Disks (Kibbeh Meshwiyeh), *167*, 167–69, *169*
    Lamb Kebabs (Lahm Meshwi), 111
    Shawarma, 112–13
    Vegetarian Kibbé Disks (Bou Emneh), 172

H
Habbar bil-Hibr, 228
Hadi, Sheikh, *189*, 343
Halawet el-Jibn, 295, *296*, *297*
Halici, Nevin, 94
Halim, Bhamdoun, *115*
Hallab, Rafaat al, 306
Hallab, Tripoli, 287, 294
hallüm cheese, 21–22
    Sweet Cheese Pie, 298–99, *299*
Handkerchief Bread, 30–31, *31*
Hand Pies, Meat-filled, from Baalbek, 44–45, *45*
Hazim, Joumana, 137, *137*, *187*
herb(s), 19
    Kibbé, Nayla's, 180–81
    Mixed, and Toasted Pita Salad, 86, *87*
Hindbeh bil-Zeyt, 128
H'leywat Ghanam, 248
Hokayem, Fadia, 272, 273, 342
Hokayem, Sumy, *123*, *174*, *251*, *258*, *259*, 272, 342
hommaydah, 23
Hommus (Hommus bi-Tahini), 68
hospitality, tradition of, 294
Hourani, Zelfa, 198, 344
H'risseh ala Djej, 240–41, *241*

I
Ibrahim, Moussa, 17, 235, 342
ice cream:
    Apricot Leather, 339, *338*
    Fruit (Büza ala Fawakeh), 336
    Milk (Büza ala Halib), 337
imam bayildi, 94
Intestines, Striped Tripe and, 250–52, *251*
itab al-Tibakhah (*The Book of Cookery*), 148

J
Jaber, Maher, 220
Jawaneh d'Jej Meshwiyeh (Barbecued Chicken Wings), 108, *109*
Jew's Mallow, 237–39
jibneh khadrah, 21
Jumblatt, Walid, Jr., 2, 57

K
Kafta, 110
Ka'k al-Abbas, 50, *50–51*
Ka'k al-Al'a, Tripoli, 342
Ka'k bil-Zeyt, 49
Ka'k el-Eid, 324
Ka'k Furn al-Al'a, 52–53, *53*
Kama bil-Kizbrah, 129
Kammüneh, 18
karabij, 322
Karam, Karl, 332, 343
kataifi or "hair" pastry:
    Baklava, *304*, 304–5
    King Faysal's Sweet, 306, *307*
    Sweet Cheese Pie, 298–99, *299*
kebabs:
    Chicken, 107
    Lamb, 111
Kellage, 314
Khobz Saj, 30–31, *31*
kibbé, 153–83
    baking in communal ovens, 158, *159*
    Balls (Kibbeh 'Rass), 162
    Balls, for Soup of the Feast, 62
    Balls in Tomato Sauce ('Rass Kibbeh bil-Banadüra), 174
    Balls in Yogurt Sauce (Kibbeh 'Rass bil-Laban), 163
    Chickpea (Kibbet Hommus), 173
    in Citrusy Tahini Sauce (Kibbeh Arnabiyeh), *164*, 165–66
    Disks, Grilled (Kibbeh Meshwiyeh), *167*, 167–69, *169*
    Disks, Vegetarian Grilled (Bou Emneh), 172
    Fake, in Kishk Sauce (Kibbeh Hileh bil-Kishk), 170–71
    Fish (Kibbet Samak), 177–78
    Goat Tartare (Kibbet Me'zeh Nayeh), *156*, 157
    Herb, Nayla's (Fraket Nayla), 180–81
    Lentil (Kibbet Adass), 179
    Pie (Kibbeh bil-Saniyeh), 160–61
    Potato (Kibbet Batata), 182
    Pumpkin (Kibbet La'teen), 175–76
    Stretched (Kibbeh Mamdüdeh), 158
    Tomato (Kibbet Banadüra), 183
King Faysal's Sweet, 306, *307*
kishk, 7
    and Bulgur Wheat Salad, Warm, 274
    Chicory Salad with, 88
    and Mixed Legume Soup from Mükhtara, 58, *59*
    Sauce, Fake Kibbé in, 170–71
    Soup, 63
    Topping (for Mana'ish), 35, *35*
K'nafeh bil-Jebn, 298–99, *299*
kol wa shkor, 304

L
Laban Emmoh, 144
Laban ma' Khyhar, 96
Laban Matbükh, 142, *143*
Lahm bil-Ajine, 43
Lahm bil-Khall, 287–88, *289*
Lahm Meshwi, 111
labneh (strained yogurt), 22
    in "bride" (wrap), 134
    Strained Yogurt Fatayer, 41
lamb:
    Awarma, 15
    Cannellini Bean and Meat Stew, 290–91, *291*
    Chickpeas, and Bulgur Wheat, 275
    Chops, Stuffed Vine Leaves with, *206*, 206–7
    Citrusy Peas, Carrots, and Meat Stew, 279–80, *280*
    Fatteh, 135–36
    Fava Bean Fatteh, 139–40, *141*
    and Fava Beans in Yogurt, 146–47
    Green Beans and Meat in a Tomato Sauce, 283
    Grilled Kibbé Disks, *167*, 167–69, *169*
    ground, buying from butcher or grinding your own, 110, 157
    Kafta, 110
    Kebabs, 111
    Kibbé Balls, 162
    Kibbé Balls in Tomato Sauce, 174

Kibbé in Citrusy Tahini Sauce, 164, 165–66
Kibbé Pie, 160–61
Meatballs in a Lemony Sauce, 281–82
Meat-filled Hand Pies from Baalbek, 44–45, 45
Meat "Pizza," 43
Nayla's Herb Kibbé, 180–81
Okra and Meat Stew, 284, 285
Shanks in Vinegar, 287–88, 289
Shawarma, 112–13
Soup of the Feast, 62
Spinach, Cilantro, and Meat Stew, 286
Stretched Kibbé, 158
Stuffed Zucchini in Yogurt Sauce, 145
Tiny Meat Dumplings in Yogurt Sauce, 148–49
Winter Tabbüleh, 83
in Yogurt Sauce, 144
Lamb's Liver, Raw, 247, 247
Lamb's Sweetbreads, 248
Lamb's Tongue Salad, 254
Lebanese Cooking (Mouzannar), 84
Lebanese "Parmigiana," 124
lebbah/lebba, 22
legume(s):
 Butter Bean Salad, 93
 Mixed, and Grain Soup, 57
 Mixed, and Kishk Soup from Mükhtara, 58, 59
 see also chickpea(s); fava bean(s); grains and legumes
lemons, 19
Lemony Sauce, Meatballs in, 281–82
Lemony Swiss Chard Soup, 56
Lenten dishes:
 bil-zeyt dishes, 118. *See also* olive oil, dishes cooked in
 Silky Müjaddarah (Müjaddarah m'Saffayeh), 261
 see also vegetarian and vegan options
lentil(s), 258
 Kibbé, 179
 Red Müjaddarah, 260
 "Risotto," 262
 Silky Müjaddarah, 261
 Soup, 60
liver(s):
 Chicken, Fried, 246
 Lamb's, Raw, 247, 247
Lord of Stuffed Vegetables, 208–9
Lübyeh bil-Lahmeh, 283

Lübyeh bil-Zeyt, 120, 121
Lydon, Shuna, 336

M

Ma'carün, 308
Madfüneh, 270, 271
Mafrükeh, 268, 269
Maghmür, 124
mahlep (mahlab), 17
Ma'jü'a, 294, 295
Makdüss, 14
 Fattüsh with, 87
Makhlüta, 57
Makhlütat Mükhtara, 58, 59
Mallet-el-Smid, 28, 29
Mamari, Janine and Tony, 88, 274, 343
ma'mül:
 Date Pastries ('Rass bil-Tamr), 320–21
 Walnut Pastries (Ma'Mül bil-Joz), 322–23, 323
ma'mül molds, 23, 320
Mana'ish, 34–35
 Cheese Topping for, 35, 35
 Kishk Topping for, 35, 35
 Tomato Topping for, 34, 35
 Za'tar Topping for, 35, 35
Marinade, Garlic, 107
Mar Metr (Saint Dimitri), Semolina Cream Pastries for day of, 318, 318–19
Marrow(s), Stuffed, 191–92
 in Tomato Sauce with Okra, 194–95
Marshüsheh, 272–73
Mar'ü', 30–31, 31
mastic, 7–8
Matbakh Ors el-Shams communal kitchen, Mükhtara, 2–3, 14, 31, 81, 343
maté, 294
Mat'hanet Khoury, Beirut, 17, 330
meat:
 Dumplings, Tiny, in Yogurt Sauce, 148–49
 -filled Hand Pies from Baalbek, 44–45, 45
 ground, buying from butcher or grinding your own, 110, 157
 "Pizza," 43
 Sambüsak, 40
 see also stews and braises; *specific meats*
Meatballs in a Lemony Sauce, 281–82
Meaty Stuffed Eggplants, 190–91
Megli, 330, 331
Mehshi Ammet Jenny Gebara:

 Wara' Enab wa Koussa ma Djejeh, 198–200, 199
Mehshi Are', 191–92
Mehshi Batinjan bil-Lahmeh, 190–91
Mehshi Koussa bil-Zeyt, 187–89
Mehshi Malfüf, 196–97
Mehshi Sille', 204–5
Mehshi Wara Enab ma Kastalettah, 206, 206–7
Mikati, Ziad, 52, 342
Milk Ice Cream, 337, 338
Milk Pudding, 332
Mishtah, 26–27, 27
Mixed Herb and Toasted Pita Salad, 86, 87
Mixed Legume and Grain Soup, 57
Mixed Legume and Kishk Soup from Mükhtara, 58, 59
moghrabiyeh (Lebanese couscous), 8
 Spiced, 232, 233–34, 234
Mouzannar, Ibrahim, 84
Mroue, Maha, 73, 342
m'shabbak, 309
Mudallal, Kamal, 302
Müdardarah, 262
Müffata'a, 334, 335
Mühallabiyeh, 332
müjaddarah:
 Red (Müjaddarah Hamra), 260
 Silky (Müjaddarah m'Saffayeh), 261
Müjaddarat Fassüliah, 258, 259
Mükhtara, 31, 81
 communal kitchen in, 2–3, 14, 31, 81, 343
 Mixed Legume and Kishk Soup from (Makhlütat Mükhtara), 58, 59
Mülükhiyeh, 237–39
 and Fava Bean Spread, 74–75, 75
müneh (foodstuffs), 2–3, 3, 118
 communal ovens for, 158, 159
 kishk and awarma as part of, 63
 prepared in communal kitchens, 2–3, 14, 28, 31, 81, 118, 343
müneh stores, 17, 118
Müssa'a, 122–23, 123
Mütabba'at Küssa, 126, 127
Mütabbal Shmandar, 70, 71

N

Nammürah, 310, 311
Natef, 8–9, 302–3, 303
Nayla's Herb Kibbé, 180–81

newborns, Meghli to celebrate, 330, *331*
nuts, 11–12
    Fragrant Wheat Porridge, 327
    Roast Chicken with Rice and, 242–43, *243*

O

offal, 245–55
    Braised Spleen (T'hal), 253
    Fried Chicken Livers (Asbett Djej Me'liyeh), 246
    Lamb's Sweetbreads (H'leywat Ghanam), 248
    Lamb's Tongue Salad (Salatet Lsenet), 254
    Ox Tongue Stew (Rosto), 255
    Raw Lamb's Liver (Asbeh Sawdah Nayeh), 247, *247*
    Sheep's Testicles (Beyd Ghanam), 249
    Stuffed Tripe and Intestines (Ghammeh), 250–52, *251*
oils and fats, 12–13
okra:
    and Meat Stew, 284, *285*
    Stuffed Marrows in Tomato Sauce with, 194–95
    in Tomato Sauce, 125
olive oil, 12–13, 118
    bil-zeyt ("cooked in olive oil") term and, 118
    Crackers, 28, *29*
    Galettes, 49
olive oil, dishes cooked in (bil-zeyt dishes), 117–31
    Artichokes and Potatoes in Olive Oil (Ard el-Shawkeh bil-Zeyt), 129
    Chicory in Olive Oil (Hindbeh bil-Zeyt), 128
    Desert Truffles with Cilantro (Kama bil-Kizbrah), 129
    Eggplant in Extra Virgin Olive Oil (Makdüss), 14
    Eggplant in Tomato Sauce (Müssa'a'a), 122–23, *123*
    Fava Beans and Swiss Chard with Cilantro (Fül bil-Sil'), 119
    Green Beans in Tomato Sauce (Lübyeh bil-Zeyt), 120, *121*
    Lebanese "Parmigiana" (Maghmür), 124
    Okra in Tomato Sauce (Bamyeh bil-Zeyt), 125
    Zucchini Frittatas (Ejjet Küssa), 131
    Zucchini in a Minty Tomato Sauce (Mütabba'at Küssa), *126*, 127
Omeisheh, 274
orange blossom water (ma' el-zahr), 5
Osseyran, Feryal, 14, 18, *18*, 73, *87*, 139, 146, 183, 342
Ottomans, xi, xii, xiii, 281
    Bread of the Seraglio (Aysh el-Saraya) of, 312
Owwamat, 308, 309
Ox Tongue Stew, 255

P

Pancakes, Filled, 315–16, *317*
pantry, 1–23
    concentrated ingredients, 3–5
    distilled ingredients, 5
    dried ingredients, 5–12
    fresh essentials, 19–23
    oils and fats, 12–13
    preserved ingredients, 13, 16
    spices and spice mixtures, 17–19
"Parmigiana," Lebanese, 124
parsley:
    Chickpea, and Cucumber Salad, 102, *103*
    Tabbüleh, 82
    Winter Tabbüleh, 83
pastries, savory, 36–53
    Anjar Cheese "Pizza" (Sfiha from Anjar), 46
    Meat-filled Hand Pies from Baalbek (Sfiha b'Albakiyeh), 44–45, *45*
    Meat "Pizza" (Lahm bil-Ajine), 43
    see also fatayer; galettes; sambüsak
pastries, sweet:
    Baklava (Ba'lawa), *304*, 304–5
    Clotted Cream Fritters (Kellage), 314
    Date ('Rass bil-Tamr), 320–21
    King Faysal's Sweet (Fayssaliyeh), 306, *307*
    Semolina Cream (Tamriyeh), *318*, 318–19
    Walnut (Ma'Mül bil-Joz), 322–23,
    Karabij, 322, *323*
Patrimoine Culinaire du Liban, Le (Ramzi), 194, 272
pea(s):
    Carrots, and Meat Stew, Citrusy, 279–80, *280*
    Yellow Split, Soup, 61
Pellet Fritters, 308, 309
Perry, Charles, 332
phyllo:
    Baklava, *304*, 304–5
    Semolina Cream Pastries, *318*, 318–19
    Sweet Walnut or Clotted Cream Triangles, 312
pickling solution, 13
pies:
    Kibbé, 160–61
    Sweet Cheese, 298–99, *299*
    walnut, 322
pine nuts, 11–12, 68, 304
pistachio(s), 11
    Baklava, *304*, 304–5
    King Faysal's Sweet, 306, *307*
    Pastries, 322–23, *323*
Pita, 32–33, *33*
    Toasted, and Mixed Herb Salad, 86, *87*
"pizza":
    Cheese, Anjar, 46
    Meat, 43
Pombo-Villar, Esteban, 9
pomegranate molasses, 4–5
    Dressing, 81
Porridge, Fragrant Wheat, 327
"Porridge," Whole Wheat, Chicken and, 240–41, *241*
potato(es):
    and Artichokes in Olive Oil, 129
    Kibbé, 182
poultry, 231–43
    see also chicken
poussins, 232
    Spiced Lebanese "Couscous," 233–34, *234*
Preserved Eggplants in Extra Virgin Olive Oil, 14
preserved ingredients, 13, 16
Priest's Salad, 94, *95*
puddings:
    Milk, 332
    Rezz bil-Halib, 332
    Tahini Rice, 334, *335*
Pumpkin Kibbé, 175–76
purslane:
    Mixed Herb and Toasted Pita Salad, 86, *87*
    Tomato, and Armenian Cucumber Salad, 89

R

Rachaya al-Wadi, 102
Ramadan, dishes for:
    Aniseed Fritters (Ma'carün), 308

apricot leather drink, 339
Clotted Cream Fritters (Kellage), 314
Date Pastries ('Rass bil-Tamr), 320–21
Filled Pancakes (Atayef), 315–16, *317*
Lentil Soup (Shorbet Adass), 60
Spiced Lebanese "Couscous" (Moghrabiyeh), 233–34, *234*
Ramzi, chef, 150, 194, 272, *273*
'Rass bil-Tamr, 320–21
'Rass Kibbeh bil-Banadüra, 174
Rebb el-Rümman bil-Zeyt wal-Tüm, 81
Red Müjaddarah, 260
Rezz bil-Sh'ayriyeh, 263
rice:
    Lentil "Risotto," 262
    Mixed Legume and Grain Soup, 57
    Pudding, Tahini, 334, *335*
    Rezz bil-Halib, 332
    Roast Chicken with Nuts and, 242–43, *243*
    Soup of the Feast, 62
    Stuffed Zucchini in Yogurt Sauce, 145
    Vermicelli, 263
rice flour, in Meghli, 330, *331*
"risotto":
    Cranberry Beans and Bulgur Wheat, *258*, 259
    Fish, Huda's, *224*, 224–27, *227*
    Green Bulgur Wheat, *268*, 269
    Lentil, 262
rose water, 5
Rosto, 255

S

Sabbagh, Mazen, 72
Saberi, Helen, 9, 302
Sacred Bread, 48
Safa, Denise, 264–65, 287
saffron:
    Fish Kibbé, 177–78
    grown in Bekaa, 332, 343
    Huda's Fish "Risotto," *224*, 224–27, *227*
    Milk Pudding, 332
    Yellow "Sponge" Cake, 328, *329*
Sahjouneh, *27*, 32
Saida, *19*, 65
Saida, dishes from:
    Al-Jardali's Shortbreads, 326
    Fava Beans and Lamb in Yogurt, 146–47

Kibbé in Citrusy Tahini Sauce, *164*, 165–66
sweets makers and, 294
Saint Barbara. See Eid el-Barbara
Saj Bread, 30–31, *31*
    Sweet, 47
salad dressings:
    Lemon and Garlic, 80
    Pomegranate Molasses, 81
salads, 79–101
    Arugula (Salatet Jarjir), 90
    Butter Bean (Salatet Fassülyah), 93
    Cabbage (Salatet Malfüf), 91
    Chickpea, Cucumber, and Parsley (Siff), 102, *103*
    chickpea, served as breakfast (balilah), 93
    Chicory, with Kishk (Salatet Hindbeh ma' Kishk), 88
    Colocasia (Taro) in Tahini Sauce ('El'ass bil-Tarator), 98–99
    Fava Bean, Fresh (Salatet Fül Akhdar), 92
    Lamb's Tongue (Salatet Lsenet), 254
    Mixed Herb and Toasted Pita (Fattüsh), 86, *87*
    Priest's (Salatet el-Raheb), 94, *95*
    Purslane, Tomato, and Armenian Cucumber (Salatet Ba'leh ma' Banadürah wa Me'teh), 89
    Swiss Chard Stalks in Tahini Sauce (Dlü' el-Sile' bil-Tarator), 97
    Tabbüleh, 82
    Thyme, Fresh (Salatet Za'tar), 100
    Warm Bulgur Wheat and Kishk (Omeisheh), 274
    White Tabbüleh (Tabbüleh Baidah), 84, *85*
    Winter Tabbüleh (Tabbüleh Shatawiyeh), 83
    Yogurt and Cucumber (Laban ma' Khyhar), 96
Salam, Tarfa, 119
salatet. See salads
Samak bil-Tahineh, 223
Samak Me'li, 219, *219*
Samak Meshwi bil-Melh, *229*, 229
sambüsak, 36–40
    Curd Cheese (Sambüsak Bil-Arisheh), *38*, 39
    Dough for, 36–37
    Meat (Sambüsak bil-Lahmeh), 40

Samkeh Harrah, *212*, 214–18, *217*
Samkeh ma Tarator Trabülsi, 213
Saniürat al-Jardali, 325
sauces:
    Tahini, 98–99, 112–13
    Tahini, Citrusy, *164*, 165–66
    Tajen, *224*, 225
    Tomato, 174, 209
    Yogurt, Cooked, 142, *143*
Sayyadiyeh, Huda's, *224*, 224–27, *227*
S'banegh bil-Lahmeh, 286
seasonal treats (bil-mawssam), 19–20
seasonings:
    Seven-Spice Mixture (Sabe' B'harat), 19
    Za'tar, 10
semolina, 8
    Aniseed Fritters, 308
    Cake, 310, *311*
    and Cheese Dessert, 295, *296*, 297
    Cream Pastries, *318*, 318–19
    Date Pastries, 320–21
    Easter Rings, 324
    Ma'jü'a, *294*, 295
    Shortbreads, 325
    Yellow "Sponge" Cake, 328, *329*
sesame (seeds), 8
    Galettes, Citadel Bakery's, 52–53, *53*
    galettes, in Ma'jü'a, *294*, 295
    Seven-Spice Mixture, 19
    Sfiha from Anjar, 46
    S'füf, 328, *329*
shanklish, 21
    Anjar Cheese "Pizza," 46
Shawarma, 112–13
Sh'aybiyatt, 312
Sheep's Testicles, 249
Sheikh el-Mehshi, 208–9
Shish Barak, 148–49
Shish Tawü', 107
Shorbet Adass, 60
Shorbet Adass Asfar, 61
Shorbet el-Eid, 62
Shorbet Kishk, 63
Shortbreads, 325
    Al-Jardali's, 326
Siff, 102, *103*
Silky Müjaddarah, 261
soapwort, in Natef, 8–9, 302–3, 303
Souheil, Nadine, 61, 155, *181*, 342
Souheil, Zeinab, 61, 342
soups, 55–65
    of the Feast (Shorbet el-Eid), 62

soups (cont.)
    Kishk (Shorbet Kishk), 63
    Lentil (Shorbet Adass), 60
    Mixed Legume and Grain (Makhlüta), 57
    Mixed Legume and Kishk, from Mükhtara (Makhlütat Mükhtara), 58, *59*
    Swiss Chard, Lemony (Adass bil-Hamüd), 56
    Yellow Split Pea (Shorbet Adass Asfar), 61
    Zinkol with Verjuice (Zinkol bil-Hosrüm), 64–65
Spiced Lebanese "Couscous," 233–34, *234*
spices and spice mixtures, 17–19
    Kammüneh, 18
    Megli, 330, *331*
    Seven-Spice Mixture, 19
Spinach, Cilantro, and Meat Stew, 286
Spleen, Braised, 253
"Sponge" Cake, Yellow, 328, *329*
spreads. *See* dips and spreads
Squid in Ink Sauce, 228
Stewed Spicy Fish, 218
stews and braises, 277–91
    Cannellini Bean and Meat Stew (Fassülyah bil-Lahmeh), 290–91, *291*
    Citrusy Peas, Carrots, and Meat Stew (Yakhnet Bazella wa Jazar), 279–80, *280*
    Green Beans and Meat in a Tomato Sauce (Lübyeh bil-Lahmeh), 283
    Lamb Shanks in Vinegar (Lahm bil-Khall), 287–88, *289*
    Meatballs in a Lemony Sauce (Dawüd Basha), 281–82
    Okra and Meat Stew (Bamyeh bil-Lahmeh), 284, *285*
    Ox Tongue Stew (Rosto), 255
    Spinach, Cilantro, and Meat Stew (S'banegh bil-Lahmeh), 286
Stretched Kibbé, 158
Stuffed Eggplant Fatteh, *137*, 137–38
Stuffed Spicy Fish, *212*, 216–17, *217*
Stuffed Tripe and Intestines, 250–52, *251*
stuffed vegetables, 185–209
    Cabbage Leaves (Mehshi Malfüf), 196–97
    Eggplants, Meaty (Mehshi Batinjan bil-Lahmeh), 190–91
    Eggplants, Vegetarian (Batinjen Mehshi Ate'), 202–3, *203*
    Lord of (Sheikh el-Mehshi), 208–9
    Marrow (Mehshi Are'), 191–92
    Marrows in Tomato Sauce with Okra (Mehshi Are' ma Bamiyeh), 194–95
    Swiss Chard Leaves (Mehshi Sille'), 204–5
    Vine Leaves with Lamb Chops (Mehshi Wara Enab ma Kastalettah), *206*, 206–7
    Zucchini, Vegetarian (Mehshi Koussa bil-Zeyt), 187–89
    Zucchini and Vine Leaves with Whole Chicken (Wara' Enab wa Koussa ma Djejeh), 198–200, *199*
    Zucchini in Yogurt Sauce (Ablamah), 145, 201–2
Sugar Syrup, 300
sumac, 9
    Eggplant Spread, 73
Sunni Muslims, xii–xiii, 72, 119, 165, 212, 214, 334
Sweetbreads, Lamb's, 248
sweets, 292–339
    Al-Jardali's Shortbreads (Saniürat al-Jardali), 326
    Aniseed Fritters (Ma'carün), 308
    Apricot Leather Ice Cream (Büza ala Amar el-Dinn), 339
    Baklava (Ba'lawa), *304*, 304–5
    Bread of the Seraglio (Aysh el-Saraya), 312
    Cheese and Semolina Dessert (Halawet el-Jibn), 295, *296*, *297*
    Clotted Cream (Ashtah), 301
    Clotted Cream Fritters (Kellage), 314
    Date Pastries ('Rass bil-Tamr), 320–21
    Easter Rings (Ka'k el-Eid), 324
    Filled Pancakes (Atayef), 315–16, *317*
    Fragrant Wheat Porridge (Ameh), 327
    Fruit Ice Cream (Büza ala Fawakeh), 336
    King Faysal's Sweet (Fayssaliyeh), 306, *307*
    Ma'jü'a, *294*, 295
    Megli, 330, *331*
    Milk Ice Cream (Büza ala Halib), 337, *338*
    Milk Pudding (Mühallabiyeh), 332
    Natef, 302–3, *303*
    Pellet Fritters (Owwamat), 308, *309*
    Rezz bil-Halib, 332
    Semolina Cake (Nammürah), 310, *311*
    Semolina Cream Pastries (Tamriyeh), *318*, 318–19
    Shortbreads (Ghraybeh), 325
    Sugar Syrup (Ater), 300
    Sweet Cheese Pie (K'nafeh bil-Jebn), 298–99, *299*
    Sweet Walnut or Clotted Cream Triangles (Sh'aybiyatt), 312
    Tahini Rice Pudding (Müffata'a), 334, *335*
    Walnut Pastries (Ma'Mül bil-Joz), 322–23
    Karabij, *323*
    Yellow "Sponge" Cake (S'füf), 328, *329*
Sweet Saj Bread, 47
Swiss chard:
    Fatayer, 41
    and Fava Beans with Cilantro, 119
    Leaves, Stuffed, 204–5
    Soup, Lemony, 56
    Stalks in Tahini Sauce, 97
Syrup, Sugar, 300

T

Tabbüleh, 82
    White (Tabbüleh Baidah), 84, *85*
    Winter (Tabbüleh Shatawiyeh), 83
tabe' molds, 23, 320
Tabüneh, 33, *33*
tahini:
    Cilantro Sauce, Tripolitan, Baked Fish with, 213
    Dip, 77
    Hommus, 68
    Rice Pudding, 334, *335*
    Sauce, 98–99, 112–13
    Sauce, Citrusy, *164*, 165–66
    Sauce, Colocasia (Taro) in, 98–99
    Sauce, Fish in, 223
    Sauce, Spicy Fish in, 214–15
    Sauce, Swiss Chard Stalks in, 97
Tajen Sauce, 224, *225*
Tamriyeh, *318*, 318–19
Tarator, 77

Taro (Colocasia) in Tahini Sauce, 98–99
Testicles, Sheep's, 249
T'hal, 253
thymbra spicata, 10
Thyme, Fresh, Salad, 100
tomato(es):
    Kibbé, 183
    Lebanese "Parmigiana," 124
    paste (rebb el-banadūra), 4
    Priest's Salad, 95.94
    Sauce, 209
    Sauce, Eggplant in, 122–23, *123*
    Sauce, Green Beans in, 120, *121*
    Sauce, Green Beans and Meat in, 283
    Sauce, Kibbé Balls in, 174
    Sauce, Minty, Zucchini in, *126*, 127
    Sauce, Okra in, 125
    Sauce, Stuffed Marrows in, with Okra, 194–95
    Topping (for Mana'ish), 34, *35*
    White Tabbūleh, 84, *85*
Triangles, Sweet Walnut or Clotted Cream, 312
Tridet el-Batenjan, 73
Tridet el-Küssa, 72
Tripe, Stuffed Intestines and, 250–52, *251*
Tripoli:
    Al-Haddad in, *304*, 306
    Baked Fish with a Tripolitan Tahini Cilantro Sauce from, 213
    Dabboussi in, *232*, 233, *294*
    King Faysal's Sweet from, 306, *307*
    Ma'jü'a from, *294*, 295
    samkeh harrah sandwiches in, 214, 220–22, *221*
    souks of, *88*, *90*, *91*, *96*, *232*
    sweets makers in, 294
Truffles, Desert, with Cilantro, 129
Tüm, 76
turmeric, in Yellow "Sponge" Cake, 328, *329*

U
utensils, special, 23

V
vegetable corer, 23
vegetables:
    dried (khodrah m'addadeh/ myabasseh), 6–7
    stuffed, 185–209. *See also* stuffed vegetables
vegetarian and vegan options:
    Chickpea Kibbé, 173
    Fake Kibbé in Kishk Sauce, 170–71
    Fava Bean Fatteh, 139–40
    Grilled Kibbé Disks, 172
    Kibbé in Citrusy Tahini made with Colocasia, 165–66
    Lamb Fatteh made with chickpeas, 135
    Lebanese "Parmigiana," 124
    Lentil Kibbé, 179
    Mixed Legume and Grain Soup, 57
    Potato Kibbé, 182
    Priest's Salad, 94, *95*
    Pumpkin Kibbé, 175–76
    Spinach and Cilantro Stew, 286
    Stuffed Eggplants, 202–3, *203*
    Stuffed Swiss Chard Leaves, 204–5
    for stuffed vegetables, 186
    Stuffed Zucchini, 187–89
    Tomato Kibbé, 183
    Zinkol with Verjuice, 64–65
    see also grains and legumes
verjuice, 3–4
    Zinkol with, 64–65
Vermicelli Rice, 263
Vinegar, Lamb Shanks in, 287–88, *289*
vine leaves:
    Stuffed, with Lamb Chops, *206*, 206–7
    Stuffed Zucchini and, with a Whole Chicken, 198–200, *199*

W
walnut(s), 11
    Baklava, *304*, 304–5
    Fake Kibbé in Kishk Sauce, 170–71
    Filled Pancakes, 315–16, *317*
    Fragrant Wheat Porridge, 327
    Pastries, 322–23, *323*
    Triangles, Sweet, 312
    Vegetarian Grilled Kibbé Disks, 172
wheat:
    Porridge, Fragrant, 327
    Roasted Green, Chicken with, 235–36
    see also bulgur wheat; semolina
White Tabbūleh, 84, *85*
Whole Wheat "Porridge," Chicken and, 240–41, *241*
wild greens (sli'), 22–23
    for Chicory in Olive Oil, 127
Winter Tabbūleh, 83
Wrap, Spicy Fish, 220–22, *221*

Y
Yakhnet Bazella wa Jazar, 279–80, *280*
Yellow Split Pea Soup, 61
Yellow "Sponge" Cake, 328, *329*
yogurt (laban), 22
    and Cucumber Salad, 96
    goat's-milk, 134
    Sauce, Cooked, 142, *143*
    Sauce, Kibbé Balls in, 163
    stabilizing for cooking, 134
    strained (labneh), 134
    Strained, Fatayer, 41
    strained, in "bride" (wrap with labneh), 134
yogurt dishes, 133–50
    Cooked Yogurt Sauce, 142, *143*
    Fava Bean Fatteh, 139–40, *141*
    Fava Beans and Lamb in Yogurt, 146–47
    Lamb Fatteh, 135–36
    Lamb in Yogurt Sauce, 144
    Stuffed Eggplant Fatteh, *137*, 137–38
    Stuffed Zucchini in Yogurt Sauce, 145, 201
    Tiny Meat Dumplings in Yogurt Sauce, 148–49
    Zinkol, 150

Z
Zaatari, Akram, 72, 73, 342
Zaatari, Mona, 187, 204, 341–42
Zaatari, Nazek, 72, 342
Zakhia family, Ehden, 158, *159*
za'tar (mixture of thyme, sumac, and sesame seeds), 100
    Topping (for Mana'ish), 35, *35*
    Za'tar (recipe), 10
za'tar (thyme), 100
Zeidan, Renata, *264–65*, 342
zellabya, 308
zeytun, 16
Zinkol, 150
    with Verjuice, 64–65
zucchini:
    Frittatas, 131
    in a Minty Tomato Sauce, *126*, 127
    Spread, 72
    Stuffed, in Yogurt Sauce, 145, 201–2
    Stuffed, Vegetarian, 187–89
    Stuffed Vine Leaves and, with a Whole Chicken, 198–200, *199*

Without limiting the exclusive rights of any author, contributor or the publisher of this publication, any unauthorized use of this publication to train generative artificial intelligence (AI) technologies is expressly prohibited. HarperCollins also exercise their rights under Article 4(3) of the Digital Single Market Directive 2019/790 and expressly reserve this publication from the text and data mining exception.

LEBANON. Copyright © 2026 by Anissa Helou. All rights reserved. No part of this book may be used or reproduced in any manner whatsoever without written permission except in the case of brief quotations embodied in critical articles and reviews. For information, address HarperCollins Publishers, 195 Broadway, New York, NY 10007. In Europe, HarperCollins Publishers, Macken House, 39/40 Mayor Street Upper, Dublin 1, D01 C9W8, Ireland.

HarperCollins books may be purchased for educational, business, or sales promotional use. For information, please email the Special Markets Department at SPsales@harpercollins.com.

hc.com

Ecco® and HarperCollins® are trademarks of HarperCollins Publishers.

FIRST EDITION

DESIGNED BY RENATA DE OLIVEIRA

Studio photographs by Kristin Perers.
Photographs on location by Dalia Khamissy.
Photograph on page 247 by Anissa Helou.

Library of Congress Cataloging-in-Publication Data has been applied for.

ISBN 978-0-06-333492-2

Printed in Canada.

26 27 28 29 30 TC 5 4 3 2 1